A HISTORY OF
BABYLONIA & ASSYRIA

II

BABYLON

A HISTORY OF BABYLONIA AND ASSYRIA

FROM PREHISTORIC TIMES TO THE PERSIAN CONQUEST.

By LEONARD W. KING, LITT.D., F.S.A.

Vol. I.—A HISTORY OF SUMER AND AKKAD:
An Account of the Early Races of Babylonia from
Prehistoric Times to the Foundation of the
Babylonian Monarchy.

Vol. II.—A HISTORY OF BABYLON from the Foundation of the Monarchy to the Persian Conquest.

Vol. III.—A HISTORY OF ASSYRIA from the Earliest
Period to the Fall of Nineveh.

Vol. III. is in preparation.

Each Volume separately, bound in cloth, 18s. net ; or, for the Three
Volumes (if subscribed for at one time), £2 10s.

LONDON : CHATTO & WINDUS.

MERODACH-BALADAN II. KING OF BABYLON, MAKING A GRANT OF
LAND TO BÊL-AKHÊ-ERBA, GOVERNOR OF BABYLON

A HISTORY

OF

BABYLON

FROM THE FOUNDATION OF THE MONARCHY
TO THE PERSIAN CONQUEST

BY

LEONARD W. KING, Litt.D., F.S.A.

Assistant Keeper of Egyptian and Assyrian Antiquities in the British Museum
Professor of Assyrian and Babylonian Archæology in
the University of London

WITH MAP, PLANS, AND ILLUSTRATIONS

LONDON
CHATTO & WINDUS
1919

PRINTED BY
WILLIAM CLOWES AND SONS, LIMITED
LONDON AND BECCLES, ENGLAND.

PREFACE

In the first volume of this work an account was given of the early races of Babylonia from prehistoric times to the foundation of the monarchy. It closed at the point when the city of Babylon was about to secure the permanent leadership under her dynasty of West-Semitic kings. The present volume describes the fortunes of Babylonia during the whole of the dynastic period, and it completes the history of the southern kingdom. Last autumn, in consequence of the war, it was decided to postpone its publication ; but, at the request of the publishers, I have now finished it and seen it through the press. At a time when British troops are in occupation of Southern Mesopotamia, the appearance of a work upon its earlier history may perhaps not be considered altogether inopportune.

Thanks to recent excavation Babylon has ceased to be an abstraction, and we are now able to reconstitute the main features of one of the most famous cities of the ancient world. Unlike Ashur and Nineveh, the great capitals of Assyria, Babylon survived with but little change under the Achæmenian kings of Persia, and from the time of Herodotus onward we possess accounts of her magnificence, which recent research has in great part substantiated. It is true that we must modify the description Herodotus has left us of her size, but on all other points the accuracy of his information is confirmed. The Lion Frieze of the Citadel and the enamelled beasts of the Ishtar Gate enable us to understand something of the spell she cast. It is claimed that the site has been identified of her most famous building, the Hanging Gardens of the royal palace ; and, if that should prove to be the case, they can hardly be said to have justified their reputation. Far more impressive is the Tower of Babel with its huge Peribolos, enclosing what has been aptly described as the Vatican of Babylon.

The majority of the buildings uncovered date from the Neo-Babylonian period, but they may be regarded as typical of Babylonian civilization as a whole. For temples were rebuilt again and again on the old lines, and religious conservatism retained the mud-brick walls and primitive decoration of earlier periods. Even Nabopolassar's royal palace must have borne a close resemblance to that of Hammurabi ; and the street net-work of the city appears to have descended without much change from the time of the First Dynasty. The system which Hammurabi introduced into the legis-lation of his country may perhaps have been reflected in the earliest attempt at town-planning on a scientific basis. The most striking fact about Babylon's history is the continuity of her culture during the whole of the dynastic period. The principal modification which took place was in the system of land-tenure, the primitive custom of tribal or collective proprietorship giving place to private ownership under the policy of purchase and annexation deliberately pursued by the West-Semitic and Kassite conquerors. A parallel to the earlier system and its long survival may be seen in the village communities of India at the present day.

In contrast to that of Assyria, the history of Babylon is more concerned with the development and spread of a civilization than with the military achieve-ments of a race. Her greatest period of power was under her first line of kings ; and in after ages her foreign policy was dictated solely by her commercial needs. The letters from Boghaz Keui, like those from

Tell el-Amarna, suggest that, in keeping her trade connexions open, she relied upon diplomacy in preference
to force. That she could fight at need is proved by her
long struggle with the northern kingdom, but in the
later period her troops were never a match for the
trained legions of Assyria. It is possible that Nabopolassar and his son owed their empire in great measure
to the protecting arm of Media ; and Nebuchadnezzar's
success at Carchemish does not prove that the Babylonian character had suddenly changed. A recently
recovered letter throws light on the unsatisfactory
state of at least one section of the army during
Nebuchadnezzar's later years, and incidentally it suggests that Gobryas, who facilitated the Persian occupation, may be identified with a Babylonian general of
that name. With the fall of Media, he may perhaps
have despaired of any successful opposition on his
country's part.

Babylon's great wealth, due to her soil and semi-
tropical climate, enabled her to survive successive
foreign dominations and to impose her civilization on
her conquerors. Her caravans carried that civilization
far afield, and one of the most fascinating problems of
her history is to trace the effect of such intercourse in
the literary remains of other nations. Much recent
research has been devoted to this subject, and the great
value of its results has given rise in some quarters to
the view that the religious development of Western
Asia, and in a minor degree of Europe, was dominated
by the influence of Babylon. The theory which underlies such speculation assumes a reading of the country's
history which cannot be ignored. In the concluding
chapter an estimate has been attempted of the extent
to which the assumption is in harmony with historical
research.

The delay in the publication of this volume has
rendered it possible to incorporate recent discoveries,

some of which have not as yet appeared in print.
Professor A. T. Clay has been fortunate enough to
acquire for the Yale University Collection a complete
list of the early kings of Larsa, in addition to other
documents with an important bearing on the history of
Babylon. He is at present preparing the texts for
publication, and has meanwhile very kindly sent me
transcripts of the pertinent material with full permission to make use of them. The information
afforded as to the overlapping of additional dynasties
with the First Dynasty of Babylon has thrown new
light on the circumstances which led to the rise of
Babylon to power. But these and other recent discoveries, in their general effect, do not involve any
drastic changes in the chronological scheme as a whole.
They lead rather to local rearrangements, which to a
great extent counterbalance one another. Under
Babylon's later dynasties her history and that of
Assyria are so closely inter-related that it is difficult to
isolate the southern kingdom. An attempt has been
made to indicate broadly the chief phases of the
conflict, and the manner in which Babylonian interests
alone were affected. In order to avoid needless
repetition, a fuller treatment of the period is postponed
to the third volume of this work. A combined account
will then also be given of the literature and civilization
of both countries.

I take this opportunity of expressing my thanks to
Monsieur F. Thureau-Dangin, Conservateur-adjoint
of the Museums of the Louvre, for allowing me last
spring to study unpublished historical material in his
charge. The information he placed at my disposal I
found most useful during subsequent work in the
Ottoman Museum at Constantinople shortly before
the war. Reference has already been made to my
indebtedness to Professor Clay, who has furnished me
from time to time with other unpublished material, for

which detailed acknowledgment is made in the course of this work. With Professor C. F. Burney I have discussed many of the problems connected with the influence of Babylon upon Hebrew literature; and I am indebted to Professor A. C. Headlam for permission to reprint portions of an article on that subject, which I contributed in 1912 to the *Church Quarterly Review*.

To Dr. E. A. Wallis Budge my thanks are due, as he suggested that I should write these histories, and he has given me the benefit of his advice. To him, as to Sir Frederic Kenyon and Mr. D. G. Hogarth, I am indebted for permission to make use of illustrations, which have appeared in official publications of the British Museum. My thanks are also due to Monsieur Ernest Leroux of Paris for allowing me to reproduce some of the plates from the " Mémoires de la Délégation en Perse," published by him under the editorship of Monsieur J. de Morgan; and to the Council and Secretary of the Society of Biblical Archæology for the loan of a block employed to illustrate a paper I contributed to their Proceedings. The greater number of the plates illustrating the excavations are from photographs taken on the spot; and the plans and drawings figured in the text are the work of Mr. E. J. Lambert and Mr. C. O. Waterhouse, who have spared no pains to ensure their accuracy. The designs upon the cover of this volume represent the two most prominent figures in Babylonian tradition. In the panel on the face of the cover the national hero Gilgamesh is portrayed, whose epic reflects the Babylonian heroic ideal. The panel on the back of the binding contains a figure of Marduk, the city-god of Babylon, grasping in his right hand the flaming sword with which he severed the dragon of chaos.

L. W. KING.

b

CONTENTS

CHAPTER I

INTRODUCTORY: BABYLON'S PLACE IN THE HISTORY OF ANTIQUITY

CHAPTER II

THE CITY OF BABYLON AND ITS REMAINS: A DISCUSSION OF THE RECENT EXCAVATIONS

CHAPTER III

THE DYNASTIES OF BABYLON: THE CHRONOLOGICAL SCHEME IN THE LIGHT OF RECENT DISCOVERIES

CHAPTER IV

THE WESTERN SEMITES AND THE FIRST DYNASTY OF BABYLON

CHAPTER V

THE AGE OF HAMMURABI AND ITS INFLUENCE ON LATER PERIODS

CHAPTER VI

THE CLOSE OF THE FIRST DYNASTY OF BABYLON AND THE KINGS FROM THE COUNTRY OF THE SEA

CHAPTER VII

THE KASSITE DYNASTY AND ITS RELATIONS WITH EGYPT AND THE HITTITE EMPIRE

CHAPTER VIII

THE LATER DYNASTIES AND THE ASSYRIAN DOMINATION

CONTENTS

CHAPTER IX

THE NEO-BABYLONIAN EMPIRE AND THE PERSIAN CONQUEST

CHAPTER X

GREECE, PALESTINE, AND BABYLON: AN ESTIMATE OF CULTURAL INFLUENCE

APPENDICES

LIST OF PLATES

ILLUSTRATIONS IN THE TEXT

MAPS AND PLANS

A HISTORY OF BABYLON

CHAPTER I

THE name of Babylon suggests one of the great
centres from which civilization radiated to other
peoples of the ancient world. And it is true
that from the second millennium onwards we have
evidence of the gradual spread of Babylonian culture
throughout the greater part of Western Asia. Before
the close of the fifteenth century, to cite a single
example of such influence, we find that Babylonian had
become the language of Eastern diplomacy. It is not
surprising perhaps that the Egyptian king should have
adopted the Babylonian tongue and method of writing
for his correspondence with rulers of Babylon itself or
of Assyria. But it is remarkable that he should employ
this foreign script and language for sending orders to
the governors of his Syrian and Palestinian dependencies,
and that such Canaanite officials should use the same
medium for the reports they despatched to their
Egyptian master. In the same period we find the
Aryan rulers of Mitanni, in Northern Mesopotamia,
writing in cuneiform the language of their adopted
country. A few decades later the Hittites of Anatolia,
discarding their old and clumsy system of hieroglyphs
except for monumental purposes, borrow the same
character for their own speech, while their treaties with
Egypt are drawn up in Babylonian. In the ninth
century the powerful race of the Urartians, settled in
the mountains of Armenia around the shores of Lake
Van, adopt as their national script the writing of

Assyria, which in turn had been derived from Babylon. Elam, Babylon's nearest foreign neighbour, at a very early period had, like the Hittites of a later age, substituted for their rude hieroglyphs the language and older characters of Babylon, and later on they evolved from the same writing a character of their own. Finally, coming down to the sixth century, we find the Achæmenian kings inventing a cuneiform sign-list to express the Old Persian language, in order that their own speech might be represented in royal proclamations and memorials beside those of their subject provinces of Babylon and Susiania.

These illustrations of Babylonian influence on foreign races are confined to one department of culture only, the language and the system of writing. But they have a very much wider implication. For when a foreign language is used and written, a certain know-ledge of its literature must be presupposed. And since all early literatures were largely religious in character, the study of the language carries with it some acquain-tance with the legends, mythology and religious beliefs of the race from whom it was borrowed. Thus, even if we leave out of account the obvious effects of com-mercial intercourse, the single group of examples quoted necessarily implies a strong cultural influence on contemporary races.

It may thus appear a paradox to assert that the civilization, with which the name of Babylon is asso-ciated, was not Babylonian. But it is a fact that for more than a thousand years before the appearance of that city as a great centre of culture, the civilization it handed on to others had acquired in all essentials its later type. In artistic excellence, indeed, a standard had been already reached, which, so far from being surpassed, was never afterwards attained in Mesopotamia. And although the Babylonian may justly be credited with greater system in his legislation, with an extended literature, and perhaps also with an increased luxury of ritual, his efforts were entirely controlled by earlier models. If we except the spheres of poetry and ethics, the Semite in Babylon, as elsewhere, proved himself a clever adapter, not a creator. He was the prophet of

Sumerian culture and merely perpetuated the achievements of the race whom he displaced politically and absorbed. It is therefore the more remarkable that his particular city should have seen but little of the process by which that culture had been gradually evolved. During those eventful centuries Babylon had been but little more than a provincial town. Yet it was reserved for this obscure and unimportant city to absorb within herself the results of that long process, and to appear to later ages as the original source of the culture she enjoyed. Before tracing her political fortunes in detail it will be well to consider briefly the causes which contributed to her retention of the place she so suddenly secured for herself.

The fact that under her West-Semitic kings Babylon should have taken rank as the capital city does not in itself account for her permanent enjoyment of that position. The earlier history of the lands of Sumer and Akkad abounds with similar examples of the sudden rise of cities, followed, after an interval of power, by their equally sudden relapse into comparative obscurity. The political centre of gravity was continually shifting from one town to another, and the problem we have to solve is why, having come to rest in Babylon, it should have remained there. To the Western Semites themselves, after a political existence of three centuries, it must have seemed that their city was about to share the fate of her numerous predecessors. When the Hittite raiders captured and sacked Babylon and carried off her patron deities, events must have appeared to be taking their normal course. After the country, with her abounding fertility, had been given time to recover from her temporary depression, she might have been expected to emerge once more, according to precedent, under the ægis of some other city. Yet it was within the ancient walls of Babylon that the Kassite conquerors established their headquarters; and it was to Babylon, long rebuilt and once more powerful, that the Pharaohs of the eighteenth Dynasty and the Hittite kings of Cappadocia addressed their diplomatic correspondence. During Assyria's long struggle with the southern kingdom Babylon was always the protagonist, and no raid by Aramean or Chaldean tribes ever succeeded in ousting her from that position. At the height of Assyrian power she continued to be the chief check upon that empire's expansion, and the vacillating policy of the Sargonids in their treatment of the city sufficiently testifies to the dominant *rôle* she continued to play in politics. And when Nineveh had fallen, it was Babylon that took her place in a great part of Western Asia.

This continued pre-eminence of a single city is in striking contrast to the ephemeral authority of earlier capitals, and it can only be explained by some radical change in the general conditions of the country. One fact stands out clearly : Babylon's geographical position must have endowed her during this period with a strategical and commercial importance which enabled her to survive the rudest shocks to her material prosperity. A glance at the map will show that the city lay in the north of Babylonia, just below the confluence of the two great rivers in their lower course. Built originally on the left bank of the Euphrates, she was protected by its stream from any sudden incursion of the desert tribes. At the same time she was in immediate contact with the broad expanse of alluvial plain to the south-east, intersected by its network of canals.

But the real strength of her position lay in her near neighbourhood to the transcontinental routes of traffic. When approaching Baghdad from the north the Mesopotamian plain contracts to a width of some thirty-five miles, and, although it has already begun to expand again in the latitude of Babylon, that city was well within touch of both rivers. She consequently lay at the meeting-point of two great avenues of commerce. The Euphrates route linked Babylonia with Northern Syria and the Mediterranean, and was her natural line of contact with Egypt; it also connected her with Cappadocia, by way of the Cilician Gates through the Taurus, along the track of the later Royal Road.[1] Farther north the trunk-route through

[1] Cf. Hogarth, "The Nearer East," pp. 212 ff., and Ramsay, "The Historical Geography of Asia Minor," pp. 27 ff. Herodotus (V, 52–54)

Anatolia from the west, reinforced by tributary routes from the Black Sea, turns at Sivas on the Upper Halys, and after crossing the Euphrates in the mountains, first strikes the Tigris at Diarbekr; then leaving that river for the easier plain, it rejoins the stream in the neighbourhood of Nineveh and so advances southward to Susa or to Babylon. A third great route that Babylon controlled was that to the east through the Gates of Zagros, the easiest point of penetration to the Iranian plateau and the natural outlet of commerce from Northern Elam.[1] Babylon thus lay across the stream of the nations' traffic, and in the direct path of any invader advancing upon the southern plains.

That she owed her importance to her strategic position, and not to any particular virtue on the part of her inhabitants, will be apparent from the later history of the country. It has indeed been pointed out that the geographical conditions render necessary the existence of a great urban centre near the confluence of the Mesopotamian rivers.[2] And this fact is amply attested by the relative positions of the capital cities, which succeeded one another in that region after the supremacy had passed from Babylon. Seleucia, Ctesiphon and Baghdad are all clustered in the narrow neck of the Mesopotamian plain, and for only one short period, when normal conditions were suspended, has the centre of government been transferred to any southern city.[3] The sole change has consisted in the permanent selection of the Tigris for the site of each new capital, with a decided tendency to remove it to

describes the "Royal Road" of the Persian period as passing from Ephesus by the Cilician Gates to Susa, and it obtained its name from the fact that all government business of the Persian Court passed along it; the distances, given by Herodotus in parasangs and stages, may well be derived from some official Persian document (cf. How and Wells, "Commentary on Herodotus," II, p. 21). But it followed the track of a still earlier Royal Road, by which Khatti, the capital of the old Hittite Empire, maintained its communications westward and with the Euphrates valley.

[1] At the present day this forms the great trunk-road across the highlands of Persia, by way of Kirmanshah; and, since the Moslem conquest, it has been the chief overland route from the farther East for all those making the pilgrimage to Mecca.

[2] Cf. Hogarth, op. cit., p. 260 f.

[3] See below, pp. 9 ff.

the left or eastern bank.[1] That the Euphrates should
have given place in this way to her sister river was
natural enough in view of the latter's deeper channel
and better water way, which gained in significance as
soon as the possibility of maritime communication was
contemplated.

Throughout the whole period of Babylon's supremacy the Persian Gulf, so far from being a channel
of international commerce, was as great a barrier as
any mountain range. Doubtless a certain amount of
local coasting traffic was always carried on, and the
heavy blocks of diorite which were brought to Babylonia from Magan by the early Akkadian king Narâm-
Sin, and at a rather later period by Gudea of Lagash,[2]
must have been transported by water rather than over
land. Tradition, too, ascribed the conquest of the
island of Dilmun, the modern Bahrein, to Sargon of
Akkad ; but that marked the extreme limit of Babylonian penetration southwards, and the conquest must
have been little more than a temporary occupation
following a series of raids down the Arabian coast.
The fact that two thousand years later Sargon of
Assyria, when recording his receipt of tribute from
Upêri of Dilmun, should have been so far out in his
estimate of its distance from the Babylonian coast-
line,[3] is an indication of the continued disuse of the
waters of the gulf as a means of communication. On
this supposition we may readily understand the difficulties encountered by Sennacherib when transporting
his army across the head of the gulf against certain
coast-towns of Elam, and the necessity, to which he
was put, of building special ships for the purpose.

There is evidence that in the Neo-Babylonian period
the possibilities of transport by way of the gulf had
already begun to attract attention, and Nebuchadnezzar II. is said to have attempted to build harbours

---

[1] It is not improbable that the transference from one bank to the
other was dictated by the relations of the ruling empire with Persia and
the West.

[2] See "Sumer and Akkad," p. 242.

[3] Cf. Delitzsch, "Paradies," pp. 178 ff., and Meyer, "Geschichte des
Altertums," I., ii., p. 473.

in the swamp at the mouths of the delta.[1] But his object must have been confined to encouraging coastal trade, for the sea-route between the Persian Gulf and India was certainly not in use before the fifth century, and in all probability was inaugurated by Alexander. According to Herodotus[2] it had been opened by Darius after the return of the Greek Scylax of Caryanda from his journey to India, undertaken as one of the surveying expeditions on the basis of which Darius founded the assessment of his new satrapies. But, although there is no need to doubt the historical character of that voyage, there is little to suggest that Scylax coasted round, or even entered, the Persian Gulf.[3] Moreover, it is clear that, while Babylon's international trade received a great impetus under the efficient organization of the Persian Empire, it was the overland routes which benefited. The outcrops of rock, or cataracts, which blocked the Tigris for vessels of deeper draft, were not removed until Alexander levelled them ; and the problem of Babylon's sea-traffic, to which he devoted the closing months of his life, was undoubtedly one of the factors which, having now come into prominence for the first time, influenced Seleucus in selecting a site on the Tigris for his new capital.[4]

But that was not the only cause of Babylon's deposition. For after her capture by Cyrus, new forces came into play which favoured a transference of the capital eastward. During the earlier periods of her history Babylon's chief rival and most persistent enemy had lain upon her eastern frontier. To the early Sumerian rulers of city-states Elam had been " the mountain that strikes terror,"[5] and during subsequent periods the cities of Sumer and Akkad could never be sure of immunity from invasion in that quarter. We shall see that in Elam the Western Semites of Babylon found the chief obstacle to the southward extension of their authority, and that in later periods any symptom

[1] See below, Chap. IX., p. 280.
[2] IV., 44.
[3] Cp. Myres, " Geographical Journal," VIII. (1896), p. 623, and How and Wells, " Commentary on Herodotus," Vol. I., p. 320.
[4] See Bevan, " House of Seleucus," I., pp. 242 ff., 253.
[5] Cf. " Sum. and Akk.," p. 149.

of internal weakness or dissension was the signal for renewed attack. It is true that the Assyrian danger drew these ancient foes together for a time, but even the sack of Susa by Ashur-bani-pal did not put an end to their commercial rivalry.

During all this period there was small temptation to transfer the capital to any point within easier striking distance of so powerful a neighbour; and with the principal passes for eastward traffic under foreign control, it was natural that the Euphrates route to Northern Mesopotamia and the Mediterranean coast should continue to be the chief outlet for Babylonian commerce. But on the incorporation of the country within the Persian empire all danger of interference with her eastern trade was removed; and it is a testimony to the part Babylon had already played in history that she continued to be the capital city of Asia for more than two centuries. Cyrus, like Alexander, entered the city as a conqueror, but each was welcomed by the people and their priests as the restorer of ancient rights and privileges. Policy would thus have been against any attempt to introduce radical innovations. The prestige the city enjoyed and the grandeur of its temples and palaces doubtless also weighed with the Achæmenian kings in their choice of Babylon for their official residence, except during the summer months. Then they withdrew to the cooler climate of Persepolis or Ecbatana, and during the early spring, too, they might transfer the court to Susa; but they continued to recognize Babylon as their true capital. In fact, the city only lost its importance when the centre of government was removed to Seleucia in its own immediate neighbourhood. Then, at first possibly under compulsion, and afterwards of their own free will, the commercial classes followed their rulers to the west bank of the Tigris; and Babylon suffered in proportion. In the swift rise of Seleucia in response to official orders, we may see clear proof that the older city's influence had been founded upon natural conditions, which were shared in an equal, and now in even a greater degree, by the site of the new capital.

The secret of Babylon's greatness is further

illustrated by still later events in the valley of the Euphrates and the Tigris. The rise of Ctesiphon on the left bank of the river was a further result of the eastward trend of commerce. But it lay immediately opposite Seleucia, and marked no fresh shifting of the centre of gravity. Of little importance under the Seleucid rulers, it became the chief city of the Arsacidæ, and, after the Parthian Empire had been

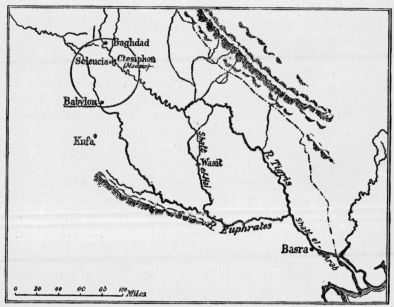

FIG. 1.

DIAGRAM TO ILLUSTRATE THE POLITICAL CENTRE OF GRAVITY IN BABYLONIA.

The circle marks the limits within which the capital shifted from the period of the First Dynasty onwards. It was only under the abnormal conditions produced by the Moslem conquest that Kûfa and Baṣra became for five generations the twin capitals of 'Irâḳ; this interval presents a parallel to the earlier period before the rise of Babylon.

conquered by Ardashīr I., it continued to be the principal city of the province and became the winter residence of the Sassanian kings. When in 636 A.D. the Moslem invaders defeated the Persians near the ruins of Babylon and in the following year captured Ctesiphon, they found that city and Seleucia, to which they gave the joint name of Al-Madâin, or "the cities," still retaining the importance their site had acquired in

the third century B.C.   Then follows a period of a
hundred and twenty-five years which is peculiarly instructive for comparison with the earlier epochs of
Babylonian history.

The last of the great Semitic migrations from
Arabia had resulted in the conquests of Islam, when,
after the death of Mohammed, the Arab armies
poured into Western Asia in their efforts to convert
the world to their faith.   The course of the movement,
and its effect upon established civilizations which were
overthrown, may be traced in the full light of history ;
and we find in the valley of the Tigris and Euphrates
a resultant economic condition which forms a close
parallel to that of the age before the rise of Babylon.
The military occupation of Mesopotamia by the Arabs
closed for a time the great avenues of transcontinental
commerce ; and, as a result, the political control of the
country ceased to be exercised from the capital of the
Sassanian kings and was distributed over more than
one area.   New towns sprang into being around the
permanent camps of the Arab armies.   Following on
the conquest of Mesopotamia, the city of Baṣra was
built on the Shatt el-ʻArab in the extreme south of the
country, while in the same year, 638 A.D., Kûfa was
founded more to the north-west on the desert side of
the Euphrates.   A third great town, Wâsiṭ, was added
sixty-five years later, and this arose in the centre of the
country on both banks of the Tigris, whose waters
were then passing along the present bed of the Shatt el-
Hai.   It is true that Madâin retained a measure of
local importance, but during the Omayyad Caliphate
Kûfa and Baṣra were the twin capitals of ʻIrâk.[1]

Thus the slackening of international connections led
at once to a distribution of authority between a north
and a south Babylonian site.   It is true that both
capitals were under the same political control, but from
the economic standpoint we are forcibly reminded of
the era of city-states in Sumer and Akkad.   Then, too,
there was no external factor to retain the centre of

[1] As such the two cities were known as ʻAl-ʻIrâkân, or Al-ʻIrâkayn,
meaning " the two capitals of ʻIrâk " ; cf. G. Le Strange, "The Lands of the
Eastern Caliphate," p. 25.

gravity in the north ; and Erech more than once secured the hegemony, while the most stable of the shifting dynasties was the latest of the southern city of Ur. The rise of Babylon as the sole and permanent capital of Sumer and Akkad may be traced, as we shall note, to increased relations with Northern Syria, which followed the establishment of her dynasty of West-Semitic kings.[1]   And again we may see history repeating herself, when Moslem authority is removed to Baghdad at the close of the first phase in the Arab occupation of Mesopotamia.   For on the fall of the Omayyad dynasty and the transference of the Abbasid capital from Damascus to the east, commercial intercourse with Syria and the west was restored to its old footing.   Basra and Kûfa at once failed to respond to the changed conditions, and a new administrative centre was required.   It is significant that Baghdad should have been built a few miles above Ctesiphon, within the small circle of the older capitals ;[2] and that, with the exception of a single short period,[3] she should have remained the capital city of 'Irâk.   Thus the history of Mesopotamia under the Caliphate is instructive for the study of the closely parallel conditions which enabled Babylon at a far earlier period to secure the hegemony in Babylonia and afterwards to retain it.

From this brief survey of events it will have been noted that Babylon's supremacy falls in the middle period of her country's history, during which she distributed a civilization in the origin of which she played no part.   When she passed, the culture she had handed on passed with her, though on Mesopotamian soil its decay was gradual.   But she had already delivered her message, and it has left its mark on the

[1] See further, Chap IV.   The fact that from time to time other cities of Akkad had secured the leadership, suggests that the forces which eventually placed Babylon at the head of the country were already beginning to be felt. They were doubtless checked in no small degree by the absence of an internal administration of any lasting stability during the acute racial conflict which characterized the period.

[2] The city was founded by the second Abbasid Caliph in 762 A.D.

[3] For a period of fifty-six years (836–892 A.D.) the Caliphate was removed to Sâmarrâ.   The circumstances which led to the transference may be traced directly to the civil war which broke out on the death of Harûn-ar-Rashîd ; cf. Le Strange, op. cit., p. 32.

remains of other races of antiquity which have come
down to us.   We shall see that it was in three main
periods that her influence made itself felt in any marked
degree beyond the limits of the home-land.   The earliest
of these periods of external contact was that of her
First Dynasty of West-Semitic rulers, though the most
striking evidence of its effect is only forthcoming after
some centuries had passed.   In the second period the
process was indirect, her culture being carried north and
west by the expansion of Assyria.   The last of the three
epochs coincides with the rule of the Neo-Babylonian
kings, when, thanks to her natural resources, the
country not only regained her independence, but for a
short time established an empire which far eclipsed her
earlier effort.   And in spite of her speedy return, under
Persian rule, to the position of a subject province, her
foreign influence may be regarded as operative, it is true
in diminishing intensity, well into the Hellenic period.

The concluding chapter will deal in some detail
with certain features of Babylonian civilization, and with
the extent to which it may have moulded the cultural
development of other races.   In the latter connexion
a series of claims has been put forward which cannot be
ignored in any treatment of the nation's history.   Some
of the most interesting contributions that have recently
been made to Assyriological study undoubtedly concern
the influence of ideas, which earlier research had already
shown to be of Babylonian origin.   Within recent years
a school has arisen in Germany which emphasizes the
part played by Babylon in the religious development
of Western Asia, and, in a minor degree, of Europe.
The evidence on which reliance has been placed to
prove the spread of Babylonian thought throughout the
ancient world has been furnished mainly by Israel and
Greece; and it is claimed that many features both in
Hebrew religion and in Greek mythology can only be
rightly studied in the light thrown upon them by
Babylonian parallels from which they were ultimately
derived.   It will therefore be necessary to examine
briefly the theory which underlies most recent speculation on this subject, and to ascertain, if possible, how far
it may be relied on to furnish results of permanent value.

But it will be obvious that, if the theory is to be accepted in whole or in part, it must be shown to rest upon a firm historical basis, and that any inquiry into its credibility should be more fitly postponed until the history of the nation itself has been passed in review. After the evidence of actual contact with other races has been established in detail, it will be possible to form a more confident judgment upon questions which depend for their solution solely on a balancing of probabilities. The estimate of Babylon's foreign influence has therefore been postponed to the closing chapter of the volume. But before considering the historical sequence of her dynasties, and the periods to which they may be assigned, it will be well to inquire what recent excavation has to tell us of the actual remains of the city which became the permanent capital of Babylonia.

CHAPTER II

THE CITY OF BABYLON AND ITS REMAINS: A DISCUSSION
OF THE RECENT EXCAVATIONS

THE actual site of Babylon was never lost in popular tradition. In spite of the total disappearance of the city, which followed its gradual decay under Seleucid and Parthian rule, its ancient fame sufficed to keep it in continual remembrance. The old Semitic name Bâb-ilî, "the Gate of the Gods," lingered on about the site, and under the form Bâbil is still the local designation for the most northerly of the city-mounds. Tradition, too, never ceased to connect the exposed brickwork of Nebuchadnezzar's main citadel and palace with his name. Kasr, the Arab name for the chief palace-mound and citadel of Babylon, means " palace " or " castle," and when in the twelfth century Benjamin of Tudela visited Baghdad, the Jews of that city told him that in the neighbouring ruins, near Hilla, the traveller might still behold Nebuchadnezzar's palace beside the fiery furnace into which Hananiah, Mishael and Azariah had been thrown. It does not seem that this adventurous rabbi actually visited the site,[1] though it is unlikely that he was deterred by fear of the serpents and scorpions with which, his informants said, the ruins were infested.

In the sixteenth century an English merchant traveller, John Eldred, made three voyages to " New Babylon," as he calls Baghdad, journeying from Aleppo down the Euphrates. On the last occasion, after describing his landing at Falûja, and how he secured a

[1] Rogers points out that the rabbi's account of Babylon seems to lack the little touches which betray the record of an eye-witness, and he compares it with the same traveller's descriptions of Mosul and Baghdad. By far the best and fullest account of the early explorers of Babylonia is that given by Rogers in his " History of Babylonia and Assyria," Vol. I., pp. 84 ff.

14

hundred asses for lack of camels to carry his goods to Baghdad, he tells us that "in this place which we crossed over stood the olde mightie citie of Babylon, many olde ruines whereof are easilie to be seene by daylight, which I, John Eldred, have often behelde at my goode leisure having made three voyages between the New Citie of Babylon and Aleppo over this desert."[1]   But it would seem probable from his further description that "the olde tower of Babell," which he visited "sundry times," was really the ruin of 'Aḳarḳûf, which he would have passed on his way to Baghdad. Benjamin of Tudela, on the other hand, had taken Birs-Nimrûd for the Tower of Babel,[2] and had noted how the ruins of the streets of Babylon still extend for thirty miles.   In fact, it was natural that several of the early travellers should have regarded the whole complex of ruins, which they saw still standing along their road to Baghdad, as parts of the ancient city ; and it is not surprising that some of the earlier excavators should have fallen under a similar illusion so far as the area between Bâbil and El-Birs is concerned.[3] The famous description of Herodotus, and the accounts other classical writers have left us of the city's size, tended to foster this conviction ; and, although the centre of Babylon was identified correctly enough, the size of the city's area was greatly exaggerated. Babylon had cast her spell upon mankind, and it has taken sixteen years of patient and continuous excavation to undermine that stubborn belief.   But in the process of shrinkage, and as accurate knowledge has gradually given place to conjecture, the old spell has reappeared unchanged.   It may be worth while to examine in

[1] See Hakluyt, "The Principall navigations voiages and discoveries of the English nation," ed. 1589, p. 232 ; ed. Goldsmid, Vol. X., "Asia," Pt. III. (1889), p. 63.

[2] He states that "the heavenly fire which struck the tower split it to its very foundation," a description which is thoroughly applicable to the present appearance of Borsippa's temple-tower at El-Birs ; see the photograph reproduced on Plate II.   Other travellers, such as Anthony Shirley in 1599 or 1600, appear to have made the same identification.   A few years later Pietro della Valle was nearer the mark in identifying the tower with the mound Bâbil, from which he carried away to Rome some of Nebuchadnezzar's stamped bricks, probably the first collection of Babylonian antiquities to reach Europe (cf. Rogers, *op. cit.*, p. 98).

[3] See p. 16, Fig. 2.

some detail the results of recent work upon the site,
and note to what extent the city's remains have
thrown light upon its history while leaving some
problems still unsolved.

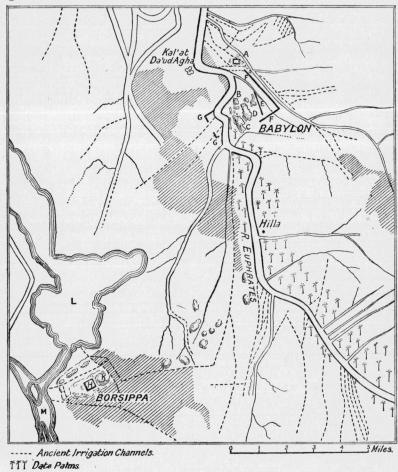

----- *Ancient Irrigation Channels.*
ↁↁↁ *Date Palms.*
///// *Desert*

FIG. 2.

MAP OF THE NEIGHBOURHOOD OF BABYLON AND BIRS-NIMRÛD.

A: The mound Bâbil.   B: The mound Ḳaṣr.   C: The mound 'Amrân-ibn-
'Ali.   D: The mound Merkes.   E: Inner City-wall of Babylon.   F: Outer City-
wall of Babylon.   G: Ruins of western walls.   H: Temple-tower of E-zida.
K: Ruins of E-zida.   L: Marsh.   M: Hindîya Canal.
[After the India Office Map.]

In view of the revolution in our knowledge of
Babylonian topography, which has been one of the

most striking results of recent work, no practical purpose would be served by tracing out the earlier but very partial examinations of the site which were undertaken successively by Rich in 1811,[1] by Layard in 1850,[2] by Oppert as the head of a French expedition in the years 1852–54,[3] and by Hormuzd Rassam, between 1878 and 1889, when he was employed on excavations for the British Museum.[4] During the last of these periods the British Museum obtained a valuable series of tablets from Babylon, some of the texts proving of great literary and scientific interest. In 1887, and again after a lapse of ten years, Dr. Robert Koldewey visited the site of Babylon and picked up fragments of enamelled bricks on the east side of the Kasr. On the latter occasion he sent some of them to Berlin, and Dr. Richard Schöne, at that time Director of the Royal Museums, recognized their artistic and archæological interest. Thus it was with the hope of making speedy and startling discoveries that the German Oriental Society began work upon the site at the end of March in the year 1899; and it is the more

[1] In addition to his incomplete plan (cf. C. J. Rich, " Narrative of a Journey to the site of Babylon in 1811," edited by his widow, London, 1839 ; opposite p. 43), and the smaller-scale plan of Major Rennet based upon it (published originally in " Archæologia," Vol. 18, and reprinted with Rich's memoir), we possess another sketch-plan, more accurate in certain details, by Sir Robert Ker Porter (cf. " Travels in Georgia, Persia, Armenia, Ancient Babylonia, etc., during the years 1817, 1818, 1819, and 1820," Vol II., 1822, opposite p. 349). Accurate surveys of large districts in Babylonia were made by Captain J. Felix Jones of the Indian Navy, who did such excellent work on Nineveh and its neighbourhood (see his " Memoirs," issued as a volume in " Bombay Government Records," No. XLIII., New Series, Bombay, 1857 ; and for the Nineveh survey, cf. " Journ. Roy. Asiat. Soc.," Vol. XV., 1853, pp. 352 ff.). The material collected by Felix Jones in Babylonia, was incorporated in the India Office Map, which was compiled by Trelawney Saunders on the basis of the surveys made between 1860 and 1865 by Commander W. Beaumont Selby, Lieut. W. Collingwood and Lieut. J. B. Bewsher, all of the Indian Navy. This was issued in 1885 under the title " Surveys of Ancient Babylon and the surrounding ruins with part of the rivers Tigris and Euphrates, the Hindiyeh Canal, the Sea of Nejf and the Shat Atshar," etc., London, 1885. It takes in the area from Baghdad to the junction of the Shatt Atshar with the Euphrates and is by far the best map, and the only one on a large scale, hitherto produced of Babylon and its neighbourhood. All plans of the mounds covering the ruins of the city itself are of course superseded by those issued by the German expedition.

[2] See " Nineveh and Babylon," London, 1853.

[3] The results of the expedition were published in two volumes under the title " Expédition scientifique en Mesopotamie," Paris, 1863.

[4] Cf. " Asshur and the Land of Nimrod," New York, 1897.

C

to the credit of the excavators that they have not allowed any difficulties or disappointments to curtail and bring to a premature close the steady progress of their research.

The extent of ground covered by the remains of the ancient city, and the great accumulation of *débris* over some of the principal buildings rendered the work more arduous than was anticipated, and consequently the publication of results has been delayed. It is true that, from the very beginning of operations, the expert has been kept informed of the general progress of the digging by means of letters and reports distributed to its subscribers every few months by the society.[1] But it was only in 1911, after twelve years of uninterrupted digging, that the first instalment was issued of the scientific publication. This was confined to the temples of the city, and for the first time placed the study of Babylonian religious architecture upon a scientific basis.[2] In the following year Dr. Koldewey, the director of the excavations, supplemented his first volume with a second, in which, under pressure from the society, he forestalled to some extent the future issues of the detailed account by summarizing the results obtained to date upon all sections of the site.[3] It has thus been rendered possible to form a connected idea of the remains of the ancient city, so far as they have been recovered.

In their work at Babylon the excavators have, of course, employed modern methods, which differ considerably from those of the age when Layard and Botta brought the winged bulls of Assyria to the British Museum and to the Louvre. The extraordinary success which attended those earlier excavators has, indeed, never been surpassed. But it is now realized that only by minuteness of search and by careful classification of strata can the remains of the past be made to reveal in full their secrets. The fine museum

---

[1] " Mitteilungen der Deutschen Orient-Gesellschaft zu Berlin," Nos. 1–54 (March, 1899–June, 1914).

[2] See Koldewey, " Die Tempel von Babylon und Borsippa," Leipzig, 1911.

[3] Cf. "Das wieder erstehende Babylon," Leipzig, 1912. A careful English translation of the work, from the pen of Mrs. Johns, has been issued under the title " The Excavations at Babylon," London, 1914.

I. THE TEMPLE-TOWER OF E-ZIDA AT BORSIPPA.
II. THE LION OF BABYLON ON THE KASR MOUND.

specimen retains its importance ; but it gains immensely in significance when it ceases to be an isolated product and takes its place in a detailed history of its period.

In order to grasp the character of the new evidence, and the methods by which it has been obtained at Babylon, it is advisable to bear in mind some of the general characteristics of Babylonian architecture and the manner in which the art of building was influenced by the natural conditions of the country. One important point to realize is that the builders of all periods were on the defensive, and not solely against human foes, for in that aspect they resembled other builders of antiquity. The foe they most dreaded was flood. Security against flood conditioned the architect's ideal : he aimed solely at height and mass. When a king built a palace for himself or a temple for his god, he did not consciously aim at making it graceful or beautiful. What he always boasts of having done is that he has made it "like a mountain." He delighted to raise the level of his artificial mound or building-platform, and the modern excavator owes much to this continual filling in of the remains of earlier structures. The material at his disposal was also not without its influence in the production of buildings "like mountains," designed to escape the floods of the plain.

The alluvial origin of the Babylonian soil deprived the inhabitants of an important factor in the development of the builder's art : it produced for them no stone. But it supplied a very effective building-material in its place, a strongly adhesive clay. Throughout their whole history the Babylonian architects built in crude and in kiln-burnt brick. In the Neo-Babylonian period we find them making interesting technical experiments in this material, here a first attempt to roof in a wide area with vaulting, elsewhere counteracting the effects of settlement by a sort of expansion-joint. We shall see, too, that it was in this same medium that they attained to real beauty of design.

Brick continued to be the main building-material in Assyria too, for that country derived its culture from the lower Euphrates valley.[1] But in the north soft

[1] Recent discoveries at Shergât prove that a Sumerian occupation of the

limestone quarries were accessible.   So in Assyria they
lined their mud-brick walls with slabs of limestone,
carved in low relief and brightly coloured ; and they set
up huge stone colossi to flank their palace entrances.
This use of stone, both as a wall-lining and in wall-
foundations, constitutes the main difference between
Babylonian and Assyrian architectural design.   Incidentally it explains how the earlier excavators were so
much more successful in Assyria than in Babylonia ;
for in both countries they drove their tunnels and
trenches into most of the larger mounds.   They could
tunnel with perfect certainty when they had these stone
linings of the walls to guide them.   But to follow out
the ground-plan of a building constructed only of
unburnt brick, with mud or clay for mortar, necessi-
tates a slower and more systematic process of examination.   For unburnt brick becomes welded into a solid
mass, scarcely to be distinguished from the surrounding
soil, and the lines of a building in this material can only
be recovered by complete excavation.

An idea of the labour this sometimes entails may be
gained from the work which preceded the identification
of E-sagila, the great temple of Marduk, the city-god of
Babylon.   The temple lies at a depth of no less than
twenty-one metres below the upper level of the hill of
débris ; and portions of two of its massive mud-brick
walls, together with the neighbouring pavements, were
uncovered by bodily removing the great depth of soil
truck by truck.   But here even German patience and
thoroughness have been beaten, and tunnelling was

site of Ashur preceded the first settlement of the Semitic Assyrians.   In a
stratum below the first Ishtar-temple (the earliest Assyrian temple yet
recovered, dating as it does from the close of the third millennium B.C.),
several examples of Sumerian sculpture were found which bear an unmistak-
ably close relationship to the earliest Sumerian work at Tello and Bismâya.
The racial type represented by the sculptures is also that of the south, and
suggests a Sumerian occupation of Assyria before the advent of the Semites.
The termination of their settlement at Ashur was probably not the work of
the Semitic conquerors of Assyria, but of another non-Semitic race akin to
the Mitannian people of Northern Mesopotamia (on this subject see further
Chap. IV., pp. 137 ff.).   But the Semites were at least indirect heirs of the
Sumerian inhabitants and derived their culture in part from them ; and the
growth of such elements in their acquired civilization would have been
fostered as intercourse with the south increased.   For a summary account
of the new discoveries at Ashur, see the "Mitteilungen der Deutschen Orient-
Gesellschaft," No. 54 (June, 1914).

eventually adopted to establish the outer limits of the ground-plan, much of the interior of which still remains unexplored.[1]

The Babylon which has now been partially cleared, though in its central portion it reaches back to the First Dynasty and to the period of Hammurabi, is mainly that of the Neo-Babylonian empire, when Nebuchadnezzar II., and Nabonidus, the last native Babylonian king, raised their capital to a condition of magnificence it had not known before. This city survived, with but little change, during the domination of the Achæmenian kings of Persia, and from the time of Herodotus onward Babylon was made famous throughout the ancient world. At that time Ashur and Nineveh, the great capitals of Assyria, had ceased to exist; but Babylon was still in her glory, and descriptions of the city have come down to us in the works of classical writers. To fit this literary tradition to the actual remains of the city has furnished a number of fascinating problems. How, for example, are we to explain the puzzling discrepancy between the present position of the outer walls and the enormous estimate of the city's area given by Herodotus, or even that of Ctesias? For Herodotus himself appears to have visited Babylon; and Ctesias was the physician of Artaxerxes II. Mnemon, who has left a memorial of his presence in a marble building on the Kaṣr.

Herodotus reckons that the walls of Babylon extended for four hundred and eighty stades, the area they enclosed forming an exact square, a hundred and twenty stades in length each way.[2] In other words, he would have us picture a city more than fifty-three miles in circumference. The estimate of Ctesias is not so large, his side of sixty-five stades giving a circumference of rather over forty miles.[3] Such figures, it has been suggested, are not in themselves impossible, Koldewey, for example, comparing the Great Wall of China which extends for more than fifteen hundred miles,

[1] See further, p. 72 f.
[2] I., 178.
[3] For references to other estimates, see How and Wells, "Commentary on Herodotus," sub I., 178.

and is thus about twenty-nine times as long as Herodotus's estimate for the wall of Babylon.[1]   But the
latter was not simply a frontier-fortification.   It was
the enclosing wall of a city, and a more apposite
comparison is that of the walls of Nanking, the largest
city-site in China, and the work of an empire even
greater than Babylon.[2]   The latter measure less than
twenty-four miles in circuit, and the comparison does
not encourage an acceptance of Herodotus's figures on
grounds of general probability.   It is true that Oppert
accepted them, but he only found this possible by
stretching his plan of the city to include the whole area
from Bâbil to Birs-Nimrûd,[3] and by seeing traces of
the city and its walls in every sort of intervening mound
of whatever period.

As a matter of fact part of the great wall, which
surrounded the city from the Neo-Babylonian period
onward, has survived to the present day, and may still
be recognized in a low ridge of earth, or series of consecutive mounds,[4] which cross the plain for a considerable
distance to the south-east of Bâbil.   The traveller
from Baghdad, after crossing the present Nîl Canal by
a bridge,[5] passes through a gap in the north-eastern wall
before he sees on his right the isolated mound of Bâbil
with the extensive complex of the Kaṣr and its neighbour, Tell 'Amrân-ibn-'Ali, stretching away in front
and to his left.[6]   The whole length of the city-wall,
along the north-east side, may still be traced by the
position of these low earthen mounds, and they prove
that the city on this side measured not quite two and
three-quarter miles in extent.   The eastern angle of the
wall is also preserved, and the south-east wall may be
followed for another mile and a quarter as it doubles
back towards the Euphrates.   These two walls, together
with the Euphrates, enclose the only portion of the
ancient city on which ruins of any importance still
exist.   But, according to Herodotus and other writers,

[1] Cf. " Das wieder erstehende Babylon," p. 5.
[2] Cf. Haverfield, " Ancient Town Planning," p. 22.
[3] See above, p. 16, Fig. 2.
[4] See the general plan of Babylon on p. 23, Fig. 3, B.
[5] Fig. 3, T.
[6] A. D. and E. on plan.

the city was enclosed by two similar walls upon the western bank, in which case the site it occupied must have formed a rough quadrangle, divided diagonally by

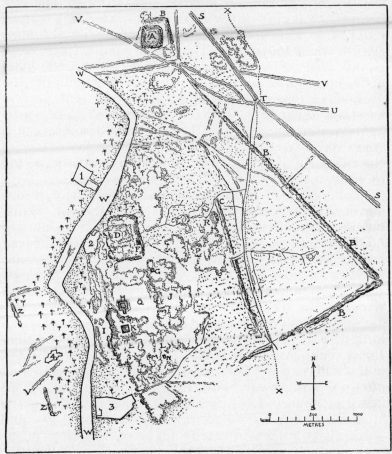

FIG. 3.

PLAN OF THE RUINS OF BABYLON.

A: The mound Bâbil. B: Outer City-wall. C: Inner City-wall. D: The Ḳaṣr mound. E: The mound 'Amrân-ibn-'Ali. F: E-makḫ, temple of the goddess Ninmakḫ. G: Temple of Ishtar of Akkad. H: E-temen-anki, the Tower of Babylon. I: Ancient bed of the Euphrates. J: The mound Merkes. K: E-sagila, the temple of Marduk. L: The mound Ishin-aswad. M: Unidentified temple known as "Z." N: E-patutila, the temple of Ninib. P: Greek theatre. Q: Sakhn, the small plain covering the precincts of the Tower of Babylon. R: The mound Homera. S: Nîl Canal. T: Bridge over Nîl Canal. U: Former bed of Nîl Canal. V: Old Canal. W: Euphrates. X: Track from Baghdad to Hilla. Z: Mounds covering the ruins of walls. 1: Village of Anana. 2: Village of Kweiresh. 3: Village of Jumjumma. 4: Village of Sinjar.

[After Koldewey and Andrae.]

the river.   No certain trace has yet been recovered of
the western walls,[1] and all remains of buildings seem to
have disappeared completely on that side of the river.
But for the moment it may be assumed that the city
did occupy approximately an equal amount of space
upon the western bank ; and, even so, its complete
circuit would not have extended for more than about
eleven miles, a figure very far short of any of those
given by Herodotus, Ctesias and other writers.

Dr. Koldewey suggests that, as the estimate of
Ctesias approximates to four times the correct measurement, we may suspect that he mistook the figure which
applies to the whole circumference for the measure of
one side only of the square.   But even if we accept that
solution, it leaves the still larger figure of Herodotus
unexplained.   It is preferable to regard all such estimates of size, not as based on accurate measurements,
but merely as representing an impression of grandeur
produced on the mind of their recorder, whether by a
visit to the city itself, or by reports of its magnificence
at second-hand.

The excavators have not as yet devoted much
attention to the city-wall, and, until more extensive
digging has been carried out, it will not be possible to
form a very detailed idea of the system of fortification.
But enough has already been done to prove that the
outer wall was a very massive structure, and consisted
of two separate walls with the intermediate space filled
in with rubble.   The outer wall, or face, which bore the

---

[1] Some traces of walls still remain near the villiage of Sinjar (see Fig. 3, 4),
and Weissbach has attempted to use them for a reconstruction of the city
plan.   As a result he makes the western portion of the city considerably
smaller than that on the eastern bank, his north-west wall meeting the
Euphrates opposite the Ḳaṣr, and being continued by the elaborate fortification-
walls to the north of the Southern Citadel ; cf. " Das Stadtbild von Babylon,"
in " Der alte Orient," V., Heft 4. This represents quite a possible arrangement.
We shall see that these remains of western walls may possibly date from a
still earlier period, and may also have defended the western extension of the
earlier city-area (see below, p. 35).   But even so they may have remained
the only fortifications on the western bank ; for the tendency to expansion
would have been more marked to the east where the main citadel offered
increased possibilities of defence.   The fact that Nebuchadnezzar's northern
citadel should also have been built on the left bank points in the same direction.   But the question can only be settled definitely when the traces of these
western walls have been examined by excavation and their relationship to the
eastern fortifications determined.

brunt of any attack and rose high above the moat
encircling the city, was of burnt brick set in bitumen.
It measured more than seven metres in thickness, and
below ground-level was further protected from the
waters of the moat by an additional wall, more than
three metres in thickness, and, like it, constructed
of burnt brick with bitumen as mortar.   Behind the
outer wall, at a distance of some twelve metres from it, was
a second wall of nearly the same thickness.   This faced
nward towards the city, and so was constructed of

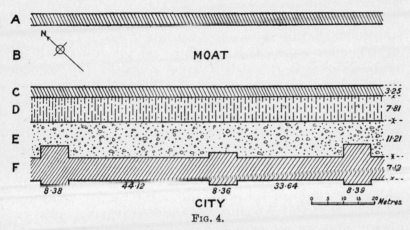

FIG. 4.

GROUND-PLAN OF PART OF THE OUTER CITY-WALL.

A : Outer moat-lining of burnt-brick. B : Moat. C : Inner moat-lining of
burnt-brick.   D : Outer wall of burnt-brick.   E : Rubble-filling.   F : Inner wall
of crude brick, with towers built at intervals across it.   The figures on the plan
give measurements in metres.

[After Koldewey and Andrae.]

crude or unburnt brick, as it would not be liable to
direct assault by a besieger; and the mortar employed
was clay.[1]   The crude-brick wall cannot be dated
accurately, but it is certainly older than the reign of
Nebuchadnezzar, and in his father's time it probably

[1] The line of mounds now marking in places the position of the city-wall
is formed, oddly enough, by the core of the mud-brick portion, which still stands
above the level of the surrounding soil.   The far stronger outer wall has completely disappeared, for its fine burnt-bricks have tempted plunderers in search
of building material.   It is only after excavation that the lower courses of its
foundation are detected when still in place.   It is possible that deep excavation may settle the position of the whole line of walls, even where no trace
of them now remains upon the surface.

formed the outer city's sole protection.[1]   The burnt-brick wall and the moat-lining in front of it date, in their present form, from the age of Nebuchadnezzar, for they are built of his square bricks, impressed with his usual stamp, which are so common over the whole site of Babylon.

At intervals along the crude-brick wall were towers projecting slightly beyond each face.[2]   Only the bases of the towers have been preserved, so that any restoration of their upper structure must rest on pure conjecture.   But, as rubble still fills the space between the two walls of burnt and unburnt brick, it may be presumed that the filling was continued up to the crown of the outer wall.   It is possible that the inner wall of crude brick was raised to a greater height and formed a curtain between each pair of towers.   But even so, the clear space in front, consisting of the rubble filling and the burnt-brick wall, formed a broad roadway nearly twenty metres in breadth, which extended right round the city along the top of the wall.   On this point the excavations have fully substantiated the account given by Herodotus, who states that " on the top, along the edges of the wall, they constructed buildings of a single chamber facing one another, leaving between them room for a four-horse chariot to turn." [3]   Even if smaller towers were built upon the outer edge, there would have been fully enough space to drive a team of four horses abreast along the wall, and in the intervals between the towers two such chariots might easily have passed each other.   It has been acutely noted that this design of the wall was not only of protection by reason of its size, but was also of great strategic value ; for it enabled the defence to move its forces with great speed from one point to another, wherever the attack at the moment might be pressed.[4]

[1] This has been deduced from the fact that a ditch, or moat, once ran immediately in front of it, of which traces only have been found.   The old ditch was filled in when Nebuchadnezzar's burnt-brick wall broadened and strengthened the whole line of fortification.

[2] It has been reckoned that there were not less than ninety towers along the north-east wall of the city, though only fifteen of these have as yet been completely excavated.

[3] I., 179.

[4] Cf. Koldewey, " Babylon," p. 2.

In fact it is only in the matter of size and extent that the description given by Herodotus of the walls of Babylon is to be discounted; and those are just the sort of details that an ancient traveller would accept without question from his local guide. His total number for the city-gates is also no doubt excessive,[1] but his description of the wall itself as built of burnt-brick tallies exactly with the construction of its outer face, which would have been the only portion visible to any one passing outside the city. Moreover, in one portion of the wall, as reconstructed by Nebuchadnezzar, its inner as well as its outer half appears to have been formed of burnt-brick. This is the small rectangular extension, which Nebuchadnezzar threw out to protect his later citadel now covered by the mound known as Bâbil.[2]

The mound of Bâbil represents Nebuchadnezzar's latest addition to the city's system of fortification, and its construction in advance of the old line of the outer walls was dictated by the desire, of which we find increasing evidence throughout his reign, to strengthen the capital against attack from the north. The mound has not yet been systematically excavated, but enough has been done to prove that, like the great citadel upon the Kaṣr, it protected a royal palace consisting of a large number of chambers and galleries grouped around open courts. From this fact it is clear that a Babylonian citadel was not simply a fortress to be used by the garrison for the defence of the city as a whole: it was also a royal residence, into which the monarch and his court could shut themselves for safety should the outer wall of the city itself be penetrated. Even in times of peace the king dwelt there, and the royal stores and treasury, as well as the national armoury and arsenal, were housed in its innumerable magazines. In the case of the Southern Citadel of

---

[1] He tells us that in the circuit of the wall there were a hundred gates, all of brass, with brazen lintels and side-posts; cf. I., 179. As yet the excavations have not determined the site of any of the gates in the outer wall; but the manner in which bronze may have been used to strengthen and decorate the doors and gateways is illustrated by the bronze lintel, or step, from E-zida, the temple of Nabû at Borsippa, now in the British Museum; cf. Plate XXVI., opposite p. 278, and see further, p. 77, n. 4.　　[2] See Fig. 3, A.

Babylon, on which excavations have now been continuously carried out for sixteen years, we shall see that it formed a veritable township in itself. It was a city within a city, a second Babylon in miniature.[1]

The Southern or chief Citadel was built on the mound now known as the Ḳasr, and within it Nebuchadnezzar erected his principal palace, partly over an earlier building of his father Nabopolassar. The palace and

FIG. 5.

CONJECTURAL RESTORATION OF THE SOUTHERN CITADEL.

The view is reconstructed from the north, the conventional mound in the foreground covering the Central Citadel now partially excavated. The Sacred Road passes through the Ishtar Gate and along the east side of the palace; further to the east and within the fortifications is the small temple of Ninmakh. The innermost wall encloses the palace of Nebuchadnezzar with its four open courts; the façade of the Throne Room, with three entrances, is visible in the Great Court. The flat roofs of the palace are broken here and there by smaller courts or light-wells. Compare the ground-plan on p. 30, Fig. 6.

[After Andrae.]

citadel occupy the old city-square or centre of Babylon, which is referred to in the inscriptions as the *irṣit Bâbili*, "the Babil place."[2] Though far smaller in extent than Nebuchadnezzar's citadel, we may conclude that the chief fortress of Babylon always stood upon this site, and the city may well have derived its name Bâb-ilî, "the Gate of the Gods," from the strategic position of its ancient fortress, commanding as it does, the main approach to E-sagila, the famous temple of the city-god.[3] The earliest ruins in Babylon, which

[1] Indeed during the Neo-Babylonian period it appears to have been known as "the City of the Dwelling of the King of Babylon;" see further, p. 41.

[2] Cf. "East India House Inscription," Col. VII., l. 40 (Rawlinson, "Cun. Inscr. West. Asia," Vol. I., pl. 57, and Langdon, "Die neubabylonischen Königsinschriften," p. 136 f.).

[3] See below, pp. 71 ff. Traces of a very ancient settlement, with much pottery (still unpublished), have been found by deep trenching in the fillings

date from the age of Hammurabi and the First Dynasty
of West-Semitic kings, lie under the mound of Merkes [1]
just to the east of E-sagila and the Tower of Babylon,
proving that the first capital clustered about the shrine
of the city-god.   The streets in that quarter suffered
but little change, and their main lines remained unaltered down through the Kassite period into Neo-
Babylonian and later times. [2]   It was natural that even
in the earlier period the citadel should have been
planted up-stream, to the north of city and temple,
since the greatest danger of invasion was always from
the north.

The outer city-wall, already described, dates only
from the Neo-Babylonian period, when the earlier and
smaller city expanded with the prosperity which
followed the victories of Nabopolassar and his son.
The eastern limits of that earlier city, at any rate toward the close of the Assyrian domination, did not
extend beyond the inner wall, which was then the only
line of defence and was directly connected with the
main citadel.   The course of the inner wall may still
be traced for a length of seventeen hundred metres by
the low ridge or embankment, [3] running approximately
north and south, from a point north-east of the mound
Homera. [4]   It was a double fortification, consisting of
two walls of crude or unburnt brick, with a space
between of rather more than seven metres.   The thicker
of the walls, on the west, which is six and a half metres
in breadth, has large towers built across it, projecting
deeply on the outer side, and alternating with smaller
towers placed lengthwise along it.   The outer or
eastern wall has smaller towers at regular intervals.
Now along the north side of the main or Southern
Citadel run a pair of very similar walls, [5] also of crude

below the south-east corner of the citadel; cf. Koldewey, "Babylon," p. 82.
Some flints and stone-implements found elsewhere are also evidence of a still
earlier prehistoric settlement.

[1] See above, p. 23, Fig. 3, J.   [2] See further, pp. 82 ff.
[3] See Fig. 3, C.   [4] Fig. 3, R.
[5] See below, p. 30, Fig. 6, where the space between the crude brick walls is
labelled K K.   The walls are distinguished, by cross-hatching, from the
structure of the palace which is of burnt-brick.   When the Ishtar Gate (H)
was built by Nebuchadnezzar, the northern of the two walls received a facing
on both sides of brick-rubble laid in mud and bitumen, indicated by a heavy

brick, and they are continued eastward of the citadel to a point where, in the Persian period, the Euphrates through a change of course destroyed all further trace

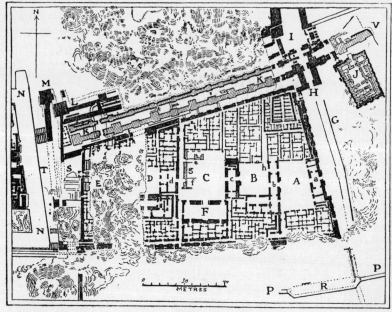

FIG. 6.

PLAN OF THE SOUTHERN CITADEL.

A : East Court of the Palace of Nebuchadnezzar. B : Central Court. C : Great Court. D : Private portion of palace built over earlier Palace of Nabopolassar. E : West extension of palace. F : Throne Room of Nebuchadnezzar. G : Sacred Road, known as Aibur-shabû. H : Ishtar Gate. I : Continuation of Sacred Road with Lion Frieze. J : Temple of Ninmakh. K : Space between the two fortification-walls of crude brick, probably Imgur-Bêl and Nimitti-Bêl. L : Older moat-wall. M : Later moat-wall. N : Later fortification thrown out into the bed of the Euphrates. P : Southern Canal, probably part of the Libil-khegalla. R : Basin of canal. S : Persian building. T : Moat, formerly the left side of the Euphrates. V : River-side embankment of the Persian period. a : Gateway to East Court. b : Gateway to Central Court. c : Gateway to Great Court. d : Double Gateway to private part of palace. e, f : Temporary ramps used during construction of palace. g : Temporary wall of crude brick. h : Broad passage-way, leading northwards to Vaulted Building.
[After Koldewey, Reuther and Wetzel.]

of them.[1]   We may confidently assume that in the time of Nebuchadnezzar[2] they were linked up with the

surrounding line upon the plan ; but originally this wall too was of crude brick.

[1] Fig. 6, V ; and see further, p. 58, n. 1.
[2] The present crude brick walls of the Ḳaṣr fortifications date from his reign or from that of his father.

inner city-wall to the north of Homera and formed its continuation after it turned at right angles on its way towards the river-bank. This line of fortification is of considerable interest, as there is reason to believe it may represent the famous double-line of Babylon's defences, which is referred to again and again in the inscriptions.

The two names the Babylonians gave these walls were suggested by their gratitude to and confidence in Marduk, the city-god, who for them was the " Bêl," or Lord, *par excellence*. To the greater of the two, the *dûru* or inner wall, they gave the name *Imgur-Bêl*, meaning " Bêl has been gracious"; while the *shalkhu*, or outer one, they called *Nimitti-Bêl*, that is, probably, " The foundation of Bêl," or " My foundation is Bêl." [1] The identification of at least one of the crude-brick walls near Homera with Nimitti-Bêl, has been definitely proved by several foundation-cylinders of Ashur-bani-pal, the famous Assyrian king who deposed his brother Shamash-shum-ukîn from the throne of Babylon and annexed the country as a province of Assyria.[2] On the cylinders he states that the walls Imgur-Bêl and Nimitti-Bêl had fallen into ruins, and he records his restoration of the latter, within the foundation or structure of which the cylinders were originally immured. Unfortunately they were not found in place, but among the *débris* in the space between the walls, so that it is not now certain from which wall they came. If they had been deposited in the thicker or inner wall, then Nimitti-Bêl must have been a double line of fortification, and both walls together must have borne the name; and in that case we must seek elsewhere for Imgur-Bêl. But it is equally possible that they came from the narrow or outer wall; and on this alternative Nimitti-Bêl may be the outer one and Imgur-Bêl the broader inner-wall with the widely projecting towers. It is true that only further excavation can settle the point; but meanwhile the fortifications on the Kaṣr have supplied further evidence which seems to support the latter view.

[1] The meaning of *nimitti* is not quite certain.
[2] In 648 B.C. ; see further, Chap. VIII.

The extensive alterations which took place in the old citadel's fortifications, especially during Nebuchadnezzar's long reign of forty-three years, led to the continual dismantling of earlier structures and the enlargement of the area enclosed upon the north and west. This is particularly apparent in its northwest corner. Here, at a considerable depth below the later fortification-walls, were found the remains of four earlier walls,[1] the discovery of which has thrown considerable light on the topography of this portion of Babylon. All four are ancient quay-walls, their northern and western faces sloping sharply inwards as they rise. Each represents a fresh rebuilding of the quay, as it was gradually extended to the north and west. Fortunately, stamped and inscribed bricks were employed in considerable quantities in their construction, so that it is possible to date the periods of rebuilding accurately.

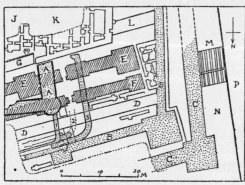

FIG. 7.

GROUND-PLAN OF QUAY-WALLS AND FORTIFICATION-WALLS IN THE N.W. CORNER OF THE S. CITADEL.

A : Sargon's quay-wall. B : Older moat-wall. C : Later moat-wall of Nebuchadnezzar. D : Intermediate wall. E : South fortification-wall of crude brick, probably Imgur-Bêl. F : North fortification-wall of crude brick, probably Nimitti-Bêl. G : North wall of the Southern Citadel. I : Ruins of building, possibly the quarters of the Captain of the Wall. J : Palace of Nabopolassar. K : West Extension of the Southern Citadel. L : Connecting wall. M : Later wall across channel with grid for water. N : Water, originally the left side of the Euphrates. P : Later fortification of Nebuchadnezzar in former bed of the Euphrates. 1–3 : Nabopolassar's quay-walls. N.B. The quays and moat-walls are distinguished by dotting.

[After Koldewey.]

The earliest of the quay-walls, which is also the earliest building yet recovered on the Kaṣr, is the most massive of the four,[2] and is strengthened at the angle

---

[1] Figs. 7 and 8, A and 1–3. Fig. 7 gives the ground-plan of this corner of the citadel. In Fig. 8 the quay-walls and fortification-walls are given in section along the north front, looking from W. to E. In Fig. 8 the quay-wall "2" cannot be shown, as it is practically a westward extension of "1."

[2] A.

with a projecting circular bastion. It is the work of Sargon of Assyria,[1] who states the object of the structure in a text inscribed upon several of its bricks. After reciting his own name and titles, he declares that it was his desire to rebuild Imgur-Bêl; that with this object he caused burnt-bricks to be fashioned, and built a quay-wall with pitch and bitumen in the depth

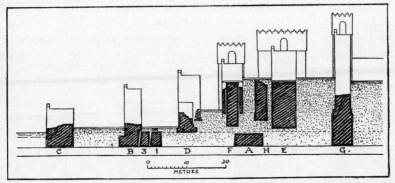

FIG. 8.

SECTION OF THE QUAY-WALLS AND FORTIFICATION-WALLS ALONG THE NORTH FRONT OF THE SOUTHERN CITADEL.

A : Sargon's quay-wall. B : Older moat-wall. C : Later moat-wall of Nebuchadnezzar. D : Intermediate wall. E : South fortification-wall of crude brick, probably Imgur-Bêl. F : North fortification-wall of crude brick, probably Nimitti-Bêl. G : North wall of Southern Citadel. H : Remains of older crude brick wall.

[After Andrae.]

of the water from beside the Ishtar Gate to the bank of the Euphrates; and he adds that he "founded Imgur-Bêl and Nimitti-Bêl mountain-high upon it."[2] The two walls of Sargon, which he here definitely names as Imgur-Bêl and Nimitti-Bêl, were probably of crude brick, and were, no doubt, demolished and replaced by the later structures of Nabopolassar's and Nebuchadnezzar's reigns. But they must have occupied approximately the same position as the two crude

[1] It was built by Sargon within the last five years of his reign, when, after his signal defeat of Merodach-baladan in 710 B.C., he ruled Babylonia as an Assyrian province. He did not ascend the throne, but contented himself with the title "Governor (shakkanaku) of Babylon," though he claimed the older title of "King of Sumer and Akkad." See further, Chap. VIII.

[2] Cf. Delitzsch's translation in Koldewey, "Babylon," p. 139; Engl. ed. p. 138. Elsewhere in the building-inscriptions the Ishtar Gate is named as belonging to Imgur-Bêl and Nimitti-Bêl.

D

brick walls above the quay of Sargon,[1] which run from
the old bank of the Euphrates to the Ishtar Gate,
precisely the two points mentioned in Sargon's text.
His evidence is therefore strongly in favour of identifying these later crude-brick walls, which we have
already connected with the inner city-wall, as the
direct successors of his Imgur-Bêl and his Nimitti-Bêl,
and therefore as inheritors of the ancient names.

We find further confirmation of this view in one
of the later quay-walls, which succeeded that of Sargon.
The three narrow walls already referred to[2] were all
the work of Nabopolassar, and represent three successive extensions of the quay westward into the bed
of the stream, which in the inscriptions upon their
bricks is given the name of Arakhtu.[3]   But the texts
make no mention of the city-walls.   No inscriptions
at all have been found in the structure of the next
extension, represented by the wall B, which, like
the latest quay-wall (C), is not rounded off in the
earlier manner, but is strengthened at the corner with
a massive rectangular bastion.   It was in this latest
and most substantial of all the quay-walls that further
inscriptions were found referring to Imgur-Bêl.   They
prove that this wall was the work of Nebuchadnezzar,
who refers in them to Nabopolassar's restoration of
Imgur-Bêl and records that he raised its banks with
bitum:n and burnt-brick mountain-high.   It is therefore clear that this was the quay-wall of Imgur Bêl,
which it supported in the manner of Sargon's earlier
structure.   That the less important Nimitti-Bêl is not
mentioned in these texts does not necessitate our placing
it elsewhere, in view of Sargon's earlier reference.

We may therefore provisionally regard the two
crude-brick walls along the Ḳaṣr's northern front[4] as
a section of the famous defences of Babylon, and picture
them as running eastward till they meet the inner

[1] E and F in Figs. 7 and 8.   In Fig. 7 it will be seen that there are
remains of a building (I) at the western end of the two walls, between them
and the quay-wall B.   This may have been the quarters occupied by the
Captain of the Wall.
[2] Nos. 1–3 in Fig. 7.
[3] On the meaning of the name, see below, p. 36.
[4] E and F in Figs. 7 and 8.

city-wall by Homera. The point at which they extended westward across the Euphrates can, as yet, only be conjectured. But it is significant that the angle of the western walls, which may still be traced under mounds to the north of Sinjar village,[1] is approximately in line with the north front of the Kaṣr and the end of the inner wall by Homera. Including these western walls within our scheme, the earlier Babylon would have been rectangular in ground-plan, about a quarter of it only upon the right bank, and the portion east of the river forming approximately a square. The Babylon of the Kassite period and of the First Dynasty must have been smaller still, its area covering little more than the three principal mounds ; and, though part of its street net-work has been recovered, no trace of its fortifications has apparently survived.

The evidence relating to the city's walls and fortifications has been summarized rather fully, as it has furnished the chief subject of controversy in connexion with the excavations. It should be added that the view suggested above is not shared by Dr. Koldewey, whose objections to the proposed identification of Imgur-Bêl rest on his interpretation of two phrases in a cylinder of Nabopolassar, which was found out of place in *débris* close to the east wall of the Southern Citadel. In it Nabopolassar records his own restoration of Imgur-Bêl, which he tells us had fallen into decay, and he states that he "founded it in the primæval abyss," adding the words, " I caused Babylon to be enclosed with it towards the four winds."[2] From the reference to the abyss, Dr. Koldewey concludes that it had deep foundations, and must therefore have been constructed of burnt, not crude, brick ; while from the second phrase he correctly infers that it must have formed a quadrilateral closed on all sides. But that, as we have seen, is precisely the ground-plan we obtain by including the remains of walls west of the river. And, in view of the well-known tendency to exaggeration in these Neo-Babylonian records, we should surely not credit any single metaphor with the accuracy of a modern architect's specification.

[1] See above, p. 23, Fig. 3. Z ; cf. also, p. 24, n. 1.
[2] Cf. Delitzsch's translation in "Babylon," p. 135 f.

If a single section of the wall had been furnished, during restoration, with a burnt-brick substructure, it would have been enough to justify the royal claim.

The manner in which the Euphrates was utilized for the defence and water-supply of the citadel has also been illustrated by the excavations. The discovery of Sargon's inscriptions proved that in his day the river flowed along the western face of his quay-wall ; [1] while the inscriptions on bricks from the three successive quay-walls of Nabopolassar [2] state, in each case, that he used them to rebuild the wall of a channel he calls the " Arakhtu," using the name in precisely the same way as Sargon refers to the Euphrates. The simplest explanation is that in Nabopolassar's time the Arakhtu was the name for that section of the Euphrates which washed the western side of the citadel, and that its use in any case included the portion of the citadel-moat, or canal, along its northern face, which formed a basin opening directly upon the river.[3] The " Arakhtu " may thus have been a general term, not only for this basin, but for the whole water-front from the north-west corner of the citadel to some point on the left bank to the south of it. It may perhaps have been further extended to include the river frontage of the Tower of Babylon, since it was into the Arakhtu that Sennacherib cast the tower on his destruction of the city. Within this stretch of water, particularly along the northern quays, vessels and *keleks* would have been moored which arrived down stream with supplies for the palace and the garrison. The Arakhtu, in fact, may well have been the name for the ancient harbour or dock of Babylon.

Some idea of the appearance of the quays may be gathered from the right-hand corner of the restoration in Fig. 5.[4] It is true that the outer quay-wall appears to have been built to replace the inner one, while in the illustration both are shown. But since the height of the citadel and of its walls was continually being raised,

---

[1] See above, p. 33.   [2] See above, p. 34.

[3] Its employment with the determinative *nâru*, " river " or " canal," does not prove that it was at this time a canal in the strict sense. According to the explanation offered in the text, it would have been a section of the river, including an open basin and probably a canal In earlier periods it may have been simply a canal, which led off from the river at this point.

[4] See above, p. 28.

the arrangement there suggested is by no means impossible. But in the later part of his reign Nebuchadnezzar changed the aspect of the river-front entirely. To the west of the quay-walls, in the bed of the river, he threw out a massive fortification with immensely thick walls, from twenty to twenty-five metres in breadth.[1] It was constructed entirely of burnt-brick and bitumen, and, from his reference to it in an inscription from Sippar, it would seem that his object in building it was to prevent the formation of sandbanks in the river, which in the past may have caused the flooding of the left bank above E-Sagila.[2] A narrow channel[3] was left between it and the old quay, along which the river water continued to flow through gratings. This no doubt acted as an overflow for the old northern moat of the citadel, since the latter fed the supply-canal, which passed round the palace and may still be traced along its south side.[4]

It is possible that the subsequent change in the course of the Euphrates may be traced in part to this huge river-fortification. Its massive structure suggests that it had to withstand considerable water-pressure, and it may well have increased any tendency of the stream to break away eastward. However that may be, it is certain that for a considerable time during the Persian and Seleucid periods it flowed round to the eastward of the Ḳaṣr, close under three sides of the

---

[1] See above, p. 30, Fig. 6, N.

[2] On a foundation-cylinder from Sippar in the British Museum (No. 91114; A. H. 82—7—14, 1042) Nebuchadnezzar writes: "For the protection of E-sagila and Babylon, that sandbanks (pa-ri-im) should not form in the bed of the Euphrates, I caused a great fortification to be made in the river, of bitumen and burnt-brick. Its foundation I laid in the abyss, and its head I raised mountain-high"; cf. Ball, "Proc. Soc. Bibl. Arch.", X., May 1888, Pl. IV., Col. ii., ll. 19—24, and Langdon, "Neubabylonischen Königsinschriften," p. 106 f.

[3] See p. 30, Fig. 6, T, and p. 32, Fig. 7, N.

[4] Fig. 6, P, R. It re-entered the river close under the citadel-wall, for its outlet has been found in the later river-wall of Nabonidus. It was perhaps the canal called in the inscriptions Libil-khegalla, "May it bring abundance." It will be seen from the plan that the remains of the canal to the south-east show a narrow channel (P), less than three metres in breadth, but widening westward of the Sacred Road (G) into a broad basin (R). This represents a reconstruction, probably of the time of Neriglissar, who built a bridge for the road across the canal. Formerly the road crossed the canal by a dam with walled embankments, of which traces have been found below the canal-walls. Beneath the embankment the water probably flowed through grated sluices like these spanning Nebuchadnezzar's narrow channel between his river-fortification and the citadel.

citadel and rejoined its former bed to the north of Marduk's temple and the Tower of Babylon. Its course east of the Ishtar Gate is marked by a late embankment sloping outwards, which supported the thicker of the crude-brick walls at the point where they suddenly break off.[1] Beyond this embankment only mud and river sediment were found. The water-course to the south of the citadel is probably the point where the river turned again towards the channel it had deserted. A trench that was dug here showed that the present soil is formed of silt deposited by water, and beyond the remains of the earlier canal no trace of any building was recovered. This temporary change in the river's course, which the excavations have definitely proved, explains another puzzle presented by the classical tradition—the striking discrepancy between the actual position of the principal ruins of Babylon in relation to the river and their recorded position in the Persian period. Herodotus,[2] for example, places the fortress with the palace of the kings (that is, the Kasr), on the opposite bank to the sacred precinct of Zeus Belus (that is, E-temen-anki, the Tower of Babylon). But we have now obtained proof that they were separated at that time by the Euphrates, until the river returned to its former and present bed, probably before the close of the Seleucid period.

The greater part of the Southern Citadel is occupied by the enormous palace on which Nebuchadnezzar lavished his energies during so many years of his reign. On ascending the throne of Babylon, he found the ancient fortress a very different place to the huge structure he bequeathed to his successors. He had lived there in his father's life-time, but Nabopolassar had been content with a comparatively modest dwelling. And when his son, flushed with his victory over the hosts of Egypt, returned to Babylon to take the hands of Bêl, he began to plan a palace that should be worthy of the empire he had secured. Of the old palace of Nabopolassar, in which at first he was obliged to dwell, very little now remains. What is left of it constitutes the earliest building of which traces now

[1] See above, p. 30, and cf. Fig. 6, V.   [2] I., 181.

THE THRONE-ROOM IN NEBUCHADNEZZAR'S PALACE AT BABYLON.

exist within the palace area.   Nebuchadnezzar describes
it, before his own building operations, as extending
from the Euphrates eastward to the Sacred Road ;
and the old palace-enclosure undoubtedly occupied
that site.   Traces of the old fortification-wall have
been found below the east front of the later palace, and
the arched doorway which gave access to its open
court, afterwards filled up and built over by Nebuchadnezzar, has been found in a perfect state of preservation.[1]

The old palace itself[2] did not reach beyond the
western side of Nebuchadnezzar's great court.[3]   The
upper structure, as we learn from the East India House
Inscription,[4] was of crude brick, which was demolished
for the later building.   But Nabopolassar, following a
custom which had survived unchanged from the time of
Hammurabi, had placed his crude-brick walls upon
burnt-brick foundations.   These his son made use of,
simply strengthening them before erecting his own
walls upon them.   Thus this section of the new palace
retained the old ground-plan to a great extent unchanged.   The strength and size of its walls are remarkable and may in part be explained by the crude-brick
upper structure of the earlier building, which necessarily
demanded a broader base for its walls.

When Nebuchadnezzar began building he dwelt in
the old palace, while he strengthened the walls of its
open court on the east and raised its level for the solid
platform on which his own palace was to rise.[5]   For a
time the new and the old palace were connected by two
ramps of unburnt-brick,[6] which were afterwards filled
in below the later pavement of the great court ; and
we may picture the king ascending the ramps with his
architect on his daily inspection of the work.   As soon
as the new palace on the east was ready he moved into
it, and, having demolished the old one, he built up his

---

[1] If we except the foundations of the Ishtar Gate, this door is the only
structure recovered on the site of Babylon which gives us an idea of what
a building looked like above ground-level.   Elsewhere the ground-plan is our
only guide.
[2] See p. 30, Fig. 6, D.   [3] Fig. 6, C.
[4] Col. vii., l. 34.   [5] Fig. 6, A—C.
[6] Fig. 6, e and f. The hatched wall, which runs between them (g), was a
temporary containing wall, also of crude brick.

own walls upon its foundations, and filled in the intermediate spaces with earth and rubble until he raised its
pavement to the eastern level.   Still later he built out
a further extension [1] along its western side.   In the
account he has left us of the palace-building the king
says : " I laid firm its foundation and raised it mountain-
high with bitumen and burnt-brick.   Mighty cedars I
caused to be stretched out at length for its roofing.   Door-
leaves of cedar overlaid with copper, thresholds and
sockets of bronze I placed in its doorways.   Silver and
gold and precious stones, all that can be imagined of
costliness, splendour, wealth, riches, all that was highly
esteemed, I heaped up within it, I stored up immense
abundance of royal treasure therein." [2]

A good general idea of the palace ground-plan, in its
final form, may be obtained from Fig. 6.   The main
entrance was in its eastern front, through a gate-way,[3]
flanked on its outer side by towers, and known as the
Bâb Bêlti, or " Lady Gate, " no doubt from its proxi-
mity to the temple of the goddess Ninmakh.[4]   The
gate-house consists of an entrance hall, with rooms
opening at the sides for the use of the palace-guard.
The eastern part of the palace is built to the north and
south of three great open courts,[5] separated from each
other by gateways [6] very like that at the main entrance
to the palace.   It will be noticed that, unlike the
arrangement of a European dwelling, the larger rooms
are always placed on the south side of the court facing
to the north, for in the sub-tropical climate of Babylonia
the heat of the summer sun was not courted, and these
chambers would have been in the shade throughout
almost the whole of the day.

Some of the larger apartments, including possibly
the chambers of the inner gateways, must have served
as courts of justice, for from the Hammurabi period
onward we know that the royal palace was the resort
of litigants, whose appeals in the earlier period were

---

[1] See above, p. 30, Fig. 6, E.
[2] East India House Inscription, Col. vii., l. 61—Col. viii., l. 18 ; cf.
Rawlinson, " Cun. Inscr. West. Asia," Vol. I., pl. 57, and Langdon, " Neubabylonischen Königsinschriften," p. 136 f.
[3] Fig. 6, a.   [4] Fig. 6, J.
[5] A, B and C.   [6] Marked b and c on the plan.

settled by the king himself,[1] and later by the judges under his supervision. Every kind of commercial business was carried on within the palace precincts, and not only were regular lawsuits tried, but any transaction that required legal attestation was most conveniently carried through there. Proof of this may be seen in the fact that so many of the Neo-Babylonian contracts that have been recovered on the site of Babylon are dated from the Al-Bît-shar-Bâbili, "the City of the King of Babylon's dwelling," doubtless a general title for the citadel and palace-area. All government business was also transacted here, and we may provisionally assign to the higher ministers and officials of the court the great apartment and the adjoining dwellings on the south side of the Central Court of the palace.[2] For many of the more important officers in the king's service were doubtless housed on the premises; and to those of lower rank we may assign the similar but rather smaller dwellings, which flank the three courts on the north and the Entrance Court upon the south side as well. Even royal manufactories were carried on within the palace, to judge from the large number of alabaster jars, found beside their cylindrical cores, in one room in the south-west corner by the outer palace-wall.[3]

It will be seen from the ground-plan that these dwellings consist of rooms built around open courts or light-wells; most of them are separate dwellings, isolated from their neighbours, and having doors opening on to the greater courts or into passage-ways running up from them. No trace of any windows has been found within the buildings, and it is probable that they were very sparsely employed. But we must not conclude that they were never used, since no wall of the palace has been preserved for more than a few feet in height, and, for the greater part, their foundations

[1] See further, Chap. V.
[2] Fig. 6, B.
[3] Such jars, or alabastra, were highly esteemed; and the royal factory need not surprise us, since the king not only employed them for his own use, but sent the larger sort away as presents. In the Persian period we know that Xerxes despatched some as royal gifts, inscribed with his own name and titles, as far afield as Egypt and the western coast of Asia Minor.

only have survived. But there is no doubt that, like the modern houses of the country, all the dwellings, whether in palace or city, had flat roofs, which formed the natural sleeping-place for their inhabitants during the greater part of the year. Towards sunset, when the heat of the day was past, they would ascend to the house-tops to enjoy the evening breeze; during the day a window would have been merely a further inlet for the sun. The general appearance of the palace is no doubt accurately rendered in the sketch already given.[1]

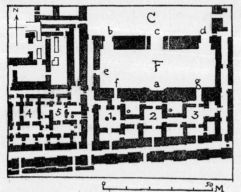

The most interesting apartment within the palace is one that may be identified as Nebuchadnezzar's Throne Room. This is the room immediately to the south of the Great Court.[2] It is the largest chamber of the palace, and since the walls on the longer sides are six metres thick, far broader than those at the ends, it is

FIG. 9.

PLAN OF THE THRONE ROOM OF NEBUCHADNEZZAR
AND PART OF THE PRIVATE PALACE.

C : Great Court. F : Throne Room. *a* : Recess in back-wall for throne. *b–d* : Entrances to Throne Room from Court. *e–g* : Entrances from side and back. 1–3 : Open courts, surrounded by rooms for the royal service. 4, 5 : Open courts in the south-east corner of the Private Palace.
[After Koldewey.]

possible that they supported a barrel-vaulting. It has three entrances from the court,[3] and in the back wall opposite the centre one is a broad niche, doubly recessed into the structure of the wall, where we may assume the royal throne once stood. During any elaborate court ceremony the king would thus have been visible upon his throne, not only to those within the chamber, but also from the central portion of the Great

[1] See above, p. 28, Fig. 5.
[2] See Fig. 6, F; this portion of the ground-plan of the palace is given on a larger scale in Fig. 9.
[3] Fig. 9, *b, c* and *d*.

Court. It was in this portion of the palace that some
traces of the later Babylonian methods of mural decoration were discovered. For, while the inner walls of
the Throne Room were merely washed over with a

Fig. 10.

DESIGN IN ENAMELLED BRICK FROM THE FAÇADE OF THE THRONE ROOM

In the drawing light and dark blue are indicated by light and heavy horizontal
shading; yellow by a dotted surface.

plaster of white gypsum, the brickwork of the outer
façade, which faced the court, was decorated with
brightly-coloured enamels.

Only fragments of the enamelled surface were dis-

covered, but these sufficed to restore the scheme of
decoration. A series of yellow columns with bright
blue capitals, both edged with white borders, stand
out against a dark blue ground. The capitals are the
most striking feature of the composition. Each consists of two sets of double volutes, one above the
other, and a white rosette with yellow centre comes
partly into sight above them. Between each member
is a bud in sheath, forming a trefoil, and linking the
volutes of the capitals by means of light blue bands
which fall in a shallow curve from either side of it.
Still higher on the wall ran a frieze of double palmettes
in similar colouring, between yellow line-borders, the
centres of the latter picked out with lozenges coloured
black and yellow, and black and white, alternately.
The rich effect of this enamelled façade of the Throne
Room was enhanced by the decoration of the court
gateway, the surface of which was adorned in a like
fashion with figures of lions. So too were the gateways of the other eastern courts, to judge from the
fragments of enamel found there, but the rest of the
court-walls were left undecorated or, perhaps, merely
received a coat of plaster. The fact that the interior
of the Throne Room, like the rest of the chambers of
the palace, was without ornamentation of any sort favours
the view that heat, and light with it, was deliberately
excluded by the absence of windows in the walls.

The chambers behind the Throne Room, reached
by two doorways in the back wall,[1] were evidently for
the king's service, and are ranged around three open
courts ; and in the south-west corners of two of them,
which lie immediately behind the Throne Room wall,
are wells, their positions indicated on the plan by
small open circles. The walls of each of these small
chambers are carried down through the foundations
to water-level, and the intermediate space is filled in

---

[1] Fig. 9, *f* and *g*. The courts (numbered on the plan 1–3) are square like
the small courts or light-wells in the rest of the palace, and like them were
evidently left open in order to give light and air to the chambers round them.
In the Persian period one of them (No. 1) was roofed over wholly or in part,
as the bases for two pillars, formed of palm-trunks, are still in place, which
were clearly intended to support roof-beams. These are indicated by solid
circles on the plan.

around the wells with rubble-packing. This device was evidently adopted to secure an absolutely pure supply of water for the royal table. But the private part of the palace, occupied by the women and the rest of the royal household, was evidently further to the west, built over the earlier dwelling of Nabopolassar. It will be seen from the ground-plan that this is quite distinct from the eastern or official portion of the palace, from which it is separated by a substantial wall and passage-way running, with the Great Court, the whole width of the palace-area. The character of the gateway-building, which formed its chief entrance and opened on the Great Court, is also significant.[1] For the towers, flanking the gateways to the official courts, are here entirely absent, and the pathway passes through two successive apartments, the second smaller than the first and with a porters' service-room opening off it. The entrance for the king's own use was in the southern half of the passage-way, and lies immediately between the side entrance to the Throne Room[2] and another doorway in the passage leading to one of the small courts behind it.[3] In two of the chambers within the private palace, both opening on to Court 5, are two more circular wells, walled in for protection, and here too the foundations of each chamber are carried down to water-level and filled in with brick-rubble, as in the case of the wells behind the Throne Room.

The same care that was taken to ensure the purity of the water-supply may also be detected in the elaborate drainage-system, with which the palace was provided, with the object of carrying off the surface-water from the flat palace-roofs, the open courts, and the fortification-walls. The larger drains were roofed with corbelled courses; the smaller ones, of a simpler but quite effective construction, were formed of bricks set together in the shape of a V and closed in at the top with other bricks

[1] See above, p. 30, Fig. 6, *d*.
[2] See p. 42, Fig. 9, *e*.
[3] Fig. 9, 1. This is the court roofed in during the Persian period (see p. 44, n. 1), evidently to secure the king a second covered passage-way when passing from the Throne Room or from some of its adjoining chambers to the private palace.

laid flat. The tops of the fortifications, both in the citadel itself and on the outer and inner city-wall, were drained by means of vertical shafts, or gutters, running down within the solid substructures of the towers; and in the case of crude-brick buildings these have a lining of burnt-brick. In some of the temples, which, as we shall see, were invariably built of crude brick,[1] this form of drainage was also adopted.

One other building within the palace deserves mention, as it has been suggested that it may represent

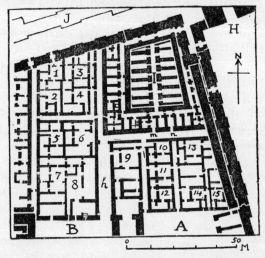

FIG. 11.

PLAN OF THE NORTH-EAST CORNER OF THE PALACE WITH THE VAULTED BUILDING.

A : East Court of the Palace. B : Central Court. H : Ishtar Gate. I : Vaulted Building. J : Southern fortification-wall of crude brick, probably Imgur-Bêl. h : Passage-way leading to the Vaulted Building. m, n : Entrances to the Vaulted Building. 1–15 : Small open courts or light-wells in official residencies. [After Koldewey.]

the remains of the famous Hanging Gardens of Babylon.[2] It is reached from the north-east corner of the Central Court[3] along a broad passage-way,[4] from which a branch passage turns off at right angles; and on the left side of this narrower passage are its two entrances.[5] It must be confessed that at first sight the ground-plan of this building does not suggest a garden

[1] See below, p. 62 f.   [2] Fig. 11, I.
[3] B, in Fig. 6 and 11.   [4] Marked h on the plans.
           [5] Fig. 11, m and n.

of any sort, least of all one that became famous as a wonder of the ancient world. It will be seen that the central part, or core, of the building is surrounded by a strong wall and within are fourteen narrow cells or chambers, seven on each side of a central gangway.[1] The cells were roofed in with semicircular arches, forming a barrel vault over each; and the whole is encircled by a narrow corridor, flanked on the north and east sides by the outer palace-wall. This part of the building, both the vaulted chambers and the surrounding corridor, lies completely below the level of the rest of the palace. The small chambers, some of them long and narrow like the vaults, which enclose the central core upon the west and south, are on the palace level; and the subterranean portion is reached by a stairway in one of the rooms on the south side.[2]

There are two main reasons which suggested the identification of this building with the Hanging Gardens. The first is that hewn stone was used in its construction, which is attested by the numerous broken fragments discovered among its ruins. With the exception of the Sacred Road and the bridge over the Euphrates, there is only one other place on the whole site of Babylon where hewn stone is used in bulk for building purposes, and that is the northern wall of the Kasr. Now, in all the literature referring to Babylon, stone is only recorded to have been used for buildings in two places, and those are the north wall of the Citadel and in the Hanging Gardens, a lower layer in the latter's roofing, below the layer of earth, being described as made of stone. These facts certainly point to the identification of the Vaulted Building with the Hanging Gardens.[3] Moreover, Berossus definitely places them within the buildings by which Nebuchadnezzar enlarged his father's palace; but this reference would apply equally to the later Central Citadel constructed by Nebuchadnezzar immediately to

---

[1] In Fig. 11 the reference letter I., to indicate the building, is marked along the gangway.

[2] It is marked on the plan, and lies between the entrance *m* and the south-east corner of the building.

[3] The κρεμαστὸς παράδεισος of Berossus, the κρεμαστὸς κῆπος of Ctesias and Strabo, the *pensiles horti* of Curtius Rufus; their descriptions are quoted at length by Koldewey, "Babylon," pp. 95 ff., Engl. ed., pp. 96 ff.

the north of his main palace.   The size of the building
is also far greater in Strabo and Diodorus than that of
the Vaulted Building, the side of the quadrangle,
according to these writers, measuring about four times
the latter's length.   But discrepancy in figures of this
sort, as we have already seen in the case of the outer
walls of the city, is easily explicable and need not be
reckoned as a serious objection.[1]

The second reason which pointed to the identification
is that, in one of the small chambers near the south-
west corner of the outer fringe of rooms on those two
sides, there is a very remarkable well.   It consists of
three adjoining shafts, a square one in the centre
flanked by two of oblong shape.   This arrangement,
unique so far as the remains of ancient Babylon are
concerned, may be most satisfactorily explained on the
assumption that we here have the water-supply for a
hydraulic machine, constructed on the principle of
a chain-pump.   The buckets, attached to an endless
chain, would have passed up one of the outside wells,
over a great wheel fixed above them, and, after emptying their water into a trough as they passed, would
have descended the other outside well for refilling.   The
square well in the centre obviously served as an
inspection-chamber, down which an engineer could
descend to clean the well out, or to remove any ob-
struction.   In the modern contrivances of this sort,
sometimes employed to-day in Babylonia to raise a
continuous flow of water to the irrigation-trenches, the
motive-power for turning the winch is supplied by
horses or other animals moving round in a circle.   In
the Vaulted Building there would have been scarcely
room for such an arrangement, and it is probable that
gangs of slaves were employed to work a couple of
heavy hand-winches.   The discovery of the well undoubtedly serves to strengthen the case for identification.

Two alternative schemes are put forward to reconstitute the upper structure of this building.   Its

---

[1] Koldewey's explanation, that the total circuit of the building has been
confused with the length of a single side, need not be invoked, in view of the
natural tendency of ancient writers to exaggeration in such matters,
especially when reproducing measurements at second or third hand.

EASTERN TOWERS OF THE ISHTAR GATE

massive walls suggest in any case that they were intended to support a considerable weight, and it may be
that the core of the building, constructed over the
subterranean vaults, towered high above its surrounding chambers which are on the palace-level.   This
would have been in accordance with the current
conception of a hanging garden ; and, since on two
sides it was bounded by the palace-wall, its trees and
vegetation would have been visible from outside the
citadel.   Seen thus from the lower level of the town,
the height of the garden would have been reinforced by
the whole height of the Citadel-mound on which the
palace stands, and imagination once kindled might have
played freely with its actual measurements.

On the other hand, the semicircular arches, still preserved within the central core, may have directly
supported the thick layer of earth in which the trees
of the garden were planted.   These would then have
been growing on the palace-level, as it were in a garden-
court, perhaps surrounded by a pillared colonnade with
the outer chambers opening on to it on the west and
south sides.   In either scheme the subterranean vaults
can only have been used as stores or magazines, since
they were entirely without light.   As a matter of fact,
a large number of tablets were found in the stair-
way-chamber that leads down to them ; and, since the
inscriptions upon them relate to grain, it would seem
that some at least were used as granaries.   But this is
a use to which they could only have been put if the
space above them was not a garden, watered continuously by an irrigation-pump, as moisture would have
been bound to reach the vaults.[1]

Whichever alternative scheme we adopt, it must be
confessed that the Hanging Gardens have not justified
their reputation.   And if they merely formed a garden-
court, as Dr. Koldewey inclines to believe, it is difficult
to explain the adjectives κρεμαστός and *pensilis*.   For
the subterranean vaults would have been completely
out of sight, and, even when known to be below the

---

[1] This objection seems to me to outweigh any correspondence in details
between the architectural structure of the Vaulted Building and the texts of
Curtius Rufus or Diodorus.

E

pavement-level, were not such as to excite wonder or to suggest the idea of suspension in the air. One cannot help suspecting that the vaulted building may really, after all, be nothing more than the palace-granary, and the triple well one of the main water-supplies for domestic use. We may, at least for the present, be permitted to hope that a more convincing site for the gardens will be found in the Central Citadel after further excavation.

In the autumn of 1901 the writer spent some time in Babylon, stopping with Dr. Koldewey in the sub-

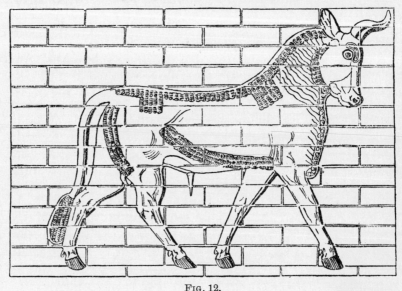

FIG. 12.

BULL IN ENAMELLED BRICK FROM THE ISHTAR GATE.

stantial expedition-house they have built with fine burnt-brick from Nebuchadnezzar's palace. At that time he had uncovered a good deal of the palace, and it was even then possible to trace out the walls of the Throne Room and note the recess where the throne itself had stood. But, beyond the fragments of the enamelled façade, little of artistic interest had been found, and on other portions of the site the results had been still more disappointing. The deep excavation of E-sagila had already been made, the temple of the goddess Ninmakh had been completely excavated, and work was in full swing on that of the god Ninib. All proved to be of unburnt brick,[1] and the principal decoration of the walls was a thin lime-wash. Their discoverer was inclined to be sceptical of Babylon's fabled splendour.

But in the following spring he made the discovery which still remains the most striking achievement of the expedition, and has rehabilitated the fame of that ancient city. This was the great Ishtar Gate, which spanned Babylon's Sacred Way, and the bulls and dragons with which it was adorned have proved that

FIG. 13.

DRAGON IN ENAMELLED BRICK FROM THE ISHTAR GATE.

the glyptic art of Babylonia attained a high level of perfection during its later period. The gate was erected at the point where the Sacred Way entered the older city. It was, in fact, the main gate in the two walls of crude brick along the north side of the Citadel, which we have seen reason to believe were the famous defences, Imgur-Bêl and Nimitti-Bêl.[2]

---

[1] For the probable reason for this practice in temple-construction, see below, p. 63.

[2] See above, pp. 31 ff.

Its structure, when rebuilt by Nebuchadnezzar, was rather elaborate.[1] It is a double gateway, consisting of two separate gate-houses,[2] each with an outer and an inner door.[3] The reason for this is that the line of fortification is a double one, and each of its walls has

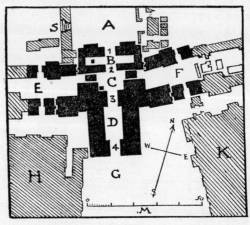

FIG. 14.

GROUND PLAN OF THE ISHTAR GATE.

The ground-plan of the gateway is indicated in black; other walls and buildings are hatched. A : Sacred Way to north of gate. B : Gate of outer wall. C : Gateway Court. D : Gate of inner wall. E : Space between west wings. F : Space between east wings. G : Sacred Way to south of gate. H : North-east corner of Palace. K : Temple of the goddess Ninmakh. S : Steps leading down from level of Sacred Way. 1, 2 : Doorways of outer gate. 3, 4 : Doorways of inner gate.

[After Koldewey.]

a gateway of its own.   But the gates are united into a single structure by means of short connecting walls, which complete the enclosure of the Gateway Court.[4]

[1] Nebuchadnezzar has left us a description of his building of the gateway in the "East India House Inscription," Col. v., l. 55–Col. vi., l. 21 (see Rawlinson, "Cun. Inscr. West. Asia," I., pl. 56, and cf. Langdon, "Neubab. Königsinschriften," p. 132 f.). He records how he decorated the building with wild oxen and dragons in enamelled brick, roofed it with cedar, and set up in it doors which he sheathed in copper and fitted with thresholds and hinges of bronze. He also set bronze oxen and dragons beside the entrances ; bases for some of these appear to have been found by the excavators.

[2] Fig. 14, B and D. In the plan the structure of the gateway, built of burnt brick, is indicated in black. The adjacent fortification-walls, of unburnt brick, are hatched ; so too are the areas covered by parts of the temple of Ninmakh and the palace.

[3] The outer gate-house (B) has doors 1 and 2 ; the doors of the inner gatehouse (D) are numbered 3 and 4.

[4] C.

Dr. Koldewey considers it probable that this court was roofed in, to protect the great pair of doors, which swung back into it, from the weather. But if so, the whole roofing of the gateway must have been at the same low level; whereas the thick walls of the inner gate-house suggest that it and its arched doorways rose higher than the outer gateway, as is suggested in the section[1] and in the reconstruction of the Citadel.[2]

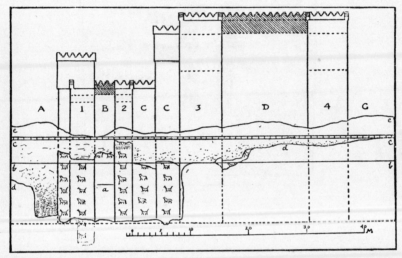

FIG. 15.

SECTION OF THE ISHTAR GATE.

The section is conjecturally restored, looking from west to east; the index capitals and figures correspond to those in Fig. 14. A: Sacred Way to north of gate. B: Gate of outer wall. C: Gateway Court. D: Gate of inner wall. G: Sacred way to south of gate. 1, 2: Doorways of outer gate. 3, 4: Doorways of inner gate. a: Traces of pavement. b: Level of second pavement. c: Level of final pavement. d: Present ground-level. e: Level of ground before excavation. It will be noticed that the portions of the gate preserved are all below the final pavement-level.

[After Andrae.]

It thus appears more probable that the court between the two gateways was left open, and that the two inner arches[3] rose far higher than those of the outer gate.[4] And there is the more reason for this, as an open court would have given far more light for viewing the remarkable decoration of the gateway upon its inner walls.

[1] Fig. 15.
[2] See above, p. 28, Fig. 5.
[3] Figs. 14 and 15, Nos. 3 and 4.
[4] Nos. 1 and 2.

It will be noticed in the plan that the central
roadway is not the only entrance through the gate;
on each side of the two central gate-houses a wing is
thrown out, making four wings in all. These also are
constructed of burnt-brick, and they serve to connect
the gate with the two fortification-walls of unburnt
brick. In each wing is a further door, giving access
to the space between the walls. Thus, in all, the gate
has three separate entrances, and no less than eight

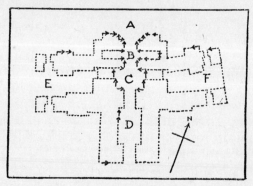

FIG. 16.

DIAGRAM TO SHOW THE ARRANGEMENT OF THE BEASTS OF THE ISHTAR GATE.

The ground-plan of the gate is shown in outline, the arrows indicating the
positions of Bulls or Dragons still in place upon its walls. The head of each
arrow points in the same direction as the beast to which it refers. Where no
beasts are preserved, the foundations of the structure are indicated by a dotted
line. The index letters correspond to those in Fig. 14.
[After Koldewey.]

doorways, four ranged along the central roadway, and
two in each double wing.

The whole wall-surface of the gateway on its
northern side, both central towers and side-wings, was
decorated with alternate rows of bulls and dragons in
brick relief, the rows ranged one above the other up
the surface of walls and towers. The decoration is
continued over the whole interior surface of the central
gateways and may be traced along the southern front
of the inner gate-house. The beasts are arranged in
such a way that to any one entering the city they
would appear as though advancing to meet him. In
the accompanying diagram,[1] which gives the ground-plan

[1] Fig. 16.

of the gate in outline, the arrows indicate the positions of beasts that are still in place upon the walls, and the head of each arrow points in the direction that animal faces. It will be noticed that along most of the walls running north and south the beasts face northwards, while on the transverse walls they face inwards towards the centre. One end-wall in chamber B is preserved, and there, for the sake of symmetry, the two animals face each other, advancing from opposite directions. It has been calculated that at least five hundred and seventy-five of these creatures were represented on the walls and towers of the gateway. Some of the walls, with their successive tiers of beasts, are still standing to a height of twelve metres. The two eastern towers of the outer gate-house are the best preserved, and even in their present condition they convey some idea of the former magnificence of the building.

In the greater part of the structure that still remains in place, it is apparent that the brickwork was very roughly finished, and that the bitumen employed as mortar has been left where it has oozed out between the courses. The explanation is that the portions of the gateway which still stand are really foundations of the building, and were always intended to be buried below the pavement level. It is clear that the height of the road-way was constantly raised while the building of the gate was in progress, and there are traces of two temporary pavements,[1] afterwards filled in when the final pavement-level [2] was reached.[3] The visible portion of the gate above the last pavement has been entirely destroyed, but among its *débris* were found thousands of fragments of the same two animals, but in enamelled brick of brilliant colouring, white and yellow against a

---

[1] Fig. 15, *a* and *b*.   [2] Fig. 15, *c*.

[3] The adornment of the gate's foundations, as well as its upper structure, with reliefs, may in part be explained by their temporary use in flanking the roadway during construction. But the decoration of sacred buildings was not intended merely for the purpose of artistic display. It had a deeper significance, based on the belief that the use of sacred emblems ensured the protection of their tutelary deities. And this perhaps offers the best explanation of the presence of the Weather-god's Bull, and of Marduk's Dragon, upon the foundation-walls of the building. The lion, Ishtar's own emblem in her character as the goddess of war, was employed, as we shall see (cf. p. 58), upon the two walls leading to her gate.

blue ground.   Some of these have been laboriously
pieced together in Berlin, and specimens are now
exhibited in the Kaiser Friedrich Museum and in the
Imperial Ottoman Museum at Constantinople.   Only

FIG. 17.

ENAMELLED FRAGMENT OF THE ISHTAR GATE STILL IN POSITION.

The fragment, which was the highest portion of the gate preserved, is from
the east side of the second doorway of the outer gate; cf. Figs. 14 and 15, No. 2.
It stands just below the final pavement-level, and only the upper portion is
enamelled.

one fragment of an enamelled portion of the wall was
found in place,[1] and that was below the final pavement.
It shows the legs of a bull above a band of rosettes
with yellow centres.[2]

[1] See Fig. 15; its position is indicated in the southern doorway (2) of the
outer gate-house.   This was the first part of the gateway to be discovered, as
it stands higher than the rest.
[2] See Fig. 17.

The delicate modelling of the figures is to some extent obscured in the foundation specimens, but the imperfections there visible are entirely absent from the enamelled series. An examination of the latter shows that the bricks were separately moulded, and, before the process of enamelling, were burnt in the usual way. The contours of the figures were then outlined in black with a vitreous paste, the surfaces so defined being afterwards filled in with coloured liquid enamels. The paste of the black outlines and the coloured enamels themselves had evidently the same fusing point, for

FIG. 18.

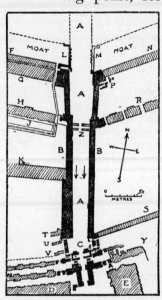

PLAN OF THE LATER DEFENCES OF THE CITADEL UPON THE NORTH, SHOWING THE WALLS WITH THE LION FRIEZE AND THE ISHTAR GATE.

A: Sacred Way. B, B: Walls with Lion Frieze flanking the Sacred Way. C: Ishtar Gate. D: North-east corner of Palace. E: Temple of Ninmakh. F: Front wall of Northern Citadel. G: North wall of Northern Citadel. H: North wall of the Principal Citadel. J: Broad Canal, fed from the Euphrates, to supply the Principal Citadel. K: Old wall of the Principal Citadel. L, M: Moat-walls supporting dam, over which the roadway passed; that on the east side has not yet been excavated. N: Eastward extension of north wall of Northern Citadel. P: Stair-case, or ramps, ascending to roadway. R: Eastward extension of wall of Principal Citadel. S: South wall of eastern outworks. T, U, V: Ends of transverse walls in Principal Citadel. Y: Riverside embankment of the Persian period. Z: Crude brick walls with doorways, forming a temporary gateway, filled in below latest pavement. N.B.—The two arrows denote the direction in which the lions are represented as advancing in the frieze.

when fired they have sometimes shaded off into one another, giving a softness and a pleasing variety of tone to the composition.[1] It should be added that the enamelled beasts, like those in plain brick, are in slight relief, the same moulds having been employed for both.

Before the Neo-Babylonian period the Ishtar Gate had defended the northern entrance to the city, and was probably a massive structure of unburnt brick without

---

[1] The same process was employed for the Lion Frieze to the north of the gateway ; see below, p. 59.

external decoration.   But, with the building of the outer city-wall, it stood in the second line of defence.   And as Nebuchadnezzar extended the fortifications of the Citadel itself upon the northern side, it lost still more of its strategic importance, and from its interior position became a fit subject for the decorator's art.   The whole course of the roadway through these exterior defences he flanked with mighty walls, seven metres thick, extending from the gate northwards to the outermost wall and moat.[1]   Their great strength was dictated by

Fig. 19.

LION FROM THE FRIEZE OF THE SACRED WAY TO THE NORTH OF THE ISHTAR GATE.

the fact that, should an enemy penetrate the outer city-wall, he would have to pass between them, under the garrison's fire, to reach the citadel-gate.   But these, like the gate itself, formed a secondary or interior defence, and so, like it, were elaborately decorated.   The side of each wall facing the roadway was adorned with a long frieze of lions, in low relief and brilliantly enamelled,

[1] See Fig. 18, B, B. The fortified areas to the west of the roadway, which Nebuchadnezzar built out as direct extensions of the Southern Citadel upon its north side, are still in course of excavation.   They have been christened the "Principal Citadel" and the "Northern Citadel" of the Ḳaṣr.   The most interesting construction yet recovered there is a broad canal (Fig. 18, J), to the north of the palace-area of the Principal Citadel; this was evidently left uncovered, and it must have drawn its water-supply from the Euphrates through grated openings in the western wall.   To the east of the roadway lines of defence were thrown out corresponding to those of the two later citadels.   The foundations of their eastern wall, approximately parallel to the roadway, have been uncovered; but the whole of this area was destroyed by the Euphrates when it changed its course, and only the main fortification-walls can now be traced below the deposit of silt.

which were represented advancing southwards towards the Ishtar Gate. The surface of each wall was broken up into panels by a series of slightly projecting towers, each panel probably containing two lions, while the plinth below the Lion Frieze was decorated with rosettes. There appear to have been sixty lions along each wall. Some were in white enamel with yellow manes, while others were in yellow and had red manes,[1] and they stood out against a light or dark blue ground. Leading as they did to the bulls and dragons of the gateway, we can realize in some degree the effect produced upon a stranger entering the inner city of Babylon for the first time.

Such a stranger, passing within the Ishtar Gate, would have been struck with wonder at the broad Procession Street,[2] which ran its long course straight through the city from north to south, with the great temples ranged on either hand. Its foundation of burnt brick covered with bitumen is still preserved, upon which, to the south of the gateway, rested a pavement of massive flags, the centre of fine hard limestone, the sides of red breccia veined with white. In inscriptions upon the edges of these paving slabs, formerly hidden by their asphalt mortar, Nebuchadnezzar boasts that he paved the street of Babylon for the procession of the great lord Marduk, to whom he prays for eternal life.[3] The slabs that are still in place are polished with hard use, but, unlike the pavements of Pompeii, show no ruts or indentations such as we might have expected from the chariots of the later period. It is possible that, in view of its sacred character, the use of the road was restricted to foot passengers and beasts of burden, except when the king and his retinue passed along it through the city. And in any case, not counting

---

[1] The red enamel has decomposed and is now green. All the lions, like the enamelled beasts of the Ishtar Gate, were found in fragments.

[2] Compare the plan on p. 30, Fig. 6, where the Procession Street, in its course past the Citadel, is lettered G.

[3] Cf. Koldewey, "Die Pflastersteine von Aiburschabu in Babylon," pp. 4 ff. The limestone is termed *shadû*, or "mountain-stone," and Koldewey suggests that it was quarried in the neighbourhood of Hît on the Euphrates. The quarries from which the *turmina-banda*, or breccia, was obtained have not yet been identified.

chariots of war and state, there was probably very little
wheeled traffic in Babylonia at any time.

When clear of the citadel the road descends by
a gradual slope to the level of the plain, and preserving
the same breadth, passes to the right of the temple
dedicated to Ishtar of Akkad.[1]   As it continues southward it is flanked at a little distance on the east by the
streets of private houses, whose foundations have been
uncovered in the Merkes mound ;[2] and on the west side
it runs close under the huge peribolos of E-temen-anki,
the Tower of Babylon.[3]   As far as the main gate of
E-temen-anki[4] its foundation is laid in burnt-brick,
over which was an upper paving completely formed of
breccia.   The inscription upon the slabs corresponds to
that on the breccia paving-stones opposite the citadel ;
but they have evidently been re-used from an earlier
pavement of Sennacherib, whose name some of them
bear upon the underside.   This earlier pavement of
Babylon's Sacred Way must have been laid by that
monarch before he reversed his conciliatory policy toward
the southern kingdom.   At the south-east corner of
the peribolos the road turns at a right angle and running between the peribolos and E-sagila, the great
temple of the city-god, passes through a gate in the
river-wall built by Nabonidus, and so over the Euphrates
bridge before turning southward again in the direction
of Borsippa.[5]   This branch road between the Tower of
Babylon and E-sagila[6] is undoubtedly the continuation
of the procession-street.   For not only was it the way
of approach to Marduk's temple, but its course has been
definitely traced by excavation.   But there can be no
doubt that the upper portion of the road, running north
and south through the city, was continued in a straight
line from the point where the Sacred Way branched
off.   This would have conducted an important stream

---

[1] The course of the Procession Street may be followed in the plan on
p. 83, Fig. 31 ; it is there marked A.   The Temple of Ishtar of Akkad is
lettered H.

[2] Fig. 30, G.

[3] Fig. 30, E, F ; compare also Fig. 27 on p. 74, with the same lettering.

[4] Fig. 27, the gate numbered 2.

[5] See Fig. 27, where the course of the road is lettered A, as in Fig. 30.

[6] Fig. 27, B and C.

THE SACRED WAY OF BABYLON.

of traffic to the main gate in the southern city-wall, passing on its way between the temples dedicated to the god Ninib and to another deity not yet identified.[1]

Apart from the royal palaces, the five temples of Babylon were the principal buildings within the city, and their excavation has thrown an entirely new light upon our ideas of the religious architecture of the country. The ground-plans of four of them have now been ascertained in their entirety, and we are consequently in a position to form some idea of the general principles upon which such buildings were arranged. The first to be excavated was the little temple E-makh, dedicated to the goddess Ninmakh, which, as we have already seen, was built on the citadel itself, in the north-east corner of the open space to the south of the Ishtar Gateway. Its principal façade faces the north-west, and, since the eastern entrance of the Ishtar Gate opens just opposite the corner of the temple, a wall with a doorway in it was thrown across, spanning the passage between temple and fortification.[2] The only entrance to the temple was in the centre of the façade; and in the passage-way immediately in front of it, surrounded by a pavement of burnt-brick, is a small crude-brick altar.[3] It is an interesting fact that the only other altar yet found in Babylon is also of crude brick and occupies precisely the same position, outside a temple and immediately opposite its main entrance;[4] while in a third temple, though the altar itself has disappeared, the paved area which surrounded it is still visible.[5] We may therefore conclude that this represents the normal position for the altar in the Babylonian cult; and it fully substantiates the statement of Herodotus that the two altars of Belus were outside his temple.[6] One of these, he tells us, was of solid gold, on which it was only lawful to offer sucklings; the other was a common altar (doubtless of crude brick) but of great size, on which

---

[1] See above, p. 23, Fig. 3, where the position of the two temples is indicated by the letters N and M. The line of the city-wall along part of the south side is indicated by the mounds lettered B.

[2] For the position of the temple in relation to the Ishtar Gate, see above, p. 30, Fig. 6, where the temple is lettered J, and the Ishtar Gate H.

[3] See p. 64, Fig. 20, *d*.   Compare also the reconstruction in Fig. 21.

[4] See below, p. 71.   [5] See below, p. 69.   [6] I., 183.

full-grown animals were sacrificed. It was also on the great altar that the Chaldeans burnt the frankincense, which, according to Herodotus, was offered to the amount of a thousand talents' weight every year at the festival of the god.

It may further be noted that this exterior position of the altar corresponds to Hebrew usage, according to which the main altar was erected in the outer court in front of the temple proper. Thus Solomon's brazen altar, which under Phœnician influence took the place of earlier altars of earth or unhewn stone,[1] stood before the temple.[2] The altar within the Hebrew temple was of cedar-wood,[3] and it was clearly not a permanent structure embedded in the pavement, for Ezekiel refers to it as a "table," and states that it "was of wood."[4] It was more in the nature of a table for offerings, and it may be inferred that in earlier times it served as the table upon which the shewbread was placed before Yahwe.[5] The complete absence of any trace of a permanent altar within the Babylonian temples can only be due to a similar practice; the altars or tables within the shrines must have been light wooden structures, and they were probably carried off or burnt when the temples were destroyed. There is of course no need to regard this resemblance as due to direct cultural influence or borrowing. But we may undoubtedly conclude that we here have an example of parallelism in religious ritual between two races of the same Semitic stock. What the Sumerian practice was in this respect we have as yet no means of ascertaining; but in such details of cult it is quite possible that the Semitic Babylonians substituted their own traditional usages for any other they may have found in the country of their adoption.

The temple of Ninmakh itself, like all the others in Babylon, was built of crude brick, and though its walls were covered with a thin plaster or wash of lime, only

---

[1] Cf. Exodus, xx., 24–26.   [2] Cf. I. Kings, viii., 64.
[3] See I. Kings, vi., 20.   [4] Ezekiel, xli., 22.
[5] Cf. I. Samuel, 6 [7]. For a discussion of the evidence relating to the Hebrew practices, see especially the article " Altar," by W. E. Addis, in the " Encyclopædia Biblica," I., Cols. 123 ff.

the simplest form of decoration in black and white was attempted, and that very sparingly.[1] The fact that the practice of building in mud-brick should have continued at a time when kiln-burnt and enamelled brick was lavished on the royal palaces, is probably to be explained as a result of religious conservatism. The architectural design does not differ in essentials from that employed for buildings of a military character. It will be seen that the long exterior walls of E-makh resemble those of a fortification, their surface being broken up by slightly projecting towers set at regular intervals.[2] Larger rectangular towers flank the gateway, and two others, diminishing in size and probably also in height, are ranged on either side of them. The vertical grooves, which traverse the exterior faces of the towers from top to bottom, constitute a characteristic form of temple embellishment, which is never found on buildings of a secular character. They may be either plain rectangular grooves, or more usually, as in E-makh, are stepped when viewed in section.[3]

In all the important doorways of the temples foundation-deposits were buried in little niches or boxes, formed of six bricks placed together and hidden below the level of the pavement. The deposits found in place are generally fashioned of baked clay, and that of most common occurrence is a small figure of the god Papsukal. One of those in Ninmakh's temple was in the form of a bird, no doubt sacred to the goddess. There is clear evidence that the object of their burial was to ensure the safety of the entrance both from spiritual and from human foes. In addition to this magical protection the entrance was further secured by double doors, their pivots shod with bronze and turning in massive stone sockets. The ordinary method of fastening such doors by bolts was supplemented in the case of E-makh by a beam propped against the doors and with its lower end fitting into a socket in the pavement. Since the

[1] See below, p. 69 f.
[2] See p. 65, Fig. 21.
[3] In some temples, as in E-zida, the temple of Nabû at Borsippa, and in the earliest remains of E-sagila (see below, pp. 71 ff.), semicircular fillets take the place of sunken grooves.

temple was within the citadel fortifications, the possibility was foreseen that it might have to be defended
from assault like the secular buildings in its immediate
neighbourhood.

Passing through the entrance-chamber of E-makh,
from which opens a service-room for the use of the

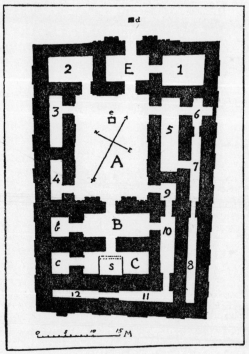

FIG. 20.

GROUND-PLAN OF E-MAKH.

A: Open Court.   B: Ante-chamber to Shrine.   C: Shrine.   E: Entrance-
chamber, or Vestibule, to temple.   b: Service-room for Ante-chamber.   c: Service-
room for Shrine.   d: Crude-brick altar.   e: Well.   s: Dais, or postament, for
statue of Ninmakh.   1: Porters' room.   2–4: Priests' apartments or Store-rooms.
5, 6, 9, 10: Chambers giving access to narrow passages.   7, 8, 11, 12: Narrow
passages, possibly containing stairways or ramps to roof.
[After Andrae.]

temple-guardians, one enters a large open court,[1] surrounded on all sides by doorways leading to priests'
apartments and store-chambers and to the shrine.   The
latter is on the south-east side, facing the entrance to

[1] Fig. 20, A. The description may be followed by means of the index
letters and figures on the plan, which are explained below it.

the court, and, like the main gateway of the temple, the façade of the shrine and the flanking towers of its doorway were adorned with stepped grooves. The shrine itself is approached through an ante-chamber, and each has a small service-apartment opening out from it to the left. Against the back wall of the shrine, immediately opposite the doors, stood the cult image of the goddess, visible from the open court; this has disappeared, but the foundations of the low dais or postament, on which it stood, are still in place.

The long narrow passage behind the shrine[1] was

FIG. 21.

CONJECTURAL RESTORATION OF E-MAKH, THE TEMPLE OF THE GODDESS NINMAKH.

The view is taken from the north. The plain finish to the tops of walls and towers is in accordance with one theory of reconstruction. The connecting wall between the temple and the east wing of the Ishtar Gate is omitted to simplify the drawing.

[After Andrae.]

thought at first by its discoverer to have served a secret purpose of the priesthood. It was suggested that it might have given access to a concealed opening in the back wall of the shrine, behind the image of the goddess, whence oracles could have been given forth with her authority. But there is a precisely similar passage along the north-east wall; and we may probably accept the more prosaic explanation that they contained the ramps or stairways that led up to the flat roof, though why two should have been required, both at the same end of the building, is not clear.[2] The precise use of

[1] In Fig. 20 the passage is numbered 11 and 12.
[2] They are so narrow that they can hardly have served as store-chambers.

F

the other chambers opening from the court cannot be identified with any certainty, as nothing was found in them to indicate whether they served as apartments for the priesthood or as magazines for temple-stores. Beyond a number of votive terracotta figures, no cult object was discovered. But around the dais for the image of the goddess, the well in the courtyard 'for lustral water, and the small crude-brick altar before the temple entrance, it is possible to picture in imagination some of the rites to which reference is made in the Babylonian religious texts.

As we have already seen was the case with the palace-buildings, the upper structure of all the temples has been completely destroyed, so that it is not now certain how the tops of walls and towers were finished off. In the conjectural restoration of Ninmakh's temple[1] the upper portions are left perfectly plain. And this represents one theory of reconstruction. But it is also possible that the walls were crowned with the stepped battlements of military architecture. In the restoration of Assyrian buildings, both secular and religious, great assistance has been obtained from the sculptured bas-reliefs that lined the palace walls. For the scenes upon them include many representations of buildings, and, when due allowance has been made for the conventions employed, a considerable degree of certainty may be attained with their help in picturing the external appearance of buildings of which only the lower courses of the walls now remain. The scarcity of stone in Babylonia, and the consequent absence of mural reliefs, have deprived us of this source of information in the case of the southern kingdom. The only direct evidence on the point that has been forthcoming consists of a design stamped in outline upon a rectangular gold plaque, found with other fragments of gold and jewellery in the remains of a sumptuous burial within the structure of Nabopolassar's palace.[2] The period of the burial is certain, for the grave in which the great pottery sarcophagus was placed had been

---

[1] See Fig. 21.
[2] The grave was hollowed out of the massive brickwork of the outer wall, in the extreme north-west corner of the palace.

closed with bricks of Nebuchadnezzar, who afterwards built his strengthening wall against it. It must therefore date from the earlier part of his reign, and Dr. Koldewey makes the suggestion that it was perhaps the tomb of Nabopolassar himself.[1] However that may be, the grave is certainly of the early Neo-Babylonian period, and the architectural design upon the gold plaque may be taken as good evidence for that time.

The plaque formed the principal decoration in a chain bracelet, small rings passing through the holes at its four corners and serving to attach it to the larger links of the chain. On it the jeweller has represented a gate with an arched door-way, flanked by towers, which rise above the walls of the main building. Each tower is surmounted by a projecting upper structure, pierced with small circular loopholes, and both towers and walls are crowned with triangular battlements. The latter are obviously intended to be stepped, the engraver not having sufficient space to represent this detail in a design on so small a scale. The outline is probably that of a fortified city-gate, and it

FIG. 22.

GOLD PLAQUE, WITH ARCHITECTURAL DESIGN, FROM A NEO-BABYLONIAN BURIAL.

The engraving on the plaque shows a city-gate with flanking towers and stepped battlements. [Enlargement after photo. by Koldewey.]

fully justifies the adoption of the stepped battlement in the reconstruction of military buildings of the period. Whether the temples were furnished in the same manner, for purely decorative purposes, is not so clear. Some idea of the appearance of one, restored on this alternative hypothesis, may be gathered from the elevation of the unidentified temple known as "Z," which is given in Fig. 24.

It is important that the ground-plans of no less than four of the temples in Babylon have been recovered, for it will be seen that the main features, already noted in

---

[1] Cf. "Babylon," p. 118 f. ; Engl. ed., p. 119 f.

Ninmakh's temple, are always repeated.[1]   In each the temple buildings are arranged around an open court, to which access is given through one or more entrances with vestibules.   The doorways to temple and to shrine are flanked by grooved towers, while within the shrine itself the cult-statue stood on a low dais, visible from the court.   Yet with this general similarity, all combine

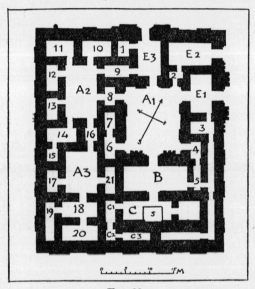

FIG. 23.

GROUND-PLAN OF THE UNIDENTIFIED TEMPLE KNOWN AS "Z."

A1: Main Court of temple. A2, A3: Subsidiary Courts. B: Ante-chamber to Shrine. C: Shrine. E1, E2, E3: Entrance-chambers, or Vestibules, to temple. c1, c2, c3: Service-rooms for Shrine. s: Dais, or postament, for cult-statue. 1–3: Porters' rooms. 4, 5: Chambers with access to narrow passage, possibly containing stairway or ramp to roof. 6, 7: Priests' apartments or store-rooms. 8, 9: Entrance-chambers to residential quarters. 10–15: Quarters for resident priesthood around N.-W. Court. 16: Entrance-chamber to Inner Court. 17–21: Quarters for resident priesthood around Inner Court.
[After Andrae.]

special features of their own.   The temple "Z," for example, is exactly rectangular in plan, and is divided into two distinct parts, the object of which may be readily surmised.   The larger and eastern portion, opening on the great court, was obviously devoted to the service of the deity.   For there, on the south side,

[1] In the ground-plans, which are here reproduced, the same lettering is employed, as far as they correspond, for the principal features of each building.

is the shrine and its ante-chamber, with the dais for the cult-image against the south wall.   The western portion is grouped around two smaller courts, and, as its arrangement resembles that of a private dwelling-house, we may regard it as the quarters of the resident priesthood. Other notable features are the three service-chambers to the shrine, and the three separate entrances to the temple itself, each with its own vestibule and porters' room.   But there is only one narrow passage, extending partly behind the shrine and containing, as suggested, a ramp or stairway to the roof.   There was probably an altar before the northern gate, as shown in the

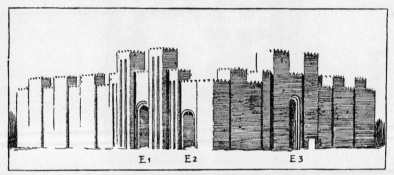

FIG. 24.

CONJECTURAL RESTORATION OF THE UNIDENTIFIED TEMPLE KNOWN AS " Z."

The view is taken from a point immediately opposite the north corner of the temple.   The stepped battlements on walls and towers, borrowed from military architecture, are here adopted in accordance with one theory of reconstruction. [After Andrae and Koldewey.]

restoration, but only the paved area on which it stood was found to be still in place.

In the temples dedicated to Ishtar of Akkad and to the god Ninib the shrines are on the west side of the great court, instead of on the south as in those we have already examined.   Thus it would seem there was no special position for the shrine, though the temples themselves are generally built with their corners directed approximately to the cardinal points.[1] In the temple of Ishtar unmistakable traces have been noted of a simple form of mural decoration that

[1] It will be noticed that this orientation is least apparent in E-sagila (see below, p. 74, Fig. 27), and in the temple of Ishtar of Akkad (Fig. 25).

appears to have been employed in all the temples of
Babylon. While the walls in general were coloured
dead white with a thin gypsum wash, certain of the
more prominent parts, such as the main entrance, the
doorway leading to the shrine and the niche behind
the statue of the goddess, were washed over with
black asphalt in solution, each blackened surface being
decorated near its edge with white strips or line-borders.
The contrast in colour presented by this black and white

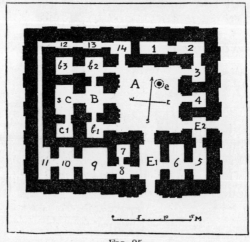

FIG. 25.

GROUND-PLAN OF THE TEMPLE OF ISHTAR OF AKKAD.

A : Open Court. B : Ante-chamber to Shrine. C : Shrine. E1, E2 : Entrance-
chambers, or Vestibules, to temple. b1, b2, b3 : Service-rooms for Ante-chamber.
c1 : Service-room for Shrine. e : Well. s : Position of statue of Ishtar, on dais
or postament against niche in back-wall of Shrine. 1–4 : Priests' apartments or
store-rooms. 5–7 : Porters' rooms. 8 : Entrance-chamber to small inner court.
9 : Small open court in which were two circular stores or granaries. 10–14 :
Chambers, probably used as store-rooms, giving access to narrow passage, which
possibly contained stairway or ramp to roof.
[After Reuther.]

decoration must have been startling in its effect; no
doubt, like the crude-brick material of the buildings, it
was an inheritance from earlier times, and owed its
retention to its traditional religious significance.

In the temple of Ninib two additional shrines flank
the principal one, each having its own entrance and a
dais or postament for a statue. It is probable that the
side shrines were devoted to the worship of subsidiary
deities connected in some way with Ninib, for the

temple as a whole was dedicated solely to him.   This
we learn from Nabopolassar's foundation-cylinders,
buried below the pavement of the shrine, which relate
how the king erected the building in his honour, on an
earlier foundation, after he had kept back the foot of

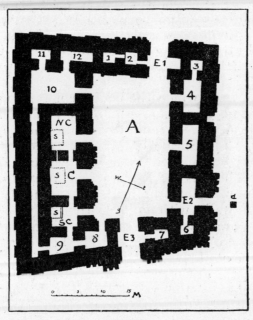

FIG. 26.

GROUND-PLAN OF THE TEMPLE OF NINIB.

A : Open Court. C : Shrine of Ninib. NC, SC : Subsidiary shrines for other
deities. s, s, s : Postaments for statues of Ninib and the other deities, set against
niches in the wall exactly opposite the entrances.   E1, E2, E3 : Entrance-
chambers or Vestibules, to temple.   d : Crude-brick altar.   1, 2, 6, 7 : Porters'
rooms.   3–5, 11, 12 : Priests' apartments or store-rooms.   10 : Small open court.
8, 9 : Chambers giving access to narrow passage behind the shrines, which
possibly contained stairway or ramp to roof.
[After Andrae.]

the Assyrian from the land of Akkad and had thrown
off his heavy yoke.[1]   It was fitting that he should have
marked his gratitude in this way to the god of war.
    The most interesting temple of Babylon is naturally
that dedicated to the worship of the city-god.   This
was the famous E-sagila, a great part of which still lies
buried some twenty-one metres below the surface of

[1] Cf. Weissbach, " Babylonische Miscellen," p. 20 f., ll. 17–21.

Tell 'Amrân.[1] Its main portion, lying to the west, is practically square in ground-plan, and like the smaller temples of the city, it consists of chambers grouped around an open court; but their arrangement here is far more symmetrical.[2] There was a great gateway in the centre of each side, where in Neriglissar's time stood the eight bronze serpents, a pair of them beside each entrance.[3] The eastern gate was no doubt the principal one, as it gives access to the inner court through a single great vestibule or entrance-chamber, in striking contrast to the smaller vestibules on the north and south sides, from which the court can be reached only through side-corridors.[4] Around the great court within, the temple doorways and towers are arranged symmetrically. The shrine of Marduk lay on its western side, as may be inferred from the façade and towered entrance. This was the E-kua of the inscriptions, which Nebuchadnezzar states he made to shine like the sun, coating its walls with gold as though with gypsum-plaster, a phrase which recalls the mud and gypsum washes of the other temples. "The best of my cedars," he says, "that I brought from Lebanon, the noble forest, I sought out for the roofing of Ekua, [Marduk's] lordly chamber; the mighty cedars I covered with gleaming gold for the roofing of Ekua."[5] The lavish employment of gold in the temple's decoration is attested by Herodotus, who states that in this, "the lower temple,"[6] was a great seated figure of Zeus, which, like the throne, the dais, and the table before it, was fashioned of gold, the metal weighing altogether eight hundred talents.[7]

[1] See above, p. 23, Fig. 3, E.   [2] See p. 74, Fig. 27, C.
[3] See Rawlinson, "Cun. Inscr. West. Asia," I., pl. 67, Col. I., ll. 21 ff., and cf. Bezold in Schrader's "Keilins. Bibl.," III., ii., p. 72 f., and Langdon, "Neubab. Königsinschriften," p. 210 f.
[4] The main entrance to the temple was approached through an annex on the east (Fig. 27, D), of which the external walls only have been traced by tunnelling, while its interior remains still unexplored. It will be noted in the plan that the main entrance to the annex is again on the east side, marked by a recess in the enclosing wall, almost opposite the main entrance to the temple. The approach to the annex was doubtless by a branch of the Procession Street, which must have left the principal roadway opposite entrance No. 4 of the Peribolos (see Fig. 27).
[5] Cf. "East India House Inscr.," Col. II., ll. 43 ff., and Col. III., ll. 21 ff.
[6] The κάτω νηός, to distinguish it from that on the temple-tower.
[7] I., 183.

TWO VIEWS OF THE TEMPLE OF NINIB IN COURSE OF EXCAVATION.

The identification of the temple was rendered certain by the discovery of inscribed bricks in earlier pavements below those of Nebuchadnezzar. Inscriptions stamped upon bricks from two pavements of Ashur-bani-pal record that this Assyrian king made " bricks of E-sagila and E-temen-anki," while on an older one which he re-used, stamped with the name of Esarhaddon, it is definitely stated that it formed part of the paving of E-sagila.[1] These pavements were reached by means of an open excavation in Tell 'Amrân, extending some forty metres each way. It took no less than eight months to remove the soil to the pavement level, and it is estimated that some thirty thousand cubic metres of earth were carted away in the course of the work. It is not surprising, therefore, that the chambers on the west side of the court, including the shrine of Marduk, still remain covered by the mound. A subsidiary shrine, on the north side of the court, has been cleared, and it would be a spot of considerable interest if, as Dr. Koldewey suggests, it was dedicated to Ea. For in the Hellenistic period Ea was identified with Serapis, and should this prove to have been his sanctuary, it was here that Alexander's generals repaired during his illness, when they enquired of the god whether he should be carried thither to be healed.[2]

To the north of Marduk's temple rose its ziggurat, the Tower of Babel, known to Babylonians of all ages as E-temen-anki, " The House of the Foundation-stone of Heaven and Earth." It stood within its Peribolos or sacred precincts, marked now by the flat area or plain which the local Arabs call Sakhn, " the pan."[3] The precincts of the tower were surrounded by an enclosing wall, decorated with innumerable grooved towers, along the east and south sides of which the track of the Sacred Way may still be followed.[4] On the inner side of the wall, in its whole circuit, stretched a vast extent of buildings, all devoted to the cult of the

[1] Cf. Koldewey, "Babylon," p. 202 f.; Engl. ed., p. 207.
[2] Cf. Koldewey, "Die Tempel von Babylon und Borsippa," p. 43.
[3] See above, p. 23, Fig. 3, Q.
[4] Marked A, A, A in Fig. 27.

city-god, and forming, in the phrase of their discoverer, a veritable Vatican of Babylon.[1]

The area so enclosed forms approximately a square,

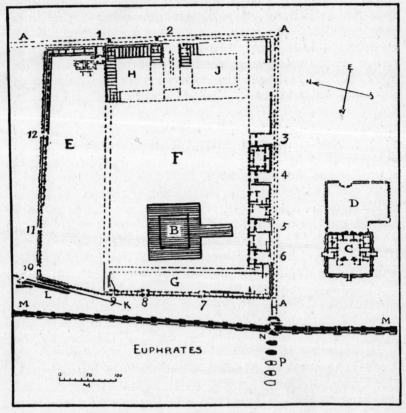

FIG. 27.

GROUND-PLAN OF E-TEMEN-ANKI AND E-SAGILA.

A : Sacred Way, or Procession Street. B : E-temen-anki, the Ziggurat or Temple-tower of Babylon. C : E-sagila, the temple of Marduk. D : Eastern Annex to E-sagila. E : Northern Court of the Peribolos or sacred precincts. F : Main Court. G : Western Court. H, J : Temple-magazines. K : Arakhtu-wall. L : Nebuchadnezzar's wall. M : River-wall of Nabonidus. N : Gateway in River-wall. P : Stone piers of Bridge over the Euphrates. 1–12 : Entrances to the Peribolos, No. 2 marking the position of the Main Entrance.
[After Wetzel.]

and is cut up by cross-walls into three separate sections

[1] Cf. Koldewey, "Babylon," p. 185; Engl. ed., p. 190. Some idea of the probable appearance of the immense enclosure may be gathered from the reconstruction in Fig. 28.

of unequal size.   Within the largest of the great courts [1] stood the temple-tower,[2] its core constructed of unburnt brick but enclosed with a burnt brick facing.[3]   In the reconstruction a single stairway is shown projecting from the southern side, and giving access to the first stage or story of the tower.   But it has lately been ascertained that three separate stairways ascended the tower on the south side, the two outer ones being built against its south-east and south-west corners, and being

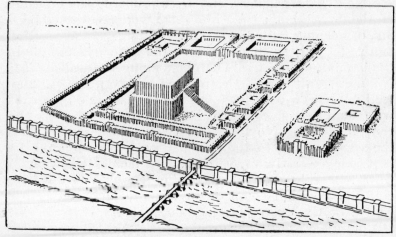

FIG. 28.

CONJECTURAL RECONSTRUCTION OF E-TEMEN-ANKI AND E-SAGILA.

The form of the Temple-tower within the Peribolos is here restored in accordance with Dr. Koldewey's theory that it consisted of a single stage or story, on which the upper Temple of Marduk rested.   According to an alternative interpretation of Herodotus, the upper Temple would have formed the last of eight receding towers or stages.   It will be noted that the two flanking stairways, recently discovered on the south side of the tower, are here not shown.
[After Andrae.]

flanked on their outer sides by stepped walls, which formed a solid breastwork or protection for any one ascending them.[4]

[1] Fig. 27, F.   [2] Fig. 27, B.
[3] During the recent excavation of the tower the outer facing of burnt brick has been uncovered along the north side, and it was seen to have been decorated with twelve tower-like projections.   A considerable fragment was also found on the west side ; and the exterior measurement of both these sides of the tower was ascertained to be ninety-one metres.   The crude-brick core measures about sixty-one metres along its north front.   See "Mitteil. der Deutsch. Orient-Gesellschaft," No. 53 (April, 1914), p. 18.
[4] The outer stairways were eight metres in breadth, and sixteen steps are

The buildings within the precincts were evidently not temples, as they present none of their characteristic features, such as the shrine or the towered façade, and any theory as to their use must be based on pure conjecture. Judging solely by their ground-plans, it would appear that the two great buildings on the east side, consisting of a long series of narrow chambers ranged around open courts, were probably the magazines and store-chambers. The buildings on the south side resemble dwelling-houses, and were probably the quarters of the priesthood; their huge size would not have been out of keeping with the privileges and dignified position enjoyed by those in control of the principal temple in the capital. The small chambers along the walls of the Northern Court,[2] and the narrow Western Court,[3] may well have been used to house the thousands of pilgrims who doubtless flocked to Babylon to worship at the central shrine. No less than twelve gateways led into the sacred precincts, the principal entrance being on the east side,[4] exactly opposite the east face of the temple-tower. The breccia paving of the Sacred Way was here continued within the area of the precincts, along the centre of the open space, or deep recess, between the temple-magazines. The great gateway probably spanned the western end of this recess, thus completing the line of the Main Court upon that side.[5]

The most striking feature of E-temen-anki was naturally the temple-tower itself, which rose high above the surrounding buildings and must have been visible from all parts of the city and from some considerable distance beyond the walls. Its exact form has been the subject of some controversy. Dr. Koldewey rejects the current view, based upon the description of Herodotus,[6] that it consisted of a stepped tower in eight stages, with the ascent to the top encircling the outside. It is true that the excavations have shown that the ascent to the first stage, at any rate, was not

still preserved of the one in the south-west corner; cf. "Mitteil. d. Deutsch. Or.-Gesells.," No. 53, p. 19.
  [1] Fig. 27, H and J.   [2] Fig. 27, E.
  [3] Fig. 27, G.   [4] Fig. 27, Entrance No. 2.
  [5] This arrangement is suggested in Fig. 28.   [6] I., 181.

of this character, consisting, as it did, of a triple stairway built against one side of the tower;[1] but, as the
ground-plan only of the building can now be traced,
there is nothing to indicate the form of its upper
structure. Dr. Koldewey does not regard the evidence
for the existence of stepped towers in Babylonia as satisfactory, and he appears to consider that they depend
solely on the description of Herodotus, who, he claims,
says nothing about stepped terraces, nor that each stage
was smaller than the one below it. He is inclined to
reconstruct the tower as built in a single stage, decorated
on its face with coloured bands, and surmounted by the
temple to which the triple-stairway would have given
direct access. This view of its reconstruction is shown
in Fig. 28, but its author considers the problem as still
unsettled, and suspends his judgment until the Ziggurat
at Borsippa, the best preserved of the temple-towers, is
excavated.

There, as at Babylon, we have a temple and a
separate temple-tower, but they both stood within the
same peribolos or sacred enclosure, along the inner side
of which were built series of numerous small chambers
resembling those of E-temen-anki. A street[2] ran along
the north-west front of the peribolos, and two gateways[3]
opened on to it from the sacred enclosure. The main
entrance both to peribolos and temple was probably on
the north-east side.[4] It will be noted that the plan of
the temple[5] follows the lines of those already described,
consisting of a complex of buildings ranged around one
great court and a number of smaller ones. The shrine
of the god Nabû stood on the south-west side of the
Great Court, the heavily-towered façade indicating
the entrance to its outer vestibule. While so much of
the temple itself and of its enclosure has been cleared, the
temple-tower[6] awaits excavation. It still rises to a
height of no less than forty-seven metres above the
surrounding plain, but such a mass of *débris* has fallen

---

[1] See above, p. 75.   [2] See Fig. 29, G.   [3] C and D.
[4] The bronze step of Nebuchadnezzar, preserved in the British Museum
(see above, p. 27, n. 1), seems to have come from the temple entrance in the
south-west front, facing the temple-tower.
[5] Fig. 29, A.   [6] Fig. 29, B.

about its base that to clear it completely would entail
a vast amount of labour. The mound of soil not only
covers the open court surrounding the temple-tower,
but extends over the inner line of chambers on the
north-west side of the peribolos. The destruction of
the temple and its surroundings by fire has vitrified the
upper structure of the ziggurat, and to this fact the
ruins owe their preservation. For the bricks are welded

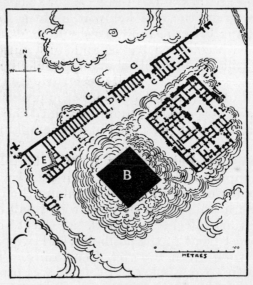

FIG. 29.

GROUND-PLAN OF E-ZIDA AND THE TEMPLE-TOWER OF NABÛ AT BORSIPPA.

A : The temple E-zida. B : The Temple-tower of Nabû. C, D : Gateways
opening from the Peribolos on to the street which ran along that side of the
sacred enclosure. E : Remains of later building. F : Chambers on south-west
side of Peribolos. G, G : Street running along the north-west face of the
Peribolos.

[After Koldewey.]

into a solid mass, and, since it is no longer possible to
separate them, they offer no attractions as building-
material and so have escaped the fate of E-temen-anki.

It is quite possible that, when Nabû's temple-tower
is excavated, it will throw some light upon the upper
structure of these massive buildings. Meanwhile we
possess a piece of evidence which should not be ignored in
any discussion of the subject. On a boundary-stone of
the time of Merodach-baladan I. are carved a number

of emblems of the gods, including those of Marduk and Nabû, which are set beside each other in the second row. That of Marduk consists of his sacred Spear-head supported by his dragon, that of Nabû being the Wedge or Stilus, also supported by a horned dragon. But while the other emblems are left sculptured in relief against the field of the stone, that of Nabû is engraved against a temple-tower.[1] It will be noticed that this rises in stages, diminishing in size and set one above the other. The rough engraving may well represent the

FIG. 30.

ROUGH ENGRAVING OF A TEMPLE-TOWER UPON A BOUNDARY-STONE.

The boundary-stone is of the period of Marduk-aplu-iddina, or Merodach-baladan I. The engraving represents a temple-tower, before which is a dragon supporting on its back an upright Wedge, the emblem of Nabû. The tower is represented as built in stories, or stepped stages, set one upon the other.
[From Brit. Mus., No. 90850.]

outward form of Nabû's temple-tower at Borsippa at the time of Merodach-baladan I. In any case, since the emblems on the boundary-stones are associated with

[1] In the engraving, in order that the wedge and the dragon should stand out in relief, the surface of the stone has been cut away round them. This gives the lowest story of the tower an appearance of having arched openings in it. It should, of course, be solid, like the other stages of the tower, the apparent openings being merely due to the exigencies of the engraver; cf. King, "Boundary-Stones and Memorial-Tablets in the British Museum," p. 25, n. 1. A photographic reproduction of this portion of the stone is given, op. cit., Pl. xli.

temples, the only building it can be intended for is
a temple-tower. It thus definitely proves the construction of this class of building in stories or stages, which
diminish in area as they ascend.

Additional evidence that this was actually the form
of the Tower of Babylon has been deduced from a tablet,
drawn up in the Seleucid era, and purporting to give
a detailed description and measurements of E-sagila and
its temple-tower. A hurried description of the text
and its contents was published by George Smith [1] before
he started on his last journey to the east, and from that
time the tablet was lost sight of. But some three years
ago it was found in Paris, and it has now been made
fully available for study.[2] It must be admitted that
it is almost impossible at present to reconcile the
descriptions on the tablet with the actual remains of
E-sagila and the Peribolos that have been recovered by
excavation. The "Great Terrace (or Court)," and the
"Terrace (or Court) of Ishtar and Zamama," which,
according to the tablet, were the largest and most
important subdivisions in the sacred area, have not been
satisfactorily identified. Dr. Koldewey was inclined to
regard the former as corresponding to the Great Court[3]
of the Peribolos, including the buildings surrounding
it, and the latter he would identify with the northern
court of the enclosure;[4] while the third great sub-
division he suggested might be the inner space of the
Great Court, which he thus had to count twice over.
Scarcely more satisfactory is M. Marcel Dieulafoy's
reconstruction, since he makes the two main areas, or
"terraces," extend to the east of the Sacred Way, over
ground which, as the excavations have shown, was
covered by the houses of the town, and thus lay beyond
the limits of the sacred area. It is possible that the
apparent discrepancies may be traced to an extensive
reconstruction of the Peribolos between the Neo-
Babylonian and the Seleucid periods. But, whatever

---

[1] In the "Athenæum," Feb. 12th, 1876.
[2] See Scheil, "Esagil ou le temple de Bêl-Marduk," in the "Mémoires
de l'Académie des Inscriptions et Belles-lettres," vol. xxxix. (1914), pp. 293 ff. ;
and cp. the "Étude arithmétique et architectonique du texte," by Dieulafoy,
ibid., pp. 309 ff.
[3] See above, p. 74, Fig. 27, F.   [4] Fig. 27, E.

explanation be adopted, a number of detailed measurements given by the tablet are best explained on the hypothesis that they refer to receding stages of a temple-tower. The tablet may thus be cited as affording additional support to the current conception of the Tower of Babylon, and there is no reason to reject the interpretation that has so long been accepted of the famous description of the tower that is given by Herodotus.[1]

There is one other structure in Babylon that deserves mention, and that is the bridge over the Euphrates, since its remains are those of the earliest permanent bridge of which we have any record in antiquity. It will be noted from the ground-plan of E-temen-anki[2] that the procession-street leads past the corner of the Peribolos to a great gate-way in the river-wall, guarding the head of the bridge which crossed the Euphrates on stone piers. The river at this point appears to have been one hundred and twenty-three metres in breadth. The piers are built in the shape of boats with their bows pointing up-stream, and their form was no doubt suggested by the earlier bridge-of-boats which they displaced. The roadway, as in boat-bridges in Mesopotamia at the present day, was laid across the boat-piers, and must have been very much narrower than the length of the piers themselves. The bridge, which is mentioned by Herodotus[3] and Diodorus,[4] was the work of Nabopolassar, as we learn from the East India House Inscription, in which Nebuchadnezzar states that his father "had built piers of burnt brick for the crossing of the Euphrates."[5] The stone used in its construction, which is referred to by Herodotus, was no doubt laid above the brick-piers, as a foundation for the flat wooden structure of the bridge itself. The later river-wall was the work of Nabonidus, and it marks an extension of the bank westwards, which was

---

[1] According to M. Dieulafoy's theory, the tower itself was built in five stages, standing on a massive base (*kigallu*), which in turn rested on a plinth, or terrace, extending over a great part of the temple-court ; thus, including the temple at the summit of the tower, the eight stages of Herodotus would be explained.

[2] See above, p. 74, Fig. 27, and cp. Fig. 28.   [3] I., 186.

[4] II., 8.   [5] Col. IV., l. 66—Col. V., l. 4.

G

rendered possible by the building of Nebuchadnezzar's fortification in the bed of the river to the west of the Southern Citadel.[1] The old line of the left bank is marked by the ruins of earlier river-walls, traces of which have been uncovered below the north-west angle of the Peribolos.[2] It was doubtless to protect the Peribolos and E-sagila from flood that the bank was extended in this way.

The buildings that have hitherto been described all date from the later Assyrian and Neo-Babylonian periods, and during their first years of work at Babylon the excavators found nothing that could be assigned to the earlier epochs in the history of the capital. It was assumed that the destruction of Babylon by Sennacherib had been so thorough that very little of the earlier city had survived. But later on it was realized that the remains of the older Babylon lay largely below the present water-level. The continual deposit of silt in the bed of the river has raised the level at which water is reached when digging on the site of the city, and it is clear that at the time of the First Dynasty the general level of the town was considerably lower than in later periods. During recent years a comparatively small body of water has flowed along the Euphrates bed, so that it has been possible on the Merkes Mound to uncover one quarter in the ancient city. There trenches have been cut to a depth of twelve metres, when water-level was reached and further progress was rendered impossible, although the remains of buildings continued still lower.

From the accompanying plan it will be seen that the street net-work has been recovered over a considerable area. The entire structure of the mound consists of the dwellings of private citizens, rising layer above layer from below water-level to the surface of the soil. The upper strata date from the Parthian period, and here the houses are scattered with wide spaces of garden or waste land between them. In striking contrast to these scanty remains are the streets of the Greek, Persian and Neo-Babylonian periods, where the houses are crowded together, and open spaces, which

[1] See above, p. 37.   [2] See p. 74, Fig. 27, K and L.

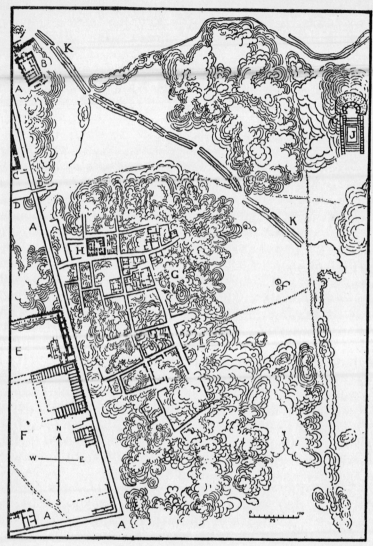

FIG. 31.

PLAN OF THE MERKES MOUND, SHOWING PART OF THE STREET NET-WORK OF
BABYLON.

A : The Sacred Way or Procession-Street of Babylon. B : E-makh, the
temple of the goddess Ninmakh. C : South-east corner of the Southern Citadel
with the Palace of Nebuchadnezzar. D : Canal and basin. E : Northern Court
of the Peribolos of E-temen-anki. F : Main Court of the Peribolos. G : The mound
Merkes. H : Temple of Ishtar of Akkad. J : Greek Theatre. K : Old canal.
[After Koldewey.]

were at one time courts or gardens, have later on been
surrendered to the builder.   We here have striking
proof of the value of house-property in Babylon during
the city's period of greatest prosperity.   Still deeper
in the mound a level can be dated to the twelfth and
thirteenth centuries, for in the houses were found
tablets inscribed in the reigns of Merodach-baladan I.,
Meli-Shipak II., and Enlil-nadin-shum.   In the northern
part of the mound, in the lowest stratum of all and
lying partly above and partly below water-level, contract-tablets of the First Dynasty were uncovered,
bearing date-formulæ of Samsu-iluna, Ammi-ditana and
Samsu-ditana.   Here the mud-brick walls of the houses,
though not very thick, all rest upon burnt-brick foundations, a method of building which, as we have seen,[1]
survived into the Neo-Babylonian period.   This is the
earliest city of which traces have been recovered, and
a thick layer of ashes testifies to its destruction by fire.
There can be no doubt that the town so destroyed was
that of Hammurabi and his immediate successors, for
the dated tablets were found lying in the layer of
ashes undisturbed.   We here have additional proof that
Babylon's First Dynasty ended in disaster.   It is
possible that the conflagration, in which the city then
perished, was the work of the Hittite raiders whose
onslaught we know took place in Samsu-ditana's reign.

This portion of the town would appear to have been
entirely residential, as it contains no open space such as
would have served as a market.   Even the temples were
without a space in front of them, and in this respect
resemble the churches in many modern cities.   It will
be noted that the temple of Ishtar of Akkad in the
north of the Merkes Mound, though not actually built
in, is approached on every side by private houses, though
on its southern face the road is rather broader than elsewhere.   Still more shut in were the temple of Ninib and
the unidentified temple known as " Z," both of which
lie in the mound Ishin-aswad.[2]   Here trenches cut
across the mound have uncovered the ruins of Babylonian houses in crude brick, the remains of different
periods lying one above the other as in Merkes, and

----

[1] See above, p. 39.   [2] See above, p. 68 ff.

they surround the temples on all sides.   The only other spot in Babylon where the same strata of streets and private houses have been found is in a low range of mounds between the Ḳasr and Tell 'Amrân, where the dwellings appear to be of an inferior character such as we might expect in a poorer quarter of the town.   It is only in the rather higher ground that satisfactory results have yet been obtained, as in the plain the earlier strata descend below water-level.   It is possible that further digging may lay bare the business-quarters of ancient Babylon, and that we may identify the markets and bazaars which formed one of the great centres of distribution in the ancient world.

Meanwhile, the Merkes Mound has yielded sufficient evidence to form a general conclusion as to the lines on which the city was built.   The street net-work shown in the plan is mainly that of the Neo-Babylonian period, but, wherever the earlier levels were preserved, it was noted that the old streets followed the same lines with but slight variations.   The main arteries run roughly north and south, parallel to the course of the Sacred Way, while others cross them at right angles.[1]   It would appear that, in spite of the absence of open spaces, we here have a deliberate attempt at town-planning on a scientific basis, the original idea of which may be traced back to the First Dynasty.   It is true that the streets are not entirely regular, but the main thoroughfares all run through, and the island-plots are all approximately rectangular.   We may probably place this achievement to the credit of the Semitic element in the population, as in the two Sumerian towns, in which private house-property has been uncovered, there is no trace of town-planning.   Both at Fâra and at Abû Hatab, the sites of the early Sumerian cities of Shuruppak and Kisurra, the streets that have been followed out are crooked and far more irregular than those of Babylon.   It has long been known that Hammurabi did much to codify the laws of his country and render

---

[1] It may be noted that this fully corroborates the statement of Herodotus (I., 180) that the streets of Babylon were straight, particularly those that ran at right angles and led to the river.   As little more than the foundations of the houses are preserved, it is not possible to control his further statement that the houses were three or four stories high.

their administration effective. It would now appear that similar system and method were introduced at the same period into the more material side of the national life.

The excavations at Babylon have thus thrown some direct light upon the condition of the city during the period at which it first became the capital. It is true that no portion of a royal or sacred building as yet identified antedates the later Assyrian Empire, and that, as the result of extensive reconstruction, the ruins of temples, palaces and city-walls are mainly those of the Neo-Babylonian period. But there was no great break in continuity between that epoch and its predecessors, so that, when due allowance has been made for certain innovations, the buildings of the later period may be treated as typical of Babylonian civilization as a whole. We have seen how the streets of Babylon followed the same lines throughout the whole of her dynastic period, and a similar spirit of conservatism no doubt characterized her architectural development. Temples were rebuilt again and again on the old sites, and even in the Neo-Babylonian period they retained the mud-brick walls and primitive decoration of their remote predecessors. Indeed, the conditions of life in Babylonia precluded any possibility of drastic change. The increased use of burnt brick in the upper structure of the royal palaces rendered possible the brilliant enamelling of the Neo-Babylonian craftsmen. But, even as late as Nabopolassar's reign, the thick mud-brick walls of the king's dwelling must have resembled those of Hammurabi himself: it was mainly in point of size that the earlier palace and city differed from those of later monarchs. And when we examine the successive periods of the country's history, we shall find that tradition exerted an equally powerful influence in retaining unaltered the essential features of the national life. It was under her earliest dynasty that Babylon worked out in detail a social organization that suited her agricultural and commercial activities ; and it is a remarkable tribute to its founders that it should have survived the shock of foreign domination and have imposed its mould upon later generations.

CHAPTER III

THE DYNASTIES OF BABYLON: THE CHRONOLOGICAL
SCHEME IN THE LIGHT OF RECENT DISCOVERIES

IT has often been said that chronology is the skeleton
of history; and it will be obvious that any flaw in
the chronological scheme must react upon our
conception of the sequence and inter-relation of events.
Perhaps the most serious defect from which Babylonian
chronology has suffered hitherto has been the complete
absence of any established point of contact between the
Babylonian dynasties and those earlier lines of rulers
who exercised authority in cities other than Babylon.
On the one hand, with the help of the Babylonian List
of Kings, we could build up from below a scheme of
the rulers of Babylon itself. On the other hand, after
the discovery of the Nippur Kings' List, it was possible
to establish the succession of the earlier dynasties of
Ur and Nîsin, and to conjecture their relation to the
still more remote rulers of Akkad and other cities in
the north and south. The two halves of the skeleton
were each articulated satisfactorily enough, but the few
bones were wanting which should enable us to fit them
together. It is scarcely necessary to say that there was
no lack of theories for filling in the gap. But every one
of the schemes suggested introduced fresh difficulties of
its own; and to writers of a more cautious temperament
it seemed preferable to avoid a detailed chronology
for those earlier ages. Approximate dates only were
suggested, for, in spite of the obvious temptations presented by the Nippur List, it was realized that any
attempt to work out the earlier dates in detail was
bound to be misleading. Such writers were content to

await the recovery of new material and meanwhile to think in periods.[1]

It is thus with some satisfaction that the announcement may be made that the connecting link, for which we have been waiting, has quite recently been established, with the result that we have now in our hands the necessary material for reconstructing the chronology on a sound basis and extending it back without a serious break, into the middle of the third millennium. The effect of the newly recovered point of contact between the earlier and the later phases in the country's history is naturally of greater importance for the former, so far as strict chronology is concerned.[2] But the information afforded, as to the overlapping of additional dynasties with that of the West-Semitic kings of Babylon, throws an entirely new light upon the circumstances which led to the rise of Babylon to power. Our picture of the capital's early history, as an independent city-state struggling for the mastery of her rivals, ceases to be an abstraction, and we may now follow her varying fortunes to their climax in Hammurabi's reign. This will form the subject of the following chapter ; but, as the new historical material is only now in course of publication, it will be advisable first to give some account of it and to estimate its effects upon the chronological scheme.

It has long been recognized that certain kings of Larsa, the city in Southern Babylonia now marked by the mounds of Senkera, were contemporaneous with the First Dynasty of Babylon. The greatest of these, Rîm-Sin, a ruler of Elamite extraction, was the contemporary of Hammurabi, and his signal defeat by Babylon was commemorated in the date-formula for the thirty-first year of the latter's reign.[3] This victory was, indeed, the chief event of Hammurabi's reign, and at one time it was thought that it freed Babylon once for all from her most powerful enemy. But the discovery of a chronicle of early Babylonian kings, while

---

[1] Cf. "Sumer and Akkad," p. 64.

[2] The new discoveries, in their general effect, do not involve any drastic changes in the accepted chronological scheme, as the local rearrangements largely counterbalance one another ; see below, p. 117 f.

[3] Cf. "Letters of Hammurabi," III., pp. lxviii, 236 f.

substantiating the fact of Hammurabi's victory, and affording the additional information that it was followed by the capture of Ur and Larsa, proved that Rîm-Sin survived into the reign of Samsu-iluna, Hammurabi's son, by whom he was finally defeated.[1] Another king of Larsa, Warad-Sin, formerly identified with Rîm-Sin, was correctly recognized as his brother, both of them sons of the Elamite Kudur-Mabuk, and successively kings of the city.[2] The names of other rulers were known from votive texts and foundation-records, and from this source it was possible to incorporate in the dynasty Gungunum, probably Sumu-ilum (a king of Ur), and Nûr-Adad or Nûr-Immer and his son Sin-idinnam. It was realized that Sin-idinnam, the correspondent to whom Hammurabi addressed his letters, was not to be identified with the king of Larsa of that name,[3] and all four rulers were provisionally regarded as having preceded Warad-Sin upon the throne.[4]

A complete list of the Larsa kings has now been recovered by Professor A. T. Clay of Yale University, who is engaged in preparing the text for publication. The dynasty is seen to have consisted of sixteen kings, and against the name of each ruler is stated the number of years he occupied the throne. The surface of the tablet is damaged in places and the figures against three of the names are wanting. But this is of no great consequence, since the scribe has added up the total number of years enumerated in the list, and states it at the close as two hundred and eighty-nine.[5] A most

[1] See "Chronicles concerning Early Babylonian Kings," I., p. 68 f.; II., p. 17 f.

[2] Cf. Thureau-Dangin, "Inscriptions de Sumer et d'Akkad," p. 300, n. 3; and "Sum. und Akkad. Königsinschriften," p. 210 f., note k.

[3] Cf. "Letters of Hammurabi," III., pp. xxvi ff.

[4] Their votive inscriptions are collected by Thureau-Dangin, "Königsinschriften," pp. 206 ff.

[5] Knowing that I was engaged upon this volume of my History and that it would probably be printed off before his own work left the press, Professor Clay very kindly sent me a transcript of his Larsa Kings' List with full permission to make use of it. To enable the reader to follow the argument with regard to the dynasty and its chronology, the following transliteration and rendering may be given of the text: "21 MU Na-ap-la-nu-um | 28 MU E-mi-ṣu | 35 MU Sa-mu-um | 9 MU Za-ba-aia | 27 MU Gu-un-gu-nu-um | 11 MU A-bi-sa-ri-e | 29 MU Su-mu-ilum | 16 MU Nu-ur-(ilu)Adad | 7 (?) MU (ilu)Sin-i-din-nam | 2 MU (ilu)Sin-i-ri-ba-am | 6(?) MU (ilu)Sin-i-ḳi-sha-am | 1 MU Ṣili(li)-(ilu)Adad | 12 MU Warad-(ilu)Sin | 61 MU (ilu)Ri-im-(ilu)Sin | 12(?) MU (ilu)Ha-am-mu-ra-bi | 12 MU Sa-am-su-i-lu-na sharru | 289 MU-BI." In the

important point about the list is that the last two kings of the dynasty are stated to have been Hammurabi and Samsu-iluna, who, as we know, were the sixth and seventh rulers of the First Dynasty of Babylon. It is true that Hammurabi is one of the three kings against whose names the figures are wanting. But we already know that he conquered Larsa in his thirty-first year,[1] so that we may confidently regard him as king of that city for the last twelve years of his reign. The two remaining kings of the dynasty whose years are missing, Sin-idinnam and Sin-iḳisham, have thirteen years to divide between them, and since they are only separated from each other by the short two-years' reign of Sin-iribam, the absence of the figures is practically immaterial. We are thus furnished with the means for establishing in detail the relationship of the earliest kings of Babylon to those of Larsa.

But like most new discoveries, this one has brought a fresh problem in its train. We already suspected that Rîm-Sin was a long-lived monarch, and we here find him credited with a reign of sixty-one years. But that fact would be difficult to reconcile with his survival into Samsu-iluna's tenth year, which, according to the figures of the new list, would have fallen eighty-three years after his accession to the throne. That Rîm-Sin did survive into the reign of Samsu-iluna seems practically certain, since the broken passage in the late chronicle, from which the fact was at first inferred, is supported by two date-formulæ which can be satisfactorily explained only on that hypothesis.[2] Thus, if he ascended the

---

translation that follows, a semicolon separates each line of the text : " 21 years Naplanum ; 28 years Emiṣu ; 35 years Samum ; 9 years Zabâia ; 27 years Gungunum ; 11 years Abi-sarê ; 29 years Sumu-ilum ; 16 years Nûr-Adad ; 7(?) years Sin-idinnam ; 2 years Sin-iribam ; 6(?) years Sin-iḳisham ; 1 year Ṣili-Adad ; 12 years Warad-Sin ; 61 years Rîm-Sin ; 12(?) years Hammurabi ; 12 years Samsu-iluna, the king ; 289 the years thereof." From the insertion of the word *sharru*, " king," after Samsu-iluna's name, we may infer that the list is a contemporaneous document, drawn up in Samsu-iluna's twelfth year. Another point of interest is that the scribe has written the determinative for divinity before the names of Rîm-Sin and Hammurabi, but not before that of Samsu-iluna. The numbers followed by a query are those suggested by Professor Clay for the three broken passages ; it will be noted that they make up the total of the figures, which is given by the scribe as two hundred and eighty-nine years.

[1] See above, p. 88.   [2] See further, p. 98 f.

BRICK OF SIN-IDINNAM, KING OF LARSA, RECORDING THE CUTTING OF A CANAL AND THE RESTORATION
OF THE TEMPLE OF THE MOON-GOD IN THE CITY OF UR.

From Mukayyar; Brit. Mus., No. 90251; photo. by Messrs. Mansell & Co.

throne of Larsa when merely a boy of fifteen, we should
have to infer from the new figures that he was leading
a revolt against Samsu-iluna in his ninety-eighth year—
a combination of circumstances which is just within the
bounds of possibility, but is hardly probable or convincing. We shall see presently that there is a comparatively simple, and not improbable, solution of the
puzzle, to which another line of evidence seems to
converge.

It will be noted that the new list of the kings of
Larsa, important as it undoubtedly is for the history of
its own period, does not in itself supply the long-desired
link between the earlier and the later chronology of
Babylonia. The relationship of the First Dynasty of
Babylon with that of Nîsin [1] is, so far as the new list is
concerned, left in the same state of uncertainty as before.
The possibility has long been foreseen that the Dynasty
of Nîsin and the First Dynasty of Babylon overlapped
each other,[2] as was proved to have been the case with
the first dynasties in the Babylonian List of Kings, and
as was confidently assumed with regard to the dynasties
of Larsa and Babylon. That no long interval separated
the two dynasties from one another had been inferred
from the character of the contract-tablets, dating from
the period of the Nîsin Dynasty, which had been found
at Nippur; for these were seen to bear a close resemblance to those of the First Babylonian Dynasty in
form, material, writing, and terminology.[3] There were
obvious advantages to be obtained, if grounds could be
produced for believing that the two dynasties were not
only closely consecutive but were partly contemporaneous. For, in such a case, it would follow that not
only the earlier kings of Babylon, but also the kings
of Larsa, would have been reigning at the same time
as the later kings of Nîsin. In fact, we should

[1] It should be noted that the name of the Babylonian city now usually
rendered as Isin should be more correctly read as Nîsin. This is suggested
by two forms of the name, which Prof. Clay tells me occur on two tablets in
the Yale Babylonian Collection, Nos. 5415 and 5417; in the date-formulæ
upon these tablets the city's name is written as *Ni-i-si-in* (KI) and *Ni-i-si-in-
na* (KI). Eventually the initial *n* was dropped; cf. p. 254, n. 2.

[2] Cf. "Chronicles," I., p. 168, n. 1.

[3] Cf. Hilprecht, "Mathematical, Metrological and Chronological
Tablets" (in "Bab. Exped.," Ser. A., Vol. X., i.), p. 55, n. 1.

picture Babylonia as still divided into a number of smaller principalities, each vying with the other in a contest for the hegemony and maintaining a comparatively independent rule within its own borders. It was fully recognized that such a condition of affairs would amply account for the confusion in the later succession at Nîsin, and our scanty knowledge of that period could then be combined with the fuller sources of information on the First Dynasty of Babylon.[1]

In the absence of any definite synchronism, such as we already possessed for deciding the inter-relations of the early Babylonian dynasties, other means were tried in order to establish a point of contact. The capture of Nîsin by Rîm-Sin, which is recorded in date-formulæ upon tablets found at Tell Ṣifr and Nippur, was evidently looked upon as an event of considerable importance, since it formed an epoch for dating tablets in that district. It was thus a legitimate assumption that the capture of the city by Rîm-Sin should be regarded as having brought the Dynasty of Nîsin to an end; such an assumption certainly supplied an adequate reason for the rise of a new era in time-reckoning. Now in the date-formulæ of the First Dynasty of Babylon two captures of the city of Nîsin are commemorated, the earlier one in that for the seventeenth year of Sin-muballiṭ, the later in the formula for Hammurabi's seventh year. Advocates have been found for deriving each of these dates from the capture of Nîsin by Rîm-Sin, and so obtaining the desired point of contact.[2] But the obvious objection to either of these views is that we should hardly expect a victory by Rîm-Sin to be commemorated in the date-formulæ of

---

[1] Cf. "Sumer and Akkad," pp. 63, 313 f.

[2] The identification of Rîm-Sin's capture of Nîsin with that referred to in Sin-muballiṭ's seventeenth year was first suggested in "Letters of Hammurabi," III., p. 228, n. 39, and it was adopted for purposes of chronology by Hilprecht, "Math., Met., and Chron. Tabl.," p. 50, note; Meyer, "Geschichte," I., ii., pp. 345, 556; Ungnad, "Orient. Lit.-Zeit.," 1908, Col. 66, and "Z.D.M.G.," LVI., p. 714, and others. Langdon has recently sought to identify Rîm-Sin's capture with that referred to in the formula for Hammurabi's seventh year; see "The Expositor," 1910, p. 131, and "Babyloniaca," 1914, p. 41, and cf. Chiera, "Legal and Administrative Documents," p. 24 f. For Chiera's own researches on the point, see below, p. 93 f.

his chief rival; and certain attempts to show that Babylon was at the time the vassal of Larsa have not proved very convincing. Moreover, if we accept the earlier identification, it raises the fresh difficulty that the era of Nîsin was not disturbed by Hammurabi's conquest of that city. The rejection of both views thus leads to the same condition of uncertainty from which we started.

A fresh and sounder line of research has recently been opened up. A detailed study has been undertaken of the proper names occurring on contract-tablets from Nippur, and it was remarked that some of the proper names found in documents belonging to the Nîsin and Larsa Dynasties are identical with those appearing on other Nippur tablets belonging to the First Dynasty of Babylon.[1] That they were borne by the same individuals is in many cases quite certain from the fact that the names of their fathers are also given. Both sets of documents were not only found at Nippur but were obviously written there, since they closely resemble one another in general appearance, style and arrangement. The same witnesses, too, occur again and again on them, and some of the tablets, which were drawn up under different dynasties, are the work of the same scribe. It has even been found possible, by the study of the proper names, to follow the history of a family through three generations, during which it was living at Nippur under different rulers belonging to the dynasties of Nîsin, Larsa and Babylon; and one branch of the family can never have left the city, since its members in successive generations held the office of "pashishu," or anointing-priest, in the temple of the goddess Ninlil.[2]

Of such evidence it will suffice for the moment to cite two examples, since they have a direct bearing on the assumption that Rîm-Sin's conquest of Nîsin put an end to the dynasty in that city. From two of the documents we learn that Zîatum, the scribe, pursued his calling at Nippur not only under Damik-ilishu, the

[1] Cf. Edward Chiera, "Legal and Administrative Documents from Nippur chiefly from the Dynasties of Isin and Larsa" (in "University of Pennsylvania Museum Publications, Babylonian Section," Vol. VIII., No. 1), pp. 19 ff.

[2] *Op. cit.*, p. 22.

last king of Nîsin, but also under Rîm-Sin of Larsa,[1]
a fact which definitely proves that Nippur passed under
the control of these two rulers within the space of one
generation.   The other piece of evidence is still more
instructive.   It has long been known that Hammurabi
was Rîm-Sin's contemporary, and from the new Kings'
List we have gained the further information that he
succeeded him upon the throne of Larsa.   Now two
other of the Nippur documents prove that Ibkushu, the
pashishu, or "anointing-priest" of the goddess Ninlil,
was living at Nippur under Damik-ilishu and also under
Hammurabi in the latter's thirty-first year.[2]   This fact
not only confirms our former inference, but gives very
good grounds for believing that the close of Damik-
ilishu's reign must have fallen within that of Rîm-Sin.
We may therefore regard it as certain that Rîm-Sin's
conquest of Nîsin, which began a new era for time-
reckoning in central and southern Babylonia, put an
end to the reign of Damik-ilishu and to the Dynasty of
Nîsin, of which he was the last member.   In order to
connect the chronology of Babylon with that of Nîsin it
therefore only remains to ascertain at what period in
Rîm-Sin's reign, as King of Larsa, his conquest of
Nîsin took place.

It is at this point that a further discovery of Prof.
Clay has furnished us with the necessary data for a
decision.   Among the tablets of the Yale Babylonian
Collection he has come across several documents of
Rîm-Sin's reign, which bear a double-date.   In every
case the first half of the double-date corresponds to
the usual formula for the second year of the Nîsin era.
On two of them the second half of the date-formula
equates that year with the eighteenth of some other era,
while on two others the same year is equated with the
nineteenth year.[3]   It is obvious that we here have

---

[1] Cf. Chiera, *op. cit.*, pl. ix., No. 15, ll. 27 ff. ; pl. xxiii., No. 35, ll. 20 ff.';
and p. 21, No. 26.

[2] *Op. cit.*, pl. vii., No. 12, ll. 29, 35 f. ; pl. xxxv., No. 81, ll. 2, 23 ff. ;
and p. 20, No. 6.

[3] Professor Clay has written to inform me that on the two tablets Y.B.C.,
Nos. 4229 and 4270, the usual formula for the second year of the Nîsin era is
followed by the words *shag mu ki XVIII-kam*, which may be rendered "within
the eighteenth year," *i.e.* corresponding to the eighteenth year. On one tablet

scribes dating documents according to a new era, and explaining that that year corresponds to the eighteenth (or nineteenth) of one with which they had been familiar, and which the new method of time-reckoning was probably intended to displace. Now we know that, before the capture of Nîsin, the scribes in cities under Rîm-Sin's control had been in the habit of dating documents by events in his reign, according to the usual practice of early Babylonian kings.[1] But this method was given up after the capture of Nîsin, and for at least thirty-one years after that event the era of Nîsin was in vogue.[2] In the second year of the era, when the new method of dating had just been settled, it would have been natural for the scribes to add a note explaining the relationship of the new era to the old. But, as the old changing formulæ had been discontinued, the only possible way to make the equation would have been to reckon the number of years Rîm-Sin had been upon the throne. Hence we may confidently conclude that the second figure in the double-dates was intended to give the year of Rîm-Sin's reign which corresponded to the second year of the Nîsin era.

It may seem strange that in some of the documents

the addition to the usual date takes the form *shag mu ki XVIII-kam in-ag* (?), but Prof. Clay is not quite certain of the reading of the sign *ag*, which, he writes, "because the tablet was cased, is badly twisted." If the reading is correct it is important, for the addition may then be rendered "within (*i.e.* corresponding to) the eighteenth year that he reigned," the word *in-ag* being the verb usually employed in Sumerian dynastic lists in sentences stating the number of years a king reigned. Two other long date-formulæ for the same year (on tablets Y.B.C., Nos. 4307 and 4481) begin as follows : *mu ki II dim*(?) *mu ki XIX giš-ku-makh Ana* (*dingir*)*En-lil* (*dingir*)*En-ki*, etc. Here the reading of the sign *dim* is not absolutely certain, but, assuming its correctness, the formula may be rendered : "The second year (corresponding to the nine-teenth year) in which with the exalted weapon of Anu, Enlil and Ea, Rîm-Sin the king took the city of Nîsin," etc. It will be seen that the readings, which are suggested by Prof. Clay for the two uncertain signs in the formulæ, give excellent sense, and, if correct, they definitely prove that the second figures in the equations were derived from Rîm-Sin's regnal years. But, even if we regard the two signs as quite uncertain, the general interpretation of the double-dates is not affected ; it would be difficult to explain them on any other hypothesis than that adopted in the text.

[1] Some of his earlier date-formulæ have been recovered; see below, p. 155.

[2] For many years past the latest date recovered of the Nîsin era was one of the thirtieth year ; see Scheil, " Recueil de travaux," XXI. (1899), p. 125, and cf. " Letters of Hammurabi," III., p. 229. Prof. Clay informs me that among the tablets of the Yale Babylonian Collection is one dated in the thirty-first year of the fall of Nîsin.

with the double-dates the second figure is given as eighteen and in others as nineteen. There is more than one way in which it is possible to explain the discrepancy. If we assume that the conquest of Nîsin took place towards the close of Rîm-Sin's seventeenth year, it is possible that, during the two years that followed, alternative methods of reckoning were in vogue, some scribes regarding the close of the seventeenth year as the first year of the new epoch, others beginning the new method of time-reckoning with the first day of the following Nisan. But that explanation can hardly be regarded as probable, for, in view of the importance attached to the conquest, the promulgation of the new era commemorating the event would have been carried out with more than ordinary ceremonial, and the date of its adoption would not have been left to the calculation of individual scribes. It is far more likely that the explanation is to be sought in the second figure of the equation, the discrepancy being due to alternative methods of reckoning Rîm-Sin's regnal years. Again assuming that the conquest took place in Rîm-Sin's seventeenth year, those scribes who counted the years from his first date-formula would have made the second year of the era the eighteenth of his reign. But others may have included in their total the year of Rîm-Sin's accession to the throne, and that would account for their regarding the same year as the nineteenth according to the abolished system of reckoning.[1] This seems the preferable explanation of the two, but it will be noticed that, on either alternative, we must regard the first year of the Nîsin era as corresponding to the seventeenth year of Rîm-Sin's reign.

One other point requires to be settled, and that is the relation of the Nîsin era to the actual conquest of the city. Was the era inaugurated in the same year as the conquest, or did its first year begin with the following first of Nisan? In the course of the fifth

[1] The fact that they had always dated by formulæ, and not by numbered years of the king's reign, is quite sufficient to explain the uncertainty as to whether the accession-year should be included in their reckoning. Thus the apparent discrepancy in the double-dates, so far from weakening the explanation put forward in the text, really affords it additional support and confirmation.

HAMMURABI, KING OF BABYLON, FROM A RELIEF IN THE BRITISH
MUSEUM.
Brit. Mus., No. 22454.

chapter the early Babylonian method of time-reckoning
is referred to, and it will be seen that precisely the
same question arises with regard to certain other
events commemorated in date-formulæ of the period.[1]
Though some features of the system are still rather
uncertain, we have proof that the greater historical
events did in certain cases affect the current date-
formula, especially when this was of a provisional
character, with the result that the event was commemorated in the final formula for the year of its
actual occurrence. Arguing from analogy, we may
therefore regard the inauguration of the Nîsin era as
coinciding with the year of the city's capture. In the
case of this particular event the arguments in favour
of such a view apply with redoubled force, for no other
victory by a king of Larsa was comparable to it in
importance. We may thus regard the last year of
Damik-ilishu, King of Nîsin, as corresponding to the
seventeenth year of Rîm-Sin, King of Larsa. And
since the relationship of Rîm-Sin with Hammurabi has
been established by the new list of Larsa kings, we are
at length furnished with the missing synchronism for
connecting the dynasties of the Nippur Kings' List
with those of Babylon.

We may now return to the difficulty introduced by
the new list of Larsa kings, on which, as we have
already noted, the long reign of Rîm-Sin is apparently
entered as preceding the thirty-second year of Hammurabi's rule in Babylon. Soon after the publication of
the chronicle, from a broken passage on which it was
inferred that Rîm-Sin survived into Samsu-iluna's reign,[2]
an attempt was made to explain the words as referring to
a son of Rîm-Sin and not to that ruler himself.[3] But
it was pointed out that the sign, which it was suggested
should be rendered as " son," was never employed with
that meaning in chronicles of the period,[4] and that we

---

[1] See below, p. 190.
[2] See " Chronicles concerning early Babylonian Kings," II., p. 18.
[3] Cf. Winckler, " Orient. Lit.-Zeit.," 1907, Col. 585 f., and Hrozný,
" Wiener Zeitschrift," Bd. 21 (1908), p. 382.
[4] Cf. " Sumer and Akkad," p. 317, n. 2. The broken line in the chronicle
reads: [.........]-zu-na-a (m)Rîm-(ilu)Sin ana [.........] illik(ik), " [.........]...
Rîm-Sin to [.........] marched." The rendering suggested by Winckler and

H

must consequently continue to regard the passage as referring to Rîm-Sin. It was further noted that two contract-tablets found at Tell Sifr, which record the same deed of sale, are dated the one by Rîm-Sin, and the other in Samsu-iluna's tenth year.[1] In both of these deeds the same parties are represented as carrying out the same transaction, and, although there is a difference in the price agreed upon, the same list of witnesses occur on both, and both are dated in the same month. The most reasonable explanation of the existence of the two documents would seem to be that, at the period the transaction they record took place, the possession of the town now marked by the mounds of Tell Sifr was disputed by Rîm-Sin and Samsu-iluna. Soon after the first of the deeds had been drawn up, the town may have changed hands, and, in order that the transaction should still be recognized as valid, a fresh copy of the deed was made out with the new ruler's date-formula substituted for that which was no longer current.[2] But whatever explanation be adopted, the alternative dates upon the documents, taken in conjunction with the chronicle, certainly imply that Rîm-Sin was living at least as late as Samsu-iluna's ninth year, and probably in the tenth year of his reign.

If, then, we accept the face value of the figures given by the new Larsa Kings' List, we are met by the difficulty already referred to, that Rîm-Sin would have been an active political force in Babylonia some eighty-three years after his own accession to the throne. And assuming that he was merely a boy of fifteen when he succeeded his brother at Larsa, he would have been taking the field against Samsu-iluna in his ninety-eighth year.[3] But it is extremely unlikely that he was so young at his accession, and, in view of the improbabilities involved, it is preferable to scrutinize the figures

Hrozný was : " [.........]zuna, the son of Rîm-Sin, to [.........] marched ; " but their translation ignored the fact that, in these late chronicles, " son " is always expressed by the sign TUR (mâru), never by A (aplu).

[1] Cf. Ungnad, " Zeits. für Assyr.," XXIII., pp. 73 ff., and Thureau-Dangin, " Journal Asiatique," xiv., 1909, pp. 335 ff.

[2] The difference in price may perhaps be traced to the political revolution, which may have enabled one of the parties to exact better terms from the other.

[3] See above, p. 90 f.

in the Larsa list with a view to ascertaining whether they are not capable of any other interpretation.

It has already been noted that the Larsa List is a contemporaneous document, since the scribe has added the title of "king" to the last name only, that of Samsu-iluna, implying that he was the reigning king at the time the document was drawn up. It is unlikely, therefore, that any mistake should have been made in the number of years assigned to separate rulers, the date-formulæ and records of whose reigns would have been easily accessible for consultation by the compiler. The long reign of sixty-one years, with which Rîm-Sin is credited, must be accepted as correct, for it does not come to us as a tradition incorporated in a Neo-Baby-lonian document, but is attested by a scribe writing within two years of the time when, as we have seen, Rîm-Sin was not only living but fighting against the armies of Babylon. In fact, the survival of Rîm-Sin throughout the period of Hammurabi's rule at Larsa, and during the first ten years of Samsu-iluna's reign, perhaps furnishes us with the solution of our problem.

If Rîm-Sin had not been deposed by Hammurabi on his conquest of Larsa, but had been retained there with curtailed powers as the vassal of Babylon, may not his sixty-one years of rule have included this period of dependence? In that case he may have ruled as independent King of Larsa for thirty-nine years, followed by twenty-two years during which he owed allegiance successively to Hammurabi and Samsu-iluna, until in the latter's tenth year he revolted and once more took the field against Babylon. It is true that, with the missing figures in the Kings' List restored as suggested by Professor Clay, the figure for the total duration of the dynasty may be cited against this expla-nation; for the two hundred and eighty-nine years is obtained by regarding the whole of Rîm-Sin's reign as anterior to Hammurabi's conquest. There are two possibilities with regard to the figure. In the first place it is perhaps just possible that Sin-idinnam and Sin-ikîsham may have reigned between them thirty-five years, in place of the thirteen years provisionally assigned to them. If that were so, the scribe's total would be twenty-two years less than the addition of his figures, and the discrepancy could only be explained by some such overlapping as suggested. But it is far more likely that the figures are correctly restored, and that the scribe's total corresponds to that of the figures in the list. On such an assumption it is not improbable that he mechanically added up the figures placed opposite the royal names, without deducting from his total the years of Rîm-Sin's dependent rule.

This explanation appears to be the one least open to objection, as it does not necessitate the alteration of essential figures, and merely postulates a natural oversight on the part of the compiler. The placing of Hammurabi and Samsu-iluna in the list after, and not beside, Rîm-Sin would be precisely on the lines of the Babylonian Kings' List, in which the Second Dynasty is enumerated between the First and Third, although, as we now know, it overlapped a part of each. In that case, too, the scribe has added up the totals of his separate dynasties, without any indication of their periods of overlapping. The explanation in both cases is, of course, that the modern system of arranging contemporaneous rulers in parallel columns had not been evolved by the Babylonian scribes. Moreover, we have evidence that at least one other compiler of a dynastic list was careless in adding up his totals; from one of his discrepancies it would seem that he counted a period of three months as three years, while in another of his dynasties a similar period of three months was probably counted twice over both as months and years.[1] It is true that the dynastic list in question is a late and not a contemporaneous document, but at least it inclines us to accept the possibility of such an oversight as that suggested on the part of the compiler of the Larsa list.

The only reason which we have as yet examined for equating the first twenty-two years of Babylon's suzerainty over Larsa with the latter part of Rîm-Sin's reign has been the necessity of reducing the duration of that monarch's life within the bounds of probability. If this had been the only ground for the assumption, it

---

[1] Cf. "Chronicles concerning Early Babylonian Kings," I., p. 184 f.

might perhaps have been regarded as more or less pro-
blematical. But the Nippur contract-tablets and legal
documents, to which reference has already been made,[1]
furnish us with a number of separate and independent
pieces of evidence in its support. The tablets contain
references to officials and private people who were
living at Nippur in the reigns of Damik-ilishu, the
last king of Nîsin, and of Rîm-Sin of Larsa, and also
under Hammurabi and Samsu-iluna of Babylon. Most
of the tablets of Rîm-Sin's period are dated by the
Nîsin era, and, since the dates of those drawn up in
the reigns of Hammurabi and Samsu-iluna can be
definitely ascertained by means of their date-formulæ,
it is possible to estimate the intervals of time separating
references to the same man or to a man and his son. It
is remarkable that in some cases the interval of time
appears excessive if the whole of Rîm-Sin's reign of
sixty-one years be placed before Hammurabi's capture
of Larsa. If, on the other hand, we regard Rîm-Sin as
Babylon's vassal for the last twenty-two years of his
rule in Larsa, the intervals of time are reduced to
normal proportions. As the point is of some importance for the chronology, it may be as well to cite one
or two examples of this class of evidence, in order that
the reader may judge of its value for himself.

The first example we will examine will be that
furnished by Ibkushu, the anointing-priest of Ninlil,
to whom we have already referred as having lived at
Nippur under Damik-ilishu and also under Hammurabi
in the latter's thirty-first year[2]; both references, it may
be noted, describe him as holding his priestly office at
Nippur. Now, if we accept the face value of the figures
in the Larsa List we obtain an interval between these
two references of at least forty-four years and probably
more.[3] By the suggested interpretation of the figures
in the List the interval would be reduced by twenty-
two years. A very similar case is that of the scribe
Ur-kingala, who is mentioned in a document dated in

---

[1] See above, p. 93 f.   [2] See above, p. 94, n. 2.
[3] If Ibkushu was appointed priest in Damik-ilishu's last year, the interval
would be exactly forty-four years ; but as Damik-ilishu reigned for twenty-
three years, Ibkushu may well have been appointed several years earlier.

the eleventh year of the Nîsin era, and again in one of
Samsu-iluna's fourth year.[1]   In the one case we obtain
an interval of fifty years between the two references,
while in the other it is reduced to twenty-eight years.
Very similar results follow if we examine references on
the tablets to fathers and their sons.   A certain Adad-
rabi, for example, was living at Nippur under Damik-
ilishu, while his two sons Mâr-irsitim and Mutum-ilu
are mentioned there in the eleventh year of Samsu-
iluna's reign.[2]   In the one case we must infer an interval
of at least sixty-seven years, and probably more, between
father and sons ; in the other an interval of forty-five
years or more is obtained.   It will be unnecessary to
examine further examples, as those already cited may
suffice to illustrate the point.   It will be noted that
the unabridged interval can in no single instance be
pronounced impossible.   But the cumulative effect produced is striking.   The independent testimony of these
private documents and contracts thus converges to the
same point as the data with regard to the length of Rîm-
Sin's life.   Several of the figures so obtained suggest that,
taken at their face value, the regnal years in the Larsa
List yield a total that is about one generation too long.
They are thus strongly in favour of the suggested method
of interpreting Rîm-Sin's reign in the Larsa succession.

We may thus provisionally place the sixty-first year of
Rîm-Sin's rule at Larsa in the tenth year of Samsu-iluna's
reign, when we may assume that he revolted and took
the field against his suzerain.   It was in that year that
Tell Ṣifr changed hands for a time.   But it is probably
a significant fact that not a single document of Samsu-
iluna's reign has been found in that district dated after
his twelfth year.   In fact we shall see reason to believe
that the whole of Southern Babylonia soon passed from
the control of Babylon, though Samsu-iluna succeeded
in retaining his hold on Nippur for some years longer.
Meanwhile it will suffice to note that the suggested

[1] See Poebel, "Babylonian Legal and Business Documents," pl. 3, No. 6,
ll. 25, 30 ff., and pl. 11, No. 23, ll. 33, 36 ff. ;   and cf. Chiera, "Legal and
Administrative Documents from Nippur," p. 21, No. 24.
[2] Cf. Chiera, op. cit., p. 22.   Chiera's own deduction from the proper names
(pp. 29 ff.) must of course be modified in view of the Larsa Kings' List ; but
his data hold good.

sequence of events fits in very well with other references in the date-lists. The two defeats of Nîsin by Hammurabi and his father Sin-muballit, which have formed for so long a subject of controversy, now cease to be a stumbling-block. We see that both took place before Rîm-Sin's capture of Nîsin,[1] and were merely temporary successes which had no effect upon the continuance of the Nîsin dynasty. That was brought to an end by Rîm-Sin's victory in his seventeenth year, when the Nîsin era of dating was instituted. That, in cities where it had been long employed, the continued use of the era alongside his own formulæ should have been permitted by Hammurabi for some eight years after his capture of Larsa, is sufficiently explained by our assumption that Rîm-Sin was not deposed, but was retained in his own capital as the vassal of Babylon. There would have been a natural reluctance to abandon an established era, especially if Babylon's authority was not rigidly enforced during the first few years of her suzerainty, as with earlier vassal states.[2]

The overlapping of the Dynasty of Nîsin with that of Babylon for a period of one hundred and eleven years, which follows from the new information afforded by the Yale tablets, merely carries the process still further that was noted some years ago with regard to the first three Dynasties of the Babylonian List of Kings. At the time of the earlier discovery considerable difference of opinion existed as to the number of years, if any, during which the Second Dynasty of the List held independent sway in Babylonia. The archæological evidence at that time available seemed to suggest that the kings of the Sea-Country never ruled in Babylonia, and that the Third, or Kassite, Dynasty

[1] On the suggested hypothesis with regard to the Larsa List, Rîm-Sin's capture of Nîsin would have taken place two years after Hammurabi's attack on that city. But, if we reject the hypothesis, the Nîsin era would have begun in Sin-muballit's seventh year.

[2] See pp. 142 ff. The survival of the Nîsin era, during the first years of Larsa's vassalage, seems to offer less difficulties than those involved in an acceptance of Rîm-Sin's sixty-one years of independent rule, followed at first by twenty-one or twenty-two years of political obscurity, and then by a period of active operations in the field. And, apart from the improbabilities involved in the length of Rîm-Sin's life, the further difficulty of the interruption of the Nîsin era by Sin-muballit's and Hammurabi's conquests of the city would still remain (see above, p. 92 f.).

followed the First Dynasty without any considerable
break.[1]   Other writers, in their endeavours to use and
reconcile the chronological references to earlier rulers
which occur in later texts, assumed a period of independence for the Second Dynasty which varied, according to their differing hypotheses, from one hundred and
sixty-eight to eighty years.[2]   Since the period of the
First Dynasty was not fixed independently, the complete absence of contemporary evidence with regard to
the Second Dynasty led to a considerable divergence of
opinion upon the point.

So far as the archæological evidence is concerned,
we are still without any great body of documents
dated in their reigns, which should definitely prove the
rule of the Sea-Country kings in Babylonia.   But two
tablets have now been discovered in the Nippur Collections which are dated in the second year of Iluma-
ilum, the founder of the Second Dynasty.[3]   And this fact
is important, since it proves that for two years at any
rate he exercised control over a great part of Babylonia.
Now among the numerous documents dated in the
reigns of Hammurabi and Samsu-iluna, which have
been found at Nippur, none are later than Samsu-
iluna's twenty-ninth year, although the succession of
dated documents up to that time is almost unbroken.
It would thus appear that after Samsu-iluna's twenty-
ninth year Babylon lost her hold upon Nippur.   It is
difficult to resist the conclusion that the power which
drove her northwards was the kingdom of the Sea-
Country, whose founder Iluma-ilum waged successful
campaigns against both Samsu-iluna and his son Abi-
eshu', as we learn from the late Babylonian chronicle.[4]
Another fact that is probably of equal significance is
that, of the tablets from Larsa and its neighbourhood,

[1] That was the view I suggested in "Chronicles concerning Early Babylonian Kings," I., pp. 96 ff., and it was adopted by Meyer, "Geschichte des
Altertums," Bd. I., Hft. ii., p. 340 f.
[2] Cf. "Sumer and Akkad," p. 63, n. 2.
[3] See Poebel, "Business Documents," pl. 40, No. 68, and Chiera, "Legal
and Administrative Documents," pl. xl., No. 89.
[4] Cf. "Chronicles," II., pp. 19 ff.   That the Sea-Country was Babylon's
most powerful rival at this time may be inferred from the inclusion of Iluma-
ilum's name in the Chronicle.   He is evidently selected for mention as the
leader of the most notable invasion of the period.

BRICK OF WARAD-SIN, KING OF LARSA, RECORDING BUILDING
OPERATIONS IN THE CITY OF UR.
Brit. Mus., No. 90055.

none have been found dated after Samsu-iluna's twelfth year, although we have numerous examples drawn up during the earlier years of his reign. We may therefore assume that soon after his twelve years of rule at Larsa, which are assigned to him on the new Kings' List,[1] that city was lost to Babylon. And again it is difficult to resist the conclusion that the Sea-Country was the aggressor. From Samsu-iluna's own date-formulæ we know that in his twelfth year "all the lands revolted" against him.[2] We may therefore with considerable probability place Iluma-ilum's revolt in that year, followed immediately by his establishment of an independent kingdom in the south.[3] He probably soon gained control over Larsa and gradually pushed north-wards until he occupied Nippur in Samsu-iluna's twenty-ninth or thirtieth year.

Such appears to be the most probable course of events, so far as it may be determined in accordance with our new evidence. And since it definitely proves that the founder of the Second Dynasty of the Kings' List established, at any rate for a time, an effective control over southern and central Babylonia, we are the more inclined to credit the kings of the Sea-Country with having later on extended their authority farther to the north. The fact that the compiler of the Babylonian List of Kings should have included the rulers of the Sea-Country in that document has always formed a weighty argument for regarding some of them as having ruled in Babylonia ; and it was only possible to eliminate the dynasty entirely from the chronological scheme by a very drastic reduction of his figures for

---

[1] See above, p. 90, note.

[2] See Schorr, "Urkunden des altbab. Ziv. und Prozessrechts," p. 595.

[3] We know that Iluma-ilum was the contemporary of Abi-eshu' as well as of Samsu-iluna. As he is credited by the Kings' List with a reign of sixty years, it is possible, if we accept that figure, that he had established his dynasty in the Sea-Country some years before attacking Larsa. His accession has been placed as early as Hammurabi's twenty-sixth year (cf. Thureau-Dangin, "Zeits. für Assyr.," XXI., pp. 176 ff.), though the same writer, by making a reduction of twenty years in his dates for the Third and Second Dynasties, afterwards assumed that he secured his throne in Samsu-iluna's fourth year (op. cit., p. 185 f.). As we have no evidence that Iluma-ilum was Hammurabi's contemporary, it is safer to place his accession in Samsu-iluna's reign ; and, in that case, the date-formula for the twelfth year appears to offer the most probable occasion for his revolt.

some of their reigns. The founder of the dynasty, for example, is credited with a reign of sixty years, two other rulers with reigns of fifty-five years, and a fourth with fifty years. But the average duration of the reigns in the dynasty is only six years in excess of that for the First Dynasty, which also consisted of eleven kings. And, in view of the sixty-one years credited to Rîm-Sin in the newly recovered Larsa List, which is a contemporaneous document and not a later compilation, we may regard the traditional length of the dynasty as perhaps approximately correct.[1] Moreover, in all other parts of the Kings' List that can be controlled by contemporaneous documents, the general accuracy of the figures has been amply vindicated. The balance of evidence appears, therefore, to be in favour of regarding the compiler's estimate for the duration of his Second Dynasty as also resting on reliable tradition.

In working out the chronological scheme it only remains therefore to fix accurately the period of the First Dynasty, in order to arrive at a detailed chronology for both the earlier and the later periods. Hitherto, in default of any other method, it has been necessary to rely on the traditions which have come down to us from the history of Berossus or on chronological references to early rulers which occur in the later historical texts. A new method of arriving at the date of the First Dynasty, in complete independence of such sources of information, was hit upon three years ago by Dr. Kugler, the Dutch astronomer, in the course of his work on published texts that had any bearing on the history and achievements of Babylonian astronomy.[2] Two such tablets had been found by Sir Henry Layard at Nineveh and were preserved in the Kouyunjik Collection of the British Museum. Of these one had long been published and its contents correctly classified as a series of astronomical omens derived from observations of the planet Venus.[3] It

---

[1] The figures are probably not absolutely accurate ; see below, p. 209, n. 1.
[2] See his " Sternkunde und Sterndienst in Babel," 1907–1913.
[3] This, the principal text, is numbered K. 160, and its text was published by George Smith in Rawlinson's " Cun. Inscr. West. Asia," III., pl. 63. Translations and studies have been given of it by Sayce, " Trans. Soc. Bibl. Arch.," III. (1874), pp. 316 ff. ; by Sayce and Bosanquet, " Monthly Notices

was certain that this Assyrian text was a copy of an earlier Babylonian one, since that was definitely stated in its colophon. The second of the two inscriptions proved to be in part a duplicate,[1] and by using them in combination Dr. Kugler was able to restore the original text with a considerable degree of certainty.[2] But a more important discovery was that he succeeded in identifying precisely the period at which the text was originally drawn up, and the astronomical observations recorded. For he noted that in the eighth section of his restored text there was a chronological note, dating that section by the old Babylonian date-formula for the eighth year of Ammi-zaduga, the tenth king of the First Babylonian Dynasty. As his text contained twenty-one sections, he drew the legitimate inference that it gave him a series of observations of the planet Venus for each of the twenty-one years of Ammi-zaduga's reign.[3]

The observations from which the omens were derived consist of dates for the heliacal rising and setting of the planet Venus. The date was observed at which the planet was first visible in the east, the date of her disappearance was noted, and the duration of her period of invisibility; similar dates were then observed of her first appearance in the west as the Evening Star, followed as before by the dates of her disappearance and her period of invisibility. The taking of such observations does not, of course, imply any elaborate astronomical knowledge on the part of the early Babylonians. This beautiful planet must have been the first, after the moon, to attract systematic observation, and thanks to her nearly circular orbit, no water-clock nor instrument

of the Royal Astronomical Society," XL. (1880), p. 566 ff., and by Schiaparelli, "Venusbeobachtungen und Berechnungen der Babylonier" (1906). For other references, see Bezold, "Catalogue," I., p. 42.

[1] The second of the two inscriptions is numbered K. 2321 + K. 3032, and its text has been published by Craig, "Astrological-Astronomical Texts," pl. 46; cf. also Virolleaud, "L'Astrologie Chaldéenne," Ishtar XII., XV. and XIV.

[2] Cf. "Sternkunde und Sterndienst in Babel," Buch II., Teil ii., Hft. 1, pp. 257 ff. In addition to broken passages occurring in the two texts, some scribal errors appear to have crept in in the course of transmission.

[3] From contemporary date-formulæ we know that Ammi-zaduga reigned for more than seventeen years. The Babylonian Kings' List ascribes him twenty-one.

for measuring angles was required. The astrologers
of the period would naturally watch for the planet's first
appearance in the glimmer of the dawn, that they might
read therefrom the will of the great goddess with whom
she was identified. They would note her gradual ascension, decline and disappearance, and then count the days
of her absence until she reappeared at sunset and repeated her movements of ascension and decline. Such
dates, with the resulting fortunes of the country, form
the observations noted in the text that was drawn up
in Ammi-zaduga's reign.

It will be obvious that the periodic return of the
same appearance of the planet Venus would not in
itself have supplied us with sufficient means for deter-
mining the period of the observations. But we obtain
additional data if we employ our information with the
further object of ascertaining the relative positions of
the sun and moon. On the one hand the heliacal
risings and settings of Venus are naturally bound up
in a fixed relationship of Venus to the sun ; on the other
hand the series of dates by the days of the month
furnishes us with the relative position of the moon with
regard to the sun on the days cited. Without the second
criterion, the first would be of very little use. But, taken
together, the combination of the sun, Venus and the
moon are of the greatest value for fixing the position of
the group of years, covered by the observations, within
any given period of a hundred years or more. Now if
we eliminate the Second Dynasty altogether from the
Babylonian Kings' List, it is certain that Ammi-zaduga's
reign could not have fallen much later than 1800 B.C. ;
on the other hand, in view of the ascertained minimum
of overlapping of the First Dynasty by the Second, it
is equally certain that it could not have fallen earlier
than 2060 B.C. The period of his reign must thus be
sought within the interval between these dates. But,
in order to be on the safe side, Dr. Kugler extended
both the limits of the period to be examined ; he conducted his researches within the period from 2080 to
1740 B.C. He began by taking two observations for
the sixth year of Ammi-zaduga, which gave the dates
for the heliacal setting of Venus in the west and her

rising in the east, and, by using the days of the month
to ascertain the relative positions of the moon, he found
that throughout the whole course of his period this particular combination took place three times.[1]   He then
proceeded to examine in the same way the rest of the
observations, with their dates, as supplied by the two
tablets, and, by working them out in detail for the
central one of his three possible periods, he obtained
confirmation of his view that the observations did cover
a consecutive period of twenty-one years.   In order to
obtain independent proof of the correctness of his figures,
he proceeded to examine the dates upon contemporary
legal documents, which could be brought into direct or
indirect relation to the time of harvest.   These dates,
according to his interpretation of the calendar, offered
a means of controlling his results, since he was able to
show that a higher or lower estimate tended to throw
out the time of harvest from the month of Nisan, which
was peculiarly the harvest month.

It must be admitted that the last part of the
demonstration stands in a different category to the
first ; it does not share the simplicity of the astronomical problem.   It formed, indeed, merely an additional
method of testing the interpretation of the astronomical
evidence, and the dates resulting from the latter were
obtained in complete independence of the farming-out
contracts of the period.   Taking, then, the three alternative dates, there can be no doubt, if we accept the
figure of the Kings' List for the Second Dynasty as
approximately accurate, that the central of the three
periods is the only one possible for Ammi-zaduga's
reign ; for either of the other two would imply too high
or too low a date for the Third Dynasty of the Kings'
List.   We may thus accept the date of 1977 B.C. as
that of Ammi-zaduga's accession, and we thereby obtain
a fixed point for working out the chronology of the
First Dynasty of Babylon, and, consequently, of the
partly contemporaneous Dynasties of Larsa and of Nîsin,
and of the still earlier Dynasty of Ur.   Incidentally

---

[1] According to this criterion, Ammi-zaduga's sixth year could have fallen
in 2036–5 B.C., or in 1972–1 B.C., or in 1853–2 B.C., thus giving for his first
year the three possible dates, 2041–40 B.C., or 1977–6 B.C., or 1858–7 B.C.

it assists in fixing within comparatively narrow limits
the period of the Kassite conquest and of the following
dynasties of Babylon.[1]   Starting from this figure as
a basis, and making use of the information already
discussed, it would follow that the Dynasty of Nîsin
was founded in the year 2339 B.C., that of Larsa only
four years later in 2335 B.C., and the First Dynasty of
Babylon after a further interval of a hundred and ten
years in 2225 B.C.[2]

It will have been seen that the suggested system of
chronology has been settled in complete independence
of the chronological notices to earlier rulers which have
come down to us in the inscriptions of some of the later
Assyrian and Babylonian kings.   Hitherto these have
furnished the principal starting points, on which reliance
has been placed to date the earlier periods in the history
of Babylon.   In the present case it will be pertinent
to examine them afresh and ascertain how far they
harmonize with a scheme which has been evolved without their help.   If they are found to accord very well
with the new system, we may legitimately see in such
an agreement additional grounds for believing we are
on the right track.   Without pinning one's faith too
slavishly to any calculation by a native Babylonian
scribe, the possibility of harmonizing such references
at least removes a number of difficulties, which it has
always been necessary either to ignore or to explain away.

Perhaps the chronological notice which has given
rise to most discussion is the one in which Nabonidus
refers to the period of Hammurabi's reign.   On one of
his foundation-cylinders Nabonidus states that Hammurabi rebuilt E-babbar, the temple of the Sun-god
in Larsa, seven hundred years before Burna-Buriash.[3]

[1] For this purpose it may be used in conjunction with the later Assyrian
synchronisms, and with the date of Burna-Buriash as obtained from Egyptian
sources (see below, p. 111).

[2] It may be worth while noting that, if we place the whole of Rîm-Sin's
reign of sixty-one years before Hammurabi's conquest of Larsa, we raise the
first two dates given in the text by twenty-two years.   On that assumption
the Dynasty of Nîsin would have been founded in 2361 B.C., and that of Larsa
in 2357 B.C.   Consequently the Dynasties of Nîsin and of Babylon would have
overlapped for a period of eighty-nine years, instead of one hundred and
eleven.   But the balance of probability is in favour of the later dates ; see
above, p. 103, n. 2.

[3] See Bezold, "Proc. Soc. Bibl. Arch.," XI., pp. 94, 99, and pl. iv.,

At a time when it was not realized that the First and Second Dynasties of the Kings' List were partly contemporaneous, the majority of writers were content to ignore the apparent inconsistency between the figures of the Kings' List and this statement of Nabonidus. Others attempted to get over the difficulty by emending the figures in the List and by other ingenious suggestions; for it was felt that to leave a discrepancy of this sort without explanation pointed to a possibility of error in any scheme necessitating such a course.[1] We will see, then, how far the estimate of Nabonidus accords with the date assigned to Hammurabi under our scheme. From the Tell el-Amarna letters we know that Burna-Buriash was the contemporary of Amen-hetep IV., to whose accession most historians of Egypt now agree to assign a date in the early part of the fourteenth century B.C.[2] We may take 1380 B.C. as representing approximately the date which, according to the majority of the schemes of Egyptian chronology, may be assigned to Amen-hetep IV.'s accession. And by adding seven hundred years to this date we obtain, according to the testimony of Nabonidus, a date for Hammurabi of about 2080 B.C. According to our scheme the last year of Hammurabi's reign fell in 2081 B.C., and, since the seven hundred years of Nabonidus is obviously a round number, its general agreement with the scheme is remarkably close.[3]

The chronological notice of Nabonidus thus serves to confirm, so far as its evidence goes, the general accuracy of the date assigned to the First Dynasty. In

85-4-30, 2, Col. II., ll. 20 ff., and Rawlinson, "Cun. Inscr. West. Asia," I., 69, Col. II., l. 4; cf. also Langdon, "Neubabylonischen Königsinschriften," p. 238 f.

[1] See "Chronicles," I., p. 87 f.

[2] An approximate date of 1430-1400 B.C. is assigned to him by Budge, "History of Egypt," Vol. IV., pp. 113 ff.; while his accession is placed in 1383 B.C. by Petrie, "History of Egypt," Vol. II., pp. 205 ff.; in 1380 B.C. by Meyer, "Ægyptische Chronologie," p. 68, and "Geschichte," I., ii., p. 335 f., and Hall, "Ancient History of the Near East," p. 228; and in 1375 B.C. by Breasted, "History of Egypt," p. 599, and "Ancient Records," Vol. I., p. 43. Maspero implies a date of about 1380 B.C.; cf. "Histoire ancienne," II., p. 337, note.

[3] According to Dr. Budge's scheme of chronology, an approximate date of 1400 B.C. for Burna-Buriash would yield for Hammurabi a date of c. 2100 B.C. (equivalent to his twenty fourth year).

the case of the Second Dynasty we obtain an equally striking confirmation, when we examine the only available reference to the period of one of its kings which is found in the record of a later ruler. The passage in question occurs upon a boundary-stone preserved in the University Museum of Pennsylvania, referring to events which took place in the fourth year of Enlil-nadin-apli.[1] In the text engraved upon the stone it is stated that 696 years separated Gulkishar (the sixth king of the Second Dynasty) from Nebuchadnezzar, who is of course to be identified with Nebuchadnezzar I., the immediate predecessor of Enlil-nadin-apli upon the throne of Babylon. Now we know from the "Synchronistic History" that Nebuchadnezzar I. was the contemporary of Ashur-rêsh-ishi, the father of Tiglath-pileser I., and if we can establish independently the date of the latter's accession, we obtain approximate dates for Nebuchadnezzar and consequently for Gulkishar.

In his inscription on the rock at Bavian Sennacherib tells us that 418 years elapsed between the defeat of Tiglath-pileser I. by Marduk-nadin-akhê and his own conquest of Babylon in 689 B.C.[2] Tiglath-pileser was therefore reigning in 1107 B.C., and we know from his Cylinder-inscription that this year was not among the first five of his reign; on this evidence the beginning of his reign has been assigned approximately to 1120 B.C. Nebuchadnezzar I., the contemporary of Tiglath-pileser's father, may thus have come to the throne at about 1140 B.C.; and, by adding the 696 years to this date, we obtain an approximate date of 1836 B.C. as falling within the reign of Gulkishar of the Second Dynasty. This date supports the figures of the Kings' List, according to which Gulkishar would have been reigning from about 1876 to 1822 B.C. But it should be noted that the period of 696 years upon the boundary-stone, though it has an appearance of great accuracy, was probably derived from a round number; for the stone refers to events which took place in Enlil-nadin-apli's fourth year, and the number 696 may have been based upon

[1] See Hilprecht, "Old Babylonian Inscriptions," Pt. I., pl. 30 f., No. 83; cf. also Jensen, "Zeits. für Assyr.," VIII., pp. 220 ff.
[2] Cf. King, "Tukulti-Ninib I.," p. 118 f.

the estimate that seven hundred years separated Enlil-nadin-apli's reign from that of Gulkishar. It is thus probable that the reference should not be regarded as more than a rough indication of the belief that a portion of Gulkishar's reign fell within the second half of the nineteenth century. But, even on this lower estimate of the figure's accuracy, its agreement with our scheme is equally striking.

One other chronological reference remains to be examined, and that is the record of Ashur-bani-pal, who, when describing his capture of Susa in about 647 B.C., relates that he recovered the image of the goddess Nanâ, which the Elamite Kudur-Nankhundi had carried off from Erech sixteen hundred and thirty-five years before.[1] This figure would assign to Kudur-Nankhundi's invasion an approximate date of 2282 B.C. As we possess no other reference to, nor record of, an early Elamite king of this name, there is no question of harmonizing this figure with other chronological records bearing on his reign. All that we can do is to ascertain whether, according to our chronological scheme, the date 2282 B.C. falls within a period during which an Elamite king would have been likely to invade Southern Babylonia and raid the city of Erech. Tested in this way, Ashur-bani-pal's figure harmonizes well enough with the chronology, for Kudur-Nankhundi would have invaded Babylonia fifty-seven years after a very similar Elamite invasion which brought the Dynasty of Ur to an end, and gave Nîsin her opportunity of securing the hegemony.[2] That Elam continued to be a menace to Babylonia is sufficiently proved by Kudur-Mabuk's invasion, which resulted in placing his son Warad-Sin upon the throne of Larsa in 2143 B.C. It will be noted that Ashur-bani-pal's figure places Kudur-Nankhundi's raid on Erech in the period between the two most notable Elamite invasions of early Babylonia, of which we have independent evidence.

Another advantage of the suggested chronological scheme is that it enables us to clear up some of the

---

[1] See Rawlinson, "Cun. Inscr. West. Asia," Vol. III., pl. 38, No. 1, Obv. l. 16.

[2] See below, p. 133.

problems presented by the dynasties of Berossus, at least
so far as concerns the historical period in his system of
chronology.   In a later historian of Babylon we should
naturally expect to find that period beginning with the
first dynasty of rulers in the capital; but hitherto the
available evidence did not seem to suggest a date that
could be reconciled with his system.   It may be worth
while to point out that the date assigned under the new
scheme for the rise of the First Dynasty of Babylon
coincides approximately with that deduced for the beginning of the historical period in Berossus.   Five of
the historical dynasties of Berossus, following his first
dynasty of eighty-six kings who ruled for 34,090 years
after the Deluge,[1] are preserved only in the Armenian
version of the Chronicles of Eusebius[2] and are the
following :—

> Dynasty II., 8 Median usurpers, ruling 224 years ;[3]
> Dynasty III., 11 kings, the length of their rule
>   wanting ;[4]
> Dynasty IV., 49 Chaldean kings, ruling 458 years ;
> Dynasty V., 9 Arab kings, ruling for 245 years ;
> Dynasty VI., 45 kings, ruling for 526 years.

It is not quite clear to what stage in the national
history Berossus intended his sixth dynasty to extend ;[5]
and in any case, the fact that the figure is wanting for
the length of his third dynasty, renders their total duration a matter of uncertainty.   But, in spite of these

---

[1] That Berossus depended on native lists of rulers in compiling his first
dynasty of semi-mythical kings has been strikingly confirmed by documents
discovered recently in the Niffer Collection of tablets preserved in the
Pennsylvania Museum.   These have been published by Poebel, "Univ. of
Pennsyl. Mus. Publications," Vol. IV., No. 1, and Vol. V., and the new
information they furnish is of great interest for the earlier history.   It may be
noted that the figure 34,090 is that given for the duration of the dynasty in
Syncellus (ed. Dindorf, p. 147) ; in the equivalent in *sars*, etc., which is added
(*i.e.* 9 *sars*, 2 *ners*, and 8 *soss* = 34,080 years), it is probable that the units are
intentionally ignored, though some would regard 34,080 as the correct figure
(see below, p. 115).   In Eusebius ("Chron. lib. I.," ed. Schoene, Col. 25) the
figure is 33,091 (probably a mistake for 34,091) ; this figure at any rate confirms the reading of ninety (against eighty) in Syncellus, cf. Meyer, "Beiträge
zur alten Geschichte (Klio)," III., p. 133 ; and see further, p. 116 f., n. 5.
[2] Eusebius, "Chron. lib. I.," ed. Schoene, Col. 25 ; see also Schwartz in
Pauly-Wissowa, "Real-Encyclopädie," III. (i.), Col. 311.
[3] In margin of MSS. 34 years.
[4] In margin of MSS. 48 years.   [5] See further, p. 115 r.

drawbacks, a general agreement has been reached as to a date for the beginning of his historical period, based on considerations independent of the figures in detail. A. von Gutschmid's suggestion that the kings after the Deluge were grouped by Berossus in a cycle of ten *sars, i e* 36,000 years,[1] furnished the key that has been used for solving the problem. For, if the first dynasty be subtracted from this total, the remaining number of years would give the total length of the historical dynasties. Thus, if we take the length of the first dynasty as 34,090 years, the duration of the historical dynasties is seen to have been 1910 years. Now the statement attributed to Abydenus by Eusebius, to the effect that the Chaldeans reckoned their kings from Alorus to Alexander,[2] has led to the suggestion that the period of 1910 years was intended to include the reign of Alexander the Great (331–323 B.C.). If therefore we add 1910 years to 322 B.C., we obtain 2232 B.C. as the beginning of the historical period with which the second dynasty of Berossus opened. It may be added that the same result has been arrived at by taking 34,080 years as the length of his first dynasty,[3] and by extending the historical period of 1920 years down to 312 B.C., the beginning of the Seleucid Era.

Incidentally it may be noted that this date has been harmonized with the figure assigned in the margin of some manuscripts as representing the length of the third dynasty of Berossus. It has usually been held that his sixth dynasty ended with the predecessor of Nabonassar upon the throne of Babylon, and that the following or seventh dynasty would have begun in 747 B.C. But it has been pointed out that, after enumerating the dynasties II.–VI., Eusebius goes on to say that after these rulers came a king of the Chaldeans whose name was Phulus[4]; and this phrase has been explained as indicating that the sixth dynasty

---

[1] Those before the Deluge are said to have reigned for a hundred and twenty *sars, i.e.* 432,000 years.

[2] Eusebius, " Chron. lib. I.," ed. Schoene, Col. 53 : " Hoc pacto Khaldæi suæ regionis reges ab Aloro usque ad Alexandrum recensent."

[3] See above, p. 114, n. 1.

[4] " Chron. lib. I.," ed. Schoene, Col. 25 : " post quos, inquit (*sc.* Polyhistor), rex Chaldæorum extitit, cui nomen Phulus est."

of Berossus ended at the same point as the Ninth
Babylonian Dynasty, in 732 B.C., that is to say, with
the reign of Nabû-shum-ukîn, the contemporary of
Tiglath-pileser IV., whose original name of Pulu is
preserved in the Babylonian List of Kings.   Thus the
seventh dynasty of Berossus would have begun with the
reign of the usurper Ukîn-zêr, who was also the contemporary of Tiglath-pileser.[1]   On this supposition the
figure " forty-eight," which occurs in the margin of
certain manuscripts of the Armenian version of Eusebius,[2] may be retained for the number of years assigned
by Berossus to his third dynasty.[3]   A further confirmation of the date 2232 B.C. for the beginning of the
historical period of Berossus has been found in a statement derived from Porphyrius, to the effect that,
according to Callisthenes, the Babylonian records of
astronomical observations extended over a period of
1903 years down to the time of Alexander of Macedon.[4]
Assuming that the reading 1903 is correct, the observations would have extended back to 2233 B.C., a date
differing by only one year from that obtained for the
beginning of Berossus' historical dynasties.

Thus there are ample grounds for regarding the
date 2232 B.C. as representing the beginning of the historical period in the chronological system of Berossus ;[5]
and we have already noted that in a late Babylonian
historian, writing during the Hellenistic period, we
should expect the beginning of his history, in the
stricter sense of the term, to coincide with the first
recorded dynasty of Babylon, as distinct from rulers
of other and earlier city-states.   It will be observed that
this date is only seven years out with that obtained
astronomically by Dr. Kugler for the rise of the First

[1] That is to say, at the point marked by the group Xίνξηρος καὶ Πῶρος in the
Ptolemaic Canon.   Ukîn-zêr is an abbreviation of Nabû-mukîn-zêr.

[2] See above, p. 114, n. 4.

[3] Cf. Meyer, "Beiträge zur alten Geschichte (Klio)," III., pp. 131 ff.

[4] The statement occurs in the commentary of Simplicius upon Aristotle's
" De Caelo," and the Greek text reads 31,000 ; cf. ed. Heiberg, p. 506.   But
in a Latin translation by Moerbeka the figure is given as 1903, and this
probably represents the original reading ; cf. Lehmann-Haupt, " Zwei
Hauptprobleme," pp. 109 f., 210, and Meyer, op. cit., p. 131.

[5] The Pennsylvania documents published by Poebel (see above, p. 114,
n. 1) suggest that variant traditions were current with regard to the number
of mythical and semi-mythical rulers of Babylonia and the duration of their

Dynasty of Babylon. Now the astronomical demonstration relates only to the reign of Ammi-zaduga, who was the tenth king of the First Dynasty; and to obtain the date 2225 B.C. for Sumu-abum's accession, reliance is naturally placed on figures for the intermediate reigns which are supplied by the contemporaneous date-lists. But the Babylonian Kings' List gives figures which were current in the Neo-Babylonian period; and, by employing it in place of contemporaneous records, we obtain the date 2229 B.C. for Sumu-abum's accession, which presents a discrepancy of only three years to that deduced from Berossus. In view of the slight inconsistencies with the Kings' List which we find in at least one of the late chronicles, it is clear that the native historians, who compiled their records during the later periods, found a number of small variations in the chronological material on which they had to rely. While there was probably agreement on the general lines of the later chronology, the traditional length of some reigns and dynasties might vary in different documents by a few years. We may conclude therefore that the evidence of Berossus, so far as it can be reconstituted from the summaries preserved in other works, may be harmonized with the date obtained independently for the First Dynasty of Babylon.

The new information, which has been discussed in this chapter, has enabled us to carry further than was previously possible the process of reconstructing the chronology; and we have at last been able to connect the earlier epochs in the country's history with those which followed the rise of Babylon to power. On the one hand we have obtained definite proof of the overlapping of further dynasties with that of the West Semitic kings of Babylon. On the other hand, the consequent reduction in date is more than compensated by new evidence pointing to the probability of a period of independent rule in Babylonia on the part of some

rule. For instance, in two of the lists drawn up under the Nisin kings, and separated from one another by an interval of only sixty-seven years, the total duration of the preceding dynasties appears to be given in one as 32,243, and in the other as 28,876 years. But this fact does not, of course, prevent the use of the figures which have come to us from Berossus, in order to ascertain the beginning of the historical period in the system he employed.

of the Sea-Country kings.   The general effect of the
new discoveries is thus of no revolutionary character.
It has resulted, rather, in local rearrangements, which
to a considerable extent are found to counterbalance
one another in their relation to the chronological
scheme as a whole.   Perhaps the most valuable result
of the regrouping is that we are furnished with the
material for a more detailed picture of the gradual rise
of Babylon to power.   We shall see that the coming
of the Western Semites effected other cities than
Babylon, and that the triumph of the invaders marked
only the closing stage of a long and varied struggle.

CHAPTER IV

THE WESTERN SEMITES AND THE FIRST DYNASTY
OF BABYLON

THE rise of Babylon to a position of pre-eminence
among the warring dynasties of Sumer and
Akkad may be regarded as sealing the final
triumph of the Semite over the Sumerian. His survival
in the long racial contest was due to the reinforcements
he received from men of his own stock, whereas the
Sumerian population, when once settled in the country,
was never afterwards renewed. The great Semitic
wave, under which the Sumerian sank and finally disappeared, reached the Euphrates from the coast-lands
of the Eastern Mediterranean. But the Amurru, or
Western Semites, like their predecessors in Northern
Babylonia, had come originally from Arabia. For it
is now generally recognized that the Arabian peninsula
was the first home and cradle of the Semitic peoples.
Arabia, like the plains of Central Asia, was, in fact,
one of the main breeding-grounds of the human race,
and during the historic period we may trace four great
migrations of Semitic nomad tribes, which successively broke away from the northern margin of the
Arabian pasture-lands and spread over the neighbouring
countries like a flood. The first great racial movement
of the kind is that of which the effects were chiefly
apparent in Akkad, or Northern Babylonia, where the
Semites first obtained a footing when overrunning the
valley of the Tigris and Euphrates. The second is distinguished from the first, as the Canaanite or Amorite,
since it gave to Canaan its Semitic inhabitants; but
how long an interval separated the one movement from
the other it is impossible to say. The process may well

have been a continuous one, with merely a change in
the direction of advance; but it is convenient to distinguish them by their effects as separate movements,
the semitization of Canaan following that of Babylonia,
but at the same time contributing to its complete
success. Of the later migrations we are not for the
moment concerned, and in any case only one of them
falls within the period of this history. That was the
third great movement, which began in the fourteenth
century and has been termed the Aramean from the
kingdom it established in Syria with its capital at
Damascus. The fourth, and last, took place in the
seventh century of our own era, when the armies of
Islam, after conquering Western Asia and Northern
Africa, penetrated even to South-Western Europe. It
was by far the most extensive of the four in the area
it covered, and, in spite of being the last of the series,
it illustrates the character and methods of the earlier
movements in their initial stages, when the desert
nomad, issuing in force from his own borders, came
within the area of settled civilization.

It is true that great tracts of Central Arabia are
to-day quite uninhabitable, but there is reason to believe
that its present condition of aridity was not so marked
in earlier periods. We have definite proof of this in
the interior of Southern Arabia, where there is still a
belt of comparatively fertile country between the flat
coastal regions and the steep mountain range, that
forms the southern boundary of the central plateau.[1]
On the coast itself there is practically no rainfall,
and even on the higher slopes away from the coast
it is very scanty. Here the herds of goats frequently
go without water for many weeks, and they have learnt
to pull up and chew the fleshy roots of a species of
cactus to quench their thirst. But further still inland
there is a broad belt of country, which is marvellously
fertile and in a high state of cultivation. The rainfall
there is regular during a portion of the year, the country
is timbered, and the main mountain range, though
possessing no towns of any size, is thickly dotted with

---

[1] Cf. Hogarth, " The Penetration of Arabia," pp. 206 ff.

strong fighting towers, which dominate the well-farmed
and flourishing villages. To the north of the range,
beyond the cultivation, is a belt roamed over by the
desert-nomads with their typical black tents of woven
goat-hair, and then comes the central desert, a region
of rolling sand. But here and there the ruins of
palaces and temples may still be seen rising from the
sand or built on some slight eminence above its level.

At the time of the Sabæan kingdom, as early as the
sixth century B.C., this region of Southern Arabia must
have been far more fertile than it is at the present
day. The shifting sand, under the driving pressure of
the simoom, doubtless played its part in overwhelming
tracts of cultivated country; but that alone cannot
account for the changed conditions. The researches of
Stein, Pumpelly, Huntington and others have shown
the results of desiccation in Central Asia,[1] and it is
certain that a similar diminution of the rainfall has
taken place in the interior of Southern Arabia.[2] To
such climatic changes, which seem, according to the
latest theories, to occur in recurrent cycles,[3] we may
probably trace the great racial migrations from Central
Arabia, which have given their inhabitants to so many
countries of Western Asia and North Africa.

It is possible to form a very clear picture of the
Semite who issued from this region, for the life of the
pastoral nomad, all the world over, is the same.[4] And
even at the present day, in the hollows of the Arabian
desert, there is enough deposit of moisture to allow
of a sufficient growth of grass for pasture-lands, capable
of supporting nomadic tribes, who move with their
flocks of sheep and goats from one more favoured area

[1] Cf. "Sumer and Akkad," pp. 352 ff.

[2] An interesting confirmation of this view has been made by General P. J.
Maitland. He points out that the great tanks at Aden, which were hewn out
of the solid rock in early Himyarite if not in Sabæan times, are at the present
day absolutely dry for four years out of five, and that the heaviest rainfalls
since they were discovered and cleared out have not filled them to an eighth
part of their capacity ; cf. his preface to G. W. Bury's "Land of Uz," p. xii. f.

[3] It has been established that these pulsations of climatic change apply to
all the great inland steppes upon the earth's surface, periods of maximum
moisture being followed by long intervals of comparative aridity ; see especially, Huntington, " The Pulse of Asia " (1907).

[4] On this subject, see especially Myres, " The Dawn of History," pp.
16 ff., 104 ff.

to another. The life of such a nomad is forced into
one mould by the conditions imposed by the desert;
for the grass-land cannot support him and he must
live on the milk and young of his flocks. He is purely
a shepherd, carrying with him the simplest and lightest
tents, tools, and weapons for his needs. The type of
society is that of the patriarchal family, for each nomad
tribe consists of a group of relatives; and, under the
direction of their chief, not only the men of the clan,
but the women and children, all take an active part in
tending the flocks and in practising the simple arts of
skin-curing and the weaving of hair and wool. So long
as the pasture-lands can support his flocks, the nomad
is content to leave the settled agriculturist beyond the
desert edge in peace. Some of the semi-nomad tribes
upon the margin of the cultivation may engage in
barter with their more civilised neighbours, and even
at times demand subsidies for leaving their crops in
peace. But the bulk of the tribes would normally
remain within their own area, while conditions existed
which were capable of supplying the needs of their
simple life. It is when the pasture lands dry up that
the nomad must leave his own area or perish, and it is
then that he descends upon the cultivation and proceeds to adapt himself to new conditions, should he
conquer the settled races whose higher culture he himself absorbs.

While still held within the grip of the desert, there
was never any prospect of his development or advance
in civilization. The only great changes that have taken
place in the life of the Arabian nomad have been due to
the introduction of the horse and the camel. But these
have merely increased his mobility, while leaving the
man himself unchanged. The Arabs of the seventh
century B.C., depicted in the reliefs from Nineveh
as fleeing on their camels before the advance of the
Assyrians, can have differed in no essential feature from
their earliest predecessors, who made their way to the
Euphrates valley on foot or with only the ass as a beast
of burden. For, having once succeeded in domesti-
cating his flocks and in living by their means upon the
rolling steppes of pasture-land, the nomad's needs are

fully satisfied, and his ways of life survive through succeeding generations. He cannot accumulate possessions, as he must be able to carry all his goods continually with him, and his knowledge of the uneventful past is derived entirely from oral tradition. The earliest inscriptions recovered in Arabia are probably not anterior to the sixth century B.C., and they were naturally not the work of nomads, but of Semitic tribes who had forsaken

FIG. 32.

ARABS OF THE SEVENTH CENTURY B.C.

From a sculpture of the reign of Ashur-bani-pal in the Nineveh Gallery of the British Museum.

their wanderings for the settled life of village and township in the more hospitable regions of the south.

The Amurru, or Western Semites, to whose incursion into Babylonia the rise of Babylon itself was directly due, had long abandoned a nomadic existence, and in addition to the higher standards of the agriculturist had acquired a civilization which had been largely influenced by that of Babylonia. Thanks to the active policy of excavation, carried out during the last twenty-five years in Palestine, we are enabled to reconstruct the conditions of life which prevailed in that country from a

very early period. It is, in fact, now possible to trace
the successive stages of Canaanite civilization back to
neolithic times.   Rude flint implements of the palæo-
lithic or Older Stone Age have also been found on the
surface of the plains of Palestine, where they had lain
since the close of the glacial epoch.   But at that time
the climate and character of the Mediterranean lands
were very different to their present condition; and a
great break of unknown length then occurs in the

Fig. 33.

ARABS OF THE SEVENTH CENTURY B.C.

From a sculpture of the reign of Ashur-bani-pal in the Nineveh Gallery of the
British Museum.

cultural sequence, which separates that primæval period
from the neolithic or Later Stone Age.   It is to this
second era that we may trace the real beginnings of
Canaanite civilization.   For, from that time onwards,
there is no break in the continuity of culture, and each
age was the direct heir of that which preceded it.

The neolithic inhabitants of Canaan, whose implements of worked and polished stone mark a great

advance upon the rough flints of their remote predecessors, belonged to the short, dark-skinned race which
spread itself over the shores of the Mediterranean.
Dwelling in rude huts, they employed for household
use rough vessels of kneaded clay which they fashioned
by hand and baked in the fire. They lived chiefly by
the cattle and flocks they had domesticated, and, to
judge by their clay spindle-whorls, they practised a
simple form of weaving, and began to clothe themselves with cloth in place of skins. Over these primitive
inhabitants a fresh tide of migration swept, probably in
the early part of the third millennium B.C. The new-
comers were Semites from Arabia, of the same stock
as those nomadic hordes who had already overrun
Babylonia and had established themselves in a great
part of that country. After they had settled in Canaan
and Syria they were known to the Babylonians as the
Amurru or Amorites. They were taller and more
vigorous than the neolithic Canaanites, and they seem
to have brought with them a knowledge of the use of
metal, acquired probably by traffic with southern
Babylonia.[1] The flint arrows and knives of their
enemies would have had little chance against weapons
of copper and bronze. But, whether helped by their
superior armament or not, they became the dominant
race in Canaan. By intermarrying with their predecessors they produced the Canaanites of history, a people
of Semitic speech, but with a varying admixture in
their blood of the dark-skinned Mediterranean race of
lower type.

Such in origin was the Canaanite branch of the
Western Semites, and it may be worth while to glance
for a moment at the main features of their culture as
revealed by excavation in Palestine.[2] One thing stands

---

[1] This view seems to be more probable than the assumption that the
Semitic inhabitants of Canaan learnt the use of metal after their first period
of settlement.

[2] For the more important monographs on the subject, see Macalister,
"The Excavation of Gezer" (1912), and Bliss and Macalister, "Excavations
in Palestine during the years 1898–1900" (1902), both issued by the Palestine
Exploration Fund; Sellin, "Tell Ta'annek," published by the Vienna
Academy in its "Denkschriften," Phil.-Hist. Kl., Bd. 50, No. 4 (1904), and
"Eine Nachlese auf dem Tell Ta'annek in Palästina," *ibid.*, Bd. 52, No. 3
(1906); Schumacher, "Tell el-Mutesellim," published by the "Deutscher

out clearly: they revolutionized conditions of life in
Canaan.   The rude huts of the first settlers were superseded by houses of brick and stone, and, in place of
villages, cities rose surrounded by massive walls.   The
city-wall of Gezer was more than thirteen feet thick
and was defended by strong towers.   That of Megiddo
was twenty-six feet in thickness, and its foot was further
protected by a slope, or *glaçis*, of beaten earth.   To
secure their water-supply in time of siege, the arrangements were equally thorough.   At Gezer, for example,
a huge tunnel was found, hewn in the solid rock, which
gave access to an abundant spring of water over ninety
feet below the surface of the ground.   Not only had
the earlier nomad adopted the agricultural life, but he
soon evolved a system of defence for his settlements,
suggested by the hilly character of his new country and
its ample supply of stone.[1]   Not less remarkable is the
light thrown by the excavations on details of Canaanite
worship.   The centre of each town was the high place,
where huge monoliths were erected, some of them,
when unearthed, still worn and polished by the kisses
of their worshippers.   At Gezer ten such monoliths
were discovered in a row, and it is worth noting that
they were erected over a sacred cave of the neolithic
inhabitants, proving that the ancient sanctuary was
taken over by the Semitic invaders.   The religious
centres inherited by the Ba'alîm, or local " Lords " of
Canaanite worship, had evidently been sanctified by
long tradition.   In the soil beneath the high places
both at Gezer and at Megiddo numbers of jars were

Palästina Verein" in 1908 ; and Sellin and Watzinger, "Jericho," a volume
issued by the "Deutsche Orient-Gesellschaft" in its "Wissenschaftliche
Veröffentlichungen," Hft. 22 (1913).   For further references and a useful
summary of the archæological results, see Driver, "Modern Research as
illustrating the Bible" (Schweich Lectures, 1908), pp. 40 ff. ; for later summaries, see especially Sayce, "Patriarchal Palestine," new ed. (1912), pp.
233 ff., and Handcock, "Latest Light on Bible Lands," 1913 ; and for an
estimate of artistic achievement, cf. Hall, "Ancient History of the Near
East" (1913), pp. 440 ff.   On the racial character of the earliest inhabitants
of Canaan, see especially Sergi, "The Mediterranean Race" (1901).
   [1] There are few data for estimating the period at which these centres of
population were first fortified.   There is no doubt that the city-walls are long
anterior to the Egyptian conquest, and from the accumulation of *débris* in the
lower strata they have been provisionally placed at an early period in the
third millennium B.C. ; in any case they preceded the age of the First Babylonian
Dynasty.

found containing the bodies of children, and we may probably see in this fact evidence of infant-sacrifice, the survival of which into later periods is attested by Hebrew tradition.   In the cultural remains of these Semitic invaders a distinct development is discernible. During the earlier period there is scarcely a trace of foreign influence, but later on we find importations from both Babylonia and Egypt.

It is but natural that southern and central Canaan should have long remained inaccessible to outside in-fluence, and that the effects of Babylonian civilization should have been confined at first to eastern Syria and to the frontier districts scattered along the middle course of the Euphrates.   Recent digging by natives so far to the north as the neighbourhood of Carchemish, for example, have revealed some remarkable traces of connexion with Babylonia at a very early period.[1]   In graves at Hammâm, a village on the Euphrates near the mouth of the Sajûr, cylinder-seals were found which exhibit unmistakable analogies to very early Babylonian work;[2] and the use of this form of seal at a period anterior to the First Dynasty of Babylon is in itself proof that Babylonian influence had reached the frontier of Syria by the great trade-route up the course of the Euphrates, along which the armies of Sargon of Akkad had already marched in their raid to the Mediterranean coast.[3]   It is not improbable, too, that Carchemish

[1] The evidence has been recovered in connexion with the excavations at Carchemish, conducted by Mr. Hogarth for the British Museum.   For dis-cussions of the problems presented by the main excavation, see his volume on "Carchemish" (1914), and "Hittite Problems and the excavation of Carchemish," in the "Proceedings of the British Academy," Vol. V.   The results of recent native digging in neighbouring mounds have been recovered on the spot by his assistants Messrs. Woolley and Lawrence, and Mr. Woolley has published an account of them in a paper on "Hittite Burial Customs," in the Liverpool "Annals of Archæology," VI., No. 4 (1914), pp. 87 ff.

[2] In view of the haphazard nature of the native diggings, the absence of cylinder-seals on some neighbouring sites is not to be taken as necessarily dis-proving Babylonian influence there.   At Amarna, for example, some eight miles to the south of Jerablus, no seals nor cylinders are reported to have been found, but at Kara Kuzal, on the Mesopotamian side of the Euphrates opposite Hammâm, where the pottery is of the Amarna type, two cylinder-seals of a later period and probably of local manufacture were recovered ; they are engraved in the style classified by Mr. Woolley as "the Syrian Geometric" (op. cit., p. 92).   The find is also of interest as proving the assimilation of the cylindrical form of seal, which had then ceased to be merely a foreign import.

[3] Cf. "Sumer and Akkad," p. 233 f.

herself sent her own products at this time to Babylon, for one class of her local pottery at any rate appears to have been valued by other races and to have formed an article of export. At the time of the later kings of the First Dynasty a special kind of large clay vessel, in use in Northern Babylonia, was known as " a Carchemisian," and was evidently manufactured at Carchemish and exported.[1] The trade was no doubt encouraged by the close relations established under Hammurabi and his successors with the West, but its existence points to the possibility of still earlier commercial intercourse, such as would explain the occurrence of archaic Babylonian cylinder-seals in early graves in the neighbourhood.

But, apart from such trade relations, there is nothing to suggest that the early culture of Carchemish and its adjacent districts had been effected to any great extent by that of Babylon, nor is there any indication that the inhabitants of the early city were Semites. Indeed, the archæological evidence is entirely in favour of the opposite view. The bronze age at Carchemish and its neighbourhood is distinguished from the preceding period by the use of metal, by different burial customs, and by new types of pottery, and must be regarded as marking the advent of a foreign people. But throughout the bronze age itself at Carchemish, from its beginning in the third millennium to its close in the eleventh century B.C., there is a uniform development.[2] There is no sudden outcrop of new types such as had marked its own beginning, and, since in its later periods it was essentially Hittite, we may assume that it was neither inaugurated nor interrupted by the Semites. Its earlier representatives, before the great Hittite migration from Anatolia, may well have been a branch of that proto-Mitannian stock, itself possibly of Anatolian origin, evidence of whose presence we shall note at Ashur before the rise of Babylon's First Dynasty.[3]

[1] One of these large vessels is mentioned in an inventory among the belongings of a votary of the Sun-god, of which we possess two copies dating from the period of the First Dynasty of Babylon; see " Cun. Texts in the Brit. Mus.," II., pl. 1, Obv., l. 8, and pl. 6, l. 11 ; and cf. Hogarth, " Carchemish," p. 17. The vessel was of large size, as it is stated to have been of two-thirds of a *gur*, the greatest Babylonian measure of capacity ; it may have been used for grain.

[2] Cf. Woolley, *op. cit.*, pp. 88 f., 92 ff.   [3] See below, pp. 137 ff.

THE CITADEL MOUND OF CARCHEMISH FROM THE NORTH-WEST.

After Hogarth, Carchemish, pl. Ia.

Carchemish lies out of the direct road from Babylon to Northern Syria, and it is remarkable that any trace of early Babylonian influence should have been found so far to the north as the mouth of the Sajûr. It is farther down stream, after the Euphrates has turned eastward towards its junction with the Khâbûr, that we should expect to find evidence of a more striking character; and it is precisely there, along the river route from Syria to Akkad, that we have recovered definite proof, at the time of the First Dynasty of Babylon, of the existence of Amorite or West-Semitic settlements with a culture that was Babylonian in its essential features. The evidence is drawn mainly from one district, the kingdom of Khana, which lay not far from the mouth of the Khâbûr. One of the chief towns, and probably the capital of the kingdom, was Tirḳa, the site of which probably lay near Tell 'Ashar or Tell 'Ishar, a place situated between Dêr ez-Zôr and Sâli îya and about four hours from the latter. The identification is certain, since an Assyrian inscription of the ninth century was found there, recording the rebuilding of the local temple which is stated in the text to have been " in Tirḳa." [1] From about this region three tablets have also been recovered, all dating from the period of the First Dynasty of Babylon and throwing considerable light on the character of West Semitic culture in a district within the reach of Babylonian influence.

One of these documents records a deed of gift by which Isharlim, a king of Khana, conveys to one of his subjects a house in a village within the district of Tirḳa.[2] On a second document is inscribed a similar deed of gift by which another king of the same district, Ammi-baïl, the son of Shunu'-rammu, bestows two plots of land on a certain Pagirum, described as " his servant," evidently

---

[1] Cf. Condamin, " Zeits. für Assyr.," XXI. (1908), pp. 247 ff. The votive inscription was drawn up by Shamshi-Adad IV.

[2] See Thureau-Dangin, " Rev. d'Assyr," IV. (1898), p. 85 f., and pl. xxxii., No. 85, and Schorr, " Urkunden des altbabylonischen Zivil- und Prozessrechts," p. 302 f. Both Thureau-Dangin and Ungnad (" Beitr. z. Assyr.," VI., No. 5, p. 26) had regarded it as a deed of sale, but the ten manehs mentioned in the text is not a sale-price but a fine to be imposed for any infringement of the deed.

in return for faithful service ;[1] and, as one of the plots
was in Tirka, it is probable that the deed was drawn up
in that city. The third document is perhaps the most
interesting of the three, since it contains a marriage-
contract and is dated in the reign of a king who bears
the name of Hammurabih. This last ruler has by some
been confidently regarded as identical with Hammurabi
of the First Dynasty of Babylon, and it has been
assumed that it was drawn up at a time when Khana
had been conquered and annexed by that monarch, of
whose advance into that region we have independent
evidence.[2] But since the tablet appears to be the
latest of the three, it is clear that Khana had been subject to Babylonian influence long before Hammurabi's
conquest. And, even if we regard Hammurabih as no
more than a local king of Khana, the document has
furnished us with a West-Semitic variant of Hammurabi's name, or one that is closely parallel to it.

The remarkable fact about all these texts is that they
are drawn up in the style of legal documents of the
period of the First Dynasty of Babylon. But, while the
terminology is much the same, it has been adapted to
local conditions. The early Babylonian method of
dating by events [3] has been taken over, but the formulæ
are not those in use at this period in Babylonia, but
are peculiar to the kingdom of Khana. Thus the first
deed of gift is dated in the year when Isharlim, the king,
built the great gate of the palace in the city of Kash-
dakh; the second was drawn up in the year in which
Ammi-baïl, the king, ascended the throne in his father's
house ; while the marriage-contract is dated in the year
that Hammurabih, the king, opened the canal Khabur-
ibal-bugash from the city of Zakku-Isharlim to the city
of Zakku-Igitlim.[4] The names of the months, too, are

---

[1] See Ungnad, "Vorderasiat. Schriftdenkmäler," VII., No. 204, and
" Beitr. z. Assyr.," VI., No. 5 (1909), pp. 26 ff. The tablet was purchased
by Prof. Sarre at Dêr ez-Zôr, and is said to have been found at Raḥaba some
hours to the south-east of the mouth of the Khâbûr.

[2] See below, pp. 157, 159 ; Hammurabi also bore the title " King of
Amurru " (cf. " Letters," III., p. 195).   [3] See below, p. 190 f.

[4] The city of Zakku-Isharlim may have derived the second part of its name
from the king referred to in the first deed of gift ; in that case Igitlim may
perhaps have been the name of another king of Khana. The canal evidently
supplied one of the cities with water from the Khâbûr. The last element in

not those of Babylon,[1] and we find evidence that local
laws and customs were in force.   Each of the deeds of
gift, for example, provides that any infringement of the
rights bestowed by the king is to be punished by a
money-fine of ten manehs of silver, and in addition the
delinquent is to undergo the quaint but doubtless very
painful process of having his head tarred with hot tar.
From the list of witnesses we gather that the community was already organized much on the lines of a
provincial district of Babylonia.   For, though we find a
cultivator or farmer occupying an important position,
we meet also a superintendent of the merchants, another
of the bakers, a chief judge, a chief seer, and members
of the priesthood.   It is interesting, too, to note that
the kings of Khana were still great landowners, to judge
from the fact that the lands conveyed in the deeds of
gift were surrounded on almost every side by palace-
property.   At the same time the chief gods of Khana
are associated with the king in the oath-formulæ, since
the royal property was also regarded as the property of
the Ba'al, or divine " Lord " of the soil.

The two chief Ba'alîm or " Lords " of Khana were
the Sun-god and the West-Semitic deity, Dagon.   The
latter is constantly referred to in the documents under
the Babylonian form of his name, Dagan.   He stood
beside Shamash on the royal seal and in the local oath-
formulæ, and is associated in the latter with Iturmer,
who may well have been the old local god of Tirka,
deposed after the invasion of the Semites.   His temple
in Tirka, which we know survived until the ninth
century,[2] was probably the chief shrine of the city, and
the great part he played in the national life is attested
by the constant occurrence of his title as a component
part of personal names.[3]   Later evidence proves that

its name is suggestive of Kassite influence, and the script of this document
points to a period rather later than that of Hammurabi ; for its publication,
see Johns, "Proc. Soc. Bibl. Arch.," XXIX. (1907), pp. 177 ff.

[1] They are the months Teritum, Kinunu, and Birizzarru. For other West-
Semitic month-names, cf. "Letters of Hammurabi," p. xxxvi. f., n. ;
the majority of the "seltenere Monatsnamen," referred to by Schorr,
"Urkunden," p. 577, are to be included in this category.

[2] The votive inscription of Shamshi-Adad IV. (see above, p. 129, n. 1)
records its restoration.

[3] We find at Khana such personal names as Amursha-Dagan, Iazi-Dagan,

Dagon was peculiarly the god of Ashdod, and the princely writer of two of the letters from Tell el-Amarna, who bore the name Dagan-takala, must have ruled some district of northern or central Canaan. The Khana documents prove that already at the time of the First Dynasty his cult was established on the Euphrates, and, in view of this fact, the occurrence of two early kings of the Babylonian Dynasty of Nîsin with the names of Idin-Dagan and Ishme-Dagan is certainly significant. We know, too, that the original home of Ishbi-Ura, the founder of the Dynasty of Nîsin, was Mari, a city and district on the middle Euphrates.[1]   We may conclude, then, that the Dynasties of Nîsin and Babylon, and probably that of Larsa, were products of the same great racial movement, and that, more than a century before Sumu-abum established his throne at Babylon, Western Semites had descended the Euphrates and had penetrated into the southern districts of the country.

The new-comers probably owed their speedy success in Babylonia in great part to the fact that many of the immigrant tribes had already acquired the elements of Babylonian culture. During their previous residence within the sphere of settled civilization they had adopted a way of life and a social organization which differed but little from that of the country into which they came. That they should have immigrated at all in a south-easterly direction, in preference to remaining within their own borders, was doubtless due to racial pressure to which they themselves had been subjected. Canaan was still in a ferment of unrest in consequence of the arrival of fresh nomad tribes within her settled districts, and, while many were doubtless diverted southwards towards the Egyptian border, others pressed northwards into Syria, exerting an outward pressure in their advance. That the West-Semitic invasion of Babylonia differed so essentially from that of Egypt by the Hyksos is to be explained by this fringe of civilized settlements and petty kingdoms, which formed a check upon the nomad hordes behind them and dominated such of them as

Turi-Dagan, Bitti-Dagan and Iashma(?)-Dagan, in addition to the city-name Ia'mu-Dagan ; cf. Ungnad, *op. cit.*, p. 27 f.

[1] Cf. Poebel, " Historical Texts," p. 137.

succeeded in breaking through.   In Egypt the damage
wrought by the Semitic barbarians was remembered for
generations after their expulsion,[1] whereas in Babylonia
the invaders succeeded in establishing a dynasty which
gave its permanent form to Babylonian civilization.

Nîsin, the city in which, as we have seen, we first
obtain an indication of the presence of West-Semitic
rulers, probably lay in Southern Babylonia, and we
may picture the earlier immigrants as descending the
course of the Euphrates until they found an opportunity of establishing themselves in the Babylonian
plain.   The Elamite conquest, which put an end to the
dynasty of Ur, and stripped Babylonia of her eastern
provinces,[2] afforded Nîsin the opportunity of claiming
the hegemony.   Ishbi-Ura, the founder of the new
dynasty of kings, established his own family upon the
throne for nearly a century, and we may probably
regard his success in bringing his city to the front as
due to the Semitic elements in Southern Babylonia,
recently reinforced by fresh accretions from the north-
west.   The centralization of authority under the later
kings of Ur had led to abuses in the administration,
and to the revolt of the Elamite provinces ; and when
an invading army appeared before the capital and
carried the king, whom his courtiers had deified, to
captivity in Elam,[3] Sumerian prestige received a blow
from which it never recovered.

Shortly after Ishbi-Ura had established himself in
Nîsin, we find another noble, who bore the Semitic name
Naplanum, following his example, and founding an
independent line of rulers in the neighbouring city of
Larsa.   But, in spite of the Semitic names borne by
these two leaders and by the kings who succeeded them
in their respective cities, it is clear that no great change
took place in the character of the population.   The
commercial and administrative documents of the Nîsin
period closely resemble those of the Dynasty of Ur, and

---

[1] Cf. Breasted, "History of Egypt," pp. 215 ff.
[2] Cf. "Sumer and Akkad," p. 304.
[3] The tradition to this effect, which was incorporated in the later augural
literature (cf. Boissier, "Choix de textes," II., p. 64 ; and Meissner, "Orient.
Lit.-Zeit.," 1907, col. 114, n. 1) may be accepted as historically accurate ; cf.
"Sumer and Akkad," p. 304.

evidently reflect an unbroken sequence in the course of the national life.[1] The great bulk of the southern Babylonians were still Sumerian, and we may regard the new dynasties both at Nîsin and Larsa as representing a comparatively small racial aristocracy, which by organizing the national forces in resistance to the Elamites, had succeeded in imposing their own rule upon the native population. At Nîsin the unbroken succession of five rulers is evidence of a settled state of affairs, and though Gimil-ilishu reigned for no more than ten years, his son and grandson, as well as his father, Ishbi-Ura, all had long reigns. At Larsa, too, we find Emiṣu and Samum, who succeeded Naplanum, the founder of the dynasty, each retaining the throne for more than a generation. It is probable that the Sumerians accepted their new rulers without question, and that the latter attempted to introduce no startling innovations into their system of administrative control.

Of the two contemporaneous dynasties in Southern Babylonia, there is no doubt that Nîsin was the more important. Not only have we the direct evidence of the Nippur Kings' List that it was to Nîsin the hegemony passed from Ur,[2] but what votive texts and building-records have been recovered prove that its rulers extended their sway over other of the great cities of Sumer and Akkad. A fragmentary text of Idin-Dagan, the son and successor of Gimil-ilishu, found at Abû Habba, proves that Sippar acknowledged his authority,[3] and inscribed bricks of his own son Ishme-Dagan have been found in the south at Ur.[4]

In all their inscriptions, too, the kings of Nîsin lay claim to the rule of Sumer and Akkad, while Ishme-Dagan and his son Libit-Ishtar[5] adopt further descriptive

[1] Cf. Huber, "Die Personennamen . . . aus der Zeit der Könige von Ur und Nisin" (1907), *passim*. It was this fact that at one time seemed to suggest the probability that the kings of Nîsin, like the bulk of their subjects, may have been Sumerians (cf. "Sumer and Akkad," p. 303); but we may preferably regard them as representing the first wave of the movement which was soon to flood Northern Babylonia.

[2] Cf. Hilprecht, "Math., Met., and Chron. Tablets," p. 46 f., pl. 30, No. 47.

[3] See Scheil, "Rec. de trav.," XVI., pp. 187 ff.

[4] Cf. "Cun. Texts in the Brit. Mus.," XXI., pl. 20 f.

[5] In the dynastic Kings' List published by Hilprecht, "Math., Met., and

titles implying beneficent activities on their part in
the cities of Nippur, Ur, Erech and Eridu. The
recently published inscriptions of Libit-Ishtar, which
were recovered during the American excavations at
Nippur, prove that in his reign the central city and
shrine of Babylonia were under Nîsin's active control.
But he was the last king in the direct line from Ishbi-
Ura, and it is probable that the break in the succession
may be connected with a temporary depression in the
fortunes of the city ; for we shortly have evidence of an
increase in the power of Larsa, in consequence of which
the city of Ur acknowledged her suserainty in place of
that of Nîsin. At the time of Libit-Ishtar's death
Zabâia was reigning at Larsa, but after three years the
latter was succeeded by Gungunum, who not only bore
the titles of king of Larsa and of Ur, but laid claim to
the rule of Sumer and Akkad.

At any rate, one member of the old dynastic family
of Nîsin acknowledged these new claims. Enannatum,
Libit-Ishtar's brother, was at this time chief priest of
the Moon-temple in Ur, and on cones discovered at
Muḳayyar he commemorates the rebuilding of the Sun-
temple at Larsa for the preservation of his own life and
that of Gungunum.[1] It is possible that when Ur-Ninib
secured the throne of Nîsin, the surviving members of
Ishbi-Ura's family fled from the city to its rival, and
that Enannatum, one of the most powerful of their
number, and possibly the direct heir to his brother's
throne, was installed by Gungunum in the high-priestly
office at Ur. It would be tempting to connect Libit-
Ishtar's fall with a fresh incursion of West-Semitic
tribes, who, recking little of any racial connexion with
themselves on the part of the reigning family at Nîsin,
may have attacked the city with some success until
defeated and driven off by Ur-Ninib. We now know
that Ur-Ninib conducted a successful campaign against
the Su tribes on the west of Babylonia,[2] and in support

Chron. Tablets," pl. 30, No. 47, Libit-Ishtar is stated to have been Ishme-
Dagan's son ; but on another, recently published by Poebel, he is stated to
have been Idin-Dagan's son, and so the brother of Ishme-Dagan (cf.
" Historical Texts," pp. 94, 137).

[1] Cf. " Cun. Texts in the Brit. Mus.," XXI., pl. 22.

[2] Cf. Poebel, " Historical Texts," p. 138 ; he also notes the fact that

of the suggestion it would be possible to cite the much discussed date-formula upon a tablet in the British Museum, which was drawn up in "the year in which the Amurru drove out Libit-Ishtar." [1]   But since the Libit-Ishtar of the formula has no title, it is also possible to identify him with a provincial governor, probably of Sippar, who bore the name of Libit-Ishtar, and seems to be referred to on other documents inscribed in the reign of Apil-Sin, the grandfather of Hammurabi.[2]   The date assigned to the invasion on the second alternative would correspond to another period of unrest at Nîsin, which followed the long reign of Enlil-bani, so that on either alternative we may conjecture that the city of Nîsin was affected for a time by a new incursion of Amorites.

Whether the fall of Libit-Ishtar may be traced to such a cause or not, we now know that it was during the reigns of Ur-Ninib and Gungunum, at Nîsin and at Larsa respectively, that a West-Semitic Dynasty was established at Babylon.   Northern Babylonia now fell under the political control of the invaders, and it is significant of the new direction of their advance that the only conflict connected in later tradition with the name of Sumu-abum, the founder of Babylon's independent line of rulers, was not with either of the dominant cities in Sumer, but with Assyria in the far north.   On a late chronicle it is recorded that Ilu-shûma, King of Assyria, marched against Su-abu, or Sumu-abum,[3] and though the result of the encounter is not related, we may assume that his motive in making the attack was to check encroachments of the invaders towards the north and drive them southward into Babylonia. Ilu-shûma's own name is purely Semitic, and since the Amorite god Dagan enters into the composition of a name borne by more than one early Assyrian ruler,

Ur-Ninib successfully raided the country of Zabshali on the east of Babylonia.
    [1] See "Cun. Texts," IV., pl. 22, No. 78, 395 ; and Ranke, "Orient. Lit.-Zeit.," 1907, col. 109 ff.
    [2] Cf. "Sumer and Akkad," p. 315 f.
    [3] Cf. "Chronicles concerning Early Babylonian Kings," II., p. 14.   The Ilu-shûma, the father of Irishum or Erishu, who is referred to in building-inscriptions of Shalmaneser I. and Esarhaddon (*op. cit.*, I., pp. 118 ff.), is probably to be regarded as a later ruler than Sumu-abum's contemporary.

we may assume that Assyria received her Semitic population at about this period as another offshoot of the Amorite migration.

This assumption does not rest entirely on evidence supplied by the royal names, but finds indirect confirmation in recent archæological research. The excavations on the site of Ashur, the earliest Assyrian capital, tend to show that the first settlements in that country, of which we have recovered traces, were made by a people closely akin to the Sumerians of Southern Babylonia.[1] It was in the course of work upon a temple dedicated to Ishtar, the national goddess of Assyria, that remains were found of very early periods of occupation. Below the foundation of the later building a still older temple was found, also dedicated to that goddess. Incidentally this building has an interest of its own, for it proved to be the earliest temple yet discovered in Assyria, dating, as it probably does, from the close of the third millennium B.C. Still deeper excavation, below the level of this primitive Assyrian shrine, revealed a stratum in which were several examples of rude sculpture, apparently representing, not Semites, but the early non-Semitic inhabitants of Southern Babylonia.

FIG. 34.

HEAD OF AN ARCHAIC LIMESTONE FIGURE FROM ASHUR.

The primitive character of the sculpture is apparent, and the inlaying of the eyes with shell is characteristic of early work in Babylonia. The figure is possibly that of a female.

[After *Mitt. der Deutsch. Orient-Gesellschaft*, No. 54, p. 9.]

[1] Since the year 1903 the Deutsche Orient-Gesellschaft has been conducting excavations at Shergât, the site of Ashur, the old capital of Assyria on the middle Tigris. Monographs on some of the temples of the city and its system of fortification have already been published, and during the summer of 1913 the excavations were drawing to a close. The greater part of the palace and temple-area had been uncovered, and detailed plans had been made of all existing buildings ; it only remained to trench still deeper to the virgin rock, in order to complete the digging. This process had naturally been left till last, as it involved considerable destruction to the buildings already uncovered. It was in the course of the deeper trenching that the discoveries referred to in the text were made ; for brief reports of them by Andrae, see the "Mitteilungen der Deutschen Orient-Gesellschaft," No. 54 (June, 1914).

The extremely archaic character of the work is well illustrated by a head, possibly that of a female figure,[1] in which the inlaying of the eyes recalls a familiar practice in early work from Babylonia. But the most striking evidence was furnished by heads of male figures, which, if offered for sale without a knowledge of their *provenance*, would undoubtedly have been accepted as coming from Tello or Bismâya, the sites of the early Sumerian cities of Lagash and Adab. The racial type presented by the heads appears to be purely Sumerian, and, though one figure at least is

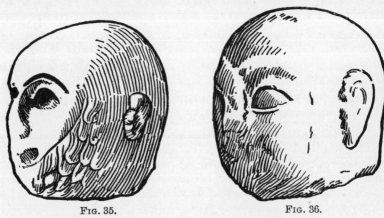

FIG. 35.   FIG. 36.

HEADS OF ARCHAIC MALE FIGURES FROM ASHUR AND TELLO.

A marked feature of both heads is the shaven scalp, exhibiting a characteristic Sumerian practice.   Fig. 35 is from Ashur, Fig. 36 from Tello.
[After *M.D.O.G.*, No. 54, p. 12, and De Sarzec, *Découvertes en Chaldée*, pl. 6, No. 1.]

bearded, the Sumerian practice of shaving the head was evidently in vogue.[2]   In other limestone figures, of which the bodies have been preserved, the treatment of the garments corresponds precisely to that in archaic Sumerian sculpture.   The figures wear the same rough woollen garments, and the conventionalized treatment of the separate flocks of wool is identical in both sets of examples.[3]   The evidence is not yet fully published, but, so far as it is available, it suggests that the Sumerians, whose presence has hitherto been traced only upon sites in Southern Babylonia, were also at a very early period in occupation of Assyria.

[1] See Fig. 34.   [2] See Figs. 35 and 36.   [3] See p. 140, Figs. 37–39.

The violent termination of their settlement at Ashur is attested by an abundance of charred remains, which separate the Sumerian stratum from that immediately above it. Had we no evidence to the contrary, it might have been assumed that their successors were of the same stock as those early Semitic invaders who dominated Northern Babylonia early in the third millennium B.C., and pushed eastward across the Tigris into Gutium. But it is recognized that the founders of the historic city of Ashur, records of whose achievements have been recovered in the early building-inscriptions, bear names which are quite un-Semitic in character. There is a good deal to be said for regarding Ushpia, or Aushpia, the traditional founder of the great temple of the god Ashir,[1] and Kikia, the earliest builder of the city's wall,[2] as representing the first arrival of the Mitannian race, which in the fourteenth century played, under new leadership, so dominant a part in the politics of Western Asia.[3] Not only have their names a Mitannian sound, but we have undoubted evidence of the worship of the Mitannian and Hittite god Teshub as early as the period of the First Dynasty of Babylon; and the fact that the Mitannian name, which incorporates that of the deity, is borne by a witness on a Babylonian contract, suggests that he came of a civilized and settled race.[4]

It is true that the name Mitanni is not met with at this period, but the geographical term Subartu is,[5] and

---

[1] The tradition has survived in the building-inscriptions of Shalmaneser I. and Esarhaddon, found at Shergât; cf. "Chronicles," I., pp. 120 ff.

[2] He is referred to on a small cone or cylinder, found at Shergât in 1904, and inscribed with a text of Ashir-rîm-nishêshu; *op. cit.*, p. 140 f.

[3] Their names have been compared with such Mitannian forms as Pindiya, Zuliya, etc.; cf. Ungnad, "Beitr. z. Assyr.," VI., No. 5, pp. 11 ff.

[4] The first witness to a loan, dated in the third year of Ammi-zaduga, bears the name Teshshub-'ari, corresponding to the later Mitannian name Ari-Teshub, meaning "Teshub has given"; cf. Ungnad, "Vorderas. Schriftdenkmäler," VII., No. 72, l. 10.

[5] A "man of Subartu" (*awîl Subarti*) is mentioned on a document of the Hammurabi period (cf. Scheil, "Rec. de trav.," XX., p. 64); and a private letter of the time gives directions for the sale into slavery of certain "Shubareans" (*Shubarî*), who had probably been captured in battle (cf. Meissner, "Beitr. z. Assyr.," II., p. 561 f., and Delitzsch, *op. cit.* IV., p. 95). On another text "a slave-girl of Shubartu (*amtum Shubaritum*) is referred to (cf. "Cun. Texts in the Brit. Mus.," VIII., pl. 46, Bu. 91–5–9, 2179, Obv., l. 20), and "a Shubarean" (*Shubarû*) is mentioned in an account-tablet among recipients of daily rations (cf. Ungnad, "Vorderas. Schriftdenk.," VII., p. 68, No. 184, Col. III., l. 3, and "Beitr. z. Assyr.," VI., No. 5, p. 19, n. 2).

in later tradition was regarded as having ranked with Akkad, Elam and Amurru as one of the four quarters of the ancient civilized world.

In the astrological and omen texts, which incorporate very early traditions, the references to Shubartu are interpreted as applying to Assyria,[1] but the term evidently had an earlier connotation before the rise of

FIG. 37.   FIG. 38.   FIG. 39.

EXAMPLES OF ARCHAIC SCULPTURE FROM ASHUR AND TELLO, EXHIBITING THE
SAME CONVENTION IN THE TREATMENT OF WOOLLEN GARMENTS.

The seated statuette (Fig. 37) is from Ashur, and the treatment of the garment is precisely similar to that in early Tello work (Figs. 38 and 39).
[After *M.D.O.G.*, No. 54, p. 18, and *Déc.*, pl. 2 (*bis*), No. 1, and pl. 21 (*ter*), No. 3.]

Assyria to power. It may well have included the North-Mesopotamian region known afterwards as the land of Mitanni, whose rulers are found in temporary occupation of Nineveh, as their predecessors may have established themselves at Ashur. But, however that may be, it is clear that the historic city of Ashur was

[1] For the purpose of interpreting lunar observations, for example, and particularly for eclipses, the face of the moon was divided into four quarters, that on the right referring to Akkad, that on the left to Elam, the upper quarter to Amurru and the lower to Subartu ; and one Assyrian astrologer, when reporting to his master an observation which related to Subartu, explains that " We are Subartu " ; cf. Thompson, " Reports of the Magicians and Astrologers," II., pp. xviii., lxxxv.

not in its origin either a Sumerian or a Semitic foundation. Its later racial character must date from the
period of the Western Semites, whose amalgamation
with an alien and probably Anatolian strain, which they
found there, may account in part for the warlike and
brutal character of the Assyrians of history, so striking
a contrast to that of the milder and more commercial
Semites who settled in the lower Euphrates valley. As
in Babylonia, the language and to a great extent the
features of the Semite eventually predominated; and
the other element in the composition of the race
survived only in an increased ferocity of temperament.

This was the people of whose attack on Sumu-abum,
the founder of Babylon's greatness, later ages preserved
the tradition. No conflict with Assyria is commemorated in Sumu-abum's date-formulæ, and it is possible
that it took place before he secured his throne in Babylon,
and built the great fortification-wall of the city with
which he inaugurated his reign. When once he was settled
there and had placed the town in a state of defence, he
began to extend his influence over neighbouring cities
in Akkad. Kibalbarru, which he fortified with a city-
wall in his third year, was probably in the immediate
neighbourhood of Babylon, and we know that Dilbat,
the fortification of which was completed in his ninth
year, lay only about seventeen miles south of the capital.[1]
The five years which separated these two efforts at
expansion were uneventful from the point of view of
political achievement, for the only noteworthy episodes
recorded were the building of a temple to the goddess
Nin-Sinna and another to Nannar, the Moon-god, in
which he afterwards set up a great cedar door. It may
be that the conflict with Assyria should be set in this
interval; but we should then have expected some sort of
reference to the successful repulse of the enemy, and it
is preferable to place it before his first year of rule.

[1] Dilbat is now marked by the mound of Dêlem, which lies about seventeen miles to the south of the Kasr, the old citadel and centre of Babylon,
and less than ten miles to the south-east of Birs Nimrûd. Many years ago
Rassam procured a few tablets there by excavation (cf. " Asshur and the Land
of Nimrod," p. 265), and in recent years large numbers have been obtained
there, as the result of native digging, and sold in Europe; they all date from
the period of the First Dynasty of Babylon.

His success in the encounter with Assyria may well
have afforded this West-Semitic chieftain the opportunity
of fortifying one of the great towns of Akkad, and of
establishing himself there as its protector against the
danger of aggression from the north ; and there is
no doubt that Babylon had long had some sort of local
governor, the traditions of whose office he inherited.
Since we have references to E-sagila in the time of the
Dynasties of Akkad and of Ur,[1] the former rulers of
Babylon were probably no more than the chief priests
of Marduk's sanctuary.   That Sumu-abum should have
changed the office to that of king, and that his successor
should have succeeded in establishing a dynasty that
endured for nearly three centuries, is evidence of the
unabated energy of the new settlers.   Even the later
members of the dynasty retained their original West-
Semitic character,[2] and this fact, coupled with the
speedy control of other cities than Babylon, suggests
that the Western Semites had now arrived in far greater
numbers than during their earlier migration farther
down the Euphrates.

It is possible to trace the gradual growth of
Babylon's influence in Akkad under her new rulers,
and the stages by which she threw out her control over
an increasing area of territory.   At Dilbat, for example,
she had no difficulties from the very first, and during
almost the whole period of the First Dynasty the
government of the city was scarcely distinguishable
from that of Babylon.   The god Urash and the goddess
Lagamal were the patron deities of Dilbat, around
whose cult the life of the city centred ; and there was
a local secular administration.   But the latter was completely subordinate to the capital, and no effort was
made, nor apparently was one required, to retain a
semblance of local independence.   The treatment of
Sippar, on the other hand, was rather different.   Here
Sumu-abum appears to have recognized the local ruler

[1] Cf. "Sumer and Akkad," pp. 226, 282.

[2] This is particularly apparent in the royal names, the foreign character
of which was first pointed out by Pognon, "Journal Asiatique," 8me sér.,
Vol. XI., pp. 544 ff., who on this evidence alone suggested that the dynasty
might be Arab or Aramean ; see further, "Letters of Hammurabi," III.,
p. lxv., and Meyer, "Geschichte des Altertums," I., ii., p. 545.

as his vassal ; and, as a further concession to its semi-independent state, he allowed the town the privilege of continuing to use its own date-formulæ, derived from local events.[1] Oaths, it is true, had to be taken in the king of Babylon's name and in that of the great Sun-god of Sippar ; but the city could arrange and use its own system of time-reckoning without reference to the capital's affairs.   Perhaps the most interesting example of Babylon's early system of provincial government is that presented by the city of Kish, for we can there trace the gradual extension of her control from a limited suzerainty to complete annexation.

Kish lay far nearer to Babylon than Dilbat,[2] but it had a more illustrious past to inspire it than the other city.   It had played a great part in the earlier history of Sumer and Akkad, and at the time of the West-Semitic occupation of Babylon it was still governed by independent kings.   We have recovered an inscription of one such ruler, Ashduni-erim, who may well have been Sumu-abum's contemporary, for the record reflects a state of affairs such as would have been caused by a hostile invasion and gradual conquest of the country.[3] Although Ashduni-erim lays claim only to the kingdom of Kish, he speaks in grandiloquent terms of the invasion, relating how the four quarters of the world revolted against him.   For eight years he fought against the enemy, so that in the eighth year his army was reduced to three hundred men.   But the city-god Zamama and Ishtar, his consort, then came to his succour and brought him supplies of food.   With this encouragement he marched out for a whole day, and then for forty days he placed the enemy's land under contribution ; and he closes his inscription rather

[1] From a local date-formula on one of the tablets from Abû Habba we have recovered the name of Narâm-Sin, a governor or vassal-ruler of Sippar in Sumu-abum's reign ; cf. Ungnad, "Vorderas. Schriftdenkmäler," VIII., No. 3.   Another vassal-ruler of Sippar, Bunutakhtun-ila, occupied the throne in Sumu-la-ilum's reign, and to the same period are to be assigned Iluma-ila and Immerum, of whom the latter cut the Ashukhi Canal ; for references, see Schorr, " Urkunden des altbabylonischen Zivil-und Processrechts," p. 611.

[2] Kish is now marked by the mounds of El-Ohêmir, or Aḥimer, which lie to the east of Babylon ; cf. " Sumer and Akkad," p. 38 f.

[3] The text is inscribed upon a clay cone from Aḥimer, and has been published by Thureau-Dangin, " Rev. d'Assyr.," VIII. (1911), pp. 65 ff.

abruptly by recording that he rebuilt the wall of Kish. The clay cone was probably a foundation-record, which he buried within the structure of the city-wall.

Ashduni-erim does not refer to his enemy by name, but it is to be noted that the hostile territory lay within a day's march of Kish, a description that surely points to Babylon. The eight years of conflict fit in admirably with the suggestion, for we know that it was in Sumu-abum's tenth year, exactly eight years after his occupation of Kibalbarru, that his suzerainty was acknowledged in Kish. Sumu-abum named that year of his reign after his dedication of a crown to the god Anu of Kish,[1] and we may conjecture that Ashduni-erim, weakened by the long conflict which he describes, came to terms with his stronger neighbour and accepted the position of a vassal. Having given guarantees for his fidelity, he would have received Sumu-abum in Kish, where the latter as the suzerain of the city performed the dedication he commemorated in his date-formula for that year. This would fully explain the guarded terms in which Ashduni-erim refers to the enemy in his inscription, the rebuilding of the city-wall having, on this supposition, been undertaken with Babylon's consent.[2]

That Kish was accorded the position of a vassal state is certain, for, among contract-tablets recovered from the city, several were drawn up in the reign of Mananâ, who was Sumu-abum's vassal. In these documents the oath is taken in Mananâ's name, but they are dated by the formula for Sumu-abum's thirteenth year, commemorating his capture of Kazallu. The importance of the latter event may be held to explain the use of the suzerain's own formula, for other documents in Mananâ's reign are dated by local events, proving that at Kish, as at Sippar, a vassal city of Babylon was allowed the privilege of retaining its own system of time-reckoning. If we are right in regarding

[1] That Sumu-abum performed the dedication in his character of suzerain is proved by a contract-tablet from Kish, which is dated by the formula for his tenth year.

[2] It is also possible that the eight years of conflict may date from Sumu-abum's accession, in which case the text would commemorate a strengthening of the wall of Kish two years before the capture of the city by Babylon; but the evidence of the date-formulæ is in favour of the tenth year.

HAMMURABI RECEIVING HIS LAWS FROM THE SUN-GOD.
After Délég. en Perse, Mém. IV, pl. 3.

Ashduni-erim as Sumu-abum's contemporary, it is clear that he must have been succeeded by Mananâ within three years of his capitulation to Babylon. During the next few years the throne of Kish was occupied by at least three rulers in quick succession, Sumu-ditana, Iawium, and Khalium,[1] for we know that by the thirteenth year of Sumu-la-ilum, who succeeded Sumu-abum on the throne of Babylon, the city of Kish had revolted and had been finally annexed.

The conquest of Kazallu, which Sumu-abum carried out in the last year but one of his reign, was the most important of Babylon's early victories, for it marked an extension of her influence beyond the limits of Akkad. The city appears to have lain to the east of the Tigris, and the two most powerful empires in the past history of Babylonia had each come into active conflict with it during the early years of their existence. Its conquest by Akkad was regarded in Babylonian tradition as the most notable achievement of Sargon's reign ; and at a later period Dungi of Ur, after capturing the Elamite border city of Dêr, had extended his empire to the north or east by including Kazallu within its borders.[2] Sumu-abum's conquest was probably little more than a successful raid, for in the reign of Sumu-la-ilum Kazallu in its turn attacked Babylon, and, by fully occupying her energies, delayed her southward expansion for some years.

In the earlier part of his reign Sumu-la-ilum appears to have devoted himself to consolidating the position his predecessor had secured and to improving the internal resources of his kingdom. The Shamash-khegallum Canal, which he cut immediately on his accession, lay probably in the neighbourhood of Sippar ;

---

[1] On one of the tablets from Kish Iawium is associated with Mananâ in the oath-formula, and from another we know that he survived Sumu-ditana, whom he probably succeeded on the throne ; Khalium may probably be placed after the other three vassal-rulers whose names have been recovered. There appears to have been a local custom at Kish for each ruler to choose a different god with whom to be associated in the oath-formulæ ; thus, while Zamama, the city-god of Kish, appears in those of Iawium's reign, his place is taken by Nannar and Sin under Mananâ and Khalium respectively. For the tablets and their dates, see Thureau-Dangin, "Rev. d'Assyr.," VIII., pp. 68 ff. ; Johns, "Proc. Soc. Bibl. Arch.," XXXII. (1910), p. 279 f. ; and Langdon, *op. cit.*, XXXIII. (1911), pp. 185 ff.

[2] Cf. "Sumer and Akkad," pp. 227, 285 f.

and later on he further improved the country's system
of irrigation by a second canal to which he gave his
own name.[1]   The policy he thus inaugurated was ener-
getically maintained by his successors, and much of
Babylon's wealth and prosperity under her early kings
may be traced to the care they lavished on increasing
the area of land under cultivation.   Sumu-la-ilum also
rebuilt the great fortification-wall of his capital, but
during his first twelve years he records only one military
expedition.[2]   It was in his thirteenth year that the
revolt and reconquest of Kish put an end to this period
of peaceful development.

The importance attached by Babylon to the suppression of this revolt is attested by the fact that for five
years it formed an era for the dating of documents,
which was only discontinued when the city of Kazallu,
under the leadership of Iakhzir-ilum, administered a
fresh shock to the growing kingdom by an invasion of
Babylonian territory.   Iakhzir-ilum appears to have
secured the co-operation of Kish by inciting it once
more to rebellion, for in the following year Babylon
destroyed the wall of Anu in that city ; and, after re-
establishing her authority there, she devoted her next
campaign to carrying the war into the enemy's country.
That the subsequent conquest of Kazallu and the defeat
of its army failed to afford a fresh subject for a nascent
era in the chronology is to be explained by the incom-
pleteness of the victory ; for Iakhzir-ilum escaped the
fate which overtook his city, and it was only after five
years of continued resistance that he was finally defeated
and slain.[3]

After disposing of this source of danger from beyond
the Tigris, Sumu-la-ilum continued his predecessor's
policy of annexation within the limits of Akkad.   In
his twenty-seventh year he commemorates the destruction and rebuilding of the wall of Cuthah, suggesting

[1] The Sumu-la-ilum Canal was first constructed in his twelfth year, and it
was recut or extended twenty years afterwards.

[2] The third year of his reign was named as that in which he slew the
Khalambû with the sword.

[3] That in the interval Babylon had no marked success to commemorate is
suggested by the naming of years after the construction of a throne for
Marduk in his temple at Babylon, and of a statue for his consort, Ṣarpanitum.

that the city had up to that time maintained its independence and now only yielded it to force of arms. It is significant that in the same year he records that he treated the wall of the god Zakar in a similar fashion, for Dûr-Zakar was one of the defences of Nippur,[1] and lay either within the city-area or in its immediate neighbourhood. That year thus appears to mark Babylon's first bid for the rule of Sumer as well as of Akkad, for the possession of the central city was regarded as carrying with it the right of suzerainty over the whole country. It is noteworthy, too, that this success appears to correspond to a period of great unrest at Nîsin in Southern Babylonia.

During the preceding period of forty years the southern cities had continued to rule within their home territory without interference from Babylon. In spite of Sumu-abum's increasing influence in Northern Babylonia, Ur-Ninib of Nîsin had claimed the control of Akkad in virtue of his possession of Nippur, though his authority cannot have been recognized much farther to the north. Like the earlier king of Nîsin, Ishme-Dagan, he styled himself in addition Lord of Erech and patron of Nippur, Ur and Eridu, and so did his son Bûr-Sin II., who succeeded his father after the latter's long reign of twenty-eight years. Of the group of southern cities Larsa alone continued to boast a line of independent rulers, the throne having passed from Gungunum successively to Abi-sarê[2] and Sumu-ilum; and in the latter's reign it would seem that Larsa for a time even ousted Nîsin from the hegemony in Sumer. For we have recovered at Tello the votive figure of a dog, which a certain priest of Lagash named Abba-dugga dedicated to a goddess on his behalf,[3] and in the inscription he refers to Sumu-ilum as King of Ur, proving that the city had passed from the control of Nîsin to that of Larsa. The goddess, to whom the

---

[1] That the two are to be identified is certain from Samsu-iluna's reference to Dûr-Zakar of Nippur as among the six fortresses built by Sumu-la-ilum and rebuilt by himself; see below, pp. 148, 204.

[2] Since Gungunum's death is recorded in a local date-formula (cf. Scheil, "Rec. de trav.," XXI., p. 125) we may infer that his end was violent; Abi-sarê's accession may thus mark a break in the direct succession at Larsa.

[3] See Thureau-Dangin, "Rev. d'Assyr.," VI., p. 69 f.

dedication was made, was Nin-Nîsin, "the Lady of
Nîsin," a fact suggestive of the further possibility that
Nîsin itself may have acknowledged Sumu-ilum for a
time.   It may be noted that in the list of Nîsin kings
one name is missing after those of Itêr-pîsha and Ura-
imitti, who followed Bûr-Sin on the throne in quick
succession.[1] According to later tradition Ura-imitti had
named his gardener, Enlil-bani, to succeed him,[2] and in
the list the missing ruler is recorded to have reigned in
Nîsin for six months before Enlil-bani's accession.   It is
perhaps just possible that we should restore his name
as that of Sumu-ilum of Larsa,[3] who may have taken
advantage of the internal troubles of Nîsin, not only
to annex Ur, but to place himself for a few months
upon the rival throne, until driven out by Enlil-bani.
However that may be, it is certain that Larsa profited
by the unrest at Nîsin, and we may perhaps also
connect with it Babylon's successful incursion in the
south.[4]

There is no doubt that Sumu-la-ilum was the real
founder of Babylon's greatness as a military power.
We have the testimony of his later descendant Samsu-
iluna to the strategic importance of the fortresses he
built to protect his country's extended frontier ;[5] and,
though Dûr-Zakar of Nippur is the only one the position of which can be approximately identified, we may
assume that the majority of these lay along the east

[1] Ura-imitti was not the son of Itêr-pisha, and since a date-formula of his
reign refers to his restoration of the city of Nippur, we may regard its previous
destruction or capture as further evidence of political trouble at Nîsin ;
cf. Poebel, "Historical Texts," p. 138 f.

[2] Cf. "Sumer and Akkad," p. 312.

[3] The name was conjecturally restored by Poebel, from a date-formula in
the Pennsylvania Museum, as Sin-ikisha (cf. "Orient. Lit.-Zeit.," 1907, col.
461 ff.).   But from Prof. Clay's new king-list we now know that that ruler
is to be identified with Sin-ikîsham, the eleventh king of the Dynasty of
Larsa ; there is no evidence to connect him with Nîsin.   On the other hand,
the six months' rule of the unknown king at Nîsin falls in the twentieth year
of Sumu-ilum's reign at Larsa, who at least for a time was recognized in Ur,
the former vassal-city of Nîsin.

[4] According to our scheme of chronology, Sumu-la-ilum's capture of Dûr-
Zakar at Nippur corresponds to the year of Ura-imitti's death and to the subsequent struggle for the throne of Nîsin.

[5] In addition to Dûr-Zakar of Nippur, these were Dûr-Padda, Dûr-Lagaba,
Dûr-Iabugani, Dûr-Gula-dûru, and Dûr-uṣi-ana-Ura.   On their reconstruction Samsu-iluna dedicated the first four to Ninmakh, Adad, Sin and Lugal-
diri-tugab, and the last two to Nergal ; cf. "Letters of Hammurabi," pp. 199 ff.

and the south sides of Akkad, where the greatest danger of invasion was to be anticipated. It does not seem that Nippur itself passed at this time under more than a temporary control by Babylon, and we may assume that, after his successful raid, Sumu-la-ilum was content to remain within the limits of Akkad, which he strengthened with his line of forts. In his later years he occupied the city of Barzi, and conducted some further military operations, details of which we have not recovered; but those were the last efforts on Babylon's part for more than a generation.

The pause in expansion gave Babylon the opportunity of husbanding her resources, after the first effort of conquest had been rendered permanent in its effect by Sumu-la-ilum. His two immediate successors, Zabum and Apil-Sin, occupied themselves with the internal administration of their kingdom and confined their military activities to keeping the frontier intact. Zabum indeed records a successful attack on Kazallu, no doubt necessitated by renewed aggression on that city's part; but his other most notable achievements were the fortification of Kâr-Shamash, and the construction of a canal or reservoir.[1] Equally uneventful was the reign of Apil-Sin, for though Dûr-muti, the wall of which he rebuilt, may have been acquired as the result of conquest, he too was mainly occupied with the consolidation and improvement of the territory already won. He strengthened the walls of Barzi and Babylon, cut two canals,[2] and rebuilt some of the great temples.[3] As a result of her peaceful development during this period the country was rendered capable of a still greater struggle, which was to free Sumer

---

[1] To this he gave the name Tâmtum-khegallum, "the Ocean (gives) abundance." He also rebuilt E-ibianu, E-sagila, and E-babbar in Sippar, installing in the last-named temple a bronze image of himself, possibly with the idea of claiming divine honours.

[2] The Sumu-dâri and Apil-Sin-khegallum Canals were both cut in his reign.

[3] The costly throne for Shamash and Shunirda, or the goddess Aia, which he dedicated in his third year, was probably for E-babbar in Sippar. Apil-Sin devoted special attention to Cuthah, the most recently acquired of Babylon's greater possessions, rebuilding on two occasions E-meslam, the temple of Nergal, the city-god. He also enriched Babylon on the material side, erecting a great city-gate in its eastern wall, and building within the city the temple E-kiku for the goddess Ishtar and another shrine for the Sun-god.

and Akkad from a foreign domination, and, by over-coming the invader, was to place Babylon for a time at the head of a more powerful and united empire than had yet been seen on the banks of the Euphrates.

The country's new foe was her old rival Elam, who more than once before had by successful invasion affected the course of Babylonian affairs. But on this occasion she did more than raid, harry, and return: she annexed the city of Larsa, and by using it as a centre of control, attempted to extend her influence over the whole of Sumer and Akkad. It was at the close of Apil-Sin's reign at Babylon that Kudur-Mabuk, the ruler of Western Elam, known at this period as the land of Emutbal, invaded Southern Babylonia and, after deposing Ṣili-Adad[1] of Larsa, installed his own son Warad-Sin upon the throne. It is a testimony to the greatness of this achievement, that Larsa had for some time enjoyed over Nîsin the position of leading city in Sumer. Nûr-Adad, the successor of Sumu-ilum, had retained control of the neighbouring city of Ur, and, though Enlil-bani of Nîsin had continued to lay claim to be King of Sumer and Akkad, this proud title was wrested from Zambia or his successor by Sin-idinnam, Nur-Adad's son.[2] Sin-idinnam, indeed, on bricks from Muḳayyar in the British Museum makes a reference to the military achievements by which he had won the position for his city. In the text his object is to record the rebuilding of the Moon-god's temple in Ur, but he relates that he carried out this work after he had made the foundation of the throne

[1] For the reading of the weather-god's name as Adad, cf. Budge and King, "Annals of the Kings of Assyria," p. lxxiv. f. The name was probably of West Semitic origin, though the form Rammânu, "the thunderer," has been noted by Prof. Sayce on a cylinder-seal beside the goddess Ashratum (cf. "Zeits. f. Assyr.," VI., p. 161), and she elsewhere appears as the spouse of the god Amurru (cf. Meyer, "Geschichte," I., ii., p. 466). The Sumerian equivalent of Adad is still uncertain ; Hrozný suggests the reading Ishkur (cf. "Zeits. f. Assyr.," XX., pp. 424 ff.), while Thureau-Dangin, Clay and others prefer Immer, suggested in "Königsinschriften," p. 208. Meanwhile it is preferable to employ the reading Adad, for periods at any rate after the West-Semitic invasion.

[2] That Sin-idinnam's assumption of the title was justified by the actual possession of Nippur is proved by a date-formula on a contract in the British Museum, in which he records the dedication of a statue of himself as an ornament for Nippur ; cf. Rawlinson, "Cun. Inscr. West. Asia," IV., pl. 36, No. 2, and Chiera, "Legal and Administrative Documents," p. 72.

of Larsa secure and had smitten the whole of his enemies with the sword.[1] It is probable that his three successors on the throne, who reigned for less than ten years between them, failed to maintain his level of achievement, and that Sin-magir recovered the hegemony for Nîsin.[2] But Ur, no doubt, remained under Larsa's administration, and it was no mean nor inferior city that Kudur-Mabuk seized and occupied.

The Elamite had seen his opportunity in the continual conflicts which were taking place between the two rival cities of Sumer. In their contest for the hegemony Larsa had proved herself successful for a time, but she was still the weaker city and doubtless more exposed to attack from across the Tigris. Hence her selection by Kudur-Mabuk as a basis for his attempt on the country as a whole. He himself retained his position in Elam as the *Adda* of Emutbal ; but he installed his two sons, Warad-Sin and Rîm-Sin, successively upon the throne of Larsa, and encouraged them to attack Nîsin and to lay claim to the rule of Sumer and Akkad. But the success which attended their efforts soon brought Babylon upon the scene, and we have the curious spectacle of a three-cornered contest, in which Nîsin is at war with Elam, while Babylon is at war in turn with both. That Sin-muballit, the son of Apil-Sin, did not combine with Nîsin to expel the invader from Babylonian soil, may have played at first into the hands of the Elamites. But it is not to be forgotten that the Western Semites of Babylon were still a conquering aristocracy, and their sympathies were far from being involved in the fate of any part of Sumer. Both Elam and Babylon must have foreseen that the capture of Nîsin would prove a decisive advantage to the victor, and each was content to see her weakened in the hope of ultimate success. When Rîm-Sin actually proved

[1] Cf. Rawlinson, *op. cit.*, I., pl. 5, No. xx. In addition to his military prowess, he reconstructed E-babbar at Larsa, built the great fortress of Dûr-gurgurri, and by canalizing the Tigris improved his country's water-supply (cf. " Cun. Texts in the Brit. Mus.," XXI., pl. 30, No. 30215 ; Delitzsch, " Beitr. zur Assyr.," I., pp. 301 ff. ; and Thureau-Dangin, " Königs-inschriften," p. 208 f.). He also built the city-gate of Mashkan-shabri ; cf. Chiera, *op. cit.*, p. 72 f.

[2] On a broken clay cone from Babylon (cf. Weissbach, " Babylonische Miscellen," p. 1, pl. 1) Sin-magir bears the title of King of Sumer and Akkad.

the victor in the long struggle, and Larsa under his
ægis inherited the traditions as well as the material
resources of the Nîsin Dynasty, the three-cornered contest was reduced to a duel between Babylon and a more
powerful Larsa.   Then for a generation there ensued a
fierce struggle between the two invading races, Elam
and the Western Semites, for the possession of the
country ; and the fact that Hammurabi, Sin-muballit's
son, should have emerged victorious, was a justification
in full of his father's policy of avoiding any alliance
with the south.   The Western Semites proved themselves in the end strong enough to overcome the conqueror of Nîsin, and thereby they were left in undisputed
possession of the whole of Babylonia.

It is possible, with the help of the date-formulæ and
votive inscriptions of the period, to follow in outline the
main features of this remarkable struggle.   At first
Kudur-Mabuk's footing in Sumer was confined to the
city of Larsa, though even then he laid claim to the
title *Adda* of Amurru, a reference to be explained
perhaps by the suggested Amorite origin of the Larsa
and Nîsin dynasties, and reflecting a claim to the
suzerainty of the land from which his northern foes at
any rate boasted their origin.[1]   Warad-Sin, on ascending
the throne, assumed merely the title King of Larsa, but
we soon find him becoming the patron of Ur, and
building a great fortification-wall in that city.[2]   He
then extended his authority to the south and east,
Eridu, Lagash, and Girsu all falling before his arms
or submitting to his suzerainty.[3]   During this period

[1] If we may identify Khallabu with Aleppo, we should find a still firmer
basis for Kudur-Mabuk's title.   For we know that, while Warad-Sin was still
King of Larsa, he dedicated a chamber in Ishtar's temple at Khallabu (cf.
"Cun. Texts in the Brit. Mus.," XXI., pl. 31, No. 91144 ; and Thureau-
Dangin, "Königsinschriften," p. 214 f.).   We should then have to assume
that, before completing his conquest of Sumer, he had already pushed up
and across the Euphrates and had captured large districts of Amurru.   It is
possible that this was so, but it should be noted that both Khallabu and Bît-
Karkara are mentioned in the Prologue to Hammurabi's Code of Laws, not
with "the settlements on the Euphrates," but immediately after Lagash and
Girsu, suggesting a Babylonian origin (see below, p. 159).
[2] Cf. Rawlinson, "Cun. Inscr. West. Asia," I., pl. 5, No. xvi. ; the
erection of the wall is also commemorated in a date-formula of his reign (cf.
Chiera, "Documents," p. 74).
[3] On a clay cone from Mukayyar, recording his building of a temple to
Nannar at Ur, Warad-Sin describes himself as "he who carries out the decrees

BRONZE CONE AND VOTIVE FIGURE.
Brit. Mus., Nos. 90951 *and* 91016.

STONE CYLINDER WITH A VOTIVE INSCRIPTION OF ARAD-SIN,
KING OF LARSA.
Brit. Mus., No. 91085.

Babylon remained aloof in the north, and Sin-muballiṭ is occupied with cutting canals and fortifying cities, some of which he perhaps occupied for the first time.[1] It was only in his fourteenth year, after Warad-Sin had been succeeded at Larsa by his brother Rîm-Sin, that we have evidence of Babylon taking an active part in opposing Elamite pretensions.

In that year Sin-muballiṭ records that he slew the army of Ur with the sword, and, since we know that Ur was at this time a vassal-city of Larsa, it is clear that the army referred to was one of those under Rîm-Sin's command. Three years later he transferred his attention from Larsa to Nîsin, then under the control of Damik-ilishu, the son and successor of Sin-magir. On that occasion Sin-muballiṭ commemorates his conquest of Nîsin, but it must have been little more than a victory in the field, for Damik-ilishu lost neither his city nor his independence. In the last year of his reign we find Sin-muballiṭ fighting on the other front, and claiming to have slain the army of Larsa with the sword. It is clear that in these last seven years of his reign Babylon proved herself capable of checking any encroachments to the north on the part of Larsa and the Elamites, and, by a continuance of the policy of fortifying her vassal-cities,[2] she paved the way for a more vigorous offensive on the part of Hammurabi, Sin-muballiṭ's son and successor. Meanwhile the unfortunate city of Nîsin was between two fircs, though for a few years longer Damik-ilishu succeeded in beating off both his opponents.

The military successes of Hammurabi fall within two clearly defined periods, the first during the five years which followed his sixth year of rule at Babylon,

and decisions of Eridu (i.e. of its oracle), who increased the offerings of E-ninnû (the temple of Ningirsu at Lagash), who restored Lagash and Girsu, and renewed the city and the land "; cf. Rawlinson, op. cit., IV., pl. 35, No. 6.

[1] During the first thirteen years of his reign Sin-muballiṭ cut three canals, the first named after himself, the Sin-muballiṭ Canal, and two others which he termed the Aia-khegallum and the Tutu-khegallum. He also built the walls of Rubatum, Zakar-dada, Dûr-Sin-muballiṭ, Bît-Karkara, and Marad. It is possible, of course, that conflicts with the south took place at this time, but, if so, the absence of any reference to them in the records is to be explained by the want of success of Babylonian arms.

[2] In this period the city walls of Nanga and Baṣu were rebuilt.

and a second period, of ten years' duration, beginning
with the thirteenth of his reign.   On his accession he
appears to have inaugurated the reforms in the internal
administration of the country, which culminated towards
the close of his life in the promulgation of his famous
Code of Laws ; for he commemorated his second year
as that in which he established righteousness in the
land.   The following years were uneventful, the most
important royal acts being the installation of the chief-
priest in Kashbaran,[1] the building of a wall for the
Gagûm, or great Cloister of Sippar, and of a temple to
Nannar in Babylon.   But with his seventh year we find
his first reference to a military campaign in a claim to
the capture of Erech and Nîsin.   This temporary success
against Damik-ilishu of Nîsin was doubtless a menace
to the plans of Rîm-Sin at Larsa, and it would appear
that Kudur-Mabuk came to the assistance of his son
by threatening Babylon's eastern border.   At any rate
Hammurabi records a conflict with the land of Emutbal
in his eighth year, and, though the attack appears to
have been successfully repulsed with a gain of territory
to Babylon,[2] the diversion was successful.   Rîm-Sin
took advantage of the respite thus secured to renew his
attack with increased vigour upon Nîsin, and in the
following year, the seventeenth of his own reign, the
famous city fell, and Larsa under her Elamite ruler
secured the hegemony in the whole of Central and
Southern Babylonia.

Rîm-Sin's victory must have been a severe blow to
Babylon, and it would seem that she made no attempt
at first to recover her position in the south, since
Hammurabi occupied himself with a raid on Malgûm [3] in
the west and with the capture of the cities of Rabikum

[1] From two recently published date-lists of Hammurabi's reign we know
that this event took place in his fifth year, while the following year appears
to have been dated by a similar priestly installation of the shepherd of
the goddess Ninaz ; cf. Boissier, "Rev. d'Assyr.," XI., No. iv. (1914),
pp. 161 ff.
[2] The territory gained on the bank of the Shu-numum-dar Canal (cf.
Boissier, op. cit.) may have lain in Emutbal.   The canal was possibly a portion
of the famous Nâr-sharri, which in the Achæmenian period was regarded as
lying " in Elam."
[3] The town lay in the neighbourhood of Sukhi on the middle Euphrates,
below the mouth of the Khâbûr and probably to the south of Khana.

and Shalibi.   But these were the last successes during
his first military period, and for nineteen years afterwards Babylon achieved nothing of a similar nature to
commemorate in her date-formulæ.   For the most part
the years are named after the dedication of statues
and the building and enrichment of temples.   One
canal was cut,[1] and the process of fortification went on,
Sippar especially being put in a thorough state of
defence.[2]   But the negative evidence supplied by the
formulæ for this period suggests that it was one in
which Babylon completely failed in any attempt she
may have made to hinder the growth of Larsa's power
in the south.

In addition to his capital, Rîm-Sin had inherited
from his brother the control of the southern group of
cities, Ur, Erech, Girsu and Lagash, all of which lay
to the east of Larsa and nearer to the coast ; and it was
probably before his conquest of Nîsin that he took
Erech from Damiḳ-ilishu, who had been attacked there
by Hammurabi two years before.   For in more than
one of his inscriptions Rîm-Sin refers to the time when
Anu, Enlil and Enki, the great gods, had given the
fair city of Erech into his hands.[3]   We also know
that he took Kisurra, rebuilt the wall of Zabilum, and
extended his authority over Kesh, whose goddess
Ninmakh, he relates, gave him the kingship over the
whole country.[4]   The most notable result of his conquest of Nîsin was the possession of Nippur, which
now passed to him and regularized his earlier claim
to the rule of Sumer and Akkad.   Thereafter he describes himself as the exalted Prince of Nippur, or as
the shepherd of the whole land of Nippur ; and we
possess an interesting confirmation of his recognition
there in a clay cone inscribed with a dedication for the

[1] The Tishit-Enlil Canal, which we now know was cut in Hammurabi's
twenty-fourth year (cf. Boissier, *op. cit.*) ; the Hammurabi-khegallum Canal
had been cut in his ninth year, at the time of Rîm-Sin's capture of Nîsin.
[2] Two years were devoted to the fortification of Sippar ; and the walls of
Igi-kharsagga, and probably of Baṣu, were built. In the vassal-city of Kibalbarru Hammurabi dedicated an image to Ninni, or Ishtar, while in Babylon
he built E-namkhe, the temple of Adad, and a shrine also for Enlil.
[3] Cf. "Dec. en Chaldée," pl. 41 ; Rawlinson, "Cun. Inscr. West. Asia,"
I., pl. 3, No. X. ; and Thureau-Dangin, " Königsinschriften," p. 216 f.
[4] See the date-formulæ cited by Chiera, " Documents," p. 80 f.

prolongation of his life by a private citizen, a certain Ninib-gamil.[1]

That Rîm-Sin's rule in Sumer was attended by great prosperity throughout the country as a whole, is attested by the numerous commercial documents which have been recovered both at Nippur and Larsa and are dated in the era of his capture of Nîsin.   There is also evidence that he devoted himself to improving the system of irrigation and of transport by water.   He canalized a section in the lower course of the Euphrates, and dug the Tigris to the sea, no doubt removing from its main channel an accumulation of silt, which not only hindered traffic but increased the danger of flood and the growth of the swamp-area.   He also cut the Mashtabba Canal, and others at Nippur and on the Khabilu river.[2]   It would seem that, in spite of his Elamite extraction and the intimate relations he continued to maintain with his father Kudur-Mabuk, he completely identified himself with the country of his adoption; for in the course of his long life he married twice, and both his wives, to judge from their fathers' names, were of Semitic descent.[3]

It was not until nearly a generation had passed, after Rîm-Sin's capture of Nîsin, that Hammurabi made any headway against the Elamite domination, which for so long had arrested any increase in the power of Babylon.[4] But his success, when it came, was complete and enduring.   In his thirtieth year he records that he defeated the army of Elam, and in the next campaign he followed

---

[1] Cf. Hilprecht, "Old Babylonian Inscriptions," Pt. II., pl. 58, No. 128.

[2] Cf. Hilprecht, *loc. cit.*, and Chiera, *op. cit.*, p. 82 f.

[3] One of his wives, Si[. . .]-Ninni, the daughter of Arad-Nannar, dedicated a temple, on his behalf and her own, to the goddess Nin-egal (cf. Thureau-Dangin, "Königsinschriften," p. 218 f.).   The other wife, who bore the name Rîm-Sin-Shala-bashtashu, was the daughter of a certain Sin-magir, and Rîm-Sin himself had a daughter named Lirish-gamlum; cf. Poebel, "Historical Texts," p. 140, who quotes the information from an inscription of Rîm-Sin-Shala-bashtashu, which Prof. Clay informs me is now in the Yale Collection. A sister of Rîm-Sin, who was a priestess, is mentioned on a cylinder of Nabonidus (cf. Scheil, "Comptes rendus de l'Académie des Inscriptions et Belles Lettres," 1912, p. 680 f.).

[4] The period would be forty-five years, instead of twenty-three, if we place the whole sixty-one years of Rîm-Sin's reign before Hammurabi's conquest of Larsa; in that case the fall of Nîsin would have taken place in Sin-muballit's seventh year.   But the available evidence is strongly in favour of curtailing Rîm-Sin's period of independent rule; see above, pp. 97 ff.

up this victory by invading the land of Emutbal, inflicting a final defeat on the Elamites, and capturing and annexing Larsa. Rîm-Sin himself appears to have survived for many years, and to have given further trouble to Babylon in the reign of Hammurabi's son, Samsuiluna. And the evidence seems to show that for a few years at least he was accorded the position of vassal ruler at Larsa.[1] On this supposition Hammurabi, after his conquest of Sumer, would have treated the old capital in the same way that Sumu-abum treated Kish.[2] But it would seem that after a time Larsa must have been deprived of many of its privileges, including that of continuing its own era of time-reckoning; and Hammurabi's letters to Sin-idinnam, his local representative, give no hint of any divided rule. We may perhaps assume that Rîm-Sin's subsequent revolt was due to resentment at this treatment, and that in Samsu-iluna's reign he seized a favourable opportunity to make one more bid for independent rule in Babylonia.

The defeat of Rîm-Sin, and the annexation of Sumer to Babylon, freed Hammurabi for the task of extending his empire on its other three sides. During these later years he twice made successful raids in the Elamite country of Tupliash or Ashnunnak, and on the west he destroyed the walls of Mari and Malgûm, defeated the armies of Turukkum, Kagmum and Subartu, and in his thirty-ninth year he records that he destroyed all his enemies that dwelt beside Subartu. It is probable that he includes Assyria under the geographical term Subartu, for both Ashur and Nineveh were subject to his rule; and one of his letters proves that his occupation of Assyria was of a permanent character, and that his authority was maintained by garrisons of Babylonian troops. Hammurabi tells us too, in the Prologue to his Code of Laws, that he subjugated " the settlements on the Euphrates," implying the conquest of such local West-Semitic kingdoms as that of Khana.[3] On the west we may therefore regard the area of his military

---

[1] This seems to follow from the continuation of the Nîsin era in the south for a few years after the fall of Larsa ; see above, p. 103.

[2] See above, p. 144.

[3] See above, pp. 129 ff. ; it was probably after these conquests that he adopted the title King of Amurru.

activities as extending to the borders of Syria. Up to the close of his reign he continued to improve the defences of his country, for he devoted his last two years to rebuilding the great fortification of Kâr-Shamash on the Tigris and the wall of Rabikum on the Euphrates, and he once again strengthened the city-wall of Sippar. His building-inscriptions also bear witness to his increased activity in the reconstruction of temples during his closing years.[1]

An estimate of the extent of Hammurabi's empire may be formed from the very exhaustive record of his activities which he himself drew up as the Prologue to his Code. He there enumerates the great cities of his kingdom and the benefits he has conferred upon each one of them. The list of cities is not drawn up with any administrative object, but from a purely religious standpoint, a recital of his treatment of each city being followed by a reference to what he has done for its temple and its city-god. Hence the majority of the cities are not arranged on a geographical basis, but in accordance with their relative rank as centres of religious cult. Nippur naturally heads the list, and its possession at this time by Babylon had, as we shall see,[2] far-reaching effects upon the development of the mythology and religious system of the country. Next in order comes Eridu, in virtue of the great age and sanctity of its local oracle. Babylon, as the capital, comes third, and then the great centres of Moon- and Sun-worship, followed by the other great cities and shrines of Sumer and Akkad, the king characterizing the benefits he has bestowed on each. The list includes some of his western conquests and ends with Ashur and Nineveh.[3] It is

---

[1] Cf., e.g., "Letters and Inscriptions of Hammurabi," pp. 180 ff. It is clear from the titles in the majority of them that they date from the latter part of his reign. It was also after his annexation of Larsa that he cut the Hammurabi-nukhush-nishi Canal, building a fortress at the head of the canal for its defence, which he named after his father Dûr-Sin-muballiṭ-abim-walidia. The erection of the granary at Babylon (op. cit., p. 192 f.) was evidently one of his earlier works.

[2] See below, p. 194 f.

[3] As the list of cities is practically a gazetteer of Hammurabi's empire during his closing years, the names will repay enumeration, together with their temples and city-gods ; they are here given in the order in which they occur in the Prologue, the names of gods, when omitted in the text, being supplied within parentheses : (1) Nippur, and Ekur, the temple of Enlil ; (2) Eridu, and É-apsû (the temple of Enki) ; (3) Babylon, and E-sagila, the

significant of the racial character of his dynasty that Hammurabi should here ascribe his victories on the middle Euphrates to "the strength of Dagan, his creator," proving that, like his ancestors before him, he continued to be proud of his West-Semitic descent.

In view of the closer relations which had now been established between Babylonia and the West, it may be interesting to recall that an echo from these troubled times found its way into the early traditions of the Hebrews, and has been preserved in the Book of Genesis. It is there related[1] that Amraphel king of Shinar, Arioch king of Ellasar, Chedorlaomer king of Elam, and Tidal king of Goiim or the "nations," acting as members of a confederation, invaded Eastern Palestine to subdue the revolted tribes of that district. Chedorlaomer is represented as the head of the confederation, and though we know of no Elamite ruler of that name, we have seen that Elam at about this period had exercised control over a great part of Southern and Central Babylonia, and that its Babylonian capital was the city of Larsa, with which the Ellasar of the Hebrew tradition is certainly to be identified.[2] Moreover, Kudur-Mabuk, the historical founder of the Elamite domination in Babylonia, did lay claim to the title of *Adda* or ruler of the Amorites.[3] Amraphel of Shinar may well be Hammurabi of Babylon himself, though, so far from acknowledging the suzerainty of the Elamites, he was their principal antagonist and brought their domination

temple of Marduk ; (4) Ur, and E-gishshirgal (the temple of Sin) ; (5) Sippar, and E-babbar (the temple of Shamash) ; (6) Larsa, and E-babbar (the temple of Shamash) ; (7) Erech, and E-anna, the temple of Anu and Ninni, or Ishtar ; (8) Nîsin, and the temple E-galmakh ; (9) Kish, and E-mete-ursag, the temple of Zamama ; (10) Cuthah, and E-meslam (the temple of Nergal) ; (11) Borsippa, and E-zida (the temple of Nabû) ; (12) Dilbat, and its god Urash ; (13) the city of Kesh ; (14) Lagash and Girsu, and E-ninnû (the temple of Ningirsu) ; (15) Khallabu, and the goddess Ninni, or Ishtar ; (16) Bît-Karkara, and E-ugalgal, the temple of Adad ; (17) Adab, and its temple E-makh ; (18) Mashkan-shabri and the temple Meslam ; (19) Malgûm ; (20) the dwellings, or settlements, on the Euphrates, and the god Dagan ; (21) Mera and Tutul ; (22) Akkad (Agade), and E-ulmash, the temple of Ishtar ; (23) Ashur, and "its favourable protecting deity" ; and (24) Nineveh, and E-mishmish, the temple of Ishtar.

[1] Gen. xiv.

[2] For the Elamite character of Chedorlaomer's name, cf. "Letters of Hammurabi," I., p. iv. f. ; but there are too many difficulties in the way of accepting the suggested identification of Arioch with Warad-Sin, the son of Kudur-Mabuk (*op. cit.*, pp. xlix. ff.). [3] See above, p. 152.

to an end. Tidal is a purely Hittite name,[1] and it is significant that the close of Hammurabi's powerful dynasty was, as we shall see presently, hastened by an invasion of Hittite tribes. Thus all the great nations which are mentioned in this passage in Genesis were actually on the stage of history at this time, and, though we have as yet found no trace in secular sources of such a confederation under the leadership of Elam, the Hebrew record represents a state of affairs in Western Asia which was not impossible during the earlier half of Hammurabi's reign.[2]

While Sumu-la-ilum may have laid the foundations of Babylon's military power, Hammurabi was the real founder of her greatness. To his military achievements he added a genius for administrative detail, and his letters and despatches, which have been recovered, reveal him as in active control of even subordinate officials stationed in distant cities of his empire. That he should have superintended matters of public importance is what might be naturally expected ; but we also see him investigating quite trivial complaints and disputes among the humbler classes of his subjects, and often sending back a case for retrial or for further report. In fact, Hammurabi's fame will always rest on his achievements as a law-giver, and on the great legal code which he drew up for use throughout his empire. It is true that this elaborate system of laws, which deal in detail with every class of the population from the noble to the slave, was not the creative work of Hammurabi himself. Like all other ancient legal codes it was governed strictly by precedent, and where it did not incorporate earlier collections of laws, it was based on careful consideration of established custom. Hammurabi's great achievement was the codification of this mass of legal enactments

---

[1] Prof. Sayce was the first to point out that Tidal is a Hittite name, and was borne by one of the last kings of the Hittite Empire, Dudkhalia ; cf. "Patriarchal Palestine," p. 60.

[2] We are not here concerned with the textual character of Gen. xiv. (on that subject, see especially Skinner, " Genesis," pp. 256 ff.), nor with the evolution of the Abrahamic traditions (see Meyer, " Die Israeliten," p. 248, and cp. Hall, " Anc. Hist. of the Near East," p. 401). It will suffice to note that, in view of the recovery of Neo-Babylonian chronicles and poetical compositions, dealing with early historical events, the employment of such a document among Hebrew literary sources seems to offer a sufficient explanation of the facts.

and the rigid enforcement of the provisions of the resulting code throughout the whole territory of Babylonia.   Its provisions reflect the king's own enthusiasm, of which his letters give independent proof, in the cause of the humbler and the more oppressed classes of his subjects.   Numerous legal and commercial documents also attest the manner in which its provisions were carried out, and we have evidence that the legislative system so established remained in practical force during subsequent periods.   It may be well, then, to pause at the age of Hammurabi, in order to ascertain the main features of early Babylonian civilization, and to estimate its influence on the country's later development.

CHAPTER V

THE AGE OF HAMMURABI AND ITS INFLUENCE ON LATER PERIODS

OF no other period in the history of Babylon have we so intimate a knowledge as that of the West-Semitic kings under whom the city first attained the rank of capital. It was a time of strenuous growth, in the course of which the long struggle with regard to language and racial dominance was decided in favour of the Semite. But the victory involved no break of continuity, for all the essential elements of Sumerian culture were preserved, the very length of the struggle having proved the main factor in securing their survival. There had been a gradual assimilation on both sides, though naturally the Sumerian had the more to give, and, in spite of his political disappearance, he continued to exert an indirect influence. This he owed in the main to the energy of the Western Semite, who completed the task of transforming a dying culture, so that in its new embodiment it could be accepted by men of a newer race.

Hammurabi's age was one of transition, and we have fortunately recovered a great body of contemporaneous evidence on which to base an analysis of its social and political structure. On the one hand the great Code of Laws supplies us with the state's administrative ideal and standard of justice.[1] On the other we have the

[1] The Code was first published and translated by Scheil, in the " Mémoires de la Délégation en Perse," Vol. IV. (1902), and the accompanying photographic facsimile remains the best authority for the text. For the fullest and best bibliography to the immense mass of literature which has grown up around it, see Johns, " Schweich Lectures," 1912, pp. 65 ff. ; the most accessible versions in English are those by Johns in " Babylonian and Assyrian Laws, Contracts and Letters " (1904), pp. 44 ff., and in Hastings' "Dictionary of the Bible," Vol. V. For the linguistic study of the text Ungnad's transliteration and glossary in Kohler and Ungnad's " Hammurabi's Gesetz," Bd. II. (1909), may be specially mentioned.

letters of the kings themselves, and the commercial and legal documents of the period,[1] to prove that the Code was no dead letter but was accurately adjusted to the conditions of the time. The possibility has long been recognized of the existence of similar codes of early Sumerian origin, and a copy of one of them, on a tablet of the Hammurabi period, has recently been recovered.[2] But the value of Hammurabi's Code rests not so much in any claim to extensive originality, but rather on its correspondence to contemporary needs. It thus forms a first-rate witness on the subjects with which it deals, and where it gives no information, the letters and contracts of the period often enable us to supply the deficiency.

For the purpose of legislation the Babylonian community was divided into three main classes or grades of society, which corresponded to well-defined strata in the social system. The highest or upper class embraced all the officers or ministers attached to the court, the higher officials and servants of the state, and the owners of considerable landed property. But wealth or position did not constitute the sole qualification distinguishing the members of the upper class from that immediately below them. In fact, while the majority of its members enjoyed these advantages, it was possible for a man to forfeit them through his own fault or misfortune and yet to retain his social standing and privileges. It would seem therefore that the distinction was based on a racial qualification, and that the upper class, or nobles, as we may perhaps term them,[3] were men of the predominant race, sprung from the West-Semitic or Amorite stock

---

[1] For the latest bibliography to the early contract-literature see Schorr, "Urkunden des altbabylonischen Zivil- und Prozessrechts" (published in the "Vorderasiatische Bibliothek," 1913), pp. xlix. ff. The great bulk of the royal letters are in the British Museum and are translated in "Letters and Inscriptions of Hammurabi, etc." (1898–1900) ; and for publications of private letters of the period, see Schorr, *op cit.*, p. lvi.

[2] See Clay, "Orient. Lit.-Zeit," 1914 (January), "A Sumerian Prototype of the Hummurabi Code." The text, of which Prof. Clay has sent me a photograph, is of the greatest importance for the study of Babylonian law ; he is at present preparing it for publication.

[3] The Babylonian name for a member of the upper class was *awîlum*, "man," and, when employed in this special sense, it is best translated by some such expression as "patrician" or "noble." But for legislative purposes, as well as in common parlance, *awîlum* could be employed in its more general meaning to include members of the middle class.

which had given Babylon its first independent dynasty.
In course of time its racial purity would tend to become
diluted by intermarriage with the older inhabitants,
especially where these had thrown in their lot with the
invaders and had espoused their cause. It is even
possible that some of the latter had from the first
obtained recognition in its ranks in return for military
or political service. But, speaking broadly, we may
regard the highest class in the social order as representing a racial aristocracy that had imposed itself.

The second class in the population comprised the
great body of free men who did not come within the
ranks of the nobles; in fact, they formed a middle class
between the aristocracy and the slaves. They bore a
title which in itself implied a state of inferiority,[1] and
though they were not necessarily poor and could possess
slaves and property, they did not share the privileges of
the upper class. It is probable that they represented
the subject race, derived in part from the old Sumerian
element in the population, in part from the Semitic strain
which had long been settled in Northern Babylonia and
by intercourse and intermarriage had lost much of its
racial purity and independence. The difference, which
divided and marked off from one another these two
great classes of free men in the population, is well illustrated by the scale of payments as compensation for
injury which they were obliged to make or were entitled
to receive. Thus if a noble should be guilty of stealing
an ox, or other animal, or a boat, which was private or
temple property, he had to pay thirty times its value as
compensation; whereas, if the thief were a member of
the middle class the penalty was reduced to ten times
the price, and, should he have no property with which
to pay, he was put to death. The penalty for man-
slaughter was also less if the assailant was a man of the
middle class; he could obtain a divorce more cheaply,

---

[1] They were known as *mushkênum*, derived from the Shafel-Piel stem of the
root [*kânu*], with the meaning "to humble oneself, to be humble." Combe
has compared the similar use of *miskín* in Arabic for a man of humble station
who is not a descendant of the prophet (cf. "Babyloniaca," III., p. 73 f.). The
word passed into Hebrew as *miskên*, and, with modifications of meaning, into
more than one European language (cf. Ital. *meschino, meschinello*, Portug.
mesquinho, French *mesquin*); see Johns, "Schweich Lectures" (1912), pp. 8, 74

and he paid his doctor or surgeon a smaller fee for a successful operation. On the other hand, these privileges were counterbalanced by a corresponding diminution of the value at which his life and limbs were assessed.

That a racial distinction underlay the difference in social position and standing is suggested by the current penalties for assault, in accordance with which a noble could demand an exact retaliation for injuries from one of his own class, whereas he merely paid a money compensation to any man of the middle class he might have injured. Thus if one noble happened to knock out the eye or the tooth of another, his own eye or his own tooth was knocked out in return, and if he broke the limb of one of the members of his own class, he had his corresponding limb broken; but, if he knocked out the eye of a member of the middle class, or broke his limb, he was fined one maneh of silver, and for knocking out the tooth of such a man, he was fined one-third of a maneh. Other regulations point to a similar cleavage in the social strata, which can best be explained by a difference in race. Thus if two members of the same class quarrelled and one of them made a peculiarly improper assault on the other, the assailant was only fined, the fine being larger if the quarrel was between two nobles. But if such an assault was made by a member of the middle class upon a noble, the assailant was punished by being publicly beaten in the presence of the assembly, when he received sixty stripes from an ox-hide scourge.

The third and lowest class in the community were the slaves, who were owned by both the upper classes, but were naturally more numerous in the households of the nobles and on their estates. The slave was his master's absolute property, and on the contract-tablets he is often referred to as "a head," as though he were merely an animal. He constantly changed hands, by sale, bequest, or when temporarily pledged for a debt. For bad offences he was liable to severe punishment, such as cutting off the ear, which was the penalty for denying his master, or for making an aggravated assault upon a noble. But, on the whole, his lot was not a particularly hard one, for he was a recognized member of his master's household, and, as a valuable piece of property, it was obviously to his owner's interest to keep him healthy and in good condition. In fact, the value of the slave is attested by the severity of the penalties exacted for abducting a male or female slave from the owner's house and removing one from the city; for the death penalty was imposed in such a case, as also on anyone harbouring and taking possession of a runaway slave. On the other hand, a fixed reward was paid by the owner to anyone by whom a runaway was captured and brought back. Special legislation was also devised with the object of rendering the theft of slaves difficult and their detection easy. Thus, if a brander put a mark upon a slave without the owner's consent, he was liable to have his hands cut off; and, if he could prove that he had done so through being deceived by another man, that man was put to death. There was a regular trade in slaves, and no doubt their numbers were constantly increased by captives taken in war.

Though the slaves, as a class, had few rights of their own, there were regulations in accordance with which, under certain circumstances, they could acquire them, and even obtain their freedom. Thus it was possible for an industrious slave, while still in his master's service, to acquire property of his own, or a slave might inherit wealth from relatives; and, in such circumstances, he was able with his master's consent to purchase his freedom. Again, if a slave were captured by the enemy and taken to a foreign land and sold, and were then brought back by his new owner to his own country, he could claim his liberty without having to pay compensation to either of his masters. Moreover, a slave could acquire certain rights while still in slavery. Thus, if the owner of a female slave had begotten children by her, he could not use her as payment for a debt; and, in the event of his having done so, he was obliged to ransom her by paying the original amount of the debt in money. It was also possible for a male slave, whether owned by a noble or by a member of the middle class, to marry a free woman, and if he did so his children were free and did not become the property of his master. His wife, too, if a free woman, retained her marriage-portion on her husband's death, and supposing the couple had acquired property during the time they lived together as man and wife, the owner of the slave could only claim half of such property, the other half being retained by the free woman for her own use and for that of her children. The mere fact that such a union was possible suggests that there was no very marked cleavage between the social status of the better class of slaves and that of the humbler members of the middle class.

The cultivation of the land, which formed the principal source of the wealth of Babylonia,[1] was carried on mainly by slave labour, under the control of the two upper classes of the population. The land itself was largely in the hands of the crown, the temples, and the great nobles and merchants who were landed proprietors; and, including that still in communal or tribal possession,[2] a very large proportion was cultivated on lease. The usual practice in hiring land for cultivation was for the tenant to pay his rent in kind, by assigning a certain proportion of the crop, generally a third or a half, to the owner, who advanced the seed-corn.[3] The tenant was bound to till the land and raise a crop, and should he neglect to do so he had to pay the owner what was reckoned as the average rent of the land, and he had also to break up the land and plough it before handing it back. Elaborate regulations were in force to adjust the landowner's duties and responsibilities on the one hand, and what was due to him from his tenant on the other. As the rent of a field was usually reckoned at harvest, and its amount depended on the size of the crop, it would have been unfair that damage to the crop from flood or storm should have been made up by the tenant; such a loss was shared equally by the owner of the field and the

---

[1] Herodotus (I., 193) bears witness to the great fertility of Babylonia, stating that of all countries of the ancient world it was the most fruitful in grain.

[2] On the early system of tribal ownership, which survived even the Kassite conquest and requisitions, see below, pp. 249 ff.

[3] In fact, the *métayer* system was in force, the landlord finding the cattle, agricultural implements, and seed for the culture of the fields; cf. Johns, "Schweich Lectures," p. 5.

farmer, though, if the latter had already paid his rent at the time the damage occurred, he could not make a claim for repayment.   There is evidence that disputes were frequent not only between farmers and landowners, but also between farmers and shepherds, for the latter, when attempting to find pasture for their flocks, often allowed their sheep to feed off the farmers' fields in spring.   For such cases a scale of compensation was fixed.   If the damage was done in the early spring, when the plants were still small, the farmer harvested the crop and received a price in kind as compensation from the shepherd.   But if it occurred later in the year, when the sheep had been brought in from the meadows and turned on to the common land by the city-gate, the damage was heavier ; in such a case the shepherd had to take over the crop and compensate the farmer heavily.

The king himself was a very large owner of cattle and sheep, and he levied tribute on the flocks and herds of his subjects.   The owners were bound to bring the young cattle and lambs, that were due from them, to the central town of the district in which they dwelt, and they were then collected and added to the royal flocks and herds.   If the owners attempted to hold back any that were due as tribute, they were afterwards forced to incur the extra expense and trouble of driving the beasts to Babylon.   The flocks and herds owned by the king and the great temples were probably enormous, and yielded a considerable revenue in themselves apart from the tribute and taxes levied upon private owners. Shepherds and herdsmen were placed in charge of them, and they were divided into groups under head-men, who arranged the districts in which the herds and flocks were to be grazed.   The king received regular reports from his chief shepherds and herdsmen, and it was the duty of the governors of the larger towns and districts of Babylonia to make tours of inspection and see that due care was taken of the royal flocks.   The sheep-shearing for all the flocks that were pastured near the capital took place in Babylon, and the king used to send out summonses to his chief shepherds to inform them of the day when the shearing would take place.[1]   Separate flocks,

[1] See the five letters of Ammi-zaduga, in " Letters of Ham.," III., pp. 162 ff.

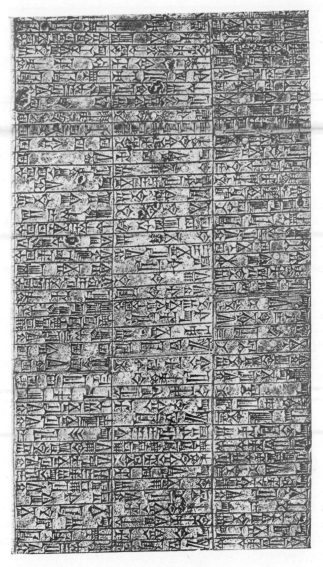

PORTION OF THE CODE OF HAMMURABI, COLS. 6-8.
After Délég. en Perse, Mém. IV, pl. 4.

that were royal and priestly property, were sometimes under the same chief officer, a fact that tends to show that the king himself exercised a considerable measure of control over the sacred revenues.

In the regulation of the pastoral and agricultural life of the community, custom played a very important part, and this was recognized and enforced by royal authority. Carelessness in looking after cattle was punished by fine, but the owner was not held responsible for damage unless negligence could be proved on his part. Thus a bull might go wild at any time and gore a man, who would have no redress against its owner. But if the beast was known to be vicious, and its owner had not blunted its horns nor shut it up, he was obliged to pay compensation for damage. On the other hand, the owner of cattle or asses, who had hired them out, could exact compensation for the loss or ill-treatment of his beasts. These were framed on the principle that the hirer was responsible only for damage or loss which he could reasonably have prevented. If, for example, a lion killed a hired ox or ass in the open country, or if an ox was killed by lightning, the loss fell upon the owner and not on the man who had hired the beast. But if the hirer killed the ox through carelessness or by beating it unmercifully, or if the beast broke its leg while in his charge, he had to restore to the owner another ox in its place. For less serious damage to the beast the hirer paid compensation on a fixed scale.[1] It is clear that such regulations merely gave the royal sanction to long-established custom.

Both for looking after their herds and for the cultivation of their estates the landed proprietors depended to a great extent upon hired herdsmen and farmers; and any dishonesty on the part of the latter with regard to cattle, provender, or seed-corn was severely punished. A theft of provender, for example, had to be made good, and the culprit ran the additional risk of having his hands cut off. Heavy compensation was exacted from any man, who, for his own profit, hired out oxen which had

---

[1] For the loss of an eye the hirer paid half the beast's value, and a quarter for a broken horn, the loss of the tail, or a torn muzzle.

been entrusted to his charge; while, if a farmer stole
the seed-corn supplied for the field he had hired, so that
he produced no crop to share with the owner, not only
had he to pay compensation but he was liable to be torn
in pieces by oxen in the field he should have cultivated.[1]
In the age of Hammurabi the heavier penalties were no
doubt largely traditional, having come down from a more
barbarous time when dishonesty could only be kept in
check by strong measures. Their retention among the
statutes doubtless acted as an effective deterrent, and a
severe sentence, if carried out occasionally in the case of
an aggravated offence, would have sufficed to maintain
respect for the regulations.

In the semi-tropical climate of Babylonia the canals
played a vitally important part for the successful prosecution of agriculture, and it was to the royal interest to
see that their channels were kept in a proper state of
repair and cleaned out at regular intervals. There is
evidence that nearly every king of the First Dynasty of
Babylon cut new canals and extended the system of
irrigation and transport by water that he had inherited.
The rich silt carried down by the rivers was deposited
partly in the canals, especially in those sections nearer
the main stream, with the result that the bed of a canal
was constantly in process of being raised. Every year
it was necessary to dig this deposit out and pile it upon
the banks. Every year the banks rose higher and
higher, until a point was reached when the labour
involved in getting rid of the silt became greater than
that required for cutting a new channel. Hence sections
of a canal were constantly being recut alongside the old
channel, and it is probable that many of the canals, the
cutting of which is commemorated in the texts, were
really reconstructions of older streams, the beds of which
had become hopelessly silted up.

At the present day the traveller in certain parts of
Babylonia comes across the raised embankments of old
canals extending across the plain within a short distance
of each other, and their parallel course is to be explained
by the process of recutting, which was put off as long as
possible, but was at last necessitated by the growing

[1] See § 256 of the Code.

height of the banks.   As the bed of a canal gradually
rose too, the high banks served the purpose of retaining
the stream, and these were often washed away by the
flood-water which came down from the hills in spring.
An interesting letter has been preserved, that was written
by Hammurabi's grandson, Abi-eshu', who describes a
sudden rise of this sort in the level of the Irnina Canal
so that it overflowed its banks.[1]   At the time the king
was building a palace in the city of Kâr-Irnina, which
was supplied by the Irnina Canal, and every year a
certain amount of work was put into the building.   At
the time the letter was written little more than a third
of the year's work had been done, when the building-
operations were stopped by flood, the canal having
overflowed its banks so that the water rose right up to
the town-wall.

It was the duty of the local governors to see that
the canals were kept in good repair, and they had the
power of requisitioning labour from the inhabitants of
villages and the owners of land situated on or near the
banks.   In return, the villagers had the right of fishing
in the waters of a canal along the section in their charge,
and any poaching by other villagers in their part of the
stream was strictly forbidden.   On one occasion in the
reign of Samsu-iluna, Hammurabi's son, fishermen from
the village of Rabim went down in their boats to the
district of Shakanim, and caught fish there contrary to
local custom.   So the inhabitants of Shakanim com-
plained to the king of this infringement of their rights,
and he sent a palace-official to the authorities of Sippar,
in the jurisdiction of which the villages in question lay,
with instructions to inquire into the matter and take
steps to prevent any poaching in the future.   Fishing
by line and net was a regular industry, and the preservation of rights in local waters was jealously guarded.

The larger canals were fed directly from the river,
especially along the Euphrates, whose banks were lower
than those of the swifter Tigris.   But along the latter
river, and also along the banks of the canals, it will be
obvious that some means had to be employed to raise
the water for purposes of irrigation from the main

[1] Cf. "Letters of Hammurabi," III., pp. 130 ff.

channel to the higher level of the land. Reference is made in the Babylonian inscriptions to irrigation-machines,[1] and, although their exact form and construction are not described, they must have been very similar to those employed at the present day. The most primitive method of raising water, which is commoner to-day in Egypt than in Mesopotamia, is the *shadduf*, which is worked by hand. It consists of a beam supported in the centre; and at one end a bucket is suspended for raising the water, while at the other end is fixed a counter-weight. Thus comparatively little labour is required to raise the bucket when full. That this contrivance was employed on the Tigris is proved by an Assyrian bas-relief, found at Kuyunjik, with representations of the *shadduf* in operation. Two of them are being used, the one above the other, to raise the water to successive levels. These were probably the contrivances usually employed by the early Babylonians for raising the water to the level of their fields, and the fact that they were light and easily removed must have made them tempting objects to the dishonest farmer. A scale of compensation was therefore in force, regulating the payments to be made to the owner by a detected thief. From the fact that these varied, according to the class and value of the machine he stole, we may infer that other contrivances, of a heavier and more permanent character, were also employed.

One of these must certainly have corresponded to a very primitive arrangement that is in general use at the present day in Mesopotamia, particularly along the Tigris, where the banks are high and steep. A recess or cutting with perpendicular sides is driven into the bank, and a wooden spindle is supported on struts in a horizontal position over the recess, which resembles a well with one side opening on to the river. A rope running over the spindle is fastened to a skin in which the water is raised from the river, being drawn up by horses, donkeys, or cattle harnessed to the other end of the rope. To empty the skin by hand into the irrigation channel would, of course, entail considerable time and labour, and, to avoid this necessity, an ingenious contrivance is employed. The

[1] They are also referred to by Herodotus (I., 193), but not described.

skin is sewn up, not in the form of a closed bag, but of a bag ending in a long narrow funnel. While the skin is being filled and drawn to the top, the funnel is kept raised by a thin line running over a lower spindle and fastened off to the main rope, so that both are pulled up together by the beasts. The positions of the spindles and the length of the ropes are so adjusted, that the end of the funnel stops just above a wooden trough on the bank below the struts, while the rest of the skin is drawn up higher and shoots its water through the funnel into the trough. The trough is usually made from half the trunk of a date-palm, hollowed out, and one end leads to the irrigation-channel on the bank. To give the beasts a better purchase in pulling up the weight of water, an inclined plane is cut in the ground, sloping away from the machine, and up and down this the beasts are driven, the skin filling and emptying itself automatically. To increase the supply of water, two skins are often employed side by side, each with its own tackle and set of beasts, and, as one is drawn up full, the other is let down empty. Thus a continuous flow of water is secured, and not more than one man or boy is required to keep each set of beasts moving. No more effective or simpler method could be devised of raising water to a considerable height, and there can be no doubt that, at the period of the First Dynasty, cattle were employed not only for ploughing, but for working primitive irrigation-machines of this character.

On the Euphrates, where the river-banks are lower, a simple form of water-wheel was probably in use then as it is to-day, wherever there was sufficient current to work one. And the advantage of this form of machine is that, so long as it is in order, it can be unlocked at will and kept working without supervision day and night. The wheel is formed of stripped boughs and branches nailed together, with spokes joining the outer rims to a roughly hewn axle. Around the outer rim are tied a series of rough earthenware cups or bottles, and a few rude paddles are fixed to the wheel, projecting beyond the rim. The wheel is then set up in place near the bank of the river, its axle resting on pillars of rough masonry. The current turns the wheel, and the

bottles, dipping below the surface, are raised up full,
and empty their water into a wooden trough at the top.
The banks of the Euphrates are usually sloping, and
the water is conducted from the trough to the fields
along a small aqueduct or earthen embankment.   Such
wheels to-day are usually set up where there is a slight
drop in the river-bed and the water runs swiftly over
shallows.   In order to span the difference in level
between the fields and the summer height of the stream
the wheels are often huge contrivances, and their rough
construction causes them to creak and groan as they
turn with the current.   In a convenient place in the
river several of these are sometimes set up side by side,
and their noise when at work can be heard at a great
distance.[1]

It is not unlikely that the later Sumerians had
already evolved these primitive forms of irrigation-
machine, and that the Babylonians of the First Dynasty
merely inherited them and passed them on to their
successors.   When once invented they were incapable
of very great improvement.   In the one the skin must
always remain a skin ; in the other the wheel must
always be lightly constructed of boughs, or the strength
of the current would not suffice to turn it.   We have seen
reason to believe that, in the palace of Nebuchadnezzar II.
at Babylon, the triple well in the north-west corner
may be best explained as having formed the water-
supply for a hydraulic machine, consisting of an endless
chain of buckets passing over a great wheel.   Such is
a very common form of raising water in Babylonia at
the present day.   It is true that in some of these
machines the wheel for the buckets is still geared by
means of rough wooden cogs to the long pole or winch,
turned by beasts, who move round in a circle.   But it is
very unlikely that the early Babylonians had evolved
the principle of the cogged wheel, and it was probably
not till the period of the later Assyrian empire that
bronze was so plentiful that it could have been used
in sufficient quantity for buckets on an endless chain.
There seems reason to believe that Sennacherib himself

[1] At Hit on the Euphrates are some of the largest water-wheels in Mesopotamia, a line of them being built across one portion of the river.

introduced an innovation when he employed metal in the construction of the machines that supplied water to his palace ;[1] and we may infer that even in the Neo-Babylonian period a contrivance of that sort was still a royal luxury, and that the farmer continued to use the more primitive machines, sanctioned by immemorial usage, which he could make with his own hands.

The manner in which the agricultural implements employed in early Babylonia have survived to the present day is well illustrated by their form of plough, which closely resembles that still in use in parts of Syria. We have no representation of the plough of

FIG. 40.

THE OLD BABYLONIAN FORM OF PLOUGH IN USE.

The drawing is taken from seal-impressions on a tablet of the Kassite period.
[After Clay.]

the First Babylonian Dynasty, but this was doubtless the same as that of the Kassite period, of which a very interesting representation has recently been recovered. On a tablet found at Nippur and dated in the fourth year of Nazi-Maruttash, are several impressions of a cylinder-seal engraved with a representation of three men ploughing.[2]   The plough is drawn by two humped bulls, or zebu, who are being driven by one of the men, while another holds the two handles of the plough and guides it.   The third man has a bag of seed-corn slung

[1] Cf. "Cun. Texts in the Brit. Mus.," XXVI., p. 26.
[2] See Fig. 40, and cf. Clay, "Documents from the Temple Archives of Nippur," in the "Museum Publications of the Univ. of Pennsylvania," Vol. II., No. 2 (1912), p. 65, from which the drawing has been taken.

over his shoulders and is in the act of feeding seed with his right hand into a tube or grain-drill, down which it passed into the furrow made by the plough.   At the top of the tube is a bowl, with a hole in the bottom opening on to the tube, which acted as a funnel and enabled the sower to drop the seed in without scattering it.   This is the earliest representation of the Babylonian plough that we possess, and its value is increased by the fact that the plough is seen in operation.   The same seed-drill occurs in three later representations. One of these also dates from the Kassite period, being found upon a boundary-stone of the period of Meli-Shipak II.,[1] on which it is sculptured as the sacred symbol of Geshtinna, the goddess of the plough.[2]   The other two are of the Assyrian period, one being represented in enamelled brick on the walls of the palace at Khorsabad,[3] the other being carved among the symbols on the Black Stone of Esarhaddon, on which he gives an account of his restoration of Babylon.[4]   Similar ploughs, with grain-drills of precisely the same structure, are still used in Syria at the present time.[5]

Before ploughing and sowing his land the Babylonian farmer prepared it for irrigation by dividing it up into a number of small squares or oblong patches, each separated from the others by a low bank of earth. Some of the banks, that ran lengthways through the field, were made into small channels, the ends of which were connected with his main irrigation-stream.   No gates nor sluices were employed, and, when he wished to water one of his fields, he simply broke away the bank opposite one of his small channels and let the water

---

[1] See Plate XXI., opposite p. 248.

[2] Cf. Frank, " Das Symbol der Göttin Geštinna," in the "Hilprecht Anniversary Volume " (1909), pp. 164 ff.

[3] Cf. Place, "Ninive et l'Assyrie," III., pl. 31 ; the plough is there depicted in yellow enamel on a blue ground.

[4] See Budge and King, "Guide to the Babylonian and Assyrian Antiquities in the British Museum," 2nd ed. (1908), p. 221, Figure.   George Rawlinson ("Ancient Monarchies," I., p. 567) had already explained the seed-drill in the plough on Esarhaddon's stone.

[5] The Babylonian word for plough, ḳanḳannu, has also survived in the Syriac kenkĕnā, and the Rabbinic ḳanḳannā ; cf. Frank, op. cit., p. 165 f. The use of the determinative erû, "copper," before the Babylonian word, suggests that metal was employed for the plough-share from a very early period.

A MODERN GUFA.
Photo. by Messrs. Underwood & Underwood.

flow into it. When it reached the part of his land he wished to water, he blocked the channel with a little earth and broke down its bank so that the water flowed over one of the small squares and soaked it.

He could then repeat the process with the next square, and so on, afterwards returning to the main channel and stopping the flow of water by blocking up the hole he had made in the bank. Such is the present process of irrigation in Mesopotamia, and there is no doubt that it was adopted by the early Babylonians. It was extremely simple, but needed care and vigilance, especially when water was being carried into several parts of an estate at once. Moreover, one main channel often supplied the fields of several farmers, and, in return for his share of the water, it was the duty of each man to keep its banks, where it crossed his land, in repair. If he failed to do so and the water forced a breach and flooded his neighbour's field, he had to pay compensation in kind for any crop that was ruined, and, if he could not pay, his goods were sold, and his neighbours, whose fields had been damaged, shared the proceeds of the sale. Similarly, if a farmer left his water running and forgot to shut it off, he had to pay compensation for any damage it might do to a neigh-bouring crop.

The date-palm formed the chief secondary source of the country's wealth, for it grew luxuriantly in the alluvium and supplied the Babylonians with one of their principal articles of diet.[1] From it, too, they made a fermented wine, and a species of flour for baking; its sap yielded palm-sugar, and its fibrous bark was suitable for weaving ropes, while its trunk furnished a light but tough building-material. The early Baby-lonian kings encouraged the laying out of date-planta-tions and the planting of gardens and orchards; and special regulations were made with that object in view. For a man could obtain a field for the purpose without paying a yearly rent. He could plant and tend it for four years, and in the fifth year of his tenancy the

---

[1] On the cultivation of the date-palm and the Babylonian method of artificial fertilization, see Herodotus, I., 193; and cp. Tylor, " Proc. Soc. Bibl. Arch.," XII. (1890), pp. 383 ff.

N

original owner of the land took half the garden in pay-ment, while the planter kept the other half for himself. Care was taken to see that the bargain was properly carried out, for, if a bare patch had been left in the plantation, it was reckoned in the planter's half; and should the tenant neglect the trees during his first four years of occupation, he was still liable to plant the whole plot without receiving his half of it, and he had to pay compensation in addition, which varied in amount according to the original condition of the land. In this way the authorities ensured that land should not be taken over and allowed to deteriorate. For the hire of a plantation the rent was fixed at two-thirds of

FIG. 41.

ASSYRIAN KELEK ON THE TIGRIS.

[After Layard.]

its produce, the tenant providing all labour and supply-ing the necessary irrigation-water.

From the royal letters of the period of the First Dynasty we know that the canals were not only used for irrigation, but also as water-ways for transport. The letters contain directions for the bringing of corn, dates, sesame-seed, and wood to Babylon, and we also know that wool and oil were carried in bulk by water. For transport of heavy goods on the Tigris and Euphrates it is possible that rafts, floated on inflated skins, were used from an early period, though the earliest evidence we have of their employment is furnished by the bas-reliefs from Nineveh. Such rafts have survived to the present day,[1] and they are specially adapted for the transport of heavy materials, for they are carried down by the current, and are kept in the main stream by means of huge sweeps or oars. Being formed only of logs of wood and skins, they are not costly, for wood was plentiful in the upper course of the rivers. At the end of the journey, after the goods were landed, they were broken up, the logs being sold at a profit, and the skins, after being deflated, were packed on donkeys to return up stream by caravan.[2] The use of such *keleks*

FIG. 42.

THE ASSYRIAN PROTOTYPE OF THE GUFA.

[From a bas-relief in the British Museum.]

can only have been general when through-river communication was general, but, since we know that Hammurabi included Assyria within his dominions, it is not impossible that they may date from at least as early a period as the First Dynasty. For purely local traffic in small bulk the *gufa*, or light coracle, may have been used in Babylonia at this time, for its representation on the Assyrian monuments corresponds exactly with its structure at the present time as used on the lower Tigris and Euphrates. The *gufa* is formed of wicker-work coated with bitumen, but some of those represented on the sculptures from Nineveh appear to

---

[1] Even the modern Arabic name for such a raft, *kelek,* is derived from the Assyrian word for the same form of vessel, *kalaku,* as was first pointed out by Johnson.

[2] This is the custom at the present day, and we know that it also existed at the time of Herodotus (cf. I., 194) ; but his description of the structure of the "boats" applies, not to the raft or *kelek*, but to the *gufa*, a small coracle, which was used only for local traffic.

have been covered with skins as in the description of Herodotus.[1]

In the texts and inscriptions of the early period ships are referred to, and these were undoubtedly the only class of vessels employed on the canals for conveying supplies in bulk by water. The size of such ships, or barges, was reckoned by the amount of grain they were capable of carrying, measured by the *gur*, the largest measure of capacity. We find vessels of very different size referred to, varying from five to seventy-five *gur* and over. The larger class probably resembled the sailing barges and ferry-boats in use to-day,[2] which are built of heavy timbers and have flat bottoms when intended for the transport of beasts. In

Fig. 43.

ASSYRIAN RAFT OF LOGS ON THE TIGRIS.

[From a bas-relief in the British Museum.]

Babylon at the time of the First Dynasty a boat-builder's fee for constructing a vessel of sixty *gur* was fixed at two shekels of silver, and it was proportionately less for vessels of smaller capacity. A boat-builder was held responsible for unsound work, and should defects develop in a vessel within a year of its being launched, he was obliged to strengthen or rebuild it at his own expense. Boatmen and sailors formed a numerous class in the community, and the yearly wage of a man in such employment was fixed at sixty *gur* of corn. Larger vessels carried crews under the command of a captain, or chief boatman, and there is evidence that the vessels owned by the king included many of the larger type, which he employed for carrying grain, wool

[1] See Fig. 42; and cf. p. 179, n. 2.   [2] See Plate XV., opposite p. 184.

and dates, as well as wood and stone for building-operations.

It is probable that there were regular officials, under the king's control, who collected dues and looked after the water-transport in the separate sections of the river, or canal, on which they were stationed. It would have been their duty to report any damage or defect in the channel to the king, who would send orders to the local governor that the necessary repairs should be put in hand. One of Hammurabi's letters deals with the blocking of a canal at Erech, about which he had received such reports. The dredging already undertaken had not been thoroughly done, so that the canal had soon silted up again and boats were prevented from reaching the city ; in his letter Hammurabi sent pressing orders that the canal was to be rendered navigable within three days.[1] Special regulations were also in force with regard to the respective responsibilities of boat-owners, boatmen and their clients. If a boat-man hired a boat from its owner, he was held responsible for it, and had to replace it should it be lost or sunk ; but if he refloated it, he had only to pay the owner half its value for the damage it had sustained. Boatmen were also responsible for the safety of goods, such as corn, wool, oil or dates, which they had undertaken to carry for hire, and they had to make good any total loss due to their own carelessness. Collisions between two vessels were also provided for, and should one of the boats have been moored at the time, the boatman of the other vessel had to pay compensation for the boat that was sunk as well as for the lost cargo, the owner of the latter estimating its value upon oath. Many cases in the courts probably arose out of loss or damage to goods in course of transport by water.

The commercial activities of Babylon at the time of the First Dynasty led to a considerable growth in the size of the larger cities, which ceased to be merely local centres of distribution and began to engage in commerce farther afield. Between Babylonia and Elam close commercial relations had long been maintained, but Hammurabi's western conquests opened up new markets

[1] Cf. "Letters," III., p. 16 f.

to the merchants of his capital.   The great trade-route
up the Euphrates and into Syria was no longer blocked
by military outposts and fortifications, placed there in
the vain attempt to keep back the invasion of Amorite
tribes ; and the trade in pottery with Carchemish, of
which we have evidence under the later kings of the
First Dynasty,[1] is significant of the new relations
established between Babylonia and the West.   The
great merchants were, as a body, members of the upper
class, and while they themselves continued to reside in
Babylon, they employed traders who carried their goods
abroad for them by caravan.

Even Hammurabi could not entirely guarantee the
safety of such traders, for attacks by brigands were then
as common in the Nearer East as at the present day ;
and there was always the additional risk that a caravan
might be captured by the enemy, if it ventured too near
a hostile frontier.   In such circumstances the king saw
to it that the loss of the goods was not borne by the
agent, who had already risked his life and liberty in
undertaking their transport.   For, if such an agent had
been forced in the course of his journey to give up some
of the goods he was carrying, he had to specify the
exact amount on oath on his return, and he was then
acquitted of all responsibility.   But if it could be
proved before the elders of the city that he had
attempted to cheat his employer by misappropriating
money or goods to his own use, he was obliged to pay
the merchant three times the value of the goods he had
taken.   The law was not one-sided and afforded the
agent equal protection in relation to his more powerful
employer ; for should the latter be convicted of an
attempt to defraud his agent, by denying that the
due amount had been returned to him, he had to pay his
agent as compensation six times the amount in dispute.
The merchant always advanced the goods or money
with which to trade, and the fact that he could, if he
wished to do so, fix his own profit at double the value
of the capital, is an indication of the very satisfactory
returns obtained at this period from foreign commerce.
But the more usual practice was for merchant and trader

[1] See above, p. 127 f.

to share the profits between them, and, in the event of the latter making such bad bargains that there was a loss on his journey, he had to refund to the merchant the full value of the goods he had received. At the time of the First Dynasty asses and donkeys were the beasts of burden employed for carrying merchandise, for the horse was as yet a great rarity and was not in general use in Babylonia until after the Kassite conquest.[1]

A large number of the First Dynasty contracts relate to commercial journeys of this sort, and record the terms of the bargains entered into between the interested parties. Such partnerships were sometimes concluded for a single journey, but more often for longer periods of time. The merchant always demanded a properly executed receipt for the money or goods he advanced to the trader, and the latter received one for any deposit or pledge he might have made in token of his good faith. In reckoning their accounts on the conclusion of a journey, only such amounts as were specified in the receipts were regarded as legal obligations, and, if either party had omitted to obtain his proper documents, he did so at his own risk. The market-places of the capital and the larger towns must have been the centres where such business arrangements were transacted, and official scribes were probably always in attendance to draw up the terms of any bargain in the presence of other merchants and traders, who acted as witnesses. These had their names enumerated at the close of the document, and since they were chosen from local residents, some were always at hand to testify in case of any subsequent dispute.

The town-life in Babylonia at this time must have had many features in common with that of any provincial town in Mesopotamia to-day, except that the paternal government of the First Dynasty undoubtedly saw to it that the streets were kept clean, and made strenuous efforts to ensure that private houses should be soundly built and maintained in proper repair. We have already followed out the lines of some of the streets in ancient Babylon,[2] and noted that, while the

[1] See below, p. 215 f.   [2] See above, pp. 82 ff.

foundations of the houses were usually of burnt brick, crude brick was invariably employed for their upper structure. They were probably all buildings of a single story, their flat mud roofs, supported on a layer of brush-wood with poles for rafters, serving as a sleeping-place for their inmates during the hot season. Contemporary evidence goes to show that, before the period of Hammurabi, private houses had not been very solidly built, for his legislation contemplates the possibility of their falling and injuring the inmates. In the case of new houses the law fixed the responsibility upon the builder, and we may infer that the very heavy penalties exacted for bad work led to a marked improvement in construction. For, when such a newly built house fell and crushed the owner so that he died, the builder him-self was liable to be put to death. Should the fall of the house kill the owner's son, the builder's own son was slain; and, if one or more of the owner's slaves were killed, the builder had to restore him slave for slave. Any damage to the owner's possessions was also made good by the builder, who had in addition to rebuild the house at his own cost, or repair any portion of it that had fallen. On the other hand, payment for sound work was guaranteed, and the fact that the scale of payment was fixed by the area of ground covered by the building, is direct evidence that the houses of the period consisted of no more than one story. The beginning of town-planning on systematic lines, with streets running through and crossing each other at right angles, of which we have noted evidence at Babylon, may perhaps date from the Hammurabi period; but no confident opinion on the point can be expressed until further excavation has been undertaken in the earlier strata of the city.[1]

We have recovered from contemporary documents a very full picture of family life in early Babylonia, for the duties of the separate members of a family to one

[1] The fact that, so far as they have yet been examined, the lines of the streets appear to have altered little during the time from the First Dynasty to the Neo-Babylonian and Persian periods, is at least presumptive evidence in favour of assigning the main lines of the street-plan on the Merkes Mound to the age of Hammurabi and his descendants; see above, p. 85 f.

I. A SMALL KELEK ON THE TIGRIS AT BAGHDAD.
II. FERRY-BOATS ON THE EUPHRATES AT BIRFJIK.

another were regulated by law, and any change in relationship was duly attested and recorded in legal form before witnesses. Minute regulations were in force with regard to marriage, divorce and the adoption and maintenance of children, while the provision and disposal of marriage-portions, the rights of widows and the laws of inheritance were all controlled by the state upon traditional lines. Perhaps the most striking feature in the social system was the recognized status of the wife in the Babylonian household, and the extremely independent position enjoyed by women in general. Any marriage to be legally binding had to be accompanied by a duly executed and attested marriage-contract, and without this necessary preliminary a woman was not regarded as a wife in the legal sense. On the other hand, when once such a marriage-contract had been drawn up and attested, its inviolability was stringently secured. Chastity on the wife's part was enforced under severe penalty;[1] but on the other hand the husband's responsibility to maintain his wife in a position suitable to their circumstances was also recognized.

The law gave the wife ample protection, and in the case of the husband's desertion allowed her, under certain conditions, to become the legal wife of another man. If the husband wilfully deserted her and left his city under no compulsion, she might remarry and he could not reclaim her on his return. But if his desertion was involuntary, as in the case of a man taken in battle and carried off as a prisoner, this rule did not apply; and the wife was allowed to shape her action during his absence in accordance with the condition of her husband's affairs. The regulations in such a case were extraordinarily in favour of the woman. If the husband was possessed of property sufficient to maintain the wife during the period of his captivity, she had no excuse for remarriage;

---

[1] In the case of proved adultery, drowning was the penalty for the guilty parties; but the husband could save his wife, if he wished to do so, by appeal to the king. If the charge was brought by the husband himself, a woman could clear herself by swearing to her own innocence; but, if others brought the charge, she had to submit to the ordeal by water. She plunged into the Euphrates, and should she be drowned, it was regarded as proof of guilt; but if she got safely to the bank her innocence was established. It was believed that the Sacred River would see that justice was done; see §§ 131 f. of the Code, and cp. § 2.

and, should she become the wife of another man, the
marriage was not regarded as legal and she was liable
to the extreme penalty for adultery. But if the husband
had not sufficient means for his wife's maintenance, it
was recognized that she would be thrown on her own
resources, and she was permitted to remarry. The returning captive could claim his wife, but the children
of the second marriage remained with their own father.
The laws of divorce, too, safeguarded the woman's
interests, and only dealt with her severely if it could be
proved that she had wasted her household and failed in
her duty as a wife; in such a case she could be divorced
without compensation, and even reduced to the condition of a slave in her husband's house. But, in the
absence of such proof, her maintenance was fully
secured; for the husband had to return her marriage-
portion, and, if there had been none, he must make her
an allowance. She also had the custody of her children,
for whose maintenance and education the husband had
to provide; and, at his death, the divorced wife and her
children could inherit a share of his estate.[1] The con-
traction of a permanent disease by the wife was also
held to constitute no grounds for a divorce.

Such regulations throw an interesting light on the
position of the married woman in the Babylonian
community, which was not only unexampled in
antiquity but compares favourably, in point of freedom
and independence, with her status in many countries
of modern Europe. Still more remarkable were the
privileges capable of attainment by unmarried women
of the upper class, who in certain circumstances were
entitled to hold property in their own names and
engage in commercial undertakings. To secure such a
position a woman took vows, by which she became a
member of a class of votaries attached to one of the
chief temples in Babylon, Sippar, or another of the
great cities.[2] The duties of such women were not

---

[1] The wife could also divorce her husband, if she could prove that her past
life had been seemly; she then took her marriage-portion and returned to her
father's house. For laws as to breach of promise (based on the payment of
the bride-price), see §§ 159–161 of the Code.

[2] There was an important guild of votaries attached to E-babbar, the
temple of the Sun-god at Sippar, a second at Ur, and another at E-sagila, the
great temple of Marduk at Babylon, where they had special privileges.

sacerdotal, and, though they generally lived together in a special building, or convent, attached to the temple, they enjoyed a position of great influence and independence in the community. A votary could possess property in her own name, and on taking her vows was provided with a portion by her father, exactly as though she were being given in marriage. This was vested in herself, and did not become the property of her order, nor of the temple to which she was attached; it was devoted entirely to her maintenance, and after her father's death, her brothers looked after her interest, and she could farm the property out. Upon her death her portion returned to her own family, unless her father assigned her the privilege of bequeathing it; but any property she inherited she could bequeath, and she had not to pay taxes on it. She had considerable freedom, could engage in commerce on her own account, and, should she desire to do so, could leave the convent and contract a form of marriage.

While securing her these privileges, the vows she took entailed corresponding responsibilities. Even when married, a votary was still obliged to remain a virgin, and, should her husband desire children, she could not bear them herself, but must provide him with a maid or concubine. But, in spite of this disability, she was secured in her position as the permanent head of the household. The concubine, though she might bear the husband children, was always the wife's inferior, and should she attempt to put herself on a level with the votary, the latter could brand her and put her with the female slaves; while in the event of the concubine proving barren, she could be sold. Unmarried votaries, too, could live in houses of their own and dispose of their time and money in their own way. But a high standard of commercial and social morality was expected from them, and severe penalties were imposed for its infringement. No votary, for example, was permitted to open a beer-shop, and should she even enter one, she ran the risk of being put to death. An unmarried votary also enjoyed the status of a married woman, and the penalty for slandering one was branding in the forehead. That the social position enjoyed by a votary was considerable is proved by the fact that many women of good family, and even members of the royal house, took vows.

It is a striking fact that women of an Eastern race should have achieved such a position of independence at the beginning of the second millennium. The explanation is perhaps to be sought in the great part already played by commerce in Babylonian life. Among contemporary races, occupied mainly by agriculture and war, woman's activity was necessarily restricted to the rearing of children and to the internal economy of the household. But with the growth of Babylonian trade and commercial enterprise, it would seem that the demand arose, on the part of women of the upper class, to take part in activities in which they considered themselves capable of joining.[1] The success of the experiment was doubtless due in part to the high standard of morality exacted, and in part to the prestige conferred by association with the religious cult.

The administration of justice at the period of the First Dynasty was carried out by duly appointed courts of law under the supervision of the king. The judges were appointed by the crown, and a check was put upon any arbitrary administration of the law by the fact that the elders of the city sat with them and assisted them in hearing and sifting evidence. When once a judgment had been given and recorded, it was irrevocable, and if any judge attempted to alter such a decision, he was expelled from his judgment-seat and debarred from exercising judicial functions in the future. The regulation was probably intended to prevent the possibility of subsequent bribery; and, if a litigant considered that justice had not been done, it was always open to him to appeal to the king. Hammurabi's letters prove that he exercised strict supervision, not only over the cases decided in the capital, but also over those which were tried in the other great cities of Babylonia, and it

---

[1] Prof. Myres, in commenting on the industrial status found for these unmarried women, remarks that, with manufactures and commerce standing so high in the economy of Babylonia, it is not to be wondered at if the social structure of the country developed some of the same features as begin to perplex our modern world : cf. "Dawn of Civilization," p. 97.

is clear that he attempted to stamp out corruption on the part of all those invested with authority. On one occasion he had been informed of a case of bribery in the town of Dûr-gurgurri, and he at once ordered the governor of the district to investigate the charge and send the guilty parties to Babylon for punishment. The bribe, too, was to be confiscated and despatched to Babylon under seal, a wise provision that would have tended to discourage those inclined to tamper with the course of justice, while at the same time it enriched the state.[1] The king probably tried all cases of appeal in person, when it was possible; but in distant cities he deputed this duty to local officials. Many of the cases that came before him arose from the extortions of money-lenders,[2] and the king had no mercy when fraud on their part was proved.

The relations maintained by the king with the numerous classes of the priesthood was also very close, and the control he exercised over the chief priests and their subordinates appears to have been as effective as that he maintained over the judicial authorities throughout the country. Under the Sumerians there had always been a tendency on the part of the more powerful members of the hierarchy to usurp the prerogatives of the crown,[3] but this danger appears to have been fully discounted under the rule of the Western Semites. One important section of the priestly body were the astrologers, whose duty it probably was to make periodical reports to the king on the conjunctions and movements of the heavenly bodies, with the object of ascertaining whether they portended good or evil to the state. The later Assyrian practice may well have had its origin at this period, and we may conclude that the regulation of the calendar was carried out in accordance with such advice. One of Hammurabi's letters has come down to us in which he writes to inform Sin-idinnam, his local governor of Larsa, that it had been decided to insert an intercalary month in the calendar. He writes that, as the year, that is the

---

[1] See " Letters of Hammurabi," III., pp. 20 ff.
[2] *Op. cit.*, III., pp. 23 ff., 26 f.
[3] Cf. " Sumer and Akkad," pp. 167 f., 172 f.

calendar, had a deficiency, the month that was beginning
was to be registered as the second Elul ; and he adds
the very practical reminder, that the insertion of the
extra month would not justify any postponement in the
payment of the regular tribute due from the city of
Larsa.[1] The lunar calendar of the Babylonians rendered
the periodical intercalation of months necessary, in order
that it should be made to correspond to the solar year ;
and the duty of watching for the earliest appearance of
the new moon and fixing the first day of each month,
was among the most important of the functions performed by the official astrologers.

In the naming of the year the priesthood must also
have played an important part, since the majority of the
events from which the years were named were of a
religious character.   The system, which was inherited
from the Sumerians, cannot have been a very convenient
one,[2] and no doubt it owed its retention to the sanctity
of the religious rites and associations attaching to it.
There can be little doubt that, normally, the naming of
the year took place at the New Year's Feast, and, when
the event commemorated in the formula was the installation of a chief priest or the dedication of temple-furniture, the royal act, we may assume, was performed on
the day the year was named.[3]   Often merely a provisional title was adopted from the preceding formula,
and then perhaps no ceremony of naming was held, unless
in the course of it a great victory, or other important
occurrence, was commemorated by the renaming of the
year.   The king must have consulted with his priestly
advisers before the close of the old year, and have settled

---

[1] Cf. "Letters," III., p. 12 f.   [2] Cf. "Sumer and Akkad," p. 57 f.
[3] Ungnad ("Beitr. z. Assyr.," VI., Hft. 3, p. 7 f.) has collected a number
of formulæ from documents, dated either on the first day of Nisan, or within
the first six days of the year, which suggest that this was the practice ;   even
the completion of the cutting of a canal might have been foreseen.   Very
rarely, a formula may have been framed from an important event of
the preceding year, perhaps occurring towards its close ; the defeat of Nîsin
in Sin-muballit's seventeenth date-formula is an instance in point, since one
document which bears the formula is dated on the sixth of Nisan.   But there
is little to be said for Poebel's theory (cf. "Babylonian Legal and Business
Documents," pp. 109 ff.), which is based on the assumption that this was the
usual practice.   For editions of the First Dynasty date-formulæ, see "Letters
and Inscriptions of Hammurabi," III., pp. 212 ff. ; Poebel, "Legal and
Business Documents," pp. 56 ff. ; Johns, "Year-Names of the First Dynasty
of Babylon" (1911) ; and Schorr, "Urkunden," pp. 582 ff.

on the new formula in good time to allow of its announcement in the outlying districts of the kingdom.

Another important religious class at this period was the guild of soothsayers, and they also appear to have been directly under the royal control.   This we gather from a letter of Ammi-ditana, one of the later kings of the First Dynasty, written to three high officials of Sippar, which illustrates the nature of their duties and the sort of occasion on which they were called upon to perform them.[1]   It had come to the king's knowledge that there was a scarcity of corn in Shagga, and since that town was in the administrative district of Sippar, he wrote to the officials concerned ordering them to send a supply thither.   But, before the corn was brought into the city, they were to consult the soothsayers, in order to ascertain whether the omens were favourable.   The method of inquiry is not specified, but it was probably liver-divination, which was in common use during all periods.[2]   Only if the omens proved favourable, was the corn to be brought into the town, and we may conclude that the king took this precaution as he feared that the scarcity of corn in Shagga was due to the anger of some local deity.   The astrologers would be able to ascertain the facts, and, in the event of their reporting un-favourably, no doubt the services of the local priesthood would have been called in.

We have already seen that flocks and herds which were owned by the great temples were sometimes pas-tured with those of the king, and there is abundant evidence that the king also superintended the collection of temple-revenues along with his own.   Collectors of both secular and ecclesiastical tribute sent reports directly to the king, and, if there was any deficit in the supply expected from a collector, he had to make it up himself.   From one of Hammurabi's letters, for example, we gather that two landowners, or money-lenders, had lent money or advanced seed-corn to certain farmers near the towns of Dûr-gurgurri and Rakhabu and along the Tigris, and in settlement of their claims had seized the crops, refusing to pay the proportion due

---

[1] See "Letters of Hammurabi," III., pp. 157 ff.
[2] See Jastrow, "Religion," Bd. II., *passim*.

to Bît-il-kittim, the great temple of the Sun-god at
Larsa.   The governor of Larsa, the principal city in the
district, had rightly, as the representative of the palace,
caused the tax-collector to make up the deficiency, but
Hammurabi, on receiving the subordinate officer's complaint, referred the matter back to the governor, and we
may infer from similar cases that the defaulting parties
had to make good the loss and submit to fines or punishment.[1]   The document throws an interesting light on
the methods of government administration, and the
manner in which the king gave personal supervision to
the smallest details.

It will be obvious that for the administration of the
country a large body of officials were required, and of
their number two classes, of a semi-military character,
enjoyed the king's special favour and protection.   They
were placed in charge of public works and looked after
and controlled the public slaves, and they probably also
had a good deal to do with the collection of the revenue.
As payment for their duties, they were each granted
land with a house and garden ; they were assigned sheep
and cattle to stock their land, and in addition they
received a regular salary.   They were, in a sense, personal retainers of the king, and were liable to be sent
at any moment on a special mission.   Disobedience was
severely punished, for if such an officer, when detailed
for special service, hired a substitute, he was liable to
be put to death and the substitute could take his office.
Sometimes an officer was sent to take charge of a distant
garrison for a long period, and when this was done his
home duties were performed by another man, who temporarily occupied his house and land, and gave it back
to the officer on his return.   If the officer had a son
old enough to perform the duty in his father's absence,
he was allowed to do so ; and, if he was too young, his
maintenance was paid for out of the estate.   Should
the officer fail to arrange, before his departure, for the
proper cultivation of his land and the discharge of his
local duties, another could take his place after the lapse

---

[1] See " Letters," III., pp. 49 ff.   From a letter of Abi-eshu' (*op. cit.*, p.
153 f.), we gather that the king held the merchants of Sippar ultimately
responsible for their city's tribute.

IMPRESSIONS OF BABYLONIAN CYLINDER-SEALS.
Brit. Mus., No. 89771, 89588. 89110, 89367.

of a year, and on his return he could not reclaim his land or office. When on garrison duty, or on special service, he ran the risk of capture by the enemy, and in that event his ransom was assured. For if his own means did not suffice, the sum had to be paid from the treasury of the local temple, and in the last resort by the state. It was specially enacted that his land, garden, and house were in no case to be sold to pay for his ransom. They were inalienably attached to the office he held, which appears to have been entailed in the male line, since he was precluded from bequeathing any of the property to his wife or daughter. They could only pass from him and his male issue through neglect or disobedience.

It is not improbable that the existence of this specially favoured class of officer dates back to the earliest settlement of the Western Semites in Babylonia. The first of their number may well have been personal retainers and followers of Sumu-abum, the founder of the dynasty. Originally soldiers, they were probably assigned lands throughout the country in return for their services to the king, and they continued to serve him by maintaining order and upholding his authority. In the course of time specified duties were assigned to them, but they retained their privileges, and they must have remained a very valuable body of officers, on whose personal loyalty the king could always rely. In the case of war, they may have assisted in mobilization; for the army was probably raised on a territorial basis, much on the lines of the *corvée* for public works which was under their control.

By contemporary documents of the period much light is thrown on other classes of the population, but, as they were all connected with various departments in the commercial or agricultural life of the community, it will be unnecessary to describe them in further detail. One class perhaps deserves mention, the surgeons, since lack of professional skill was rather heavily penalized. For if a surgeon, when called in by a noble, carried out an operation so unskilfully as to cause his death or inflict a permanent injury upon him, such as the loss of an eye, the punishment was amputation of

o

both hands.   No penalty appears to have been enacted
if the patient were a member of the middle class, but
should the slave of such a man die as the result of an
operation, the surgeon had to give the owner another
slave ; and, in the event of the slave losing his eye, he
had to pay the owner half the slave's value.   There
was, of course, no secular class in the population which
corresponded to the modern doctor, for the medicinal
use of herbs and drugs was not separated from their
employment in magic.   Disease was looked upon as
due to the agency of evil spirits, or of those that controlled them, and though many potions were doubtless
drunk of a curative nature, they were taken at the
instance of the magician, not of the doctor, and to the
accompaniment of magical rites and incantations.[1]

In the religious sphere, the rise of Babylon to the
position of capital led to a number of important
changes, and to a revision of the Babylonian pantheon.
Marduk, the god of Babylon, from being a comparatively obscure city-god, underwent a transformation in
proportion to the increase in his city's importance.
The achievements and attributes of Enlil, the chief
Sumerian deity, were ascribed to him, and the old
Sumerian sagas and legends, particularly those of the
creation of the world, were rewritten in this new spirit
by the Babylonian priesthood.   The beginning of the
process may be accurately dated to the year of Hammurabi's conquest of Rîm-Sin and his subsequent control of Nippur, the ancient centre of the old Sumerian
faith.   It does not appear that the earlier Semites,
when they conquered that city, had ever attempted
to modify the old traditions they found there, or to
appropriate them for their local gods.   But a new
spirit was introduced with the triumph of the Western
Semites.   The Sumerians were then a dying race, and
the gradual disappearance of their language as a living
tongue was accompanied by a systematic translation,
and a partial transformation, of their sacred literature.
Enlil could not be entirely ousted from the position he
had so long enjoyed, but Marduk became his greater
son.   The younger god is represented as winning his

[1] See below, p. 240.

position by his own valour, in coming to the help of the older gods when their very existence was threatened by the dragons of chaos ; and, having slain the monster of the deep, he is portrayed as creating the universe from her severed body.[1] The older legends, no doubt, continued to be treasured in the ancient cult-centres of the land, but the Babylonian versions, under royal sanction and encouragement, tended to gain wide recognition and popularity.

Under the later kings of the First Dynasty a great impetus was also given to all branches of literary activity. The old Sumerian language still bulked largely in the phraseology of legal and commercial documents, as well as in the purely religious literature of the country. And, to aid them in their study of the ancient texts, the Semitic scribes undertook a systematic compilation of explanatory lists of words and ideograms—the earliest form of dictionary,—which continued in use into the Assyrian and Neo-Babylonian periods. The Sumerian texts, too, were copied out and furnished with inter-linear Semitic translations. The astronomical and astro-logical studies and records of the Sumerian priests were taken over, and great collections were compiled in combination with the early Akkadian records that had come down to them. A study of the Babylonian litera-ture affords striking proof that the semitizing of the country led to no break, nor set-back, in Babylonian culture. The older texts and traditions were taken over in bulk, and, except where the rank or position of Marduk was affected, little change or modification was made. The Semitic scribes no doubt developed their inheritance, but expansion took place on the old lines.

In commercial life, too, Sumerian customs remained to a great extent unaltered. Taxes, rent, and prices continued to be paid in kind, and though the talent, maneh, and shekel were in use as metal weights, and silver was in partial circulation, no true currency was developed. In the sale of land, for example, even

---

[1] On the composite character of the Creation Series, and the historical lines of its development, see "The Seven Tablets of Creation," I., pp. lxvi. ff.

during the period of the Kassite kings, the purchase-
price was settled in shekel-weights of silver, but very
little metal actually changed hands.   Various items
were exchanged against the land, and these, in addition
to corn, the principal medium of exchange, included
slaves, animals, weapons, garments, etc., the value of
each item being reckoned on the same silver basis, until
the agreed purchase-price was made up.   The early
Semitic Babylonian, despite his commercial activity, did
not advance beyond the transition stage between pure
barter and a regular currency.

One important advantage conferred by the Western
Semite on the country of his adoption was an increase
in the area of its commercial relations and a political
expansion to the north and west.   He systematized its
laws, and placed its internal administration on a wider
and more uniform basis.   But the greatest and most
far-reaching change of the Hammurabi period was that
the common speech of the whole of Babylonia became
Semitic, as did the dominant racial element in the
population.   And it was thanks to this fact that all
subsequent invasions of the country failed to alter the
main features in her civilization.   Such alien strains
were absorbed in process of time, and, though they
undoubtedly introduced fresh blends into the racial
mixture, the Semitic element triumphed, and continued
to receive reinforcements from the parent stock.   The
Sumerian race and language appear to have survived
longest in the extreme south of the country, and we
shall see that the rise of the Sea-Country kings may
perhaps be regarded as their last effective effort in the
political sphere.

CHAPTER VI

THE CLOSE OF THE FIRST DYNASTY OF BABYLON AND THE KINGS FROM THE COUNTRY OF THE SEA

IN the closing years of Hammurabi's reign Babylon had reached the climax of her early power. The proud phraseology of the Prologue to his Code conveys the impression that the empire was solidly compact, and its component cities the willing recipients of his royal clemency and favour. And there can be no doubt that he owed his success in great measure to the efficient administration he had established under his personal control. His son, Samsu-iluna, inherited his father's traditions, and in his letters that have survived we have abundant evidence that he exercised the same close supervision over the judicial and administrative officers stationed in cities distant from the capital. And it would appear that the first eight years of his reign passed under the same peaceful conditions, that had prevailed at the time of his accession to the throne. He cut two canals, and the names he gave them commemorate the wealth and abundance he hoped by their means to bestow upon the people. It was in his third and fourth years that the Samsu-iluna-nagab-nukhush-nishi and the Samsu-iluna-khegallum Canals were completed, and the royal activities were then confined to the further adornment of the great temples of Babylon and Sippar. His ninth year marks the crisis, not only in Samsu-iluna's own reign, but in the early fortunes of the kingdom. It is then that we first hear of Kassite tribes appearing in force upon Babylon's eastern frontier, and, though Samsu-iluna doubtless defeated them, as he claims to have done, it is clear that their emergence from the foothills of Western

Elam, followed speedily by their penetration of Babylonian territory, was the signal for setting the empire
in a blaze.

They must have met with some success before their
onslaught was arrested by the army sent against them,[1]
and the renewal of hostilities in any form must have
aroused once more the fighting instinct of the Elamite
border tribes, which had been temporarily laid to rest by
Hammurabi's victories.   Hammurabi's old antagonist,
Rîm-Sin himself, had long been living in comparative
retirement, and, in spite of his advanced age, the news
fired him to fresh efforts.   His name was still on the
lips of those who had fought under him, and since the
death of his conqueror, Hammurabi, his prestige must
have tended to increase.   When, therefore, his native
land of Emutbal, allying itself with the neighbouring
Elamite district of Idamaraz, followed up the Kassite
onslaught by an organized invasion, Rîm-Sin raised a
revolt in Southern Babylonia, and succeeded in gaining
possession of Erech and Nîsin.   It would appear that
the Babylonian garrison in Larsa, too, was overcome,
and that the city passed once more under the independent control of its old ruler.

With the whole south of the country in arms against
him, we may conjecture that Samsu-iluna detailed sufficient forces to contain Rîm-Sin, while he dealt with the
invasion of Babylon's home-territory.   He had little
difficulty in disposing of the Elamites, and, marching
southwards, he defeated Rîm-Sin's forces and reoccupied Larsa.[2]   It may be that it was at this time he
captured, or burnt, Rîm-Sin alive,[3] and that the palace
where this took place was the rebel leader's old palace
at Larsa, which he had been making his headquarters.
But the revolt was not completely subdued.   Ur and
Erech still held out, and it was only after a further
campaign that Samsu-iluna recaptured them and razed

---

[1] We may assume that they owed the partial success of the raid to their
mobility, although on this occasion, their earliest invasion of Babylonian
territory, the horse probably played a still more useful part in the retreat;
see further, p. 215 f.

[2] Such appears to be the most probable explanation of the duplicate copies
of the sale-contract from Tell Sifr, in the neighbourhood of Larsa, with their
variant dates by formulæ of Rîm-Sin and Samsu-iluna; see above, p. 98.

[3] Cf. "Chronicles concerning early Babylonian Kings," II., p. 18.

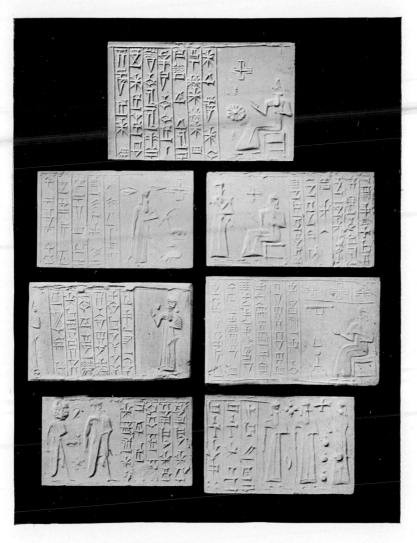

IMPRESSIONS OF KASSITE CYLINDER-SEALS.
Brit. Mus., *Nos.* 89128, 89001, 89015, 28799, 89240, 89182, 89258.

their walls. He had thus succeeded in crushing the first series of organized attacks upon the empire, but the effort of dealing simultaneously with invasion and internal revolt had evidently strained the national resources. Garrisons had probably been reduced in distant provinces, others had been cut down in order to reinforce his armies in the field, and it is not surprising that in his twelfth year these outlying districts should have followed the prevailing lead. In that year it is recorded that all the lands revolted against him.[1]

We may with some confidence trace the main source of Samsu-iluna's fresh troubles to the action of Iluma-ilum, who, probably at this time, headed a revolt in the Sea-Country on the shore of the Persian Gulf, and declared his independence of Babylon. Samsu-iluna's answer was to raise further levies and lead them against his new foe. The subsequent battle was fiercely contested on the very shore of the Gulf, for a later chronicler records that the bodies of the slain were carried off by the sea; yet it was either indecisive, or resulted in the discomfiture of the Babylonians. We may conjecture that the king was prevented from employing his full forces to stamp out the rebellion, in consequence of trouble in other quarters. For in the following two years we find him destroying the cities Kisurra and Sabum, and defeating the leader of a rebellion in the home-territory of Babylon itself.[2]

Iluma-ilum was thus afforded the opportunity of consolidating his position, and we may perhaps see evidence of his growing influence in Southern Babylonia in the fact that at Tell Sifr not a single document has been found dated in a later year of Samsu-iluna's reign than the tenth.[3] In view of the fact that the central city of Nippur eventually passed under Iluma-ilum's control, we

---

[1] Cf. the date-formula for Samsu-iluna's twelfth year, which in its full form commemorated some royal act "after all the lands had revolted." Since the success against Ur and Erech was commemorated in the preceding year, the revolt in question can hardly refer to the troubles with Rim-Sin and the Elamites, but must be taken as implying that other provinces were now making a bid for independence.

[2] The formula for his fourteenth year commemorates his overthrow of "the usurping king, whom the Akkadians had caused to lead a rebellion."

[3] The latest document from Larsa (Senkera) is dated in his twelfth year; see above, p. 104 f.

may probably assume that he was already encroaching northwards, and that territory in the south of Sumer, perhaps including the city of Larsa, passed now into his possession. In support of this suggestion it may be noted that, when Samsu-iluna, after suppressing the Akkadian usurper, began repairing the damage wrought in six years of continuous fighting, it is at Nîsin and at Sippar that he rebuilds the ruined walls, and in Emutbal that he repairs the great garrison-fortresses. Nîsin may well have marked the most southerly limit of Babylon's control, and we may picture the gradual expansion of the Sea-Country, as the power of Babylon declined. The "rebellious land," which Samsu-iluna boasts that he overthrew in his twentieth year, was perhaps the Sea-Country, for we know that he conducted a second campaign against Iluma-ilum, who this time secured a victory. If the Babylonian army succeeded in retreating in comparatively good order, it would have formed a sufficient justification for Samsu-iluna's boast that he had given the rebellious land a lesson.

The fringe of territory in the extreme south-east of Babylonia always exhibited a tendency to detach itself from the upper riverain districts of Babylonia proper. Forming the littoral of the Persian Gulf, and encroaching in its northern area upon Elam, it consisted of great stretches of rich alluvial soil interspersed with areas of marsh-land and swamps, which tended to increase where the rivers approached the coast. The swamps undoubtedly acted as a protection to the country, for while tracks and fords were known to the inhabitants, a stranger from the north-west would in many places have been completely baffled by them. The natives, too, in their light reed-boats could escape from one district to another, pushing along known passages and eluding their pursuers, when once the tall reeds had closed behind them. The later Assyrians at the height of their power succeeded in subduing a series of revolts in the Sea-Country, but it was only by enlisting the help of native guides and by commandeering the light canoes of neighbouring villages. The earlier kings of Babylonia had always been content to leave the swamp-dwellers to themselves, and at most to exact a nominal recognition of suzerainty. But it is probable that fresh energy had been lately introduced into the district, and of this Iluma-ilum doubtless took advantage when he succeeded, not only in leading a revolt, but in establishing an independent kingdom.

It is clear that the pressure exerted upon Babylonia by the West-Semitic migration must have tended to

FIG. 44.

SWAMP IN SOUTHERN BABYLONIA OR THE SEA-COUNTRY.

An Assyrian conquest of the country is here represented, amid all the difficulties presented by its swamps and reed-beds.
[After a bas-relief at Nineveh.]

displace sections of the existing population. The direction of advance was always down-stream, and the pressure continued in force even after the occupation of the country. Those strains in the population, which differed most radically from the invaders, would be the more likely to seek sanctuary elsewhere, and, with the exception of Elam, the Sea-Country offered the only

possible line of retreat.   We may assume, therefore,
that the marsh-dwellers of the south had been reinforced for a considerable period by Sumerian refugees,
and, though the first three rulers of the new kingdom
bore Semitic names and were probably Semites, the
names of later rulers of the Sea-Country suggest that
the Sumerian element in the population afterwards
secured the control,[1] no doubt with the assistance of
fresh drafts from their own kindred after their successful
occupation of Southern Babylonia.   Under the more
powerful kings of the Second Dynasty, the kingdom
may have assumed a character resembling that of its
predecessors in Babylonia.   The centre of administration was certainly shifted for a time to Nippur, and
possibly even further north, but the Sea-Country, as
the home-land of the dynasty, must have always been
regarded as a dominant province of the kingdom, and it
offered a secure refuge to its rulers in the event of their
being driven again within its borders.   In spite of its
extensive marshes, it was capable of sustaining its
inhabitants in a considerable degree of comfort, for the
date-palm flourished luxuriantly, and the areas under
cultivation must have been at least as productive as
those further to the north-west.   Moreover, the zebu, or
humped cattle of Sumer, thrived in the swamps and
water-meadows, and not only formed an important
source of supply, but were used for ploughing in the
agricultural districts.[2]

With such a country as a base of operations, protected in no small degree by its marshes, it is not
surprising that the Sea-Country kings should have met
with considerable success in their efforts at extending
the area of territory under their control.

After his second conflict with Iluma-ilum, Samsu-

---

[1] Such names as Ishkibal, Gulkishar, Peshgal-daramash, A-dara-kalama,
Akur-ul-ana and Melam-kurkura are all Sumerian.   The last king of the
dynasty, Ea-gamil, bears a Semitic name, and Shushshi, the name of
Ishkibal's brother, is probably Semitic.

[2] The zebu, or *Bos indicus*, is represented on Sumerian sculpture from
Lagash, dating from the middle of the third millennium B.C. (cf. "Sumer
and Akkad, p. 69, Fig. 21) ; men are represented ploughing with it in a
Kassite seal-impression (see above, p. 175, Fig. 40) ; and it formed one of the
most valued classes of booty from the Sea-Country at the time of the later
Assyrian empire (see Fig. 45).

iluna appears to have reconciled himself to the loss of his southern province, and to have made no further effort at reconquest. He could still boast of successes in other districts, for he destroyed the walls of Shakhnâ and Zarkhanum, doubtless after the suppression of a revolt, and he strengthened the fortifications of Kish. He also retained the control of the Euphrates route to Syria, and he doubtless encouraged the commercial enterprise of Babylon in that direction as a set-off to

FIG. 45.

THE ZEBU OR HUMPED OXEN OF THE SEA-COUNTRY.

They are here represented as being driven off from the Sea-Country, along with other booty, under a convoy of Assyrian soldiers.
[After a bas-relief from Nineveh in the British Museum.]

his losses in the south. We possess an interesting illustration of the close relations he maintained with the west in the date-formula for the twenty-sixth year of his reign, which tells us that he procured a monolith from the great mountain of the land of Amurru. This must have been quarried in the Lebanon, and transported overland to the Euphrates, and thence conveyed by *kelek* to the capital. From the details he gives us of its size, it appears to have measured some thirty-six feet in length, and it was no small achievement to have brought it so far to Babylon.

During this period of comparative tranquillity Samsu-iluna devoted himself once more to rebuilding and beautifying E-sagila and the temples of Kish and Sippar; but in his twenty-eighth year Babylon suffered a fresh shock, which appears to have resulted in still further loss of territory. In that year he claims to have slain Iadi-khabum and Muti-khurshana, two leaders of an invasion, or a revolt, of which we have no details. But it is clear that the victory, if such it was, resulted in further trouble, for in the following two years no fresh date-formulæ were promulgated, and it is probable that the king himself was absent from the capital. It is significant that no document has been recovered at Nippur which is dated after Samsu-iluna's twenty-ninth year, although in the preceding period, from the thirty-first year of Hammurabi onward, when the city first passed into Babylon's possession, nearly every year is well represented in the dated series.[1] It is difficult not to conclude that Samsu-iluna now lost the control of that city, and, since one of the documents from Nippur is dated in Iluma-ilum's reign, it can only have passed into the latter's possession. Further evidence of the diminishing territory of Babylon may be seen in the fact that Samsu-iluna should have rebuilt the old line of fortresses, founded by his ancestor Suma-la-ilum at a time when the kingdom was in its infancy.[2] This work was doubtless undertaken when he foresaw the necessity of defending the Akkadian border, and he must have lost one at least of the fortresses, Dûr-Zakar, when Nippur was taken. His activitives during his closing years were confined to the north and west, and to the task of keeping open the Euphrates route. For he cut a canal beside Kâr-Sippar, recovered possession of Saggaratum, and probably destroyed the cities of Arkum and Amal. His defeat of an Amorite force

[1] Cf. Poebel, " Legal and Business Documents," p. 119; and Chiera, " Legal and Administrative Documents," p. 25.
[2] See above, p. 148 f.

some two years before his death is of interest as proving that the Western Semites of Akkad, nearly two centuries after their settlement in the country, were experiencing the same treatment from their own stock that they themselves had caused to the land of their adoption.

Samsu-iluna, with the possible exception of Ammi-ditana, was the last great king of the West-Semitic dynasty. It is true that his son Abi-eshu' made a fresh attempt to dislodge Iluma-ilum from his hold upon Central and Southern Babylonia. A late chronicle records that he took the offensive and marched against Iluma-ilum.[1] It would seem that his attack was in the nature of a surprise, and that he succeeded in cutting off the king and part of his forces, possibly on their return from some other expedition. It is clear that he came into touch with him in the neighbourhood of the Tigris, and probably forced him to take refuge in a fortress, since he attempted to cut off his retreat by damming the river. He is said to have succeeded in damming the stream, but he failed to catch Iluma-ilum. The chronicle records no further conflict between the two, and we may assume that he then adopted his father's later policy of leaving the Sea-Country in possession of its conquered territory. In some of his broken date-formulæ we have echoes of a few further campaigns, and we know that he cut the Abi-eshu' Canal, and built a fortress at the gate of the Tigris, which he also named after himself, Dûr-Abi-eshu'. This was probably a frontier fortification, erected for the defence of the river at the point where it passed from Babylon's area of control to that of the Sea-Country. He also built the town of Lukhaia on the Arakhtu Canal in the immediate neighbourhood of Babylon. But both Abi-eshu' and his successors on the throne give evidence of having become more and more engrossed in cult-observances. The supply of temple-furniture begins to have for them the importance that military success had for their fathers. And it is a symptom of decadence that, even in the religious sphere, they are as much concerned with their own worship as with that of the gods.

[1] Cf. "Chronicles concerning Early Kings," II., p. 21.

It is significant that Abi-eshu' should have named one of his years of rule by his decoration of a statue of Entemena, the early patesi of Lagash, who had been accorded divine honours, and, at some period after Hammurabi's occupation of that city, had received a cult-centre of his own in Babylon. For the act indicates an increased interest, on Abi-eshu's part, in the deification of royalty. This honour was peculiarly associated with the possession of Nippur, the central city and shrine of the country, and Babylon had adopted the practice of deification for her kings after Nippur had been annexed by Hammurabi. Though the city had now passed from Babylon's control, Abi-eshu' did not relinquish the privilege his father and grandfather had legitimately enjoyed. Since Babylon no longer possessed the central shrine of Enlil, in which his own divine statue should have been set up, he dedicated one in Enlil's local temple at Babylon. But not content with that he fashioned no less than five other statues of himself, which he set up in the temples of other gods at Babylon, Sippar and elsewhere.[1]

His three successors followed the same practice, and Ammi-ditana and Ammi-zaduga, his son and grandson, have left descriptions of some of these cult-images of themselves.[2] A favourite character, in which the king was often represented, was holding a lamb for divination, and another was in the attitude of prayer. The later kings of the First Dynasty love, too, to dwell on

[1] One of these statues was set up in E-gishshirgal, a name which corresponds to that of the old Moon-temple at Ur; and on this evidence Poebel has assumed that Abi-eshu' succeeded in getting control of Southern Babylonia (cf. "Legal and Business Documents," p. 120). But a fuller form of the date has since been recovered, showing that this E-gishshirgal, and doubtless the temple of Enlil coupled with it, were in Babylon. It would seem therefore that after Samsu-iluna had lost his hold upon the great centre of the Moon cult in the south, a local temple for the Moon-god's worship was established at Babylon, under the ancient name, in which the old cult-practices were reproduced as far as possible. Similarly, having lost Nippur, a new shrine to Enlil was built at Babylon, or an old one enlarged and beautified. By such means it was doubtless hoped to secure a continuance of the gods' favour, and an ultimate recovery of their cities; and the continual dedication of royal images, though doubtless a sign of royal deification, must also have been intended to bring the king's claims to the divine notice.

[2] As Ammi-ditana appears to have recovered Nippur for a time towards the end of his reign, and as Ammi-zaduga probably retained it during his earlier years (see below, p. 208 f.), Babylon could legitimately claim her former privileges during the period of occupation.

their sumptuous votive offerings. Marduk is supplied with innumerable weapons of red gold, and the Sun-god's shrine at Sippar is decorated with solar disks of precious *dushû*-stone, inlaid with red gold, lapis-lazuli, and silver. Great reliefs, with representations of rivers and mountains, were cast in bronze and set up in the temples; and Samsu-ditana, the last of his line, records among his offerings to the gods the dedication to Sarpanitum of a rich silver casket for perfumes.

Incidentally, these references afford striking proof of the wealth Babylon had now acquired, due no doubt to her increased commercial activities. Elam on the one side and Syria on the other [1] had furnished her with imports of precious stone, metal, and wood; and her craftsmen had learnt much from foreign teachers. In spite of the contraction of Hammurabi's empire, the life of the people in both the town and country districts of Akkad was not materially altered. The organized supervision of all departments of national activity, pastoral, agricultural and commercial, which the nation owed in great measure to Hammurabi, was continued under these later kings; and some of the royal letters that have been recovered show that orders on compara-tively unimportant matters continued to be issued in the king's name. We know, too, of a good many public works carried out by Ammi-ditana, Abi eshu's son. He cut only one canal, and he built fortresses for the protection of others, and named them after himself. Thus, in addition to the Ammi-ditana Canal, we learn of a Dûr-Ammi-ditana, which he erected on the Zilakum Canal, and another fortress of the same name on the Mê-Enlil Canal. He strengthened the wall of Ishkun-Marduk, which was also on the Zilakum, and built Mashkan-Ammi-ditana and the wall of Kâr-Shamash, both on the bank of the Euphrates. [2]

---

[1] The bronze-casting may well have been learnt from Elam; and we have striking evidence of increased relations with the west in the fact that under Ammi-zaduga a district of Sippar was known as Amurrî, from its Amorite quarter or settlement; cf. Meissner, "Altbabylonisches Privatrecht," p. 41 f., No. 42, and Meyer, "Geschichte," I., ii., p. 467 f.

[2] His other building activities included the founding of a royal suburb at Babylon, named Shag-dugga, on the bank of the Arakhtu Canal, where he built himself a palace; while at Sippar he once more rebuilt the Gagûm, or spacious Cloister attached to the temple of the Sun-god.

The systematic fortification of the rivers and canals may perhaps be interpreted as marking an advance of the frontier southward, in consequence of which it was advisable to protect the crops and the water-supply of the districts thus recovered from the danger of sudden raids. On two occasions Ammi-ditana claims, in rather vague terms, to have freed his land from danger, once by restoring the might of Marduk, and later on by loosing the pressure from his land; and that, in his seventeenth year, he should have claimed to have conquered Arakhab, perhaps referred to as "the Sumerian,"[1] is an indication that the Sea-Country kings found ready assistance from the older population of the South. Moreover, of the later West-Semitic kings, Ammi-ditana alone appears to have made headway against the encroachments of the Sea-Country. The most conclusive proof of his advance is to be seen in the date-formula for his thirty-seventh year, which records that he destroyed the wall of Nîsin,[2] proving that he had penetrated to the south of Nippur. That Nippur itself was held by him for a time is more than probable, especially as one of his building-inscriptions, still unpublished, is said to have been found there[3]; and we know also, from a Neo-Babylonian copy of a similar text, that he claimed the title "King of Sumer and Akkad."[3] Under him, then, Babylon recovered a semblance of her former strength, but we may conjecture that the Sea-Country retained its hold on Larsa and the southern group of cities.

We are furnished with a third valuable synchronism between the dynasties of Babylon and of the south by the reference to Ammi-ditana's destruction of the wall of Nîsin, for the date-formula adds that this had been erected by the people of Damki-ilishu. The ruler referred to is obviously the third king in the dynasty of the Sea-Country, who succeeded Itti-ili-nibi upon the

---

[1] Cf. Poebel, "Legal and Business Documents," p. 121, and Schorr, "Urkunden," p. 602.

[2] For references, see Schorr, op. cit., p. 604.

[3] According to a verbal communication made by Prof. Hilprecht to Dr. Poebel.

[4] Cf. "Letters and Inscriptions of Hammurabi," III., p. 207 f.; in the same inscription he also lays claim to the rule of Amurru.

throne.[1] We may conclude that it was in his reign, or shortly after it, that Ammi-ditana succeeded in recovering Nîsin, after having already annexed Nippur on his southward advance. In his thirty-fourth year, two years before the capture of Nîsin, he had dedicated an image of Samsu-iluna in the temple E-namtila, and we may perhaps connect this tribute to his grandfather with the fact that in his reign Babylon had last enjoyed the distinction conferred by the suzerainty of Nippur.

In the year following the recovery of Nîsin Ammi-zaduga succeeded his father on the throne, and since he ascribes the greatness of his kingdom to Enlil, and not to Marduk or any other god, we may see in this a further indication that Babylon continued to control his ancient shrine. But the remaining date-formulæ for Ammi-zaduga's reign do not suggest that Ammi-ditana's conquests were held permanently. A succession of religious dedications is followed in his tenth year by the conventional record that he loosed the pressure of his land, suggesting that his country had been through a period of conflict; and, though in the following year he built a fortress, Dûr-Ammi-zaduga " at the mouth of the Euphrates," the nearly unbroken succession of votive acts, commemorated during his remaining years and in the reign of his son Samsu-ditana, makes it probable that the kings of Sea-Country were

[1] It is most improbable that he should be identified with Damik-ilishu, the last king of the earlier Dynasty of Nîsin, who perished one hundred and thirty-seven years before this time. It is true that Nabonidus, to judge from his building-inscriptions, evinces an interest in the past, but in many ways he was a unique monarch and he lived in a later age. These early date-formulæ, on the other hand, always refer to contemporaneous events, not to matters of archæological interest. We know definitely that Iluma-ilum (the first Sea-Country king) was the contemporary of Samsu-iluna and Abi-eshu', and it is not unreasonable to find a reference to Damik-ilishu (the third Sea-Country king) in the last year of Ammi-ditana, Abi-eshu's son. Granting this assumption, there follows the important inference that the exceptionally long period of one hundred and fifteen years, assigned by the Kings' List to the reigns of the first two kings of the Sea-Country, is a little exaggerated. The accuracy of some of the longer figures assigned in the List to kings of this dynasty has long been called in question (cf. " Chronicles," I., pp. 111 ff., and see above, p. 106), and the synchronism justifies this doubt. While the historical character of the Second Dynasty has been amply confirmed, we must not regard the total duration assigned to it in the Kings' List as more than approximately correct. Under these circumstances detailed dates have not been assigned to members of that dynasty in the Dynastic List of Kings ; see Appendix II., p. 320.

P

gradually regaining some of the territory they had temporarily lost.[1]

But it was not from the Sea-Country that the West-Semitic Dynasty of Babylon received its death-blow. In the late chronicle, which has thrown so much light on the earlier conflicts of this troubled period, we read of another invasion, which not only brought disaster to Babylon but probably put an end to her first dynasty. The chronicler states that during the reign of Samsu-ditana, the last king of the dynasty, " men of the land of Khatti marched against the land of Akkad," in other words, that Hittites from Anatolia [2] marched down the Euphrates and invaded Babylonia from the north-west. The chronicle does not record the result of the invasion,[3] but we may probably connect it with the fact that the Kassite king Agum-kakrime brought back to Babylon from Khanî, the old Khana on the middle Euphrates,[4] the cult-images of Marduk and Sarpanitum and installed them once more with great pomp and ceremony within their shrines in E-sagila. We may legitimately conclude that they were carried off by the Hittites during their invasion in Samsu-ditana's reign.

If the Hittites succeeded in despoiling Babylon of

---

[1] Success doubtless fluctuated from one side to the other, Ammi-zaduga in one of his later years commemorating that he had brightened his land like the Sun-god, and Samsu-ditana recording that he had restored his dominion with the weapon of Marduk. How far these rather vague claims were justified it is impossible to say. Apart from votive acts, the only definite record of this period is that of Ammi-zaduga's sixteenth year, in which he celebrates the cutting of the Ammi-zaduga-nukhush-nishi Canal.

[2] We may confidently regard the phrase as referring to the Anatolian Hittites, whose capital at Boghaz Keui must have been founded far earlier than the end of the fifteenth century when we know that it bore the name of Khatti. It is true that, after the southern migration of the Hittites in the twelfth century, Northern Syria was known as " the land of Khatti," but, if the invasion of Babylonia in Samsu-ditana's reign had been made by Semitic tribes from Syria, no doubt the chronicler would have employed the correct designation, Amurru, which is used in an earlier section of the text for Sargon's invasion of Syria. In the late omen-literature, too, the use of the early geographical terms is not confused. Both chronicles and omen-texts are transcripts of early written originals, not late compilations based on oral tradition.

[3] The reason for the omission is that the whole of this section of the text had evidently been left out by the scribe in error, and he afterwards only had room to insert the first line ; cf. " Chronicles," II., p. 22, n. 1.

[4] This district was in the path of the Hittite raid, and its occupation by a section of the invaders was evidently more permanent than that of Babylon.

BRICK OF SIN-GASHID, KING OF ERECH, RECORDING THE BUILDING OF
HIS PALACE IN THAT CITY

From Warka; Brit. Mus., No. 90268; photo. by Messrs. Mansell & Co.

her most sacred deities, it is clear that they must have raided the city, and they may even have occupied it for a time. Thus the West-Semitic Dynasty of Babylon may have been brought to an end by these Hittite conquerors, and Samsu-ditana himself may have fallen in defence of his own capital. But there is no reason for supposing that the Hittites occupied Babylon for long. Even if their success was complete, they would soon have returned to their own country, laden with heavy spoil ; and they doubtless left some of their number in occupation of Khana on their withdrawal up the Euphrates. Southern Babylonia may also have suffered in the raid, but we may assume that its force was felt most in the north, and that the kings of the Sea-Country profited by the disaster. We have as yet no direct evidence of their occupation of Babylon, but, as their kingdom had been Babylon's most powerful rival prior to the Hittite raid, it may well have increased its borders after her fall.

To this period we may probably assign a local dynasty of Erech, represented by the names of Sin-gashid, Sin-gamil and An-am. From bricks and foundation-records recovered at Warka, the site of the ancient city, we know that the first of these rulers restored the old temple of E-anna and built himself a new palace.[1] But the most interesting of Sin-gashid's records is a votive cone, commemorating the dedication of E-kankal to Lugal-banda and the goddess Ninsun, for, when concluding his text with a prayer for abundance, he inserts a list or tariff, stating the maximum-price which he had fixed for the chief articles of commerce during his reign.[2] Sin-gamil was An-am's immediate predecessor on the throne of Erech, and during his reign the latter dedicated on his behalf a temple to Nergal in the town of Usipara.[3] An-am was the son of a certain

[1] Cf. "Cun. Texts in the Brit. Mus.," XXI., pl. 12, and King, "Proc. Soc. Bibl. Arch.," XXXVII., p. 22 f.
[2] See "Cun. Texts," XXI., pl. 15 ff., and cf. Thureau-Dangin, "Königs-inschriften," p. 222 f. The purchasing power of one shekel of silver is fixed at three *gur* of corn, or twelve manehs of wool, or ten manehs of copper, or thirty *ka* of wood. The chief interest of the record is its proof that at this period the values of copper and silver stood in the ratio of 600 : 1 (cf. Meyer, "Geschichte," I., ii., p. 512).
[3] Cf. "Cun. Texts," XXI., pl. 17.

Bêl-shemea, and his principal work was the restoration of the wall of Erech, the foundation of which he ascribes to the semi-mythical ruler Gilgamesh.[1]

Doubtless other local kingdoms arose during the period following Babylon's temporary disappearance as a political force, but we have recovered no traces of them,[2] and the only fact of which we are certain is the continued succession of the Sea-Country kings. To one of these rulers, Gulkishar, reference is made upon a boundary stone of the twelfth century, drawn up in the reign of Enlil-nadin-apli, an early king of the Fourth Dynasty. On it he is given the title of King of the Sea-Country, which is also the late chronicler's designation for E-gamil, the last member of the dynasty, in the account he has left us of the Kassite invasion. Such evidence seems to show that the administrative centre of their rule was established at those periods in the south ; but the inclusion of the dynasty in the Kings' List is best explained on the assumption that at least some of its later members imposed their suzerainty over a wider area.[3] They were evidently the only stable line of rulers in a period after the most powerful administration the country had yet known had been suddenly shattered. The land had suffered much, not only from the Hittite raid, but also during the continuous conflicts of more than a century that preceded the final fall of Babylon. It must have been then that many of the old Sumerian cities of Southern and Central Babylonia were deserted, after being burned down and destroyed ; and they were never afterwards

---

[1] See Hilprecht, "Old Bab. Inscriptions," I., pl. 15, No. 26. A tablet has been recovered dated in the reign of An-am, and another of the same type is dated in the reign of Arad-shasha, whom we may therefore regard as another king of this local dynasty ; cf. Scheil, "Orient. Lit.-Zeit.," 1905, col. 351, and Thureau-Dangin, *op. cit.*, p. 238. The style of writing on these tablets is rather later than that of the First Dynasty of Babylon.

[2] For Pukhia, son of Asiru and king of the land of Khurshitu, see "Sum. and Akk.," p. 287. Khurshitu may have been the name of a district on the Ak-su, a tributary of the Adhem, since a brick from his palace is said to have been found at Tuz-khurmati on that stream ; cf. Scheil, "Rec. de trav.," XVI., p. 186 ; XIX., p. 64. The region of King Manabaltel's rule (cf. Pinches, "Proc. Soc. Bibl. Arch.," XXI., p. 158) is quite uncertain, but the archaic style of the writing of the tablet, dated in his reign, suggests that he was a contemporary of one of the earlier West-Semitic kings.

[3] See above, p. 105 f.

re-occupied. Lagash, Umma, Shuruppak, Kisurra and Adab play no part in the subsequent history of Babylonia.

Of the fortunes of Babylon at this time we know nothing, but the fact that the Kassites should have made the city their capital shows that the economic forces, which had originally raised her to that position, were still in operation. The Sumerian elements in the population of Southern Babylonia may now have enjoyed a last period of influence, and their racial survival in the Sea-Country may in part explain its continual striving for independence. But in Babylonia as a whole the effects of three centuries of West-Semitic rule were permanent. When, after the Kassite conquest, Babylon emerges once more into view, it is apparent that the traditions inherited from her first empire have undergone small change.

CHAPTER VII

THE KASSITE DYNASTY AND ITS RELATIONS WITH
EGYPT AND THE HITTITE EMPIRE

THE Kassite conquest of Babylonia, though it met with immediate success in a great part of the country, was a gradual process in the south, being carried out by independent Kassite chieftains. The Sea-Country kings continued for a time their independent existence; and even after that dynasty was brought to an end, the struggle for the south went on. It was after a further period of conflict that the Kassite domination was completed, and the administration of the whole country centred once more in Babylon. It is fortunate for Babylonia that the new invaders did not appear in such numbers as to overwhelm the existing population. The probability has long been recognized that they were Aryan by race, and we may with some confidence regard them as akin to the later rulers of Mitanni, who imposed themselves upon the earlier non-Iranian population of Subartu, or Northern Mesopotamia. Like the Mitannian kings, the Kassites of Babylonia were a ruling caste or aristocracy, and, though they doubtless brought with them numbers of humbler followers, their domination did not affect the linguistic nor the racial character of the country in any marked degree. In some of its aspects we may compare their rule to that of Turkey in the Tigris and Euphrates valley. They give no evidence of having possessed a high degree of culture, and though they gradually adopted the civilization of Babylon, they tended for long to keep themselves aloof, retaining their native names along with their separate nationality. They were essentially a practical people and produced successful administrators. The chief gain they brought to Babylon was an improved method of time-reckoning. In place of the unwieldy system of date-formulæ, inherited by the Semites from the Sumerians, under which each year was known by an elaborate title taken from some great event or cult-observance, the Kassites introduced the simpler plan of dating by the years of the king's reign. And we shall see that it was directly owing to the political circumstances of their occupation that the old system of land tenure, already to a great extent undermined by the Western Semites, was still further modified.

But, on the material side, the greatest change they effected in the life of Babylonia was due to their intro-duction of the horse. There can be little doubt that they were a horse-keeping race,[1] and the success of their invasion may in large part be traced to their greater mobility. Hitherto asses and cattle had been employed for all purposes of draught and carriage, but, with the appearance of the Kassites, the horse suddenly becomes the beast of burden throughout Western Asia. Before their time "the ass of the mountain," as it was designated in Babylonia, was a great rarity, the earliest reference to it occurring in the age of Hammurabi.[2] In that period we have evidence that Kassite tribes were already forming settlements in the western districts of Elam, and when from time to time small parties of them made their way into the Babylonian plain to be employed as harvesters,[3] they doubtless carried their

---

[1] Proof that the Aryans were horse-keepers may be seen in the numerous Iranian proper names which include *asva* (*aspa*), "horse," as a component; see Justi, "Iran. Namenbuch," p. 486, and cf. Meyer, "Geschichte," I., ii., p. 579.

[2] It is on a text of that period that we find the first mention of the horse in antiquity; cf. Ungnad, "Orient. Lit.-Zeit.," 1907, col. 638 f., and King, "Journ. of Hellenic Studies," XXXIII., p. 359. A reference to one also occurs in a letter of the early Babylonian period (cf. "Cun. Texts in the Brit. Mus.," IV., pl. 1), but, to judge from the writing, this is probably rather later than the time of Hammurabi. It is immediately after the Kassite period that we have evidence of the adoption of the horse as a divine symbol, doubt-less that of a deity introduced by the Kassites; see Plate XXII., opposite p. 254.

[3] Some First Dynasty tablets record the issue of rations to certain Kassites, who were obviously employed as labourers, probably for getting in the harvest (cf. Ungnad, "Beitr. zur Assyr.," VI., No. 5, p. 22); and in a list of proper names of the same period (cf. "Cun. Texts," VI., pl. 23) a Kassite man, (*awîl*) *ṣâbum Kashshû*, bears the name Warad-Ibari, perhaps a Semitic rendering of an original Kassite name.

goods with them in the usual way.   The usefulness
of horses imported in this manner would have ensured
their ready sale to the Babylonians, who probably
retained the services of their owners to tend the strange
animals.   But the early Kassite immigrants must have
been men of a simple and unprogressive type, for in all
the contract-literature of the period we find no trace of
their acquiring wealth, or engaging in the commercial
activities of their adopted country.   The only evidence
of their employment in other than a menial capacity is
supplied by a contract of Ammi-ditana's reign, which
records a two-years' lease of an uncultivated field taken
by a Kassite for farming.[1]

The Kassite raid into Babylonian territory in Samsu-
iluna's reign[2] may have been followed by others of a
like character, but it was only at the time of the later
kings of the Sea-Country that the invaders succeeded in
effecting a permanent foothold in Northern Babylonia.
According to the Kings' List the founder of the Third
Dynasty was Gandash, and we have obtained confirmation of the record in a Neo-Babylonian tablet purporting
to contain a copy of one of his inscriptions.[3]   The
Babylonian king, whose text the copy reproduces, there
bears the name Gaddash, evidently a contracted form
of Gandash as written in the Kings' List ; and the
record contains an unmistakable reference to the Kassite
conquest.   From what is left of the inscription it may
be inferred that it commemorated the restoration of the
temple of Bêl, that is, of Marduk, which seems to have
been damaged " in the conquest of Babylon."   It is clear,
therefore, that Babylon must have offered a strenuous
opposition to the invaders, and that the city held out
until captured by assault.   It would seem, too, that
this success was followed up by further conquests of
Babylonian territory, for in his text, in addition to
styling himself King of Babylon, Gaddash adopts the
other time-honoured titles of King of the four quarters
(of the world), and King of Sumer and Akkad.   We
may see evidence in this that the kingdom of the Sea-

---

[1] Cf. Ungnad, " Vorderas. Schriftdenkmäler," VII., pl. 27, No. 64.
[2] See above, p. 195 f.
[3] Cf. Winckler, " Untersuchungen," p. 156, No. 6.

Country was now restricted within its original limits, though some attempts may have been made to stem the tide of invasion. Ea-gamil, at any rate, the last king of the Second Dynasty, was not content to defend his home-territory, for we know that he assumed the offensive and invaded Elam. But he appears to have met with no success, and after his death a Kassite chieftain, Ula-Burariash or Ulam-Buriash, conquered the Sea-Country and established his dominion there.[1]

The late chronicler, who records these events, tells us that Ulam-Buriash was the brother of Kashtiliash, the Kassite, whom we may probably identify with the third ruler of the Kassite Dynasty of Babylon. There Gandash, the founder of the dynasty, had been succeeded by his son Agum, but after the latter's reign of twenty-two years Kashtiliash, a rival Kassite, had secured the throne.[2] He evidently came of a powerful Kassite tribe, for it was his brother, Ulam-Buriash, who conquered the Country of the Sea. We have recovered a memorial of the latter's reign in a knob or mace-head of diorite, which was found during the excavations at Babylon.[3] On it he terms himself King of the Sea-Country, and we learn from it, too, that he and his brother were the sons of Burna-Burariash, or Burna-Buriash, who may have remained behind as a local Kassite chieftain in Elam, while his sons between them secured the control of Babylonia. After a certain interval the Sea-Country must have revolted from Ulam-Buriash, for its reconquest was undertaken by Agum, a younger son of Kashtiliash, who is recorded to have captured the city of Dûr-Enlil and to have destroyed E-malga-uruna,

---

[1] Cf. "Chronicles," II., p. 22 f. For discussions of the manner in which we may reconcile the chronicler's account of the Kassite conquest of the Sea-Country with the known succession of the early Kassite kings of Babylon, see op. cit., I., pp. 101 ff., and cf. Thureau-Dangin, "Journal des Savants," Nouv. Sér., VI., No. 4, pp. 190 ff., and "Zeits. für Assyr.," XXI., pp. 176 ff. The established genealogy of Agum-kakrime renders it impossible to identify the Agum of the chronicle, who was a son of Kashtiliash the Kassite, with either of the Kassite kings of Babylon who bore that name. He can only have raided or ruled in the Sea-Country, probably at the time his eldest brother Ushshi (or perhaps his other brother, Abi-rattash) was king in Babylon.

[2] Agum-kakrime describes Kashtiliash as aplu, probably "the inheritor," not mâru, "the son," of Agum I. (cf. Thureau-Dangin, "Journ. Asiat.," XI., 1908, p. 133 f.).

[3] See Weissbach, "Babylonische Miscellen," p. 7, pl. 1, No. 3.

the local temple of Enlil.[1] The eldest son of Kashtiliash
had meanwhile succeeded his father on the throne of
Babylon, and, if Agum established his rule in the Sea-
Country, we again have the spectacle of two brothers,
in the next generation of this Kassite family, dividing
the control of Babylonia between them. But as the
chronicler does not record that Agum, like his uncle
Ulam-Buriash, exercised dominion over the Sea-Country
as a whole, he may have secured little more than a local
success. The throne of Babylon then passed to the
second son of Kashtiliash, Abi-rattash, and it was possibly
by him, or by one of his successors, that the whole
country was once more united under Babylon's rule.

We know of two more members of the family of
Kashtiliash, who carried on his line at Babylon. For
Abi-rattash was succeeded by his son and grandson,
Tashshi-gurumash and Agum-kakrime, of whom the
latter has left us the record already referred to, commemorating his recovery of the statues of Marduk and
Sarpanitum from the land of Khanî.[2] And then there
occurs a great break in our knowledge of the history of
Babylon. For a period extending over some thirteen
reigns, from about the middle of the seventeenth to the
close of the fifteenth century B.C., our native evidence
is confined to a couple of brief records, dating from the
latter half of the interval, and to one or two historical
references in later texts. By their help we have
recovered the names of a few of the missing kings,
though their relative order, and in one or two cases
even their existence, are still matters of controversy.
In fact, were we dependent solely upon Babylonian
sources, our knowledge of the country's history, even
when we can again establish the succession, would have
been practically a blank. But, thanks in great part to
the commercial relations established with Syria since
the age of the West-Semitic kings, the influence of
Babylonian culture had travelled far afield. Her method
of writing on the convenient and imperishable clay
tablet had been adopted by other nations of Western

[1] Cf. "Chronicles," II., p. 24.
[2] See above, p. 210. From his titles we gather that he ruled Padan,
Alman, Gutium and Ashnunnak as subject provinces ; cf. Jensen in Schrader's
"Keilins. Bibl.," III., i., p. 136 f.

Asia, and her language had become the *lingua franca* of the ancient world. After her conquest of Canaan, Egypt had become an Asiatic power, and had adopted the current method of international intercourse for communication with other great states and with her own provinces in Canaan. And thus it has come about that some of our most striking information on the period has come to us, not from Babylon itself, but from Egypt.

The mounds known as Tell el-Amarna in Upper Egypt mark the site of a city which had a brief but brilliant existence under Amen-hetep IV., or Akhenaten, one of the later kings of the Eighteenth Dynasty. He was the famous " heretic " king, who attempted to suppress the established religion of Egypt and to substitute for it a pantheistic monotheism associated with the worship of the solar disk. In pursuance of his religious ideas he deserted Thebes, the ancient capital of the country, and built a new capital further to the north, which he called Akhetaten,[1] the modern Tell el-Amarna. Here he transferred the official records of his own government and those of his father, Amen-hetep III., including the despatches from Egypt's Asiatic provinces and the diplomatic correspondence with kings of Mesopotamia, Assyria and Babylon. Some twenty-seven years ago a large number of these were discovered in the ruins of the royal palace, and they form one of the most valuable sources of information on the early relations of Egypt and Western Asia.[2] More recently they have been supplemented by a still larger find of similar documents at Boghaz Keui in Cappadocia, a village built beside the site of Khatti, the ancient capital of the Hittite empire. The royal and official archives had been stored for safety on the

---

[1] That is, "The Glory of the Disk," in honour of his new cult. For detailed histories of the period, see Budge, " History of Egypt," Vol. V., pp. 90 ff. ; Breasted, " History of Egypt," pp. 322 ff., and Hall, "Ancient History of the Near East," pp. 297 ff.

[2] For the texts, see Budge and Bezold, " The Tell el-Amarna Tablets in the British Museum " (1892), and Winckler, " Der Thontafelfund von El Amarna " (1889–90) ; and for translations, see Winckler, " Die Thontafeln von Tell el-Amarna " in Schrader's " Keilins. Bibl.," Bd. V., Engl. ed. 1896, and Knudtzon's " Die El-Amarna Tafeln " in the " Vorderasiatische Bibliothek," 1907–12, with an appendix by Weber, annotating and discussing the contents of the letters.

ancient citadel, and the few extracts that have as yet
been published, from the many thousands of documents
recovered on the site, have furnished further information
of the greatest value from the Hittite standpoint.[1]

From these documents we have recovered a very
full picture of international politics in Western Asia
during two centuries, from the close of the fifteenth to
the later years of the thirteenth century B.C.   We can
trace in some measure the dynastic relations established
by Egypt with the other great Asiatic states, and the
manner in which the balance of power was maintained,
largely by diplomatic methods.   During the earlier
part of this period Egyptian power is dominant in
Palestine and Syria, while the kingdom of Mitanni, under
its Aryan dynasty, is a check upon Assyrian expansion.
But Egypt was losing her hold upon her Asiatic
provinces, and the rise of the Hittite empire coincided
with her decline in power.   Mitanni soon fell before the
Hittites, to the material advantage of Assyria, which
began to be a menace to her neighbours upon the west
and south.   After a change of dynasty, Egypt had meanwhile in part recovered her lost territory in Palestine,
and once more took her place among the great nations of
Western Asia.   And it is only with the fall of the Hittite
empire that the international situation is completely
altered.   Throughout Babylon stands, so far as she may,
aloof, preoccupied with commerce rather than with
conquest;[2] but in the latter half of the period her eyes
are always fixed upon her Assyrian frontier.

---

[1] Winckler's preliminary account of the documents in the "Mitteil. d.
Deutsch. Orient-Gesellschaft," No. 35, Dec. 1907, is still the only publication
on the linguistic material that has appeared.   The topographical and part of
the archæological results of the excavations have now been published ; see
Puchstein, "Boghasköi," 1912.

[2] Among the royal letters from Tell el-Amarna are eleven which directly
concern Babylon.   Two of these are drafts, or copies, of letters which Amen-
hetep III. despatched to Kadashman-Enlil of Babylon (cf. Kundtzon, *op. cit.*,
pp. 60 ff., 74 ff.) ; three are letters received by Amen-hetep III. from the
same correspondent (*op. cit.*, pp. 66 ff., 68 ff., 72 ff.) ; five are letters written by
Burna-Buriash of Babylon to Amen-hetep IV. or Akhenaten (*op. cit.*, pp.
78 ff.) ; and one is a letter from Burna-Buriash, which may have been
addressed to Amen-hetep III. (*op. cit.*, 78 f.).   We also possess a letter, from a
princess in Babylon to her lord in Egypt, on a purely domestic matter (*op. cit.*,
pp. 98 ff.), as well as long lists of presents which passed between Akhenaten
and Burna-Buriash (*op. cit.*, pp. 100 ff.) ; one of the letters also appears to be
a Babylonian passport for use in Canaan (see below, p. 225, n. 3).   The letters

HEAD FROM A COLOSSAL STATUE OF AMEN-HETEP III.
Brit. Mus., N. Eg. Gall., No. 416; photo. by Messrs. Mansell & Co.

From the Tell el-Amarna correspondence we see how the kings of Mitanni, Assyria and Babylon gave their daughters to the Egyptian king in marriage and sought to secure his friendship and alliance. Apparently Egypt considered it beneath her dignity to bestow her princesses in return, for in one of his letters to Amen-hetep III. Kadashman-Enlil remonstrates with the King of Egypt for refusing him one of his daughters and threatens to withhold his own daughter in retaliation.[1] Another of the letters illustrates in a still more striking manner the intimate international intercourse of the period. At the height of its power the kingdom of Mitanni appears to have annexed the southern districts of Assyria, and for a time to have exercised control over Nineveh, as Hammurabi of Babylon had done in an earlier age. It was in his character of suzerain that Dushratta sent the holy statue of Ishtar of Nineveh to Egypt, as a mark of his esteem for Amen-hetep III. We have recovered the letter he sent with the goddess, in which he writes concerning her:[2] "Indeed in the time of my father the lady Ishtar went into that land; and, just as she dwelt there formerly and they honoured her, so now may my brother honour her ten times more than before. May my brother honour her and may he allow her to return with joy." We thus gather that this was not the first time Ishtar had visited Egypt, and we may infer from such a custom the belief that a deity, when stopping in a foreign country with his or her own consent, would, if properly treated, confer favour and

thus fall in the reigns of two Kassite rulers, Kadashman-Enlil I. and Burna-Buriash, but from one of Burna-Buriash's letters to Akhenaten we gather that Amen-hetep III. had corresponded with a still earlier king in Babylon, Kara-indash I.; for the letter begins by assuring the Pharaoh that "since the time of Kara-indash, when their fathers had begun to correspond with one another, they had always been good friends" (cf. Knudtzon, *op. cit.*, pp. 90 ff.). We have recovered no letters of Kurigalzu, the father of Burna-Buriash, though Amen-hetep III. maintained friendly relations with him (see below, p. 224). In a letter of Amen-hetep III. to Kadashman-Enlil reference is also made to correspondence between the two countries in the time of Amen-hetep III.'s father, Thothmes IV. (*op. cit.*, p. 64 f.).

[1] The Babylonian king expresses his willingness to receive any beautiful Egyptian woman, as no one would know she was not a king's daughter (*op. cit.*, p. 72 f.). Amen-hetep III. married a sister of Kadashman-Enlil, though the Babylonian court was not satisfied with the lady's treatment in Egypt (*op. cit.*, p. 60 f.).

[2] *Op. cit.*, pp. 178 ff.

prosperity upon that land. We shall see later on that Rameses II. sent his own god Khonsu on a similar mission to Khatti, in order to cure the epileptic daughter of the Hittite king, who was believed to be possessed by a devil.[1] We could not have more striking proofs of international intercourse. Not only did the rulers of the great states exchange their daughters but even their gods.

But the letters also exhibit the jealousy which existed between the rival states of Asia. By skilful diplomacy, and, particularly in the reign of Akhenaten, by presents and heavy bribes, the Egyptian king and his advisers succeeded in playing off one power against the other, and in retaining some hold upon their troublesome provinces of Syria and Palestine. In paying liberal bounties and rewards to his own followers and party in Egypt itself, Akhenaten was only carrying out the traditional policy of the Egyptian crown;[2] and he extended the principle still more in his dealings with foreign states. But peculation on the part of the ambassadors was only equalled by the greed of the monarchs to whom they were accredited, and whose appetite for Egyptian gold grew with their consumption of it. Much space in the letters is given up to the constant request for more presents, and to complaints that promised gifts have not arrived. In one letter, for example, Ashur-uballit of Assyria writes to Akhenaten that formerly the king of Khanirabbat had received a present of twenty manehs of gold from Egypt, and he proceeds to demand a like sum.[3] Burna-Buriash of Babylon, his contemporary, writes in the same strain to Egypt,[4] reminding Akhenaten that Amenophis III. had been far more generous to his father. "Since the time my father and thine established friendly relations with one another, they sent rich presents to one another, and they did not refuse to one another any desired object. Now my brother has sent me as a present two manehs of gold. Send now much gold, as much as thy father; and if it is less, send but half that of thy father. Why hast thou sent only two

---

[1] See below, p. 240.
[2] Cf. Breasted, "Hist. of Egypt," p. 367 f.
[3] See Knudtzon, op. cit., p. 128 f.
[4] Op. cit., p. 88 f.

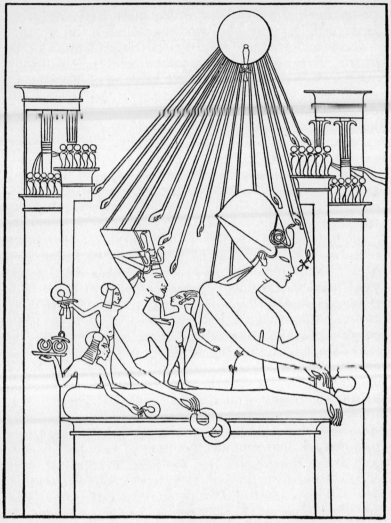

FIG. 46.

AKHENATEN, WITH HIS QUEEN AND INFANT DAUGHTERS, ON THE BALCONY
OF THEIR PALACE.

The king and his family are here represented throwing down collars and
ornaments of gold to Aÿ, the Priest of Aten and Master of the Horse, who has
called at the palace with his wife, attended by a large retinue. The Aten, or
Solar Disk, the object of the royal worship, is caressing the king with its rays
and giving him life.

[After N. de G. Davies.]

manehs of gold? For the work in the temple is great,
and I have undertaken it and am carrying it out with

vigour ; therefore send much gold. And do thou send for whatsoever thou desirest in my land, that they may take it thee."

Though a great part of the royal letters from Tell el-Amarna is taken up with such rather wearisome requests for gold, they also give valuable glimpses into the political movements of the time. We gather, for instance, that Egypt succeeds in preventing Babylon from giving support to the revolts in Canaan, but she does not hesitate to encourage Assyria, which is now beginning to display her power as Babylon's rival. Burna-Buriash makes this clear when he complains that Akhenaten has received an embassy from the Assyrians, whom he boastfully refers to as his subjects ; and he contrasts Babylon's own reception of Canaanite proposals of alliance against Egypt in the time of his father Kurigalzu. " In the time of Kurigalzu, my father," he writes, "the Canaanites sent to him with one accord, saying, ' Let us go down against the border of the land and invade it, and let us form an alliance with thee.' But my father replied to them, saying, ' Desist from seeking to form an alliance with me. If ye are hostile to the king of Egypt, my brother, and ally yourselves with one another, shall I not come and plunder you ? For with me is he allied.' My father for thy father's sake did not hearken to them." [1]   But Burna-Buriash does not trust entirely to the Egyptian's sense of gratitude for Babylon's support in the past. He reinforces his argument by a present of three manehs of lapis-lazuli, five yoke of horses and five wooden chariots. Lapis-lazuli and horses were the two most valuable exports from Babylon during the Kassite period, and they counterbalanced to some extent Egypt's almost inexhaustible supply of Nubian gold.

Babylon at this time had no territorial ambitions outside the limit of her own frontiers. She was never menaced by Mitanni, and it was only after the fall of the latter kingdom that she began to be uneasy at the increase of Assyrian power.[2] Apart from the defence of her frontier, her chief preoccupation was to keep the trade-routes open, especially the Euphrates route to

[1] Knudtzon, *op. cit.*, pp. 88 ff.   [2] See below, p. 241.

Syria and the north. Thus we find Burna-Buriash remonstrating with Egypt when the caravans of one of his messengers, named Salmu, had been plundered by two Canaanite chiefs, and demanding compensation.[1] On another occasion he writes that Babylonian merchants had been robbed and slain at Khinnatuni in Canaan,[2] and he again holds Akhenaten responsible. " Canaan is thy land," he says, " and its kings are thy servants ; " and he demands that the losses should be made good and the murderers slain.[3] But Egypt was at this period so busy with her own affairs that she had not the time, nor even the power, to protect the commercial interests of her neighbours. For in the majority of the Tell el-Amarna letters we see her Asiatic empire falling to pieces.[4] From Northern Syria to Southern Palestine the Egyptian governors and vassal rulers vainly attempt to quell rebellion and to hold back invading tribes.

The source of a good deal of the trouble was the great Hittite power, away to the north in the mountains of Anatolia. The Hittite kings had formed a confederation of their own peoples north of the Taurus, and they were now pressing southwards into Phœnicia and the Lebanon. They coveted the fertile plains of Northern Syria, and Egypt was the power that blocked their path. They were not at first strong enough to challenge Egypt by direct invasion of her provinces, so they confined themselves to stirring up rebellion among the native princes of Canaan. These they encouraged to throw off the Egyptian yoke, and to attack those cities which refused to join them. The loyal chiefs and governors

[1] Cf. Knudtzon, *op. cit.*, p. 84 f.

[2] This was a Canaanite city built by Akhenaten, and named by him Akhet-aten, in honour of the Solar Disk.

[3] *Op. cit.*, p. 86 f. An interesting little letter addressed " to the kings of Canaan, the servants of my brother," was apparently a passport carried by Akia, an ambassador, whom the Babylonian king had sent to condole with the king of Egypt, probably on the death of his father Amen-hetep III. In it the king writes, " let none detain him ; speedily may they cause him to arrive in Egypt " (cf. *op. cit.*, pp. 268 ff.).

[4] We are not here concerned with this aspect of the letters, as Babylon had but a remote interest in the internal politics of Canaan. Her activities in the west at this time were mainly commercial ; and the resulting influence of her civilization in Palestine is discussed in a later chapter (see below, pp. 289 ff.). The letters will be treated more fully in the third volume of this history, when tracing the gradual expansion of Assyria in the west, and the forces which delayed her inevitable conflict with Egypt.

Q

appealed for help to Egypt, and their letters show that they generally appealed in vain.   For Akhenaten was a weak monarch, and was far more interested in his heretic worship of the Solar Disk than in retaining the foreign empire he had inherited.   It was in his reign that the Anatolian Hittites began to take an active part in the politics of Western Asia.

Until the discovery of the documents at Boghaz Keui, it had only been possible to deduce the existence of the Hittites from the mark they had left in the records of Egypt and Assyria ; and at that time it was

FIGS. 47 AND 48.

REPRESENTATIONS OF HITTITES IN EGYPTIAN SCULPTURE.

The two Figures are parts of the same scene from a relief found at Karnak, representing the introduction of Asiatic ambassadors by an Egyptian prince to Rameses II.   The bearded Semites are readily to be distinguished from their Hittite colleagues, clean-shaven and with their long plaits of hair, or pig-tails, hanging down the back.

[After Meyer.]

not even certain whether we might regard as their work the hieroglyphic rock-inscriptions, which are scattered over a great part of Asia Minor.   But it is now possible to supplement our material from native sources, and to trace the gradual extension of their power by both conquest and diplomacy.   They were a virile race, and their strongly marked features may be still seen, not only on their own rock-sculptures, but also in Egyptian reliefs beside those of other Asiatics.[1]   In facial

[1] See Figs. 47 and 48.   The relief was found by M. Legrain at Karnak ; cf. Meyer, " Reich und Kultur der Chetiter," pl. i.   The inscription in Fig. 47

type, too, they are quite distinct, for the nose, though prominent and slightly curved, is not very fleshy, mouth and chin are small, and the forehead recedes abruptly, with the hair drawn back from it and falling in one, or possibly in two plaits, or pig-tails, on the shoulders.[1] It is still not certain to which of the great families of nations they belonged. The suggestion has been made that their language has certain Indo-European characteristics, but for the present it is safer to regard them as an

FIG. 49.

HITTITE FOOT-SOLDIERS AT THE BATTLE OF KADESH.

The figure illustrates the facial type of the Hittite, with his prominent and slightly curved nose and strongly receding brow.
[After Meyer.]

indigenous race of Asia Minor.[2] Their facial type in any case suggests comparison as little with Aryan as with Semitic stock.

Their civilization was strongly influenced by that of Babylonia, perhaps through the medium of Assyrian trading settlements, which were already established in Cappadocia in the second half of the third millennium. From these early Semitic immigrants, or their successors, they borrowed the clay tablet and the cuneiform system

labels the ambassadors as "*mariana* of Naharain (*i.e.* Northern Syria)," the term *mariana* being the Aryan word for "young men, warriors," doubtless borrowed from the ruling dynasty of Mitanni (see below, n. 2). That in Fig. 48 contains the end of a list of Hittite cities, including [Car]chemish and Aruna, the latter probably in Asia Minor.

[1] See Figs. 49 and 50.

[2] The Mitannian people were probably akin to them, though in the fifteenth century they were dominated by a dynasty of Indo-European extraction, bearing Aryan names and worshipping the Aryan gods Mitra and Varuna, Indra and the Nàsatya-twins (cf. Winckler, "Mitteil. d. Deutsch. Orient-Gesellschaft," No. 35, p. 51, and Meyer, *op. cit.*, p. 57 f.). In spite of Scheftelowitz's attempt to prove the Mitannian speech Aryan (cf. "Zeits. f. vergl. Sprachf.," xxxviii., pp. 260 ff.), it has been shown by Bloomfield to be totally non-Indo-European in character; see "Amer. Journ. of Philol.," xxv., pp. 4 ff., and cf. Meyer, "Zeits. f. vergl. Sprachf.," xlii., 21, and King, "Journ. for Hellen. Stud.," xxxiii., p. 359.

of writing.   But they continued to use their own picture-characters for monumental records ; and even in the later period, when they came into direct contact with the Assyrian empire, their art never lost its individual character.   Some of the most elaborate of their rock-sculptures still survive in the holy sanctuary at Yasili Kaya, not far from Boghaz Keui.   Here on the rock-face, in a natural fissure of the mountain, are carved the figures of their deities, chief among them the great Mother-goddess of the Hittites.   She and Teshub, the

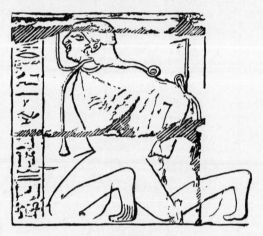

FIG. 50.

HITTITE CHIEFTAIN, A CAPTIVE OF RAMESES III.

A relief of the twelfth century, perhaps the finest representation of a Hittite on the Egyptian monuments ; it is evidently a portrait sculpture, so far as the head is concerned.   It illustrates, too, the manner in which the heavy plait of hair ends in a curled tail.

[After Meyer.]

principal male deity, are here represented meeting, with their processions of deities and attendants.   Whether it was from precisely this area that the Hittite tribes descended on their raid down the Euphrates, which hastened the fall of Babylon's First Dynasty and perhaps brought it to an end, we have as yet no means of judging.[1]   But during the subsequent centuries we

[1] Khatti may well have been an important centre from a very early period, and the use of the name " Hittites " by the late chronicler, in describing the conflicts of the First Babylonian Dynasty, is in favour of this view ; see above, p. 210, n. 2.

may certainly picture a slow but uninterrupted expansion of the area under Hittite control; and it is probable that authority was divided among the various local kingdoms and chieftainships, which occupied the valleys and upland stretches to the north of the Taurus.

At the time of their empire, their capital and central fortress was Khatti, which lay to the east of the Halys,

FIG. 51.

FIGURE, PROBABLY OF A HITTITE KING, FROM THE ROYAL GATE AT KHATTI.

The pose of the figure, slightly leaning to the right, is due to the sloping side of the gateway, beside which it is sculptured in relief.
[After a photo by Puchstein.]

on the Anatolian plateau some three thousand feet above sea-level. It occupied a strong position near the crossing of the great lines of traffic through Asia Minor; and expansion from this area must have begun to take place at an early period beyond the west bank of the river, where the country offered greater facilities for pasturage.   Another line of advance was southward to the coast-plains beneath the Taurus, and it is certain that Cilicia was occupied by Hittite tribes before any attempt was made on Northern Syria.   That at first the Hittites were scattered, without any central organization, among a number of independent city-states, may be inferred from their later records.   For when a land is referred to in their official documents, it is designated " the country of the city of so and so," suggesting that each important township had been the centre of an independent district to which it gave its name.   Some of the Hittite states attained in time to a considerable degree of importance.   Thus we find Tarkundaraba of Arzawa sufficiently eminent to marry a daughter of Amen-hetep III. of Egypt.[1]   Another city was Kussar, one of whose kings, Khattusil I., was the father of Shubbiluliuma, under whom the Hittites were organized into a strong confederacy which endured for nearly two hundred years.   It must have been owing to its strategic importance that Shubbiluliuma selected Khatti as his capital in place of his ancestral city.

Quite apart from its name, and from the traditions attaching to it, there can be no question but that from this time forward Khatti was the centre of Hittite power and civilization ; for it is by far the most extensive Hittite site in existence.   It covers the high ground, including the hill-top, above Boghaz Keui, which lies in the valley below ; and it is fortunate that the greater part of the modern village was built clear of the outer boundaries of the ancient city, as the ruins have in consequence run far less risk of destruction.[2] It was placed high for purely strategic purposes, commanding as it does the Royal Road from the west and the great trunk-road from the south as they approach the city-walls.   The citadel was formed by a flat-topped hill,[3] which dominates the walled city to the north,

---

[1] This we gather from a letter Amen-hetep wrote to him in the Arzawa language, which was found at Tell el-Amarna ; cf. Knudtzon, "Die el-Amarna Tafeln," pp. 270 ff., No. 31.

[2] A portion of the village is built over an extension of the outer fortification-walls on the north-west.

[3] Now known as Beuyuk Kale.   For an account of the excavations, see Puchstein, " Boghasköi : die Bauwerke " (1912) ; and for the best earlier description of the site, see Garstang, " Land of the Hittites," pp. 196 ff.

west, and south of it. Its precipitous slopes descend
on the north-east side to a mountain stream outside
the walls; and a similar stream, fed by shallow gullies,
flows north-westward through the city-area. From the
point where they rise in the south, to their junction
below the city, the ground falls no less than a thousand
feet, and the uneven surface has been fully utilized for
its defence. The wall which surrounded the southern
and higher half of the city is still comparatively well
preserved, and forms three sides of a rough hexagon,

FIG. 52.

THE ROYAL GATE OF KHATTI, THE CAPITAL OF THE HITTITES, VIEWED FROM THE
OUTSIDE.

The massive walls are preserved in their lower courses, but in the sketch the
upper portions are restored in outline. The arched gateway with its sloping sides
is characteristic of Hittite work.

[After Puchstein.]

but the falling and broken ground to the north prevented a symmetrical completion of the circuit. A
series of interior fortification-walls, following the slope
of the ground, enclosed a number of irregular areas,
subsidiary forts being constructed on four smaller hills
along the most southerly cross-wall, which shut in the
highest part of the city.

The city's greatest length from north to south was
about a mile and a quarter, and its greatest width some

three-quarters of a mile, the whole circuit of the existing defences, including the lower-lying area, extending
to some three and a half miles.   This is a remarkable
size for a mountain city, and although some portions of
the area cannot have been occupied by buildings, the
fortification of so extensive a site is an indication of the
power of the Hittite empire and its capital.   About
fourteen feet in thickness, the wall is preserved in many
places to a hight of more than twelve feet.   It consists
of an inner and an outer wall, filled in with a stone
packing.   The outer face was naturally the stronger of

Fig. 53.

CONJECTURAL RESTORATION OF A HITTITE GATEWAY VIEWED FROM INSIDE.

It is possible that brick was employed for the upper structure of the city-
wall and its towers, as suggested in the restoration. In such a case it is not
unlikely that the stepped battlements of Mesopotamia were also adopted.
[After Puchstein.]

the two, and huge stones, sometimes five feet in length,
have been employed in its construction.   The wall was
strengthened by towers, set at more or less regular
intervals along it, their position being sometimes
dictated by the contour of the ground.   Round a
great part of the circuit there are traces of an outer
defensive wall of lighter construction and with smaller
towers, but this was not continuous, being omitted
wherever the natural fall of the ground was a sufficient
protection to the main wall.

Projecting towers also flanked the main gateways, which exhibit a characteristic feature of Hittite architecture. This is the peculiar form of the gateway, consisting of a pointed arch with gently sloping sides, the latter formed by huge monoliths bonded into the structure of the wall.[1] It would seem that brick was probably employed for the upper structure of both wall and towers; and in other buildings of the city, such as the great temple to the north-west of the citadel, brick was used for the upper structure of the walls upon a stone foundation. Whenever the use of brick was adopted in one of the northern lands of Mesopotamia, where stone is plentiful, the latter was always used in the foundations. It is not improbable, therefore, that the stepped battlements of Assyria and Babylon were also borrowed, as that was the most convenient and decorative way of finishing off the upper courses of a fortification-wall built of that material.

In the earlier years of Shubbiluliuma the city was doubtless very much smaller than it subsequently became. But he used it effectively as a base, and, as much by diplomatic means as by actual conquest, he succeeded in making the power of the Hittites felt beyond their own borders. The Syrian revolts in the reign of Amen-hetep III., by which the authority of Egypt was weakened in her Asiatic provinces, undoubtedly received Hittite encouragement. Shubbiluliuma also crossed the Euphrates and ravaged the northern territory of Mitanni, the principal rival of the Hittites up to that time. Later he invaded Syria in

---

[1] In the Lion-Gateway at Khatti the face of each monolith is carved to represent a lion, facing any one approaching the entrance from without (cf. Puchstein, " Boghasköi," pl. 23 f.). The figure sculptured in relief on the inner side of the Royal Gateway (see p. 229, Fig. 51) preserves an interesting feature of the best Hittite work,—an unusual combination of minute surface-adornment with great boldness of design. The hatching and scroll-work on the garment are only roughly indicated in the small drawing, and other detail is omitted. Hair on the breast of the figure, for example, doubtless regarded as a sign of strength and virility, is conventionally rendered by series of minute overlapping curls, which form a diapered pattern traced with the point. This can only be detected on the original stone, or in a large-size photograph, such as that reproduced by Puchstein, *op. cit.*, pl. 19. The Royal Gateway is in the S.E. corner of the city, near the palace and the smaller temples. The great temple, by far the largest building on the site, lies on the lower ground to the north.

force and returned to his mountain fastness of Khatti, laden with spoil and leading two Mitannian princes as captives in his train. On the accession of Akhenaten, Shubbiluliuma wrote him a letter of congratulation; but, when the Syrian prince Aziru acknowledged the suzerainty of Egypt, Shubbiluliuma defeated him and laid the whole of Northern Syria under tribute, subsequently confirming his possession of the country by treaty with Egypt. The state of Mitanni, too, submitted to Shubbiluliuma's dictation, for, on the murder of its powerful king Dushratta, he espoused the cause

Fɪɢ. 54.

LONGITUDINAL SECTION OF THE LOWER WESTERN GATEWAY AT KHATTI.

The diagram, based on the conjectural restoration, indicates the massive construction of the gate-house, and the manner in which both it and the wall were adapted to the rising ground. The passage-way along the battlements must have passed through the towers.

[After Puchstein.]

of Mattiuaza, whom he restored to his father's throne after marrying him to his daughter. We have recovered the text of his treaty with Mitanni, and it reflects the despotic power of the Hittite king at this time. Referring to himself in the third person he says, " The great king, for the sake of his daughter, gave the country of Mitanni a new life." [1]

It was not until the reign of Mursil, a younger son of Shubbiluliuma, that the Hittite empire came into armed conflict with Egypt. A change of dynasty in

[1] Cf. Winckler, " Mitteil. d. Deutsch. Orient-Gesellschaft," No. 35, p. 36.

the latter country, and the restoration of her old religion, had strengthened the government, and now led to renewed attempts on her part at recovering her lost territory. On the first occasion the Hittites were defeated by Seti I. in the north of Syria, and Egypt reoccupied Phœnicia and Canaan. Later on, probably in the reign of Mutallu, Mursil's son, Rameses II. attempted to recover Northern Syria. At the battle of Kadesh, on the Orontes, he succeeded in defeating the Hittite army, though both sides lost heavily and at an early stage of the fight Rameses himself was in imminent

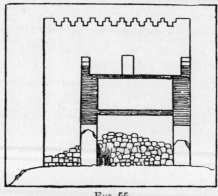

Fig. 66.

TRANSVERSE SECTION OF THE LOWER WESTERN GATEWAY AT KHATTI.

The exterior projection of each flanking tower beyond the wall is indicated in the diagram.

[After Puchstein.]

danger of capture. Episodes in the battle may still be seen pictured in relief on the temple-walls at Luxor, Karnak and Abydos.[1]

The Egyptian war was continued with varying success, though it is certain that the Hittites were

[1] The disastrous opening of the battle was largely due to the over-confidence of Rameses and his complete miscalculation of the enemy's strength and resources ; for the Egyptians had never yet met so powerful an enemy as the Hittites proved themselves to be. With the help of the reliefs it is possible to follow the tactics of the opposing armies in some detail. The accompanying inscriptions are very fragmentary, but they are supplemented by a historical account of the battle, introducing a poem in celebration of the valour of Rameses, preserved on a papyrus in the British Museum. For a detailed account of the battle, illustrated by plans and accompanied by translations of the texts, see Breasted, "Ancient Records of Egypt," Vol. III., pp. 123 ff. ; cp. also Budge, "History," Vol. V., pp. 26 ff., and Hall, "Near East," p 360 f.

eventually successful in the north.   But in the reign of
Khattusil, the brother of Mutallu, both sides were
weary of the conflict, and an elaborate treaty of peace
and alliance was drawn up.   This, when engraved upon
a silver tablet, was carried to Egypt by an ambassador
and presented to Rameses.   The contents of the treaty
have long been known from the Egyptian text, engraved on the walls of the temple at Karnak ; and
among the tablets found at Boghaz Keui was a broken
copy of the original Hittite version,[1] drawn up in
cuneiform characters and in Babylonian, the language
of diplomacy at the period.   Khattusil also maintained
friendly relations with the Babylonian court, and he
informed the king of Babylon of his treaty with the
king of Egypt.   It is clear from a copy of the letter,
recovered at Boghaz Keui, that the Babylonian king
had heard about the treaty and had written to enquire
concerning it.   Khattusil replies that the king of
Egypt and he had formed a friendship and had concluded
an alliance : " We are brothers, and against a foe will
we fight together, and with a friend will we together
maintain friendship."[2]   And his next remark enables
us to identify his Kassite correspondent ; for he adds,
" and when the king of Egypt [formerly] attacked
[Khatti], then did I write to inform thy father Kadashman-turgu."   Khattusil was thus the contemporary of
two Kassite kings, Kadashman-turgu and Kadashman-
Enlil II., the twenty-fourth and twenty-fifth rulers of
the dynasty.

Another section of this letter is of considerable
interest, as it shows that an attempt by Khattusil to
intervene in Babylonian politics had been resented,
and had led to a temporary estrangement between the
two countries.   Khattusil is at pains to reassure
Kadashman-Enlil as to the unselfishness of his motives,
explaining that the action he had taken had been
dictated entirely by the Kassite king's own interests.
The episode had occurred on the death of Kadashman-
turgu, and, according to Khattusil's account, he had at
once written to Babylon to say that, unless the succession of Kadashman-Enlil, who was then a boy, was

---

[1] Cf. Winckler, *op. cit.*, p. 20 f.   [2] *Op. cit.*, p. 23 f.

recognized, he would break off the alliance he had concluded with the late king, Kadasman-Enlil's father. The Babylonian chief minister, Itti-Marduk-balâtu, had taken offence at the tone of the letter, and had replied that the Hittite king had not written in the tone of brotherhood, but had issued his commands as though the Babylonians were his vassals. As a result, diplomatic negotiations had been broken off during the young king's minority; but he had now attained his majority, and had taken the direction of affairs from his minister's hands into his own. The long communication from Khattusil must have been written shortly after the resumption of diplomatic intercourse.

After giving these explanations of his present relations with Egypt, and of his former discontinuance of negotiations with Babylon, Khattusil passes on to matters which doubtless had furnished the occasion for his letter. Certain Babylonian merchants, when journeying by caravan to Amurru and Ugarit, a town in Northern Phœnicia, had been murdered; and, as the responsibility lay on the Hittite empire in its character of suzerain, Kudashman-Enlil had apparently addressed to Khattusil the demand that the guilty parties should be handed over to the relatives of the murdered men. The reference is of interest, as it gives further proof of Babylon's commercial activities in the West, and shows how, after Egypt had lost her control of Northern Syria, the Kassite rulers addressed themselves to its new suzerain to secure protection for their caravans.

We have evidence that such diplomatic action was thoroughly effective, for not only had Babylon's language and system of writing penetrated Western Asia, but her respect for law and her legislative methods had accompanied them, at any rate within the Hittite area. The point is well illustrated by one of the last sections in this remarkable letter, which deals with a complaint by the Babylonian king concerning some action of the Amorite prince, Banti-shinni. The Amorite, when accused by Khattusil of having "troubled the land" of Kadashman-Enlil, had replied by advancing a counterclaim for thirty talents of silver against the inhabitants of Akkad. After stating this fact, Khattusil

continues in his letter: " Now, since Banti-Shinni
has become my vassal, let my brother prosecute the
claim against him ; and, concerning the troubling of my
brother's land, he shall make his defence before the god [1]
in the presence of thy ambassador, Adad-shar-ilâni.
And if my brother will not conduct the action (himself), then shall thy servant come who has heard that
Banti-Shinni harassed my brother's land, and he shall
conduct the action.   Then will I summon Banti-Shinni

FIG. 56.

ONE OF THE TWO SACRED BOATS OF KHONSU, THE EGYPTIAN MOON-GOD, WHO
JOURNEYED INTO CAPPADOCIA TO CAST OUT A DEVIL FROM A HITTITE PRINCESS.

A priest is offering incense before the shrine and sacred boat, which is
being carried on the shoulders of other priests. In the accompanying inscription
on the original stele, the god is referred to in his character as " Plan-Maker in
Thebes " and " Smiter of Evil Spirits."
[After Rosellini.]

to answer the charge.   He is (my) vassal.   If he
harasses my brother, does he not then harass me ? " [2]
It may be that Hittite diplomacy is here making use of
the Babylonian respect for law, to find a way out of a
difficult situation ; but the mere proposal of such a trial
as that suggested proves that the usual method of
settling international disputes of a minor character

[1] That is, under oath, according to the regular Babylonian practice.
[2] Winckler, op. cit., p. 24.

was modelled on Babylon's internal legislative system. It is clear that the Hittite was anxious to prevent strained relations with Babylon, for he goes on to urge Kadashman-Enlil to attack a common enemy, whom he does not name. This must have been Assyria, whose growing power had become a menace to both states, and had caused them to draw together for mutual support.

The account that has been given of this lengthy document will have indicated the character of the royal correspondence discovered at Boghaz Keui. In

Fig. 57.

RAMESES II. OFFERING INCENSE TO ONE OF THE BOATS OF KHONSU BEFORE HE STARTED ON HIS JOURNEY.

The sacred boat of Khonsu is here being borne by a larger retinue of priests into the presence of the king, who did not accompany the god on his journey. [After Rosellini.]

some respects it closely resembles that from Tell el-Amarna, but it exhibits a pleasing contrast by the complete absence of those whining petitions for gold and presents, which bulk so largely in the earlier documents. The Egyptian policy of doles and bribery had brought out the worst side of the Oriental character. The Hittite did not believe in doles, and in any case he had not them to give; as a consequence, his correspondence confines itself in great measure to matters of state and high policy, and exhibits far greater dignity and self-respect. And this applies equally, so far as we can

see, to the communications with Egypt, who had recovered from her temporary decadence. There can be
little doubt that the royal Hittite letters, when published,
will enable us to follow the political movements of the
period in even greater detail.

One other act of Khattusil may be referred to, as it
illustrates in the religious sphere the breaking down of
international barriers which took place. A few years
after the completion of his great treaty, Khattusil
brought his daughter to Egypt, where she was married
to Rameses with great pomp and circumstance. An
intimate friendship continued to exist between the two
royal families, and when Bentresh, his sister-in-law, fell
ill in Khatti and was believed to be incurably possessed
by a devil, Rameses hastened to send his physician to
cure her.[1] But his efforts proving fruitless, the Pharaoh
despatched the holy image of Khonsu, the Egyptian
Moon-god, to Cappadocia, in order to cure her. The
god duly arrived at the distant capital, and, while he
wrought with the evil spirit, it is said that the Hittite
king "stood with his soldiers and feared very greatly."[2]
But Khonsu was victorious, and the spirit having
departed in peace to the place whence he came, there
was great rejoicing. The episode forms an interesting
parallel to Ishtar's journey into Egypt in the reign of
Amenhetep III.

There is no doubt that the son and grandson of
Khattusil, Dudkhalia and Arnuanta, carried on their
father's policy of friendliness towards Babylon, who had
no reason politically to resent the intrusion of Egyptian

[1] This is not the only occasion on which we hear of the despatch of
physicians from one foreign country to another at this period. Naturally
they were supplied by Egypt and Babylon, as the two great centres of science
and learning. Thus Khattusil refers to a physician (asû) and an exorcist
(ashipu), who had formerly been sent from Babylon to the Hittite king
Mutallu but had not returned. Kadashman-Enlil had evidently written to
enquire about them, and Khattusil replies that the exorcist is dead, but that
the physician will be sent back ; cf. Winckler, op. cit., p. 26. Medicine at
this time was, of course, merely a branch of magic, and the asû a practising
magician ; see above, p. 194.

[2] We possess no contemporary reference to Khonsu's journey. The tale
is recorded on a stele, now in the Bibliothèque Nationale, which was engraved
and set up in the Persian or Hellenic period by the priests of Khonsu at
Thebes (cf. Breasted, "Ancient Records," III., pp. 188 ff.). At the head of
the stele is a relief showing the two sacred boats of Khonsu borne on the
shoulders of priests (see p. 238 f., Figs. 56 f.).

HITTITE HIEROGLYPHIC INSCRIPTION.
After Hogarth, Carchemish, pl. B, 6.

influence at Khatti.[1] But Arnuanta is the last king
of Khatti whose name has been recovered, and it is
certain that in the following century the invasion of
Anatolia by the Phrygians and the Muski put an end
to Hittite power in Cappadocia. The Hittites were
pressed southward through the passes, and they continued to wield a diminished political influence in
Northern Syria. Meanwhile Assyria profited by their
downfall and disappearance in the north. She had
already expanded at the expense of Mitanni, and now
that this second check upon her was removed, the
balance of power ceased to be maintained in Western
Asia. Babylon's history from this time forward is in
great part moulded by her relations with the northern
kingdom. Even at the time of the later Hittite kings
she failed to maintain her frontier from Assyrian encroachment, and the capital itself was soon to fall. We
are able to follow the course of these events in some
detail, as, with the reign of Kara-indash I., the earliest
of Amen-hetep III.'s correspondents,[2] our sources of information are increased by the so-called " Synchronistic
History " of Assyria and Babylonia,[3] which furnishes a
series of brief notices concerning the relations maintained
between the two countries.

In the long period between Agum-kakrime[4] and
Kara-indash, the names of three Kassite rulers only have
recovered. From a kudurru,[5] or legal document, of the
reign of Kadashman-Enlil I. we learn of two earlier
Kassite kings, Kadashman-Kharbe and his son Kurigalzu,[6] and it is possible that a son of the latter,

[1] Evidence of increased Egyptian influence may be seen in the fact that,
to judge from the seals upon a Hittite document (cf. Winckler, *op. cit.*,
p. 29), Arnuanta appears to have adopted the Egyptian custom of marrying
his sister.

[2] See above, p. 221.

[3] Cf. " Cun. Texts in the Brit. Mus.," Pt. XXXIV. (1914), pl. 38 ff., and
Schrader, " Keilins. Bibl.," I., pp. 194 ff. ; and cp. Budge and King, " Annals
of the Kings of Assyria," pp. xxii. ff.

[4] See above, p. 218.

[5] See below, p. 245 f.

[6] Kurigalzu I. is recorded to have made a grant of certain land, in the
possession of which Kadashman-Enlil I. confirmed a descendant of the former
owner ; see King, " Babylonian Boundary Stones and Memorial Tablets in
the British Museum," p. 3 f. The document is of considerable importance, as
the reading of Kadashman-Enlil's name upon it has cleared up several points
of uncertainty connected with the vexed subject of the Kassite succession.

R

Meli-Shipak, succeeded his father on the throne. We know nothing of Babylon's relations to Assyria at this time, and our first glimpse of their long struggle for supremacy is in the reign of Kara-indash, who is recorded to have made a friendly agreement with Ashur-rîm-nishêshu with regard to their common boundary.[2] That such an agreement should have been drawn up is in itself evidence of friction, and it is not surprising that a generation or so later Burna-Buriash, the correspondent of Amen-hetep III., should have found it necessary to conclude a similar treaty with Puzur-Ashur, the contemporary Assyrian king.[3] We may regard these agreements as marking the beginning of the first phase in Babylon's subsequent dealings with Assyria, which closes with friendly agreements of a like character at the time of the Fourth Babylonian dynasty. During the intervening period of some three centuries friendly relations were constantly interrupted by armed conflicts, which generally resulted in a rectification of the frontier to Babylon's disadvantage. On only one occasion was she victorious in battle, and twice during the period the capital itself was taken. But Assyria was not yet strong enough to dominate the southern kingdom for any length of time, and at the close of the period Babylon may still be regarded as in occupation of a great part of her former territory, but with sorely diminished prestige.

To appreciate the motives which impelled Assyria from time to time to intervene in Babylonian politics, and to attempt spasmodically a southward expansion, it would be necessary to trace out her own history, and note the manner in which her ambition in other quarters reacted upon her policy in the south. As that would be out of place in the present volume, it will suffice

[1] A red marble mace-head, discovered at Babylon (cf. Weissbach, "Bab. Miscellen," pp. 2 ff.), is inscribed with his name and that of his father. Neither bears a royal title in the text, but, as this is sometimes omitted in the Kassite period, Meli-Shipak may be provisionally regarded as the successor of Kurigalzu I.; cf. Thureau-Dangin, "Journ. Asiat.," XI. (1908), p. 119 f.

[2] Cf. "Annals," p. xxii.

[3] *Op. cit.*, p. xxiii. In the interval between Kara-indash I. and Burna-Buriash are to be set Kadashman-Enlil I. and his son, [. . . .-Bu]riash (see Hilprecht, "Old Bab. Inscr.," I., i., pl. 25, No. 68, and cp. Thureau-Dangin, *op. cit.*, pp. 122 ff.), as well as Kurgalzu II. the father of Burna-Buriash (see above, pp. 221, 224).

here to summarize events so far as Babylon was affected. The friendly attitude of Puzur-Ashur to Burna-Buriash was maintained by the more powerful Assyrian king Ashur-uballit, who cemented an alliance between the two countries by giving Burna-Buriash his daughter Muballitat-Sherûa in marriage. On the death of Burna-Buriash, his son Kara-indash II., who was Ashur-uballit's grandson, ascended the throne, and it was probably due to his Assyrian sympathies that the Kassite party in Babylon revolted, slew him and set Nazi-bugash in his place. Ashur-uballit invaded Babylonia, and having taken vengeance on Nazi-bugash, put Kurigalzu III., another son of Burna-Buriash, upon the throne.[1] But the young Kurigalzu did not fulfil the expectations of his Assyrian relatives, for after Ashur-uballit's death he took the initiative against Assyria,[2] and was defeated at Sugagi on the Zabzallat by Enlil-nirari, to whom he was obliged to cede territory. A further extension of Assyrian territory was secured by Adad-nirari I., when he defeated Kurigalzu's son and successor, Nazi-marut-tash, at Kâr-Ishtar in the frontier district of Akarsallu.[3]

We have already seen from the Boghaz Keui correspondence how the Hittite Empire and Babylon were drawn together at this time by dread of their common foe, doubtless in consequence of the aggressive policy of Shalmaneser I. We do not know whether Kadash-man-Enlil II. followed the promptings of Khattusil, and it is not until the reign of Kashtiliash II.[4] that we have record of fresh conflicts. Then it was that Babylon suffered her first serious disaster at Assyrian hands. Up to this time we have seen that two Assyrian kings had

[1] Cf. "Annals," p. xxvii. The account given by the Synchronistic History is certainly to be preferred to that of the Chronicle 82–7–4, 38. The discrepancies are best explained on the assumption that the latter's editor has confused Kurigalzu, the young son of Burna-Buriash, with Kuri-galzu I., the son of Kadashman-Kharbe I., to whom the chronicler's ascription of success against the Sutû should be transferred (see Thureau-Dangin, "Journ. Asiat.," XI., 1908, pp. 125 ff., and cp. Knudtzon, "Die El-Amarna-Tafeln," p. 34, n. 2).

[2] He was no doubt elated by his successful war with Elam, in the course of which he captured Khurpatila, the Elamite king; cf. Delitzsch, "Das Bab. Chron.," p. 45.

[3] "Annals," pp. xxviii., xxxii.

[4] The successor of his father and grandfather, Shagarakti-Shuriash and Kudur-Enlil upon the Babylonian throne.

defeated Babylonian armies, and had exacted cessions of territory as the result of their victories. Tukulti-Ninib I. was only following in their steps when he in turn defeated Kashtiliash. But his achievement differed from theirs in degree, for he succeeded in capturing Babylon itself, deported the Babylonian king, and, instead of merely acquiring a fresh strip of territory, he subdued Karduniash [1] and administered it as a province of his kingdom till his death.[2] The revolts which closed Tukulti-Ninib's reign and life [3] were soon followed by Babylon's only successful campaign against Assyria.

Adad-shum-uṣur, who owed his throne to a revolt of the Kassite nobles against the Assyrian domination, restored the fortunes of his country for a time. He defeated and slew Enlil-kudur-uṣur in battle, and, when the Assyrians retreated, he followed them up and fought a battle before Ashur. This successful reassertion of Babylon's initiative was maintained by his direct descendants Meli-Shipak II. and Marduk-aplu-iddina, or Merodach-baladan I. ; and the kudurru-records of their reigns, which have been recovered, have thrown an interesting light on the internal conditions of the country during the later Kassite period. But Assyria once again asserted herself under Ashur-dan I., who defeated Zamama-shum-iddin and succeeded in recovering her lost frontier provinces.[4] The Kassite dynasty did not long survive this defeat, although it received its death-blow from another quarter. Shutruk-Nakhkhunte, the Elamite king, invaded Babylonia, defeated and slew Zamama-shum-iddin, and, aided by son Kutir-Nakhkhunte, he sacked Sippar and carried away much

[1] The unification of Babylonia under the Kassites was symbolized by the name Karduniash, which they bestowed on the country as a whole. But the older territorial divisions of Sumer and Akkad still survived as geographical terms and in the royal titles.

[2] Cf. King, " Records of Tukulti-Ninib I.," pp. 96 ff.

[3] The short reigns of Enlil-nadin-shum, Kadashman-Khabe II. and Adad-shum-iddin must be regarded as falling partly within the period of Tukulti-Ninib's troubled years of suzerainty, partly in the reign of Tukulti-Ashur, when the statue of Marduk, carried off by Tukulti-Ninib, was restored to Babylon. The reign of Enlil-nadin-shum was cut short by Kidin-Khutrutash of Elam, who sacked Nippur and Dêr, while a few years later the same Elamite monarch penetrated still further into Babylonia after defeating Adad-shum-iddin ; cf. Delitzsch, " Das Bab. Chron.," p. 46.

[4] " Annals," p. xli

spoil to Elam. The name of the last Kassite ruler, who reigned for only three years, is broken in the Kings' List, but it is possible that we may restore it as Bêl-nadin-akhi,[1] whom Nebuchadnezzar I. mentions after referring to the invasion which cost Zamama-shum-iddin his life. Whether we accept the identification or not, we may certainly connect the fall of the Kassite Dynasty with aggression on the part of Elam, such as so often before had changed the course of Babylonian politics.

Apart from the tablets of the Kassite period discovered at Nippur,[2] our principal source of information on economic conditions in Babylonia at this time is to be found in the kudurru-inscriptions, or boundary-stones, to which reference has already been made.[3] The word *kudurru* may be rendered accurately enough as "boundary-stone," for the texts are engraved on conical blocks or boulders of stone; and there is little doubt that many of the earlier stones must have been set up on landed estates, whose limits and ownership they were intended to define and commemorate. Even at a time when the stone itself had ceased to be employed to mark the boundary and was preserved in the owner's house, or in the temple of his god, as a charter or title-deed to which he could appeal in case of need, the text preserved its old formulæ setting out the limits and orientation of the plot of land to which it referred.

---

[1] The name in the Kings' List reads *Bêl-nadin*-[. . . .]; and in the fragmentary inscription in which Nebuchadnezzar records how he turned the tables upon Elam, he refers to a ruler, between [Zamama]-shum-iddin and himself, as (*ilu*)ʙᴇ-*nadin-akhi* (see Rawlinson, "Cun. Inscr. West Asia," III., pl. 38, No. 2, and cf. Winckler, "Altorientalische Forschungen," I., pp. 534 ff.). The divine ideogram (*ilu*)ʙᴇ was read as Ea by the Babylonians and as Enlil by the Assyrians. And the identification of the two royal names has been called in question on the grounds that the Assyrian copy, in which Nebuchadnezzar's text has come down to us, would have reproduced the Babylonian orthography of its original, and that in any case it is doubtful whether Enlil, like Marduk, ever bore the synonymous title of Bêl (cf. Thureau-Dangin, "Journ. Asiat.," XI., p. 132 f.). If we reject the identification, we should read the name of the last king of the Kassite Dynasty as Ea-nadin-[. . . .], and regard Bêl-nadin-akhi as probably the second or third ruler of the Fourth Dynasty.

[2] The contracts and letters of this period closely resemble those of the time of the First Dynasty. The dated documents have furnished a means of controlling the figures assigned in the Kings' List to the later Kassite rulers; see Clay, "Documents from the Temple Archives of Nippur," in the " Bab. Exped." Series, Vol. XIV. f., and for a number of contemporary letters, see Radau, *ibid.*, Vol. XVII., i.

[3] See above, pp. 241, 244.

The importance of these records is considerable, not only in their legal and religious aspects, but also from a historical point of view.   Apart from the references to Babylonian kings and to historical events, which they contain, they form in many cases the only documents of their period which have come down to us.   They thus serve to bridge the gap in our knowledge of Euphratean civilization between the Kassite epoch and that of the Neo-Babylonian kings ; and, while they illustrate the development which gradually took place in Babylonian law and custom, they prove the continuity of culture during times of great political change.[1]

The kudurru or boundary-stone had its origin under the Kassite kings, and, while at first recording, or confirming, a royal grant of land to an important official or servant of the king, its aim was undoubtedly to place the newly acquired rights of the owner under the protection of the gods.   A series of curses, regularly appended to the legal record, was directed against any interference with the owner's rights, which were also placed under the protection of a number of deities whose symbols were engraved upon the blank spaces of the stone.   It has been suggested that the idea of placing property under divine protection was not entirely an innovation of the Kassites.   It is true that the foundation-cones of the early Sumerian patesi Entemena may well have ended with elaborate curses intended to preserve a frontier-ditch from violation.[2]   But the cones themselves, and the stele from which they were copied, were intended to protect a national frontier, not the boundaries of private property.   Gate-sockets, too, have been treated as closely related to boundary-stones, on the ground that the threshold of a temple might be regarded as its boundary.[3]   But the main object of the gate-socket was to support the temple-gate, and its prominent position and the durable nature of its material

---

[1] For the kudurru-inscriptions in the British Museum, see " Babylonian Boundary-Stones and Memorial Tablets in the Brit. Mus." (1912) ; and for references to and discussions of other texts, cf. Hincke, " A New Boundary-Stone of Nebuchadnezzar I." (1907), pp. xvi. ff., 16 ff.

[2] Cf. "Sumer and Akkad," p. 165.

[3] See Hincke, op. cit., p. 4.

no doubt suggested its employment as a suitable place for a commemorative inscription. The peculiarity of the boundary-stone is that, by both curse and sculptured emblem, it invokes divine protection upon private property and the rights of private individuals.

In the age of Hammurabi we have no evidence of such a practice, and the Obelisk of Manishtusu,[1] the far earlier Semitic king of Akkad, which records his extensive purchases of land in Northern Babylonia, is without the protection of imprecatory clauses or symbols of the gods. The suggestion is thus extremely probable that the custom of protecting private property in this way arose at a time when the authority of the law was not sufficiently powerful to guarantee respect for the property of private individuals.[2] This would specially apply to grants of land to favoured officials settled among a hostile population, especially if no adequate payment for the property had been made by the Kassite king. The disorder and confusion which followed the fall of the First Dynasty must have been renewed during the Kassite conquest of the country, and the absence of any feeling of public security would account for the general adoption of such a practice as placing land in private possession under the protection of the gods.

The use of stone stelæ for this purpose may well have been suggested by a Kassite custom; for in the mountains of Western Persia, the recent home of the Kassite tribes before their conquest of the river-plain, stones had probably been used to mark the limits of their fields, and these may well have borne short inscriptions giving the owner's name and title.[3] The employment of curses to secure divine protection was undoubtedly of Babylonian, and ultimately of Sumerian origin, but the idea of placing symbols of the gods

---

[1] Cf. "Sumer and Akkad," pp. 206 ff.

[2] Cf. Cuq, "Nouvelle Revue Historique," 1907, p. 707 f., 1908, p. 476 f.

[3] Resemblances have been pointed out between the boundary-records of ancient Egypt and those of Babylonia; but of course no inference of borrowing need be inferred from them. The method of marking out the limits of a field or estate by means of boundary-stones, or boundary-tablets, is common among peoples who have abandoned nomad life for agriculture; and the further idea of inscribing the owner's name and title to the land is one that would naturally suggest itself.

upon the stone was probably Kassite.[1]   Moreover, the
kudurru was not the original title-deed recording the
acquisition of the land to which it refers.   As in
the earlier Babylonian periods, clay tablets continued to
be employed for this purpose, and they received the
impression of the royal seal as evidence of the king's
sanction and authority. The text of the tablet, generally
with the list of witnesses, was later on recopied by the
engraver upon the stone, and the curses and symbols
were added.[2]

A boundary-stone was sometimes employed to commemorate a confirmation of title, and, like many modern
legal documents, it recited the previous history of the
property during a long period extending over several
reigns.   But the majority of the stones recovered commemorate original grants of land made by the king to
a relative, or to one of his adherents in return for some
special service. Perhaps the finest of this class of charters
is that in which Meli-Shipak makes a grant of certain
property in Bît-Pir-Shadû-rabû, near the old city of
Akkad or Agade and the Kassite town Dûr-Kurigalzu,
to his son Merodach-baladan I., who afterwards succeeded him upon the throne.[3]   After giving the size
and situation of the estates, and the names of the high
officials who had been entrusted with the duty of drawing up the survey, the text defines the privileges granted
to Merodach-baladan along with the land.   As some of
these throw considerable light on the system of land
tenure during the Kassite period, they may be briefly
summarized.

The king, in conferring the ownership of the land
upon his son, freed it from all taxes and tithes, and forbade the displacement of its ditches, limits, and boundaries.

[1] This is suggested by the fact that the symbols and curses so often do not
correspond ; had they both been bound up in a like origin, we should
have expected the one to illustrate the other more closely.

[2] It was quite optional on the part of a Kassite landowner to engrave
a boundary-stone, and, if he did so, it was simply to secure additional protection for his title.   This is well illustrated by a kudurru of the reign of
Nazi-maruttash (see Plate XXI.), which was only engraved after the original
clay title-deed had been destroyed by the fall of the building in which it had
been preserved.

[3] See Plate XXI., opposite ; and cp. Scheil, "Textes Élam.-Sémit.," I.,
pp. 99 ff., pl. 21 ff.

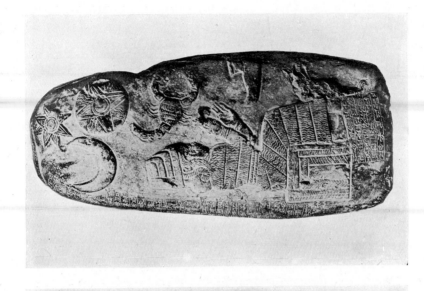

KASSITE BOUNDARY-STONES SET UP IN THE REIGNS OF MELI-SHIPAK AND NAZI-MARUTTASH.

After Délég, en Perse, Mém. I, pl. xvi and xiv.

He freed it also from the *corvée*, and enacted that none of the people of the estate were to be requisitioned among the gangs levied in its district for public works, for the prevention of flood, or for the repair of the royal canal, a section of which was maintained in working order by the neighbouring villages of Bît-Sikkamidu and Damik-Adad. They were not liable to forced labour on the canal-sluices, nor for building dams, nor for digging out the canal-bed. No cultivator on the property, whether hired or belonging to the estate, was to be requisitioned by the local governor even under royal authority. No levy was to be made on wood, grass, straw, corn, or any sort of crop, on the carts and yokes, on asses or man-servants. No one was to use his son's irrigation-ditch, and no levy was to be made on his water-supply even during times of drought. No one was to mow his grass-land without his permission, and no beasts belonging to the king or governor, which might be assigned to the district, were to be driven over or pastured on the estate. And, finally, he was freed from all liability to build a road or a bridge for the public convenience, even though the king or the governor should give the order.

From these regulations it will be seen that the owner of land in Babylonia under the later Kassite kings, unless granted special exemption, was liable to furnish forced labour for public works both to the state and to his local district ; he had to supply grazing and pasture for the flocks and herds of the king and the governor, and to pay various taxes and tithes on land, irrigation-water, and crops. We have already noted the prevalence of similar customs under the First Dynasty,[1] and it is clear that the successive conquests to which the country had been subjected, and its domination by a foreign race, had not to any appreciable extent affected the life and customs of the people nor even the general character of the administrative system.

On one subject the boundary-stones throw additional light, which is lacking at the period of the First Dynasty, and that is the old Babylonian system of land tenure. They suggest that the lands, which formed

[1] See above, pp. 167 ff.

the subject of royal grants during the Kassite period, were generally the property of the local *bîtu*, or tribe.[1] In certain cases the king actually purchased the land from the *bîtu* in whose district it was situated, and, when no consideration was given, we need merely assume that it was requisitioned by royal authority. The primitive system of tribal or collective proprietorship, which is attested by the Obelisk of Manishtusu,[2] undoubtedly survived into the Kassite period, when it co-existed with the system of private ownership, as it had doubtless done at the time of the West-Semitic kings. The *bîtu* must often have occupied an extensive area, split up into separate districts or groups of villages. It had its own head, the *bêl bîti*, and its own body of local functionaries, who were quite distinct from the official and military servants of the state. In fact, agricultural life in Babylonia during the earlier periods must have presented many points of analogy to such examples of collective proprietorship as may be seen in the village communities of India at the present day. As the latter system has survived the political changes and revolutions of many centuries, so it is probable that the tribal proprietorship in Babylonia was slow to decay.

The principal factor in its disintegration was undoubtedly the policy, pursued by the West-Semitic and Kassite conquerors, of settling their own officers and more powerful adherents on estates throughout the country. Both these periods thus represent a time of transition, during which the older system of land tenure gradually gave way in face of the policy of private ownership, which for purely political reasons was so strongly encouraged by the crown. There can be no doubt that under the West-Semitic kings, at any rate from the time of Hammurabi onwards, the policy of confiscation was rarely resorted to. And even the earlier rulers of that dynasty, since they were of the same racial stock as a large proportion of their new subjects, would have

---

[1] Cf. Cuq, "Nouv. Rev. Hist.," 1906, pp. 720 ff., 1908, p. 474 f. This view appears preferable to the theory that the land granted by the Kassite kings was taken from communal or public land of a city, or district, of which the king had the right to dispose (cf. Hincke, "Boundary Stone of Nebuchadnezzar I.," p. 16).

[2] See above, p. 247.

been the more inclined to respect tribal institutions which may have found a parallel in their land of origin. The Kassites, on the other hand, had no such racial associations to restrain them, and it is significant that the kudurrus were now for the first time introduced, with their threatening emblems of divinity and their imprecatory clauses. At first employed to guard the rights of private ownership, often based on high-handed requisition by the king, they were afterwards retained for transfers of landed property by purchase. In the Neo-Babylonian period, when the boundary-stones recorded long series of purchases by means of which the larger landed estates were built up, the imprecations and symbols had become to a great extent conventional survivals.

But that period was still far distant, and the vicissitudes the country was to pass through were not conducive to security of tenure, whether the property were held under private or collective ownership. We have seen that Assyria, as early as the thirteenth century, had succeeded in capturing and sacking Babylon, and, according to one tradition, had ruled the city for seven years. She was shortly to renew her attempts to subjugate the southern kingdom; but it was Elam, Babylon's still older foe, that brought the long and undistinguished Kassite Dynasty to an end.

CHAPTER VIII

THE LATER DYNASTIES AND THE ASSYRIAN
DOMINATION

THE historian of ancient Babylonia has reason to be grateful to Shutruk-Nakhkhunte and his son for their raids into the Euphrates valley, since certain of the monuments they carried off as spoil have been preserved in the mounds of Susa, until the French expedition brought them again to light. Thanks to Babylon's misfortunes at this time, we have recovered some of her finest memorials, including the famous Stele of Narâm-Sin, Hammurabi's Code of Laws, and an important series of the Kassite kudurrus, or boundary-stones, which, as we have seen, throw considerable light upon the economic condition of the country. These doubtless represent but a small proportion of the booty secured by Elam at this period, but they suffice to show the manner in which the great Babylonian cities were denuded of their treasures. Under the earlier kings of the Fourth Dynasty it would seem that Elam continued to be a menace, and it was not until the reign of Nebuchadnezzar I. that the land was freed from further danger of Elamite invasion. We possess two interesting memorials of his successful campaigns, during which he not only regained his own territories, but carried the war into the enemy's country. One is a charter of privileges, which the king conferred upon Ritti-Marduk, the Captain of his chariots, for signal service against Elam. The text is engraved on a block of calcareous limestone, and on one side of it are a series of divine symbols, sculptured in high relief, in order to place the record under the protection of the gods, in accordance with the custom introduced during the Kassite period.

The campaign in Elam which furnished the occasion

for the charter was undertaken, according to the text,[1] with the object of " avenging Akkad," that is to say, in retaliation for the Elamite raids in Northern Babylonia. The campaign was conducted from the frontier city of Dêr, or Dûr-ilu, and, as it was carried out in the summer, the Babylonian army suffered considerably on the march. The heat of the sun was so great that, in the words of the record, the axe burned like fire, the roads scorched like flame, and through the lack of drinking-water " the vigour of the great horses failed, and the legs of the strong man turned aside." Ritti-Marduk, as Captain of the chariots, encouraged the troops by his example, and eventually brought them to the Eulæus, where they gave battle to the Elamite confederation which had been summoned to oppose them.

The record describes the subsequent battle in vivid phraseology. " The kings took their stand round about and offered battle. Fire was kindled in their midst; by their dust was the face of the sun darkened. The hurricane sweeps along, the storm rages; in the storm of their battle the warrior in the chariot perceives not the companion at his side." Here again Ritti-Marduk did good service by leading the attack. " He turned evil against the King of Elam, so that destruction overtook him; King Nebuchadnezzar triumphed, he captured the land of Elam, he plundered its possessions." On his return from the campaign Nebuchadnezzar granted the charter to Ritti-Marduk, freeing the towns and villages of Bît-Karziabku, of which he was the headman, from the jurisdiction of the neighbouring town of Namar. In addition to freedom from all taxation and the *corvée*, the privileges secured the inhabitants from liability to arrest by imperial soldiers stationed in the district, and forbade the billeting of such troops upon them. This portion of the text affords an interesting glimpse of the military organization of the kingdom.

The second memorial too has a bearing on this war, since it exhibits Nebuchadnezzar as a patron of Elamite refugees. It is a copy of a deed recording a grant of land and privileges to Shamûa and his son Shamâia, priests of the Elamite god Rîa, who, in fear of the

[1] Cf. "Boundary-Stones in the Brit. Mus.," pp. 29 ff.

Elamite king, fled from their own country and secured Nebuchadnezzar's protection. The text states that, when the king undertook an expedition on their behalf, they accompanied him and brought back the statue of the god Rîa, whose cult Nebuchadnezzar inaugurated in the Babylonian city of Khuṣṣi, after he had introduced the foreign god into Babylon at the Feast of the New Year. The deed records the grant of five estates to the two Elamite priests and their god, and it exempts the land in future from all liability to taxation and forced labour.[1]

Though Nebuchadnezzar restored the fortunes of his country, he was not the founder of his dynasty.[2] Of his three predecessors, the name of one may now be restored as Marduk-shapik-zêrim. His name has been read on a kudurru-fragment in the Yale Collection, which is dated in the eighth year of Marduk-nadin-akhê, and refers to the twelfth year of Marduk-shapik-zêrim.[3] That he cannot be identified with Marduk-shapik-zêr-mâti is certain, since we know from the "Synchronistic History" that the latter succeeded Marduk-nadin-akhê upon the throne of Babylon, the one being the contemporary of Tiglath-pileser I., the other of his son Ashur-bêl-kala.[4] The close sequence of the reigns of Nebuchadnezzar I., Enlil-nadin-apli, and Marduk-nadin-akhê has long been recognized from the occurrence of the same officials on legal documents of the period.[5] We must therefore place the newly recovered ruler in the gap before Nebuchadnezzar I.; he must be one of the first three kings of the dynasty, possibly its founder, whose name in the Kings' List begins with the divine title Marduk, and who ruled for seventeen years according to the same authority. Another of these missing rulers may perhaps be

[1] See "Boundary-Stones in the Brit. Mus.," pp. 96 ff.
[2] The Fourth Dynasty was known as that of Isin, and the fact that its founder should have come from there is to be explained by the magnitude of the disaster to Northern Babylonia. The city had been known as Nîsin in the earlier period (see above, p. 91, n. 1), but even then there was a tendency to drop the initial n.
[3] I owe this information to Prof. Clay, who is preparing the text for publication.
[4] See below, p. 256.
[5] Op. cit., p. 37.

DIVINE EMBLEMS ON A CHARTER OF NEBUCHADNEZZAR I.
Brit. Mus., No. 90858.

restored as Ea-nadin-[. . . .], if the royal name in the broken inscription of Nebuchadnezzar I., to which reference has already been made,[1] is to be read in that way and not identified as that of the last member of the Kassite Dynasty.   During the earlier years of the Dynasty of Isin Babylonia must have been subject to further Elamite aggression, and portions of the country may for a time have acknowledged the suzerainty of her rulers.

Nebuchadnezzar's successes against Elam and the neighbouring district of Lulubu[2] no doubt enabled him to offer a more vigorous defence of his northern frontier; and, when Ashur-rêsh-ishi attempted an invasion of Babylonian territory, he not only drove the Assyrians back, but followed them up and laid siege to the frontier fortress of Zanki.   But Ashur-rêsh-ishi forced him to raise the siege and burn his siege-train; and, on Nebuchadnezzar's return with reinforcements, the Babylonian army suffered a further defeat, losing its fortified camp together with Karashtu, the general in command of the army, who was taken to Assyria as a prisoner of war. Babylon thus proved that, though strong enough to recover and maintain her independence, she was incapable of a vigorous offensive on a large scale.   It is true that Nebuchadnezzar claimed among his titles that of "Conqueror of Amurru,"[3] but it is doubtful whether we should regard the term as implying more than a raid into the region of the middle Euphrates.[4]

That within her own borders Babylon maintained an effective administration is clear from a boundary-stone of the period of Nebuchadnezzar's successor, Enlil-nadin-apli, recording a grant of land in the district of Edina in Southern Babylonia by E-anna-shum-iddina, a governor of the Sea-Country, who administered that

---

[1] See above, p. 245, n. 1.

[2] Nebuchadnezzar laid claim to the title, "Conqueror of the mighty land of Lulubu"; see "Boundary Stones," p. 31, l. 9.

[3] *Ibid.*, l. 10.

[4] A current exaggeration of Babylon's dominion in the West under Nebuchadnezzar I. appears to have arisen from a confusion as to the authorship of Nebuchadnezzar II.'s fragmentary inscription at the Nahr-el-Kelb, which is written in archaistic characters.

district under the Babylonian king and owed his appointment to him.[1]   But in the reign of Marduk-nadin-akhê,
she was to suffer her second great defeat at the hands
of Assyria.   She fought two campaigns with Tiglath-
pileser I., in the latter part of his reign, after his
successes in the North and West.[2]   In the first she
met with some success,[3] but on the second occasion
Tiglath-pileser completely reversed its result, and followed up his victory by the capture of Babylon itself
with other of the great northern cities, Dûr-Kurigalzu,
Sippar of Shamash, Sippar of Anunitum, and Opis.
But Assyria did not then attempt a permanent occupation, for we find Tiglath-pileser's son, Ashur-bêl-kala,
on friendly terms with Marduk-shapik-zêr-mâti ; and
when the latter, after a prosperous reign,[4] lost his throne
to the Aramean usurper Adad-aplu-iddina,[5] he further
strengthened the alliance by contracting a marriage with
the new king's daughter.[6]

Thus closed the first phase of Babylon's relations
with the growing Assyrian power.   A state of alternate
conflict and temporary truce had been maintained
between them for some three centuries, and now for
more than half a century the internal condition of
both countries was such as to put an end to any policy
of aggression.   The cause of Babylon's decline was the
overrunning of the country by the Sutû, semi-nomad
Semitic tribes from beyond the Euphrates,[7] who made
their first descent during Adad-aplu-iddina's later years,

---

[1] Cf. "Boundary-Stones in the Brit. Mus.," pp. 76 ff.

[2] Tiglath-pileser was the first Assyrian monarch, with the possible exception of Shamshi-Adad III., to carry Assyrian arms to the coast of the
Mediterranean ; and in consequence he attracted Egyptian notice.

[3] It was then that Marduk-nadin-akhê must have carried off the statues
of Adad and Shala from Ekallâti, which Sennacherib afterwards recovered on
his capture of Babylon in 689 B.C. ; cf. "Records of Tukulti-Ninib I.,"
p. 118 f.

[4] A later chronicle credits him with having established his suzerainty over
a large number of petty kings and rulers, and adds that they "beheld
abundance " ; cf. King, "Chronicles," I., p. 190, II., p. 57 f.

[5] The "Synchronistic History" makes Adad-aplu-iddina the son of
E-sagil-shadûni, a man of humble origin ; but, according to a Babylonian
tradition, his father was Itti-Marduk-balâtu, the Aramean (op. cit., I., p. 191,
II., p. 59), and this is more probably correct.

[6] See "Annals of the Kings of Assyria," pp. liii. ff.

[7] On the Sutû and their connexion with the Arameans, see Streck,
"Klio," VI., pp 209 ff.

and, according to a Neo-Babylonian chronicle, carried off with them the spoil of Sumer and Akkad. This was probably the first of many raids, and we may see evidence of the unsettled condition of the country in the ephemeral Babylonian dynasties, which followed one another in quick succession.[1]

The later ruler, Nabû-aplu-iddina, when recording his rebuilding of the great temple of the Sun-god at Sippar,[2] has left us some details of this troubled time ; and the facts he relates of one of the great cities of Akkad may be regarded as typical of the general condition of the country. The temple had been wrecked by the Sutû, doubtless at the time of Adad-aplu-iddina, and it was not until the reign of Simmash-Shipak, who came from the Country of the Sea and founded the Fifth Dynasty,[3] that any attempt was made to re-establish the interrupted service of the deity. His successor, Ea-mukîn-zêr, did not retain the throne for more than five months, and in the reign of Kashshû-nadin-akhi, with whom the dynasty closed, the country suffered further misfortunes, the general distress, occasioned by raids and civil disturbance, being increased by famine. Thus the service of the temple again suffered, until under E-ulmash-shakin-shum of Bît-Bazi, who founded the Sixth Dynasty, a partial re-endowment of the temple took place. But its half ruinous condition continued to attest the poverty of the country and of its rulers, until the more prosperous times of Nabû-aplu-iddina. E-ulmash-shakin-shum was succeeded by two members of his own house, Ninib-kudur-uṣur

---

[1] For a discussion of the evidence supplied by the Kings' List and the fragmentary Assyrian Dynastic Chronicle with regard to the Fifth, Sixth, and so-called Seventh Dynasties, see " Chronicles," I., pp. 183 ff.

[2] See below, p. 260 f.

[3] We know little more than the names of Adad-aplu-iddina's three successors, Marduk-akhi-erba, Marduk-zêr-[. . . .], and Nabû-shum-libur, with whose reign the Fourth Dynasty closed (cf. King, " Proc. Soc. Bibl. Arch.," p. 221). The dynasty founded by Simmash-Shipak has by some been regarded as of Chaldean origin ; and it is possible that Chaldean tribes, though not mentioned in the inscriptions before the period of Ashur-naṣir-pal and Shalmaneser, had already begun to overrun the southern districts of Babylonia. For a discussion of a passage in a religious chronicle, which may possibly record a solar eclipse in Simmash-Shipak's seventh year, see King, " Chronicles," I., pp. 232 ff., and Cowell, " Monthly Notices of the Roy. Astr. Soc.," LXV., pp. 865, 867.

and Shilanum-Shuḳamuna ; but they reigned between them less than four years, and the throne then passed for six years to an Elamite,[1] whose rule is regarded by the later chroniclers as having constituted in itself the Seventh Babylonian Dynasty.

A stable government was once more established in

Fig. 58.

SCENE REPRESENTING NABÛ-MUKÎN-APLI SANCTIONING A TRANSFER OF LANDED PROPERTY.

Arad-Sibitti, accompanied by his sister, receives the royal sanction to the transfer of an estate, situated in the district of Sha-mamîtu, to his daughter as her dowry.

[From Boundary-Stone No. 90835 in the British Museum.]

Babylonia by Nabû-mukîn-apli, the founder of the Eighth Dynasty,[2] though even in his reign Aramean tribes con-

---

[1] For the possible restoration of his name as Ae-aplu-uṣur, see " Chronicles," I., p. 200 f.

[2] There were about thirteen kings of the Eighth Dynasty, and, though their names are completely wanting in the Kings' List, some of them are preserved in records concerning their relations with Assyria. In the gap between Nabû-mukîn-apli and Shamash-mudammik we may probably place Sibir, a Babylonian king whom Ashur-naṣir-pal mentions as having founded Atlila, a city in Zamua, which he himself rebuilt as a royal residence and

tinued to give trouble, holding the Euphrates in the neighbourhood of Babylon and Borsippa, cutting communications, and raiding the country-side. On one occasion they captured the Ferry-Gate of Kâr-bêl-mâtâti and prevented the king from holding the New Year's Festival, as the statue of the god Nabû could not be transported across the river to Babylon.[1] A rude portrait of this monarch is preserved on a boundary-stone of his reign, on which he is represented giving the royal sanction to the transfer of an estate in the district of Sha-mamîtu; and it may be added that considerable friction subsequently took place, with regard to the validity of the title, between the original owner Arad-Sibitti and his son-in-law, a jewel-worker named Burusha.[2] The coarse style of the engraving is probably to be explained by the fact of its provincial origin, though there can be little doubt that the standard of Babylonian art had been adversely affected by the internal condition of the country during the preceding period.

It was at the time of the Eighth Dynasty that the renaissance of Assyria took place, which culminated in the victories of that ruthless conqueror Ashur-naṣir-pal and of his son Shalmaneser III. Its effect was first felt in Babylon in the reign of Shamash-mudammiḳ, who suffered a serious defeat in the neighbourhood of Mt. Ialman at the hands of Adad-nirari III., Ashur-naṣir-pal's grandfather. Against Nabû-shum-ishkun I., the murderer and successor of Shamash-mudammiḳ, Adad-nirari secured another victory, several Babylonian cities with much spoil falling into his hands. But we subsequently find him on friendly terms with Babylon, and allying himself with Nabû-shum-ishkun, or possibly with his successor, each monarch marrying the other's daughter.[3] His son Tukulti-Ninib II. of Assyria,

renamed Dûr-Ashur (cf. "Annals," p. 325). It is improbable that Sibir was one of the missing rulers of the Kassite Dynasty, the only other period to which his reign could be assigned. For the broken name [. . . . -akh]ê-iddina, possibly that of another ruler of this period, see "Chronicles," II., p. 63.

[1] *Op. cit.*, II., p. 81 f.
[2] See Fig. 58; and cf. "Boundary-Stones in the Brit. Mus.," pp. 51 ff.
[3] Cf. "Annals," pp. lvii. ff. Nabû-shum-ishkun's name, attested by Syn. Hist.," III., 9 ff., appears to be given as [Nabû-sh]um-ukîn in "Chron.," II., p. 64.

profiting by the renewed sense of security from attack
upon his southern border, began to make tentative
efforts at expanding westwards into Mesopotamia.   But
it was reserved for Ashur-naṣir-pal, his son, to cross the
Euphrates and lead Assyrian armies once more into
Syrian territory.   After securing his frontier to the east
and north of Assyria, Ashur-naṣir-pal turned his attention to the west.   The Aramean states of Bît-Khadippi
and Bît-Adini, both on the left bank of the Euphrates,
fell before his onslaught.   Then crossing the Euphrates
on rafts of skins, he received the submission of Sangar
of Carchemish, and marched in triumph through Syria
to the coast.

Babylon naturally viewed this encroachment on the
Euphrates route to the west as a danger to her commercial connexions, and it is not surprising that Nabû-
aplu-iddina should have attempted to oppose Ashur-
naṣir-pal's advance by allying himself with Shadudu of
Sukhi.[1]   But the armed forces he sent to support the
people of Sukhi in their resistance were quite unable to
withstand the Assyrian onslaught, and his brother
Ṣabdanu and Bêl-aplu-iddin, the Babylonian leader, fell
into Ashur-naṣir-pal's hands.   In recording his victory
the Assyrian king refers to the Babylonians as the
Kassites,[2] a striking tribute to the fame of the foreign
dynasty which had ended more than three centuries
before.   Nabû-aplu-iddina evidently realized the futility
of attempting further opposition to Assyrian aims, and
he was glad to establish relations of a friendly character,
which he continued in the reign of Shalmaneser.   He
attempted to forget the failure of his military expedition
by repairing the damage inflicted during the numerous
Aramean raids upon the ancient cult-centres of
Babylonia.

He is the king who restored and re-endowed so
richly the temple of Shamash at Sippar, digging in the
ruins of former structures till he found the ancient

---

[1] Sukhi lay on the middle Euphrates, near the mouth of the Khâbûr.   Its
position is accurately indicated by Tiglath-pileser I., who records that he
plundered the Aramean Akhlamî from the neighbourhood of Sukhi up to
Carchemish in one day (cf. "Annals," p. 73).   For a later monument from
the district, see below, p. 265 f.

[2] Cf. "Annals," p. 351 f.

MEMORIAL-TABLET OF NABÛ-APLU-IDDINA, RECORDING HIS
RESTORATION OF THE SUN-TEMPLE AT SIPPAR.
Brit. Mus., No. 91000.

image of the god. He redecorated the shrine, and with much ceremony re-established the ritual and offerings for the god, placing them under the control of Nabû-nadin-shum, a descendant of the former priest E-kur-shum-ushabshi, whom Simmash-Shipak had installed at Sippar. The sculptured scene on the stone memorial-tablet, which records the re-endowment of the temple, represents Nabû-aplu-iddina being led by the priest Nabû-nadin-shum and the goddess Aia into the presence of the Sun-god, who is seated in his temple E-babbar. Before the god is the solar disk resting upon an altar supported by attendant deities, whose bodies spring from the roof of the shrine.[1]

FIG. 59.

MARDUK AND HIS DRAGON FROM A VOTIVE OFFERING OF MARDUK-ZAKIR-SHUM.

[After Weissbach.]

The skill of the Babylonian craftsmen at this period is also attested by a cylinder of lapis-lazuli, engraved in low relief with a figure of Marduk and his dragon, which was dedicated in E-sagila at Babylon by Marduk-zakir-shum, the son and successor of Nabû-aplu-iddina. It was originally coated with gold, and the design and execution of the figure may be compared with those of the Sun-god Tablet, as an additional example of the decorative character of Babylonian stone-engraving in the ninth century.

It was in Marduk-zakir-shum's reign that Assyria capped her conquests of this period by becoming the suzerain of Babylon. Under Ashur-naṣir-pal and Shalmaneser the military organization of the country had been renewed, and both made effective use of their

---

[1] See Plate XXIII. For a translation of the memorial, see "Bab. Boundary-Stones and Memorial Tablets in the Brit. Mus.," pp. 120 ff. The tablet was found in a clay coffer, in which it had been placed at a later period by Nabopolassar, together with clay impressions of the sculptured scene, to preserve the design of the relief in case the tablet itself should eventually be broken.

extraordinarily efficient armies. Ashur-naṣir-pal's policy
was one of annihilation, and the speed with which he
struck ensured his success. Thus when he crossed the
Euphrates after taking Carchemish, the king of
Damascus, the most powerful and important state in
Syria, made no attempt to oppose him or to organize a
defence. He had evidently been taken by surprise.

But Syria then learned her lesson, and at the battle
of Ḳarḳar in 854 B.C. Shalmaneser found himself
opposed by a confederation of the northern kings, and,

FIG. 60.

THE ASSYRIAN ARMY IN CHALDEA, 851 B.C.

In the upper register Assyrian foot-soldiers and cavalry are seen crossing
a stream by a bridge of boats, while below the army is represented leaving its
fortified camp.

[From the Gates of Shalmaneser in the British Museum.]

though he eventually succeeded in ravaging the territory
of Damascus, the city itself held out. In fact, the stubborn resistance of Damascus prevented any further
attempt on Assyria's part at this period to penetrate
further into Southern Syria and Palestine. So Shalmaneser had to content himself with marching northwards across Mt. Amanus, subjugating Cilicia and
exacting tribute from districts north of the Taurus.
He also conducted a successful campaign in Armenia,
from which quarter one of Assyria's most powerful
enemies was about to arise. But it was in Babylonia

that he secured his principal political success.   He has
left us a pictorial record of his campaigns on the bronze
sheathing of two cedar-wood doors of his palace ; and,
as one of the bands commemorates his triumphal march
through Chaldea in 851 B.C., it gives us some indication
of the condition of the country at this time.

The occasion for Shalmaneser's intervention in Babylonian affairs was furnished by internal dissension.[1] When
Marduk-bêl-usâte, the brother of Marduk-zakir-shum,
revolted, and divided the country into two armed camps,
Shalmaneser readily responded to the latter's appeal
for help, and marching southwards succeeded in defeating
the rebels and in ravaging the districts under their control.   On a second expedition in the following year he
completed his work by slaying Marduk-bêl-usâte in

FIG. 61.

A CHALDEAN TOWN OF THE NINTH CENTURY B.C.

The male inhabitants are represented leaving with cattle and tribute for
Shalmaneser III., while the women watch them from the walls.
[From the Gates of Shalmaneser.]

battle, and he was then acknowledged by Marduk-zakir-
shum as his suzerain.   In this capacity he toured
through the principal cities of Akkad, offering sacrifices
in the famous temples of Cuthah, Babylon, and Borsippa.
He also led his army into Chaldea, and, after storming
its frontier fortress of Baḳâni, received the submission
of its ruler, Adini, and heavy tribute from him and from
Iakin, the Chaldean king of the Sea-Country further to
the south.   In his representation of the campaign Shalmaneser is portrayed marching through the country,

[1] See King, "The Gates of Shalmaneser," pp. 18 ff., 31 f.

and receiving tribute from the Chaldeans, which they
carry from their cities and ferry across streams to deposit
in the presence of the king and his officials.

But Babylon did not long endure the position of a
vassal state, and Shalmaneser's son and successor,
Shamshi-Adad IV., attempted her reconquest, plundering many cities before he met with serious opposition.
Marduk-balâtsu-ikbi, the Babylonian king, had meanwhile collected his forces, which included armed levies

Figs. 62 and 63.

THE TRIBUTE OF THE CHALDEANS.

In Fig. 62 Chaldeans are represented conveying tribute across a stream in
boats ; in Fig. 63 they deposit it at a bridge-head held by the Assyrians.
[From the Gates of Shalmaneser.]

from Elam, Chaldea, and other districts. The two
armies met near the city of Dûr-Papsukal, the Babylonians were totally defeated, and a rich booty fell to
their conqueror. During a subsequent interregnum
Erba-Marduk, the son of Marduk-shakin-shum, secured
the throne, owing his election to his success in driving
Aramean raiders from the cultivated fields of Babylon
and Borsippa.[1] But he did not reign for long, and when

---

[1] Cf. "Chronicles," II., p. 66 ff.

Babylon continued to give trouble to Assyria, Adad-nirari IV., the successor of Shamshi-Adad, again sub-jugated a considerable portion of the country, carrying away Bau-akhi-iddina, the Babylonian king, as a captive to Assyria, together with the treasures of his palace.[1]

During the following half-century our knowledge of Babylonian affairs is a blank, and we have not as yet recovered even the names of the last members of the Eighth Dynasty. This epoch corresponds to a period of weakness and inaction in the northern kingdom, such as more than once before had followed a forward movement on her part. The expansion of Assyria, in fact, took place in a series of successive waves, and when one had spent itself, a recoil preceded the next advance. The principal cause of her con-traction, after the brilliant reigns of Shalmaneser III. and his father, may undoubtedly be traced to the rise of a new power in the mountains of Armenia. From their capital on the shore of Lake Van, the Urartians marched southward and menaced the northern frontier of Assyria itself. Her kings could no longer dream of further adventures in the West, which would leave their home territory at the mercy of this new foe. Urartu became now the principal drag on Assyria's ambitions, a part which was afterwards so effectively played by Elam in alliance with Babylon.

It is to this period we may probably assign an inte-resting provincial monument, discovered in Babylon,[2] which illustrates the independent position enjoyed by the rulers of local districts at a time when the central control of either kingdom, and particularly of Assyria, was relaxed. The monument commemorates the prin-cipal achievements of Shamash-rêsh-usur, governor of the lands of Sukhi and Mari on the middle Euphrates.[3] He may have owed his appointment to Assyria, but

---

[1] Cf. "Keilins. Bibl.," I., p. 202 f. At this point the record of the "Synchronistic History" ceases; and it is only with the reign of Nabo-nassar, the second king of the Ninth Dynasty, that our knowledge of the Babylonian succession becomes fuller. In addition to the evidence afforded by the Kings' List, the information contained in the Babylonian Chronicle and the Ptolemaic Canon then becomes available.

[2] See Weissbach, "Babylonische Miscellen," pp. 9 ff.

[3] See above, p. 260, n. 1.

he speaks like a reigning monarch and dates the record
in his thirteenth year.   On it he records his suppression
of a revolt of the Tu'mânu tribe, who threatened his
capital Ribanish, while he was holding festival in the
neighbouring town of Baka.   But he attacked them
with the people who were with him, slew three hundred
and fifty of them, and the rest submitted.   He also
records how he dug out the Sukhi Canal, when it had

FIG. 64.

BAS-RELIEF OF SHAMASH-RÊSH-UŞUR, GOVERNOR OF THE LANDS OF SUKHI AND
MARI.

The scene represents Shamash-rêsh-uṣur standing before the god Adad and
the goddess Ishtar.   The stone was set up in Gabbari-ibni, a city he had founded,
and it commemorates his achievements, the one of which he was most proud
being the introduction of honey-bees into the land of Sukhi.
[After a photo. by Weissbach.]

silted up, and how he planted palm-trees in his palace at
Ribanish.   But his most notable act, according to his
own account, was the introduction of bees into Sukhi,
which his improved irrigation of the district doubtless
rendered possible.   "Bees which collect honey," he tells
us, "which no man had seen since the time of my
fathers and forefathers, nor had brought to the land of

Sukhi, I brought down from the mountains of the Khabkha-tribe and I put them in the garden of Gabbari-ibni." The text closes with an interesting little note upon the bees: "They collect honey and wax. The preparing of honey and wax I understand, and the gardeners understand it." And he adds that in days to come a ruler will ask the elders of his land, "Is it true that Shamash-rêsh-uṣur, governor of Sukhi, brought honey-bees into the land of Sukhi?" The monument may well have been carried to Babylon by Nebuchadnezzar II., when he incorporated the district within his empire.

The subsequent period shows a gradual tightening of Assyria's grasp upon the southern kingdom, varied by comparatively ineffective struggles and revolts on Babylon's part to avoid her loss of independence. The temporary decline of Assyrian power enabled Babylon for a time to regain something of her former position under Nabu-shum-ishkun II., an early king of the Ninth Dynasty, and his successor Nabonassar. But the military revolt in Assyria, which in 745 B.C. placed Tiglath-pileser IV. upon the throne,[1] put a speedy end to Babylon's hopes of any permanent recovery of power. His accession marks the beginning of the last period of Assyrian expansion, and the administrative policy he inaugurated justifies us in ascribing the term "empire" to the area conquered by him, and his successors, in the last half of the eighth and the first half of the seventh centuries B.C. But it was an empire which carried in itself from the outset the seeds of decay. It was based on a policy of deportation, Assyria's final answer to her pressing problem of how to administer the wide areas she annexed. Former Assyrian kings had carried away the conquered into slavery, but Tiglath-pileser IV. inaugurated a regular transference of nations. The policy certainly effected its immediate object: it kept the subject provinces quiet. But as a permanent method of administration it was bound to be a failure. While destroying patriotism and love of country, it put an end

[1] He was an Assyrian general named Pulu, the leader of the revolt, and he took the famous name of Tiglath-pileser to mark his assumption of royal rank; but he retained his own name in Babylon (see p. 268).

at the same time to all incentives to labour.   The subject country's accumulated wealth had already been
drained for the benefit of Assyrian coffers ; and in the
hands of its half-starved colonists it was not likely to
prove a permanent source of strength, or of wealth, to
its suzerain.

Tiglath-pileser's first object, before launching his
armies to the north and west, was to secure his
southern frontier, and this he effected by invading
Babylonia and forcing from Nabonassar an acknowledgment of Assyrian control.   During the campaign
he overran the northern districts, and applied his policy
of deportation by carrying away many of their inhabitants.   The distress in the country, due to the Assyrian
inroads, was aggravated by internal dissension.   Sippar
repudiated Nabonassar's authority, and the revolt was
subdued only after a siege of the city.[1]   The Ninth
Dynasty ended with the country in confusion ; for
Nabû-nadin-zêr, Nabopolassar's son, after a reign of
only two years, was slain in a revolt by Nabû-shum-ukîn,
the governor of a province.[2]   The dynasty soon came to
an end after the latter's accession.   He had not enjoyed
his position for more than a month, when the kingdom
again changed hands, and Nabû-mukîn-zêr secured the
throne.

From the fall of the Ninth Dynasty, until the rise of
the Neo-Babylonian Empire, Babylonia was completely
overshadowed by the power of Assyria.   She became
merely a subject province of the empire, and her Tenth
Dynasty is mainly composed of Assyrian rulers or
their nominees.   Nabû-mukîn-zêr had reigned only
three years when Tiglath-pileser again invaded Babylonia, took him captive, and ascended the throne of
Babylon, where he ruled under his name of Pulu.[3]
On his death, which occurred two years later, he was
succeeded by Shalmaneser V., who, as suzerain of
Babylon, adopted the name of Ululai.   But Babylonia

[1] Though we only possess a few contract-tablets of this period, the fact
that the Ptolemaic Canon begins with the reign of Nabonassar (see above, p.
265, n. 1) is evidence that it marked a revival of literary activity, accompanied
by a study of the chronology and possibly by a revision of the calendar.
[2] So "Bab. Chron.," I., 16 ; in the Kings' List he is described as the son
of Nabû-nadin-zêr.
[3] See above, p. 267, n. 1.

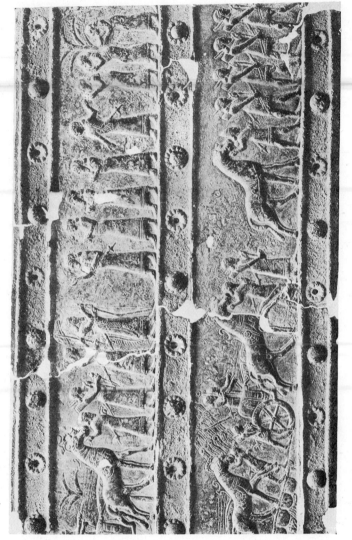

SHALMANESER III RECEIVING THE SUBMISSION OF THE CHALDEANS.

From the Gates of Shalmaneser in the Brit. Mus.

soon demonstrated her power of hindering Assyrian plans, for, after the close of Shalmaneser's reign, when Sargon's army had secured the capture of Samaria, he was obliged to recall his forces from the West by the menace of his southern province.   Merodach-baladan, a Chaldean chief of Bît-Iakin[1] at the head of the Persian Gulf, now laid claim to the throne of Babylon.   By himself he would not have been formidable to Assyria, but he was backed by an unexpected and dangerous ally.   Elam had not meddled in Babylonian affairs for centuries, but she had gradually become alarmed at the growth of Assyrian power.   So Khumbanigash, the Elamite king, allying himself with Merodach-baladan, invaded Babylonia, laid siege to the frontier fortress of Dêr or Dûr-ilu on the Lower Tigris, and defeated Sargon and the Assyrian army before its walls.   Merodach-baladan was acknowledged by the Babylonians as their king, and he continued to be a thorn in the side of Assyria.

After the defeat of Shabaka and the Egyptians at Raphia, Sargon was occupied with the final subjugation of Urartu in the north, which had for so long been a danger to Assyria.   But Urartu had to fight, not only the Assyrians, but also a new enemy, the Cimmerians, who now made their appearance from the north and east.   In fact, Sargon's conquest of Urartu resulted in the destruction of that people as a buffer state, and laid Assyria open to the direct attack of the barbarian invaders, though it was not until the reign of Esarhaddon that their activity began to be formidable.   Meanwhile, having subjugated his other foes, Sargon was able to turn his attention once more to Babylon, from which he expelled Merodach-baladan. His appearance was welcomed by the priestly party, and, entering the city in state, he assumed the title of Governor and for the last seven years of his life he ruled in Babylon virtually as king.   A memorial of his occupation survives to-day in the quay-wall, which he

[1] Merodach-baladan claimed descent from Erba-Marduk, the king of the Eighth Dynasty who secured the throne of Babylon by his services against the Arameans (see above, p. 264).   He made himself popular in Babylon by restoring to its former owners property confiscated by the Assyrians.   In the Frontispiece to this volume he is portrayed making a grant of land to his governor of Babylon.

constructed along the north front of the Southern Citadel.[1]

On Sargon's death in 705 B.C. the subject provinces of the empire rebelled. The revolt was led by Babylon, where Merodach-baladan reappears with Elamite support,[2] while Hezekiah of Judah headed a confederation of the states of Southern Syria. Sennacherib was first occupied with Babylon, where he had little difficulty in defeating Merodach-baladan and his allies. He was then free to deal with Syria and Palestine ; and at Eltekeh, near Ekron, he routed the Egyptian army, which had come to the support of the rebel states. He then received the submission of Ekron, and took Lachish after a siege, though Tyre resisted. After his expulsion from Babylon Merodach-baladan had sought safety by hiding himself in the Babylonian swamps, where he allied himself with the Chaldean prince Mushezib-Marduk ; and Babylon had been left in charge of Bêl-ibni, a young native Babylonian, who had been brought up at the Assyrian court. A rising, headed by Mushezib-Marduk, brought Sennacherib again into the country, who, after defeating the rebels, carried off Bêl-ibni and his nobles to Assyria, leaving his own son Ashur-nadin-shum upon the throne.

The country was in a state of continual disaffection, and after a few years a fresh revolt was headed by a Babylonian, Nergal-ushezib. But he ruled for little more than a year, being defeated by Sennacherib and sent in chains to Nineveh. This took place after the return of the Assyrian army from Nagitu, whither it had been conveyed by Sennacherib, across the head of the Persian Gulf, against the Chaldeans whom Merodach-baladan had settled there.[3] Sennacherib then turned his forces against Elam, and, after plundering

[1] See above, p. 32 f.

[2] According to the Ptolemaic Canon, the two years following Sargon's death formed a period of interregnum, though the Kings' List assigns the throne to Sennacherib. However this may be, we know that in 703 Marduk-zakir-shum proclaimed himself king ; but he had only reigned for one month when he was murdered by Merodach-baladan.

[3] In spite of Sennacherib's devastation of Chaldea, Merodach-baladan had assisted Mushezib-Marduk in his revolt ; but he had then fled with his followers in ships to the coast of Elam, where he died. Sennacherib built ships on the Tigris and dragged them overland to the Euphrates, where his troops embarked.

a considerable portion of the country, he was stopped in his advance into the interior by the setting in of winter. In his absence the Chaldean Mushezib-Marduk seized the throne of Babylon, and allied himself with Elam. But the combined armies were defeated at Khalule, and after the death of Umman-menanu, the Elamite king, in 689, Sennacherib seized Babylon.   Exasperated at her disaffection, he attempted to put an end for all time to her constant menace by destroying the city.   He succeeded in doing an enormous amount of damage, and, by deflecting the course of the Euphrates, wiped out large areas and turned them into swamps.[1] For the last eight years of Senna-cherib's reign the country was given over to a state of anarchy.

In 681 Sennacherib was mur-dered by his sons, and, after a struggle for the succession, Esar-haddon secured the throne.   His first thought was to reverse com-pletely his father's Babylonian policy, and by rebuilding the city and restoring its ancient privileges to placate the priestly party, whose support his grandfather, Sargon, had secured.[2]   In 668 B.C. the statue of Marduk was restored to its shrine, and Esarhaddon's son, Shamash-shum-ukîn, was proclaimed King of Babylon.   At the same time Esarhaddon sought to reconcile the military and ag-gressive party in his own capital by crowning Ashur-bani-pal, his eldest son, as king in Assyria.   But

Fig. 65.

THE GOD ADAD FROM A VOTIVE OFFERING DEDICATED IN E-SAGILA BY ESARHADDON.

[After Weissbach.]

---

[1] An interesting description of the state of Babylon on Esarhaddon's accession is given in the recently published cylinder, inscribed in the year of his accession ; cf. King, "Kouyunjik Catalogue (Supplement)," pp. xviii. f., 7 f., and "Cun. Texts in the Brit. Mus.," XXXIV., pl. 1 f.

[2] We have recovered a lapis-lazuli cylinder-seal, engraved with a figure of "Adad of E-sagila," which he dedicated in that temple ; see Fig. 65, and cf. Weissbach, "Bab. Misc.," p. 17.

Babylon was still taught to look upon Assyria as her suzerain, and the spirit of disaffection was only driven for the moment underground. Esarhaddon's aim had been to retain the territory already incorporated in the Assyrian empire, and, had he been able to confine his country's energies within these limits, its existence as a state might have been prolonged. But he was unable to curb the ambitions of his generals, and, in his effort to find employment for the army, he achieved the ultimate object of his father's western campaigns, the conquest of Egypt.

It was soon apparent that Esarhaddon's occupation of that country had been merely nominal, and it thus fell to his son Ashur-bani-pal to continue the Egyptian war, and to complete the work his father had left unfinished. And though he met with far greater success, he too in the end found the task of any permanent conquest beyond his power.[1] For he soon had his hands full with troubles nearer home, in consequence of which his hold on Egypt gradually relaxed. Urtaku of Elam, who invaded Babylonia, does not appear to have followed up his success; and the subsequent invasion of the country by Teumman was only followed by that ruler's defeat and death in battle. But the strength of Elam was not broken by this reverse, and, when Shamash-shum-ukîn revolted, he received active Elamite support.

Not only in Elam, but also throughout the territory controlled by Assyria, Shamash-shum-ukîn found support in his rebellion, a fact significant of the detestation of Assyrian rule in the scattered provinces of the empire, which continued to be held together only by fear. But the force at Ashur-bani-pal's disposal was still powerful enough to stamp out the conflagration and head off disaster for a time. He marched into Babylonia, besieged and captured Babylon, and his brother Shamash-shum-ukîn met his death in the flames of his palace in 648 B.C. The Assyrian king then

---

[1] Esarhaddon had plundered Memphis, but in a few months it had been recovered by Egypt and the Assyrian garrison massacred. On his final Egyptian campaign in 661, Ashur-bani-pal sacked and destroyed Thebes, and for some years afterwards Egypt continued to acknowledge Assyrian control.

ASHUR-BANI-PAL AS THE RESTORER OF E-SAGILA,
THE TEMPLE OF MARDUK AT BABYLON.
Brit. Mus., No. 90864.

invaded Elam, and, capturing its cities as he advanced, he laid the country under fire and sword. Susa was protected by its river, then in flood, but the Assyrian army effected a crossing, and the ancient capital lay at the mercy of the invaders. Having taken the city, Ashur-bani-pal determined to break its power for ever after the manner Sennacherib had dealt with Babylon, He not only stripped the temples and carried off the treasures of the palace, but he even desecrated the royal tombs, and completed his work of destruction by fire. So Susa was plundered and destroyed, and in Babylon itself Ashur-bani-pal continued to be supreme until his death.[1]

Babylonia had proved herself no match for the legions of Assyria at the height of the latter's power ; but the industrial and commercial life of her cities, based ultimately on the rich return her soil yielded to her agricultural population, enabled her to survive blows which would have permanently disabled a country less favoured by nature. Moreover, she always regarded the Assyrians as an upstart people, who had borrowed her culture, and whose land had been a mere province of her kingdom at a time when her own political influence had extended from Elam to the borders of Syria. Even in her darkest hour she was buoyed up by the hope of recovering her ancient glory, and she let no opportunity slip of striking a blow at the northern kingdom. She was consequently always a drag on Assyria's advance to the Mediterranean, for, when the latter's armies marched westward, they left Babylon and Elam in their rear.

In her later dealings with Babylon Assyria had tried the alternative policies of intimidation and indulgence, but with equal want of success ; and they reached their climax in the reigns of Sennacherib and Esarhaddon. It is quite possible that either of these policies, if consistently pursued, would have been equally futile in its aim of coercing or placating Babylonia. But their alternation was a far worse blunder, as it only

---

[1] The subject of Ashur-bani-pal's probable identification with Kandalanu, and the subsequent relations of Babylon to Ashur-etil-ilâni, Sin-shum-lishir, and Sin-shar-ishkun will be treated in the third volume of this history.

T

succeeded in revealing to the Babylonians their own power, and in confirming them in their obstinate resistance. To this cause we may trace the long revolt under Shamash-shum-ukîn, when Babylon with Elam at her back struck a succession of blows which helped in a material degree to reduce the power of the Assyrian army, already weakened by the Egyptian campaigns. And in 625 B.C., when the Scythians had overrun the Assyrian empire, and her power was on the wane, we find Nabopolassar proclaiming himself king in Babylon and founding a new empire which for nearly seventy years was to survive the city of Nineveh itself.

CHAPTER IX

THE NEO-BABYLONIAN EMPIRE AND THE PERSIAN CONQUEST

FREED from her Assyrian oppressors, Babylon now renewed her youth, and the city attained a material splendour and magnificence such as she had not achieved during the long course of her earlier history. But it took her more than a generation to realize to the full her newly awakened ambitions. After his declaration of independence, Nabopolassar's influence did not extend far beyond the walls of Babylon and Borsippa. The other great cities, both in the north and south, continued for a time to acknowledge Assyrian supremacy. But the sons of Ashur-bani-pal, who succeeded him upon the throne, had inherited a reduced empire, whose sole support, the Assyrian army, was now largely composed of disheartened mercenaries. In Ashur-bani-pal's reign there had been signs of coming change and of the appearance of new races before whom the Assyrians were doomed to disappear. The destruction of Urartu had removed a vital barrier against the incursion of the nomad tribes, and with its disappearance we find new racial elements pressing into Western Asia, of the same Indo-European family as that of the Medes and their Iranian kinsfolk. These were the Scythians, who in the middle of the seventh century had driven the Cimmerians before them into Asia Minor, and it was they who a generation later struck the death-blow of the Assyrian empire, pouring across it in resistless hordes. Assyria had no force in reserve with which to oppose their progress or repair their ravages.

For centuries this great military power had struck terror throughout Western Asia ; but insatiable lust for

dominion now met with its due reward. Since Sennacherib's day the ranks of the army had been filled with
levies drawn from her subject peoples or with mercenary
troops, and these were a poor substitute for the race of
hardy fighters who had been sacrificed in their country's
countless wars. So when the Medes invested Nineveh,
with the possible assistance of the Scythians, and the
passive encouragement of Babylon, the capital could
look for no assistance from her provinces. According
to Herodotus[1] the Medes had already twice invaded
Assyria before the final investment; and it was natural
that Nabopolassar should have regarded them as his
allies, and have concluded a definite alliance with them
by marrying his son Nebuchadnezzar to the daughter
of Cyaxares, the Median king.[2] Sennacherib's mighty
walls kept the enemy at bay for three years, but in 606
B.C. the city was taken by storm, and later ages preserved the tradition that Sin-shar-ishkun, the Sarakos of
the Greeks, perished in the flames of his palace, rather
than fall alive into the besiegers' hands.

Though he does not appear to have taken any active
part in the long siege of Nineveh, Nabopolassar was not
slow in securing his share of the dismembered empire.
The northern territory of Assyria, including Northern
Mesopotamia,[3] fell to the Medes, while the southern
districts became parts of Nabopolassar's empire under a
possible Median suzerainty.[4] But Babylon was soon to
put her newly organized army to the test. Two years
before the fall of Nineveh Egypt had seized the opportunity, afforded her by Assyria's impotence, of occupying Palestine and Syria.[5] She had crushed Josiah and
his Hebrew army at Mégiddo, and, though it is not
certain whether Judah had the support of other allies,

[1] I., 102 f.

[2] According to Abydenus in Eusebius, "Chron., lib. I.," ed. Schoene,
col. 37; the account is preserved in the Armenian version.

[3] This would seem to follow from Nabonidus' references to E-khulkhul,
the temple of Sin in Harran, and its destruction by the Umman-manda after
the fall of Nineveh (cf. Langdon, "Neubab. Königsinschriften," pp. 220 f.,
272 ff.); see Hogarth, "The Ancient East," p. 123. The term Manda is
loosely employed in the inscriptions.

[4] See below, pp. 278 f., 282.

[5] After throwing off the Assyrian yoke Egypt, under the XXVIth
Dynasty, entered on a last period of independence, and it was natural that
she should dream once more of Asiatic empire.

it is clear that Necho encountered no effective opposition on his advance to the Euphrates.   But Nabopolassar did not intend to allow this portion of the Assyrian empire to fall to Egypt unchallenged, and he despatched a Babylonian force north-westwards along the Euphrates under the command of the crown-prince, Nebuchadnezzar.   The two armies met at Carchemish in 604 B.C., where the Egyptians were utterly routed and driven back through Palestine.[1]   But Nebuchadnezzar did not press his pursuit beyond the borders of Egypt, for news reached him at Pelusium of Nabopolassar's death, and he was obliged to return at once to Babylon in order to carry out at the capital the necessary ceremonies attending his accession to the throne.

In spite of his withdrawal from the country, the greater part of Syria and Palestine lost no time in transferring their allegiance to Babylon.   The little state of Judah was an exception, for, though she paid her tribute at first, she soon put the warnings of the prophet Jeremiah at defiance, and her short-sighted revolt led to the capture of Jerusalem by Nebuchadnezzar in 596 B.C., and to the carrying away of a large portion of her population into captivity.   A few years later Egypt made her last attempt to reoccupy Palestine and Syria, and Judah joined the Phœnician cities of Sidon and Tyre in rallying to her support.   In 587 Nebuchadnezzar advanced into Northern Syria and took up a strong strategic position at Riblah on the Orontes, whence he despatched a part of his army to besiege Jerusalem.   An attempt by Apries, the Egyptian king, to relieve the city was unsuccessful, and in 586 Jerusalem was once more taken and the greater part of the remnant of the Jews followed their fellow-countrymen into exile.[2] The Babylonian army then occupied Phœnicia, though the city of Tyre offered an obstinate resistance and only

[1] The Egyptian army at this time must have been a very mixed host, drawn in great part from the African provinces of Egypt, and its stiffening of Greek and Carian mercenaries was probably untrustworthy; cf. Maspero, "Histoire ancienne," III., p. 530 f., and Hall, "Ancient History of the Near East," p. 543 f.

[2] Zedekiah, the last of the kings of Judah, paid dearly for his rebellion. He was captured on his flight from Jerusalem, and carried to Riblah, where Nebuchadnezzar slew his sons before his eyes, blinded him, and then sent him in chains to Babylon (II. Kings, xxv., 1 ff.).

acknowledged its allegiance to Babylon after a long siege, which is said to have lasted for thirteen years.[1]

Thus Nebuchadnezzar completed the work begun by his father, Nabopolassar, and, by the skilful and vigorous prosecution of his campaigns, established the Neo-Babylonian empire on a firm basis, so that its authority was unquestioned from the Persian Gulf to the Egyptian frontier. Of his later campaigns nothing has yet been published, beyond a fragmentary reference to a conflict with Amasis of Egypt in the thirty-seventh year of his reign.[2] Though we do not know the circumstances under which it took place, we may assume that the Babylonian army was again victorious against the Egyptian troops and the Greek mercenaries who fought in their ranks. A tradition is indeed preserved by Josephus that Nebuchadnezzar made Egypt a Babylonian province, and although this is certainly an exaggeration, the evidence suggests that he may well have conducted at least one successful campaign on Egyptian territory. The troubles of Apries in consequence of his ill-advised expedition against Cyrene, followed by the revolt of Amasis and his own deposition and death, may well have furnished the occasion for a successful invasion of the country by Nebuchadnezzar.

A very large number of inscriptions have been recovered of the Neo-Babylonian kings, but, unlike the foundation-records of Assyria, they contain no accounts of military expeditions, but confine themselves to commemorating the restoration or erection of temples and palaces in Babylon and the other great cities in the land. Considering his military successes, this is surprising in Nebuchadnezzar's case, and the suggestion has been made that he may have told us so little of his expeditions and battles because they were perhaps undertaken at the bidding of Media as his suzerain.[3] Cyaxares was his kinsman, and the part played by Babylon in the conflict of Media with Lydia may well be explained on that hypothesis.

[1] From 585 to 573 B.C.

[2] For the text of the tablet, see Strassmaier, "Nabuchodonosor," p. 194, No. 329, and for a full discussion of its contents, cf. Winckler, "Altorient. Forsch.," I., pp. 511 ff.; in Rev., l. 1, it mentions "[Am]âsu, king of Egypt."

[3] Cf. Hogarth, "The Ancient East," p. 124 f.

BRONZE DOOR-STEP FROM E-ZIDA, THE TEMPLE OF NABÛ AT BORSIPPA, INSCRIBED WITH THE NAME AND TITLES OF NEBUCHADNEZZAR II.

Brit. Mus. No. 90851.

With the passing of Assyrian power the political importance of Lydia had risen considerably, and under Sadyattes and Alyattes, the successors of Ardys upon the Lydian throne, the ravages of the Cimmerian invasion were repaired. These monarchs had conducted a long series of attacks upon the cities and states of Ionia, and, though they were in the main successful, they used up the resources of the nation without obtaining material advantages in return. Handicapped to this extent, Lydia entered upon a five years' struggle with the growing power of Cyaxares, who pushed back her eastern frontier. Matters came to a head in 585 B.C., when the great battle was fought on the Halys between Cyaxares and Alyattes on May 28th. The battle is famous for the total eclipse of the sun, which took place on that day, and is said to have been foretold by the Greek astronomer Thales of Miletus.[1] By the subsequent treaty the Halys was fixed as the frontier between Lydia and the Median empire, and, according to Herodotus, it was arranged in part through the mediation of Nebuchadnezzar.[2] The intervention of Babylon must have been undertaken in the Median interest, and it is possible that Cyaxares could count on Nebuchadnezzar for more than benevolent neutrality in case of need.

Nebuchadnezzar appears in his inscriptions as a mighty builder, and we have already seen how he transformed the city of Babylon. He entirely rebuilt and enlarged his father's royal palace,[3] and in the course of his reconstructions raised its terraced platform to so great a height above the surrounding city and plain, that its Hanging Garden became one of the seven wonders of the ancient world.[4] He rebuilt the great temples of E-zida at Borsippa and of E-sagila at Babylon, and the Sacred Procession-street within the city he

[1] Herodotus (I., 74) relates that the Medes and Lydians, when they perceived the day suddenly changed into night, ceased fighting (evidently taking it as a portent from the gods) and were anxious for terms of peace.

[2] The Babylonian king must have been Nebuchadnezzar, though the name given by Herodotus as "Labynetus" is best explained as a corruption of Nabonidus (*Nabû-na'id*).

[3] See above, pp. 38 ff.

[4] For a suggested identification of the Hanging Gardens with a building in the north-east corner of the palace on the Southern Citadel, see above, pp. 46 ff.

sumptuously paved, spanning it between the temple of
Ninmakh and his own palace with the famous Ishtar
Gate, adorned with bulls and dragons in enamelled
relief.[1]   The fortifications of the city he also greatly
strengthened by the extension of its double line of walls
and the erection of new citadels.[2]   During his long reign
of forty-two years he devoted his energies and the new
wealth of his kingdom to this work of rebuilding, both
in the capital and in the other ancient religious centres
of Babylonia.[3]   The decoration of the façade of Nebuchadnezzar's own palace reflects the influence of the West
upon Babylonian art ; and we may picture her markets
and quays as thronged with foreign caravans and merchandise.   Evidence of her extended horizon at this
period may also be traced in the interest which Nebuchadnezzar showed in the sea-traffic on the Persian Gulf,
which doubtless led him to construct a harbour in the
swamps, and to protect it against Arab raids by the
erection of the town of Teredon to the west of the
Euphrates, as an outpost on the desert frontier.[4]

Nebuchadnezzar's son, Amêl-Marduk, was an un-
worthy successor to his father.   During his short reign
he was restrained neither by law nor decency,[5] and it is
not surprising that in less than three years the priestly
party should have secured his assassination and have set
Neriglissar, his brother-in-law, in his place, a man of far
stronger character and a soldier.[6]   The son of a private
Babylonian, Bêl-shum-ishkun, Neriglissar had married a
daughter of Nebuchadnezzar, and we may certainly
identify him with Nergal-sharezer, the Rab-mag or
Babylonian general who was present at the siege of
Jerusalem.[7]   A striking proof that Neriglissar enjoyed

---

[1] See above, pp. 51 ff.   [2] See above, pp. 24 ff., 58.
[3] For a discussion of the temples in Babylon, which Nebuchadnezzar in
great part rebuilt, see above, pp. 61 ff.   His building activity in other cities
is attested by his foundation-records ; cf. Langdon, "Neubab. Königsinschriften," pp. 70 ff.
[4] Cf. Abydenus, in Eusebius, "Chron. lib. I.," ed. Schoene, Col. 39 f., or
Müller, "Fragm. Hist. Græc.," IV., p. 284, which may perhaps reproduce
a statement of Berossus ; see Bevan, "House of Seleucus," I., p. 247.
[5] According to Berossus he reigned ἀνόμως καὶ ἀσελγῶς (cf. Josephus c.
Apion. I., 20, in Müller, op. cit., p. 507).
[6] Evidence that he owed his election to the priestly party may be seen
in the approval accorded him by Nabonidus ; cf. Nab. Stele, Col. IV.,
ll. 24 ff. (Langdon, "Neubab. Königsinschriften," p. 276 f.).
[7] Jer. xxxix., 3, 13.

high military rank in Nebuchadnezzar's reign has recently been obtained in a letter from Erech, which was written by a captain in charge of a body of troops stationed in the neighbourhood of that city.[1] The date of the letter is certain, since the captain refers to soldiers on the roll of Nebuchadnezzar and Neriglissar ; and incidentally it gives us a glimpse of the unsatisfactory condition of the Babylonian army during Nebuchadnezzar's closing years. The captain is anxious that the depleted state of his company, and the measures he contemplates in order to fill its ranks, should not be known to Gubaru, who exercised a high command in Nebuchadnezzar's army. It is possible that we may identify this general with the governor of Gutium, who played so prominent a part in the Persian conquest. Knowing, as he doubtless did, the unsatisfactory condition of his country's forces, he may perhaps have regarded the task of opposing the invaders as quite beyond their powers.[2]

Neriglissar's death, less than four years after his accession, must certainly have been the death-blow to any hopes his generals may have entertained of placing the country's military organization and defence upon a sound footing. For his son was little more than a child, and after nine months' reign the priestly party at the capital succeeded in deposing him in favour of one of their own number, Nabonidus, a man of priestly descent [3] and thoroughly imbued with the traditions of the hierarchy. The new king carried on Nebuchadnezzar's tradition of temple-reconstruction with enthusiasm, but he had none of his great predecessor's military aptitude. To his own priestly detachment he added the unpractical character of the archæologist, loving to occupy himself in investigating the past history of the temples he rebuilt, in place of controlling his country's administration. The bent of his mind is well reflected in the account he has left us of the dedication of his daughter, Bêl-shalti-Nannar, as head of the college of votaries attached to the Moon-temple at Ur.[4] It is clear that

---

[1] Cf. Scheil, " Rev. d'Assyr.," XI., No. iv. (1914), pp. 165 ff.
[2] See below, p. 283.
[3] Cf. Dhorme, " Revue Biblique," 1908, pp. 131 ff.
[4] Cf. Dhorme, " Rev. d'Assyr.," XI., No. iii. (1914), pp. 105 ff.   A

this act and the accompanying ceremonial interested him far more than the education of his son ; and any military aptitude Belshazzar may have developed was certainly not fostered by his father or his father's friends. It was only when the enemy was at the frontier that the king must have realized his own fatuity.

Thus with the accession of Nabonidus the close of Babylon's last period of greatness is in sight.   But the empire did not crumble of its own accord, for in one of his foundation-records the king boasts that the whole of Mesopotamia and the West, as far as Gaza on the Egyptian border, continued to acknowledge his authority.[1] It required pressure from without to shatter the decaying empire, which from the first must have owed its success in no small measure to the friendly and protective attitude of Media.   When that essential support was no longer forthcoming, it lay at the mercy of the new power before which Media herself had already gone down.

The Persian kingdom of Cyrus, rising on a new wave of the Indo-European migration, had had little difficulty in absorbing that of the Medes.[2]   Five years after the accession of Nabonidus, Cyrus had deposed Astyages, and, uniting his own followers from the south of Iran with their Median kinsfolk, he proceeded to deal with Crœsus of Lydia.   Under her last king, the successor of Alyattes, the power of Lydia had risen to its greatest height, and the fame of Crœsus' wealth had attracted many of the more cultured Greeks to his court at Sardis.   But when Cyrus made himself master of the Median empire, Crœsus began to fear his growing power.   In 547 B.C. he fought an indecisive battle with

duplicate account of the dedication will appear in Prof. Clay's forthcoming " Miscellaneous Inscriptions in the Yale Babylonian Collection," No. 45.

[1] See his cylinder in the British Museum, 82–7–4, 1025, recording his restoration of the temples in Harran and Sippar, Col. I., ll. 38 ff. ; cf. Langdon, " Neubab. Königsinschriften," p. 220 f.

[2] Though Cyrus was at first merely king of Anshan in Elam, with Susa as his capital, he was undoubtedly of Aryan descent. The rise of the southern or Persian group of the Iranians coincided with the westward expansion of the Median empire, and the fusion of the two branches may well have been fostered by disaffection in the north, due to the favour shown by the Median kings to their Scythian subjects. This would in great measure account for the ease with which Cyrus possessed himself of the Median empire ; cf. Hogarth, " The Ancient East," pp. 159 ff.

I. BAKED CLAY FOUNDATION-CYLINDER OF NABONIDUS, REFERRING TO
THE DEFEAT OF ASTYAGES BY CYRUS [Brit. Mus. No. 91109].
II. BAKED CLAY FOUNDATION-CYLINDER OF CYRUS, RECORDING HIS
ENTRY INTO BABYLON "WITHOUT BATTLE AND WITHOUT FIGHTING."
[Brit. Mus., No. 90920].

the Persians at Pteria in Cappadocia, near the site of the old Hittite capital, and he then retreated on Sardis. Here he sent for assistance to Sparta, Egypt and Babylon. But Cyrus did not delay before renewing his attack, and he appeared unexpectedly before the capital. The Lydian army was now signally defeated ; Sardis, in which Crœsus had taken refuge, was captured after a siege, and the Lydian empire brought to an end. Cyrus was then free to turn his attention to Babylon.

If we should be right in identifying Gobryas or Gubaru, the governor of Gutium, with the Babylonian general of that name, who had held high position under Nebuchadnezzar,[1] we may trace the speed and ease of the Persian conquest of Babylonia directly to his action in espousing the cause of the invader. Foreseeing that the only hope for his country lay in its speedy submission, he may have considered that he would be acting in its best interests if he did not oppose its incorporation within the Persian empire, but rendered the revolution so far as possible a peaceful one. That would explain the action of Cyrus in entrusting the invasion largely to his hands ; and the subsequent revolt of Sippar is the more easily accounted for if a Babylonian general with Gubaru's reputation had appeared as the envoy of the Persian king. In any case we must assume that a large section of the Akkadian population was of that way of thinking, quite apart from the opposition to himself that Nabonidus had aroused in the priestly party of the capital.

The defence of the country was entrusted by Nabonidus to his son Belshazzar, who met the advancing Persians at Opis, where he was defeated ; and, as often as he attempted to rally his forces, they were again dispersed.[2] Sippar then opened its gates without fighting, Nabonidus fled, and Gubaru advancing on the capital secured its peaceful surrender. The native chronicler of these events records that, during the early days of the Persian occupation of the city, the shields of Gutium surrounded the doors of E-sagila, so that no man's spear entered the sacred shrines and no

---

[1] See above, p. 281.
[2] See the " Nabonidus-Cyrus Chronicle," Rev., Col. III., ll. 12 ff. ; and cp. Hagen, " Beitr. zur Assyr.," II., p. 222 f.

military standard was brought in.[1] The record gains
fresh meaning if we may assume that the governor
of Gutium was himself of native origin and a former
general of the Babylonian army.   On the third day of
the following month Cyrus made his state entry into
the capital, being received by all classes, and especially
by the priesthood and the nobles, as a liberator.   He
appointed Gubaru his governor of Babylon, and the
latter appears to have stamped out further resistance
by pursuing Belshazzar and putting him to death.[2]
Nabonidus had already been taken, when the capital
surrendered.

It is perhaps remarkable that the native priesthood,
from whose ranks Nabonidus himself had sprung, should
have welcomed the Persian king as their country's
deliverer, whose victory had been brought about by
Marduk, the national god.   But, after securing the
secular control, Nabonidus had given free rein to his
priestly ambition, and, as a consequence, had estranged
his own party.   His imagination may have been fired by
some ill-advised scheme of centralizing worship ; but,
whatever his motive, the king had collected many of
the cult-images throughout the country into the capital,
little recking that he thereby tore the gods from their
ancient habitations.   By restoring the gods to their
local shrines, Cyrus gained in popularity, and completely
won over the priesthood, by far the most powerful
political section of the community.[3]   Thus it happened
that Babylon made no further struggle to retain her
freedom, and the whole of the territory she had enjoyed
was incorporated without resistance in the Persian
empire.

With the permanent loss of Babylon's independence,
the period covered by this history draws to an end.
The epoch forms a convenient stopping-place ; but,
unlike the fall of the Assyrian empire, her conquest
made but little difference to the life and activities of

---

[1] Cf. "Nab.-Cyr. Chron.," Col. III., ll. 16 ff.

[2] The passage in the Chronicle, which appears to record this act on
Gubaru's part (Col. III., l. 22 f.), is broken and its reading is not certain ;
but the fact that the next entry relates to a period of national mourning in
Akkad is in favour of the interpretation suggested.

[3] Cf. "Nab.-Cyr. Chron.," Col. III., ll. 18 ff.

the population as a whole. It may therefore be permissible to glance ahead a little, and note her subsequent fortunes as a subject province, under the foreign domination of the powers which succeeded one another in the rule of that region of Western Asia. The tranquillity of the country under Cyrus formed a striking contrast to the unrest and intrigue which characterized its attitude under Assyrian rule ; and this was due to the fact that the policy he inaugurated in the provinces of his empire was a complete reversal of Assyrian methods. For the nationality of each conquered race was respected, and it was encouraged to retain its own religion and its laws and customs. Hence Babylon's commercial life and prosperity suffered no interruption in consequence of the change in her political status. Taxation was not materially increased, and little was altered beyond the name and title of the reigning king in the dates upon commercial and legal documents.[1]

This state of things would doubtless have continued, had not the authority of the Persian empire itself been rudely shaken during the reign of Cambyses, Cyrus' son and successor. The conquest of Egypt and its incorporation as an integral part of the Achæmenian empire, to which he directed his main energies, were achieved after the battle of Pelusium and the fall of Memphis. But when attempting to extend his sway over Nubia in the south, he received news of revolt in Persia. Before his departure for Egypt he had murdered his brother Bardiya, known to the Greeks as Smerdis. The murder had been kept a secret, and the revolt against the absent king was now headed by a Magian, named Gaumata, who gave himself out as the missing Smerdis and the true heir to the throne.[2] Cambyses made preparations to repress the revolt, but died on his return journey in Syria in 522. The death of the king gave a fresh impetus to the forces of rebellion, which now began to spread through the provinces of the Persian empire. But

[1] The enormous number of these that have been recovered attest the continued prosperity of the country.
[2] Cf. King and Thompson, "Sculptures and Inscription of Darius," pp. 6 ff.

Gaumata, the Persian rebel, soon met his fate. For after Cambyses' death, the Persian army was led back by Darius, a prince of the same house as Cyrus and his son; Gaumata was surprised and murdered, and Darius firmly established on the throne. Darius continued to act with extraordinary energy, and in the course of a single year succeeded in quelling the rebellions in Babylon and in the various provinces.[1] On the rock-face of Behistun in Persia, on the road from Babylon to Ecbatana, he has left us sculptured portraits of himself and the rebel leaders he subdued. The latter include Nidintu-Bêl and Arakha, the two pretenders to the Babylonian throne.[2]

The sieges of Babylon by Darius mark the beginning of the city's decay. Her defences had not been seriously impaired by Cyrus, but they now suffered considerably. The city was again restless during Darius' closing years,[3] and further damage was done to it in the reign of Xerxes, when the Babylonians made their last bids for independence.[4] For Xerxes is said not only to have dismantled the walls, but to have plundered and destroyed the great temple of Marduk itself. Large areas in the city, which had been a wonder of the nations, now began to lie permanently in ruins. Babylon entered on a new phase in 331 B.C., when the long struggle between Greece and Persia was ended by the

[1] Cf. Weissbach, "Zeits. für Deutsch. Morgenländ. Gesellschaft," Bd. LXII. (1908), pp. 631 ff. The majority of the national revolts were probably suppressed during the accession-year of Darius and the early part of his first year. The later revolts of Susiania and Scythia also gave little difficulty; Weissbach (ib., p. 641) suggests a restoration of the Persian text of the Behistun Inscription which would place them in the fourth and fifth year of Darius' reign.

[2] See King and Thompson, op. cit., Plates iii., xv. and xvi.

[3] It was only towards the end of Darius' reign, after the Egyptian revolt, that we have evidence pointing to a renewal of Babylonian unrest (see below, n. 4). The fear inspired by Darius on his accession was evidently felt throughout his Asiatic provinces, and it was the revolt of Egypt, not Asia, that checked his activities against the Greeks.

[4] For a list of documents dated in the brief reigns of Bel-simanni, Shamash-erba, and two other Babylonian usurpers of this period, see Weissbach, op. cit., p. 644. The extraordinary variants in writing the Babylonian form of Xerxes' name show the difficulty the Babylonians had in pronouncing it; but Akshimakshu can hardly be regarded as such a variant, and may well be that of a rebel who secured a brief period of power (cf. also Boissier, "Orient. Lit.-Zeit.," 1913, p. 390). On the evidence of the proper names occurring in the contracts, he and the others are all to be placed in the reign of Xerxes or in the last years of Darius.

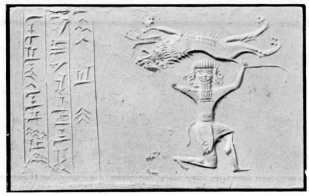

IMPRESSIONS OF NEO-BABYLONIAN AND PERSIAN CYLINDER-SEALS.
Brit. Mus., Nos. 18249, 89140, 89352.

defeat of Darius III. at Gaugamela. For Susa and Babylon submitted to Alexander, who on proclaiming himself King of Asia, took Babylon as his capital. We may picture him gazing on the city's great buildings, many of which now lay ruined and deserted. Like Cyrus before him, he sacrificed to Babylon's gods; and he is said to have wished to restore E-sagila, Marduk's great temple, but to have given up the idea, as it would have taken ten thousand men more than two months to remove the rubbish from the ruins. But he seems to have made some attempt in that direction, since a tablet has been found, dated in his sixth year, which records a payment of ten manehs of silver for " clearing away the dust of E-sagila." [1]

While the old buildings decayed, some new ones arose in their place, including a Greek theatre for the use of the large Greek colony.[2] Many of the Babylonians themselves adopted Greek names and fashions, but the more conservative elements, particularly among the priesthood, continued to retain their own separate life and customs. In the year 270 B.C. we have a record that Antiochus Soter restored the temples of Nabû and Marduk at Babylon and Borsippa,[3] and the recent diggings at Erech have shown that the old temple in that city retained its ancient cult under a new name.[4] In the second century we know that, in a corner of the great temple at Babylon, Marduk and the God of Heaven were worshipped as a two-fold deity under the name of Anna-Bêl; and we hear of priests attached to one

[1] Cf. Oppert, "Comptes rendus," 1898, pp. 414 ff.
[2] See above, p. 83, Fig. 31, J. The theatre was built of mud-brick; for the pillars and their bases a sort of concrete was employed, made of burnt-brick rubble and gypsum mortar, washed over with white plaster.
[3] Cf. Rawlinson, "Cun. Inscr. West. Asia," V., pl. 66.
[4] In contract-tablets from the site, dating from the third and second centuries B.C., the old temple E-anna is always referred to under the name Bît-rêsh, "Chief Temple," or "Chief Building" (cf. Clay, "Babylonian Records in the Library of J. Pierpont Morgan," Pt. II., 1913). Prof. Clay has recently sent me a transcript of a very interesting building-inscription from the same site, drawn up in the year 244 B.C., which will appear as No. 52 in his forthcoming "Miscellaneous Inscriptions." It records the rebuilding of Bît-rêsh by a certain Anu-uballit, the second prefect (shanû) of Erech, who also bore the Greek name Νικαρκος (Nikiḳarḳusu, Nikarḳusu); it was clearly a privilege to bear a Greek name, as he tells us he was given his by "Antiochus, king of the lands." The text furnishes additional evidence of the survival of the literary language of Babylon for official records, and of the conservatism of the religious cult.

of Babylon's old shrines as late as the year 29 B.C.
Services in honour of the later forms of the Babylonian
gods were probably continued into the Christian era.

The life of the ancient city naturally flickered longest
around the ruined temples and seats of worship.   On
the secular side, as a commercial centre, she was then
but a ghost of her former self.   Her real decay had set
in when Seleucus, after securing the satrapy of Babylon
on Alexander's death, had recognized the greater advantages offered by the Tigris for maritime communication.   On the foundation of Seleucia, Babylon as a city
began rapidly to decay.   Deserted at first by the official
classes, followed later by the merchants, she decreased
in importance as her rival grew.   Thus it was by a
gradual and purely economic process, and through no
sudden blow, that Babylon slowly bled to death.

CHAPTER X

GREECE, PALESTINE AND BABYLON: AN ESTIMATE OF
CULTURAL INFLUENCE

DURING the Persian and Hellenistic periods
Babylon exerted an influence upon contemporary races of which we may trace some survivals in the civilization of the modern world. She was
the mother of astronomy, and the twelve divisions on
the dial of our clocks and watches were ultimately derived, through Greek channels, from her ancient system
of time-division. It was under the Neo-Babylonian
kings that the Hebrew race first came into close contact
with her culture, and there can be no doubt that the
Jews, in the time of their captivity, renewed their interest
in her mythology when they found it presented some
parallels to their own. But in the course of this history
it has been shown that, during far earlier periods, the
civilization of Babylon had penetrated throughout a
great part of Western Asia. It is admitted that, as a
result of her westward expansion at the time of the First
Dynasty, her culture had spread during subsequent
periods to the Mediterranean coast-lands, and had
moulded to some extent the development of those
peoples with whom it came in contact. And since the
religious element dominated her own activities in a
greater measure than was the case with most other
races of antiquity, it has been urged that many features
in Hebrew religion and in Greek mythology can only
be rightly explained by Babylonian beliefs in which they
had their origin. It is the purpose of this chapter to
examine a theory of Babylon's external influence, which
has been propagated by a school of writers and has
determined the direction of much recent research.

U

It is scarcely necessary to insist on the manner in which material drawn from Babylonian and Assyrian sources has helped to elucidate points in the political and religious history of Israel. Scarcely less striking, though not so numerous, are the echoes from Babylonian legends which have long been recognized as existing in Greek mythology. The best known example of direct borrowing is undoubtedly the myth of Adonis and Aphrodite, the main features of which correspond closely to the Babylonian legend of Tammuz and Ishtar. In this case not only the myth, but the accompanying festival and rites were also borrowed, passing to Greece by way of Byblos on the Syrian coast and Paphos in Cyprus, both centres of Astarte worship.[1] Another Greek legend, obviously of Babylonian origin, is that of Actæon, who is clearly to be identified with the shepherd, loved by Ishtar and changed by her into a leopard, so that he was hunted and killed by his own hounds.[2]

Some parallels have also long been pointed out between the national heroes Heracles and Gilgamesh. It is true that most races of antiquity possess stories of national heroes of superhuman strength and power, but there are certain features in the traditions concerning Heracles which may have some ultimate connexion with the Gilgamesh cycle of legends.[3] Less convincing is the analogy which has been suggested between Icarus and Etana, the Babylonian hero or demi-god, who succeeded in flying to the highest heaven only to fall

[1] The cult of Adonis travelled to Greece not later than the seventh century, B.C., and there is evidence that his rites were subsequently celebrated both in Argos and in Attica ; see Frazer, " Adonis, Attis, Osiris," I., pp. 13 ff., 226 f. For the Sumerian origin of the legend, see Zimmern, "Sumerisch-babylonische Tamūzlieder" (1907), and Langdon, "Tammuz and Ishtar' (1913).

[2] Though Actæon was changed into a stag by Artemis, the main features of the Babylonian myth, viz. the angry goddess, the changing of the hero into a beast, and his death due to his own hounds, persist in the various versions of the Greek story.

[3] Apart from other detailed resemblances, the labours and sufferings to which Heracles is exposed through Hera's hatred, a feature common to all forms of the Greek legend, find a close parallel in the persecution and trial of Gilgamesh by Ishtar. For the most recent discussion of the possible influence of the Gilgamesh legends on Hebrew traditions, see the additional note on "The mythical element in the Story of Samson," in Prof. Burney's forthcoming volume on "Judges," in the "Oxford Church Biblical Commentary."

headlong to the earth. For in Etana's case there is no question of human flight: he was carried to heaven by his friend the Eagle, to whose wings he clung while they mounted to heaven's gates. But the examples already referred to may suffice to illustrate the way in which it has long been agreed that Babylonian mythology may have left its impress on that of Greece.

But the views now held by a considerable body of scholars suggest a much broader extension of Babylonian influence than is implied by a series of isolated and fortuitous connexions; and, as the character of this influence is *ex hypothesi* astronomical, any attempt to define its limits with precision is a matter of some difficulty. For it will be obvious that, if we may assume an astronomical basis or background to any two mythologies, we at once detect a great number of common features the existence of which we should not otherwise have suspected. And the reason is not far to seek; for the astronomical phenomena with which we go to work are necessarily restricted in number, and they have to do duty many times over as a background in each system.[1] In spite of this disadvantage, which is inherent in their theory, Winckler and his school have rendered good service in working out the general relationship which was believed by the Babylonians to exist between the heavenly bodies and the earth.[2] He has shown sound reasons for assuming that, according to the tenets of Babylonian astrology, events and institutions on earth were in a certain sense copies of heavenly prototypes.

It is well known that the Babylonians, like the Hebrews, conceived the universe as consisting of three parts: the heaven above, the earth beneath, and the waters under the earth. The Babylonians gradually elaborated this conception of the universe, and traced in the heavens a parallel to the threefold division of earth, separating the universe into a heavenly and an earthly world. The earthly universe consisted as before

---

[1] It is precisely this laxity of application, and the consequent temptation to abuse it, that have led many of their critics to deny all value to the researches of the late Hugo Winckler and his followers.

[2] For the chief literature in which their astral theory is expounded, see below, p. 292, n. 3.

of three divisions, that is to say the heaven (limited to the air or atmosphere above the earth), the earth itself, and the waters beneath it.   Those corresponded in the heavenly world to the Northern heaven, the Zodiac, and the Southern heaven or heavenly ocean.   By the later Babylonian period the greater gods had long become identified with the planets, and the lesser gods with the fixed stars, each deity having his special house or star in heaven in addition to his temple on earth. This idea appears to have been carried still further by the later Greek astrologers, by whom lands and cities in addition to temples were thought to have their cosmic counterparts.[1]   But even for the Babylonians the moving stars were not merely symbols serving as interpreters to men of the divine will ; their movements were the actual cause of events on earth.   To use an apposite simile of Winckler, heaven was believed to be related to earth much as a moving object seen in a mirror was related to its reflection.[2]

In order to illustrate the way in which these astral ideas are said to have supplied material to Greek mythology, a test instance may be selected, the suggested explanation of which involves one of the essential features of Winckler's astral system as he eventually elaborated it.[3]   We will take the story of the Golden

[1] On this subject, cf. Cumont, "La plus ancienne géographie astrologique" in "Klio," IX. (1909), Hft. 3, pp. 263 ff.

[2] A striking instance of the way in which this astral conception of the universe, as current at any rate among the later school of Babylonian astrologers, has left its imprint on Hebrew literature may be seen in Is. xxvii., 1, an eschatological prophecy of post-exilic date, where the imagery is clearly drawn from Babylonian sources.   The "winding" or "crooked serpent" of the passage is the constellation Draco, which winds about the North Pole ; Serpens, a little to the north of the ecliptic, is " the fugitive serpent" ; while Hydra, the water-snake, dwelling in the southern heaven or heavenly ocean, is " the dragon that is in the sea."   The passage was first explained in this way by Burney, "Journ. Theol. Stud.," XI. (1910), pp. 443 ff.

[3] Stucken's "Astralmythen" (1896–1907) appears to have strongly influenced Winckler, whose theory attracted general attention on its exposition in the "Preussische Jahrbücher" in 1901 (Bd. 104, pp. 224 ff.) and in "Himmels- und Weltenbild der Babylonier als Grundlage der Weltanschauung und Mythologie aller Völker," in " Der alte Orient," III., 2–3.   He elaborated special points in his " Altorientalische Forschungen " (1902–1905) ; see also Winckler and Jeremias, " Im Kampfe um den alten Orient," Leipzig, 1907–8. For a defence of the astronomical assumptions of the theory, see especially Jeremias, " Das Alter der babylonischen Astronomie " (op. cit., Hft. 3, 1908) ; and cf. Weidner, " Orient. Lit.-Zeit.," 1911, Col. 345 ff., and 1913, Nos. 1 and 2 (Sonderabdruck, 16 pp.) ; see further, pp. 304, 308.

LIMESTONE STATUE OF THE GOD NABÛ AT NIMRÛD.

Lamb of Atreus and Thyestes, which is introduced by Euripides into one of the choruses in his *Electra*.[1] According to the story, which is referred to, but not explicitly told, by Euripides, the Lamb with the Golden Fleece was brought by Pan to Atreus, and was regarded by the Argives as a sign that he was the true king. But his brother Thyestes, with the help of Atreus' wife, stole it and claimed to be king ; so strife ensued, good was turned to evil, and the stars were shaken in their courses. It is curious that the theft of the Lamb should have such a special effect upon the heavens and the weather, for this is definitely stated in the second strophe and antistrophe of the chorus.[2] Though details are obscure, it is clear that we here have a legend with strongly marked astrological elements. The theft of the Lamb changes the sun's course, and from other lines in the chorus we gather that the alteration led to the present climatic conditions of the world, the rain-clouds flying northward and leaving " the seats of Ammon "—that is, the Libyan desert—parched and dewless.

In its original form the legend may well have been a story of the First Sin, after which the world was changed to its present state, both moral and atmospheric.[3] There is definite evidence that the Golden Lamb was identified with the constellation Aries ; and since Babylon was admittedly the home of astrology, it is not an improbable suggestion, in spite of the reference to Ammon, that we should regard it as one of the lost legends of Babylon. According to Winckler's theory of the Babylonian religion, we should go further, and trace the origin of the legend to a convulsion in Babylonian thought which took place in the ninth and eighth centuries B.C. At this period, it is asserted, the sun at the vernal equinox was moving from the constellation Taurus into Aries. The bull, according to the theory, was identified with Marduk, the god of

---

[1] Winckler's explanation of the passage is cited by Prof. Gilbert Murray in his " Electra of Euripides," p. 91 f., and by Prof. Burrows in his " Discoveries in Crete," p. 133.

[2] Ll. 726 ff.

[3] Cf. Murray, *op. cit.*, p. 91.

Babylon,[1] and all the time he was yielding his place to the Ram, Babylon was declining before the power of Assyria. The disorganization of the calendar and the seasons, due to the imperfect method of time-reckoning in vogue, was associated with this event, giving an impetus to a fresh birth of legends, one of which has found its way in a Greek dress into this chorus of Euripides. Or, as it has been put rather differently, the story is a piece of Babylonian astronomy misunderstood.

The theory underlying this interpretation of the legend is based on the axiom that the Babylonian religion was essentially a star-worship, and that behind every department of the national literature, secular as well as religious, lay the same astral conception of the universe. Before treating the theory in greater detail, it may be well to ascertain how far the history of the country substantiates this view. In the earliest period of which we have recovered material remains there can be no doubt that image-worship formed a characteristic feature of the Babylonian religious system, though we have no means of tracing its gradual evolution out of the fetish and stock-and-stone worship which necessarily preceded it.[2] The extraneous civilization, which the Sumerians introduced, most probably included cult-images of their gods, and these may well have been already anthropomorphic. Fashioned in the god's form, the image was believed to enshrine his presence, and for the Babylonians of all periods it never lost this animistic character.

A tribal or city-god, in his earliest stage of development, was doubtless wholly identified with his cult-image. No more than one image of each was worshipped, and the idea of a god's existence apart from this visible form must have been of gradual growth.[3] The

---

[1] The bull was actually associated with Adad, the Weather-god, and naturally symbolized the God of Thunder.

[2] Cf. Taylor, "Primitive Culture," II., pp. 143 ff.

[3] It is possible to conjecture circumstances which would have tended to encourage speculation in that direction. The capture and deportation of a god, if followed by the substitution of another figure in its place and the subsequent recovery of the original, would have led to the incorporation of two figures within one shrine. And a king's ambition to rebuild or beautify a temple might have been extended to the image itself, if the latter had suffered damage or decay.

misfortunes of the material image, especially if unaccompanied by national disaster, would have fostered a belief in the god's existence apart from his visible body of wood or stone.   And such a belief eventually developed into the Babylonian conception of a heavenly division of the universe, in which the great gods had their dwelling, making their presence manifest to men in the stars and planets that moved across the sky.   But this development marked a great advance upon pure image-worship,

FIG. 66.   FIG. 67.   FIG. 68.

THE WEATHER-GOD AND TWO GODDESSES FROM AN ASSYRIAN BAS-RELIEF.

The goddesses wear the horned headdresses of Babylonian deities, and, as they are represented being carried by soldiers, they had probably been taken from a captured Babylonian town.

[After Layard.]

and undoubtedly followed the growth of a pantheon out of a collection of separate and detached city-gods.   We have no means of dating the association of some of the greater gods with natural forces.   It would seem that, in the earlier Sumerian period, religious centres in the country were already associated with lunar and solar cults and with other divisions of nature-worship.   But it is quite certain that, during all subsequent stages of Babylonian history, the divine image never degenerated into a mere symbol of divinity. Without consciously postulating a theory in explanation of his belief, the Babylonian found no difficulty in reconciling a localization of the divine person with his presence at other cult centres and ultimately with a separate life in the heavenly sphere.

That this was actually the case is proved by a number of historical examples. With the rise of Babylon we may note the important part which the actual image of

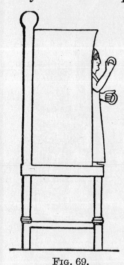

FIG. 69.

FIGURE OF DEITY IN
SHRINE.
[After Layard.]

Marduk played in each coronation ceremony and in the renewal of the king's oath at every subsequent Feast of the New Year; the hands of no other image than that in E-sagila would serve for the king to grasp. In Hammurabi's reign we see the Babylonian's conception of his visible gods reflected in his treatment of foreign images.[1] The international exchange of deities in the fourteenth and thirteenth centuries has already been referred to,[2] and the recovery of captured images was always recorded with enthusiasm.[3] For the images themselves constituted a nation's chief weapon of offence, and there was always the chance that, if properly treated by their captors, they might transfer their influence to the other side. This close connexion between the god and his image survived into the Neo-Babylonian period,

---

[1] It was not merely as booty, but in order to gain their favour, that Sin-idinnam and his army carried off certain Elamite goddesses to their own land, conveying them carefully as in their shrines; and on the restoration of the images to Elam the goddesses themselves returned thither (cf. "Letters of Hammurabi," III., pp. 6 ff.). It was in the same spirit that Nebuchadnezzar I. gave sanctuary to the refugee priests from Elam, and introduced their god Rîa into Babylon (see above, p. 253 f.).

[2] See above, pp. 221 f., 240.

[3] Agum-kakrime's recovery of the images of Marduk and Ṣarpanitum is an instance in point (see above, pp. 210, 218). But perhaps the most striking example is Ashur bani-pal's recovery of Nanâ's image from Susa, which had been carried off from Erech sixteen hundred and thirty-five years before (see above, p. 113). He probably found her installed in her Susian shrine, perhaps within the temple of Shushinak, the national god.

DIVINE EMBLEMS ON A CHARTER OF NEBUCHADNEZZAR I.
Brit. Mus., No. 90858.

and Nabonidus' offence in the eyes of the priesthood was simply that he ignored the feeling. Historical evidence thus suggests that the astral aspect of divinity in Babylonia was not an original feature of its religious system, and that it was never adopted to the exclusion of more primitive ideas.

A similar result follows if we examine the relation of a Babylonian deity to his sculptured emblem, by means of which his authority or presence could in certain circumstances be secured or indicated. The origin of such emblems was not astrological, nor is it to be sought in liver-augury : they were not derived from fancied resemblances to animals or objects, presented either by constellations in heaven, or by markings on the liver of a victim. It is clear that they arose in the first instance from the characters or attributes assumed by the gods in the mythology ; their transference to constellations was a secondary process, and their detection in liver-markings resulted, not in their own origin but in that of the omen.[1] In the earliest period the emblem of a city-god might symbolize his city's power,[2] and those of other deities expressed some quality in the character of their possessor, or were drawn from a weapon, object or animal with which they were associated in tradition.[3]

Another class of images were the animal forms, also drawn largely from the mythology, which adorned the earlier temples and were reproduced in enamelled brickwork on secular buildings by the Neo-Babylonian kings. Most of these, in the later as in the earlier periods, were placed near temple-entrances, and where stone was so plentiful that it could be used in bulk in the structure

---

[1] The Spear-head of Marduk was a fit emblem for the slayer of Tiamat, the demon of chaos, and the Stilus, or Wedge, of Nabû suits the god of writing and architecture. The emblems of some of the great nature-gods were naturally astrological, such as the Lightning-fork of Adad, and the lunar and solar disks for the Moon-god and Sun-god ; but this character was not shared by the majority of the emblems.

[2] The emblem of Ningirsu of Lagash, for example, was a lion-headed eagle grasping lions ; cf. "Sumer and Akkad," p. 100.

[3] Some divine emblems were purely animal, such as the Dog of Gula, the Walking Bird of Bau, and the Scorpion of Ishkhara. It may be added that in these cases there is nothing to indicate a totemistic origin, and the analogy of the Goat-fish of Enki or Ea, the god of the Deep, suggests that they are not to be traced beyond the mythological stage.

of buildings, the doorways themselves were carved in
the same way. That animal forms were employed to
symbolize sound is suggested by the representation of a
great harp or lyre on a Sumerian-bas-relief, in which
the figure of a bull surmounting the sound-case is
evidently intended to suggest the peculiarly deep and
vibrant tones of the instrument.[1] Moreover, on cylinder-
seals engraved with the figure of the Sun-god emerging
from the Eastern Gate of heaven, two lions are often
set immediately above the opening doors, and in one

FIG. 70.

SUMERIAN HARP.

[After *Dec. en Chald.*, pl. 23.]

specimen the gate-pivots rest upon a second pair
arranged symmetrically below them.[2]

The symbolism of these and similar monsters may
well have been suggested by the grinding of the heavy
doors in their stone sockets and the shrieking of their
bolts.[3] The noises suggested the cries of animals, which,

[1] See Fig. 70; and cp. Heuzey, "Musique chaldéenne" in the "Rev.
d'Assyr.," IX., No. iii. (1912), pp. 85 ff. M. Heuzey supports his suggestion
by quoting a description of a similar instrument of music from a contemporary text: "The 'portico' of the lyre was like a bellowing bull."

[2] See p. 299, Fig. 71, and cp. Plate XVI. (No. 89110), opposite p. 192.

[3] Heuzey (*loc. cit.*) cites the following description of the doors set up by
Gudea in the temple of Ningirsu : "The doors of cedar-wood, installed in the

in accordance with the tenets of primitive animism, were thought to inhabit the doors and gateways and to guard them. We may probably trace to this ancestry the colossal lions and winged bulls which flanked the doorways of Assyrian and Persian palaces, and, like the enamelled monsters of Babylon and Persepolis, continued to be reproduced as divine guardians of a building after their primitive associations had been forgotten or modified.[1]

Archæological evidence thus supports the view, already deduced from historical considerations, that astrology did not dominate the religious activities of

Fig. 71.

THE GUARDIAN LIONS OF THE EASTERN GATE OF HEAVEN.
[After Heuzey.]

Babylon. And an examination of the literature points to the same conclusion. Magic and divination bulk largely in the texts recovered, and in their case there is nothing to suggest an underlying astrological element.[2] We are the less inclined, therefore, to accept the axiom that an astral conception of the universe permeated and coloured Babylonian thought to such an extent, that

gateway, were like the God of Thunder thundering in the heavens ; the bolt of the temple of E-ninnû was like a savage dog ; the pivots were like a lion ; . . . on the . . ., placed above the doors, he (Gudea) caused a young lion and a young panther to dwell " (cf. Thureau-Dangin, " Sum. und Akkad. Königsinschriften," p. 118 f., Col. 26, ll. 20 ff.).

[1] Cf. " Proc. Soc. Bibl. Arch.," XXXIV. (1912), pp. 276 ff.

[2] Our knowledge of Babylonian literature has been derived in great measure from Assyrian sources, and, as the civilization of both countries was intimately connected, the two branches of the subject will be treated together at the close of the third volume of this history. It will then also be possible to speak more confidently on the relative part played by Sumerian and Semite in the development of Babylonian law, after the publication of the recently discovered Sumerian code (see above, p. 163, n. 2). Incidentally the document will throw light on the extent to which primitive Semitic custom, shared possibly by the Hebrews, may have moulded some of the provisions of Hammurabi's Code.

not only myths and legends, but even historical events, were recorded in terms which reflect the movements of the sun, moon and planets and the other phenomena of the heavens. If we once grant this assumption, it might perhaps have followed, as the astral mythologists claim, that the beliefs of the Babylonian star-worshippers became the prevailing doctrine of the ancient East and left their traces broadcast upon the records of antiquity. But the original assumption appears to be unsound, and

FIG. 72.

WINGED MONSTER ON ENAMELLED FRIEZE AT PERSEPOLIS.
[After Dieulafoy.]

the theory can only find support by treating late evidence as applicable to all stages of Babylonian history.

The roots of the theory are placed in a purely imaginary age, where evidence for or against it is lacking. Thus the oldest monuments which have been recovered upon Babylonian sites are not considered relics of the early stages of Babylonian culture.[1] It is asserted that in the periods behind them there existed an elaborate

---

[1] The rude inscriptions from such a mound as Fâra (cf. "Sumer and Akkad," pp. 24 ff.), the site of the city of Shuruppak which is mentioned in the Deluge-story, are not regarded as archaic. The shell seals, copper weapons, and rough stone necklaces from the graves beneath the city are treated with scant attention. All are assigned to a comparatively late stage of development.

and highly developed civilization, lying back in the darkness beyond the earliest extant records. In the total absence of material evidence, it is no difficult task to paint this age in colours which are shared by no other early or primitive race in the world's history. It is assumed that war and violence had no existence in Babylonia in this prehistoric time. Intellect dominated and controlled the passions of the primæval but highly gifted people, and in particular one form of intellectual conception based on a scientific knowledge of astronomy. It is postulated that a purely astronomical theory of the universe lay at the root of their civilization, and governed their whole thought and conduct. This was no teaching of a learned priesthood, but was a universally held belief which permeated every branch of the national and individual life. The theory in its perfect and uncorrupted state had perished with the other relics of its inventors. But it was inherited by the Semitic immigrants into Babylonia, and, though employed by them in an altered and corrupted form, has, it is said, left its traces in the later records. In this way the astral mythologist would explain the fragmentary character of his data, from which he claims to reconstruct the original beliefs in their entirety.

One such belief has been preserved by Seneca,[1] who, giving Berossus as his authority, refers to a Chaldean theory of a great year, a long cosmical period having, like the year, a summer and a winter. The summer is marked by a great conflagration produced by the conjunction of all the planets in Cancer, and the winter is characterized by a universal deluge caused by a similar conjunction of all the planets in Capricorn. The idea is evidently based on the conception that, as the succession of day and night corresponds to the changes of the seasons, so the year itself must correspond to greater cycles of time. Though Berossus is our earliest authority, the doctrine is regarded as a primitive Babylonian one. It is further argued that, even in the earliest period, the inhabitants of Babylonia conceived the history of the world to have been evolved in a series of successive

[1] "Quæst. Natur.," III., 29, ed. Haase, p. 235.

ages, bearing the same relation to these æons of the world-cycle as the year bore to them.

The theory of Ages of the World is familiar enough from the classical conception, first met with in Hesiod's "Works and Days,"[1] which profoundly influenced later Greek speculation. There is nothing particularly astral about Hesiod's conception of four ages, distinguished by the principal metals and showing progressive deterioration. But it is claimed that Hesiod's theory, and all parallel conceptions of World-Ages, are derived from a Babylonian prototype, Hesiod's Golden Age reflecting the general condition of prehistoric Babylonia. Assuming a close correspondence between the zodiac and the earth in early Babylonian thought, it is argued that the inhabitants of the country from the earliest periods divided the world's history into ages of about two thousand years each, according to the particular sign of the zodiac in which the sun stood each year at the vernal equinox, when the New Year's Festival was celebrated.[2] Although these ages are never named nor mentioned in the inscriptions, they are referred to by the astral mythologists as the Ages of the Twins, the Bull, and the Ram,[3] from the zodiacal constellations of Gemini, Taurus, and Aries.

This is a vital point of the theory and it postulates on the part of the early Babylonians a highly accurate knowledge of astronomy : it assumes a knowledge of the procession of the equinoxes, which could only be based on a very rigid system of astronomical observation and record.[4] But the ancient Babylonians are supposed to have been quite familiar with these facts, and to have traced a close connexion between them and the world's history. Certain myths are supposed to have charac-terized each of these world ages, not only affecting religious beliefs, but so obsessing Babylonian thought

[1] Ll. 108 ff.

[2] This was the most important festival in the Babylonian calendar ; see above, pp. 190, 296.

[3] See above, p. 293 f.

[4] The position of the sun at the vernal equinox varies, of course, only very slightly from year to year. Its displacement amounts to only a day in about seventy-two years ; and, if we assign thirty degrees to each of the twelve ecliptic constellations, it takes 2151 years to pass, in this way, through a single figure of the zodiac.

TWO VIEWS OF A CLAY MODEL OF A SHEEP'S LIVER, ANNOTATED
FOR PURPOSES OF DIVINATION.

Brit. Mus., No. 92668.

that they influenced historical writings. As the sun at the vernal equinox gradually progressed through the ecliptic constellations, so, according to the theory, the history of the world was believed to be evolved in harmony with its course, and the pre-ordained fate of the universe was slowly unrolled.

Up to this point the astral theory is very complete and, granting its original hypotheses, it goes smoothly enough. But as soon as its authors try to fit the existing legends to their theory, difficulties begin. In Babylonian mythology we find no pair of heroes who present any resemblance to the Dioscuri. But lunar cults were prominent in the earliest Babylonian epoch, and, in default of any closer parallel, the two phases of the waxing and the waning moon have been treated as characterizing the myths and legends of the Age of the Twins. Borrowing a term from music, they are described as the characteristic *motif* of the age. The second Age, that of the Bull, begins roughly with the rise of Babylon to power. There is very slender evidence for connecting Marduk, the god of Babylon, with the zodiacal constellation of the Bull, but the connexion is confidently assumed.[1] The Third Age, that of the Ram, presents even more difficulties than its two predecessors, for no amount of ingenuity can discover material for a Ram *motif* at Babylon. But Jupiter Ammon was represented with the head of a ram, and he is assumed to have been identical in his nature with Marduk. Thus the new reckoning is supposed to have passed over to Egypt, while Babylon remained unaffected.[2] The explanation put forward is that the Ram Age began at a time when the power of Babylon was on the decline; but why the Babylonians should therefore have ignored

---

[1] The fact that the bull was employed to decorate Ishtar's Gate at Babylon affords no grounds for connecting the bull with the city-god. The bull is always associated with the God of Thunder (see above, p. 294, n. 1), whereas Marduk was essentially a solar deity. This latter fact is made use of by the mythologists, who argue that an Age of the Sun would naturally follow an Age of the Moon, and that solar myths are to be looked for as characteristic of this second period.

[2] The admission that the Marduk-myths were unaffected by the Ram is difficult to reconcile with the importance attached by the astral mythologists to the advent of a new Age.

the true position of the sun at the vernal equinox is not quite obvious.

The foreign influence of Babylon's conception of the universe is said to have left its strongest imprint on Hebrew historical writing. It is claimed that the Biblical narratives relating to the earlier history of the Hebrews have in particular been influenced by the Babylonian myths of the universe, and that a great number of passages have in consequence an astral significance. This side of the subject has been worked out in detail by Dr. Alfred Jeremias,[1] and a few examples will suffice to illustrate the system of interpretation which is suggested. We will take one of the Babylonian legends which is said to be most frequently encountered in the Hebrew narratives, the Descent of the goddess Ishtar into the Underworld in search of her youthful husband Tammuz, which in its Babylonian form is unquestionably a nature-myth. There can be little doubt that in the myth Tammuz represents the vegetation of spring; this, after being parched up by the summer-heat, is absent from the earth during the winter months, until restored by the goddess of fertility. There is also no doubt that the cult of Tammuz eventually spread into Palestine, for Ezekiel in a vision saw women at the north gate of the temple at Jerusalem weeping for Tammuz.[2] We have already noted its arrival in Greece in the story of Adonis and Aphrodite.[3] In its Greek form the contest between Aphrodite and Persephone for the possession of Adonis reproduces the struggle between Ishtar and Ereshkigal in the Abode of the

[1] See his "Das alte Testament im Lichte des alten Orients" (1st ed., Leipzig, 1904), and more especially the revised and enlarged English edition published in 1911 in the "Theological Translation Library." In his introduction to this edition of the work Canon Johns, while stating that it is not the province of the writer of an introduction to combat any of the opinions of the author, admits that he differs from Dr. Jeremias' opinions on many points. A reviewer of the volumes in the "Church Quarterly Review," Vol. LXXIV., No. 147 (April, 1912), pp. 166 ff., comments on "the apologetic impulse which is as marked in Dr. Jeremias as its form is peculiar." Readers who might be inclined to see in the work grounds for condemning the results obtained by the literary criticism of the Old Testament are warned by Canon Johns in his introduction that they "would be ill-advised to lean too heavily on this staff of Babylonia."

[2] Ezek. viii., 14.

[3] See above, p. 290.

Dead ; and the annual disappearance and reappearance of Tammuz gives rise in the Greek version to the decision of Zeus that Adonis should spend one part of the year above ground with Aphrodite and the other part underground with Persephone.[1] Such are the main facts, which are not disputed, concerning this particular Babylonian myth. We may now note the manner in which it is said that *motifs* from it are interwoven in the Old Testament with traditions concerning the early history of the Hebrews.

It is well known that in early Christian writings, such as the Syriac "Hymn of the Soul," a Gnostic composition of the second or third century A.D.,[2] the land of Egypt is sometimes referred to in a metaphorical or allegorical sense. It is suggested that the story of Abraham's journey with his wife Sarah into Egypt[3] may have been written, by a parallel system of allegory, in terms reflecting a descent into the underworld and a rescue from it. It is true that in the story Pharaoh's house is plagued, probably with sterility, a feature that recalls the cessation of fertility on earth while the goddess of love remains in the underworld. But the same *motif* is traced in the rescue of Lot from Sodom : here Sodom is the underworld. The pit into which Joseph is thrown by his brethren and the prison into which Potiphar casts him also represent the underworld ; and his two fellow-prisoners, the chief baker and the chief butler, are two minor deities in Marduk's household.[4] The cave at Makkedah, in which the five kings of the Amorites hid themselves after their defeat by Joshua,[5] is said to have the same *motif* underlying it. In short, any cave, or prison, or state of misery mentioned in the Hebrew narratives may, according to astral interpretation, be taken as representing the underworld.[6]

[1] On the close correspondence of the Greek form of the legend with its Babylonian original, see Frazer, "Adonis Attis Osiris," I., pp. 6 ff.

[2] Ed. Bevan in "Texts and Studies," V., 3.

[3] Gen. xii.

[4] Cf. Jeremias, "Old Testament," I., p. 60, II., p. 65. These were the gods Minâ-ikul-bêli, "What-will-my-lord-eat?", and Minâ-ishti-bêli, "What-will-my-lord-drink?" (cf. King, "Cun. Texts," XXIV., 1908, p. 5) ; but there is nothing to connect the Hebrew story with them.

[5] Josh. x., 10, 16.

[6] In support of such astral *motifs* evidence of direct worship of Ishtar is traced in unexpected quarters. Thus the men of Gilead are explained to

The one other *motif* we will take from the Babylonian mythology is the Dragon-combat, since this illustrates the principal pattern, or system, on which the astral mythologist arranges his material.   In the Babylonian story of the Creation it will be recalled how Tiamat, the dragon of chaos, revolted with Apsû, the god of the abyss, against the new and ordered ways of the gods; how Marduk, the champion of the gods, defeated her, and, cutting her body in half, used one half of her as a firmament for the heaven, and then proceeded to carry out his other works of creation.[1] The probability has long been noted that the Dragon-combat may have suggested certain metaphorical phrases or descriptions in Hebrew poetical and prophetic literature.[2]   But the astral mythologist uses it as the dominant *motif* of his Age of Taurus; and, since this age began, according to his theory, before the period of Abraham, the Marduk myths are traced more frequently than any others in the Old Testament.   The astral god plays the part of a deliverer in the mythology : hence any Biblical hero who is recorded to have rescued any one, or to have delivered his family or people, forms a convenient peg on which to hang a *motif*.   So too the birth of the founder of a dynasty, or of the inaugurator of a new age, is said to reflect the solar *motif* of the birth ot the spring sun.[3]

In this process of detecting hidden *motifs*, numbers play an important part.   To take one example, they are

have chosen the word *shibboleth*, "ear of grain," as a password for the Ephraemites, not because it was a common word containing the required sibilant, but in honour of the goddess Ishtar, the heavenly Virgin with the ears of corn.   And, though the veil was part of the ordinary attire of Hebrew women, a natural act such as that told of Rebecca, who is said to have veiled herself at the approach of Isaac, is held to reflect the Ishtar cult.

[1] Cf. " Seven Tablets of Creation," I., pp. 32 ff.

[2] See especially Gunkell, "Schöpfung und Chaos in Urzeit und Endzeit," pp. 16 ff.

[3] Moses, for instance, is peculiarly a deliverer and the inaugurator of a new age in Israel's history ; the traditions about him thus bristle with astral *motfis*.   When he is persecuted by Pharaoh in Egypt, Pharaoh is the Dragon ; when he is rescued as a babe from the Nile, Pharaoh's daughter is Ishtar, Queen of heaven, and we have a Tammuz-Ishtar *motif*.   When he leads Israel out of Egypt, we have the *motif* of victory over the Dragon.   The crossing of the Red Sea is the cleaving of the Dragon in half, and so too is Joshua's passage of the Jordan.   In short, Joshua in his character of deliverer rivals Moses in the number of *motifs* which are said to cluster round him.

said to indicate that David's fight with Goliath reflects the myth of the Year-Cycle. The forty days during which Goliath, who is identified with the Dragon Tiamat,[1] drew near to the Israelites morning and evening are symbolical of winter. In the Hebrew text his height is given as six cubits and a span ;[2] the figure is emended to read five cubits and a span, since otherwise the number would not correspond to the five and a quarter epagomenal days.[3] With the best will in the world to be convinced one cannot help feeling that, even assuming the soundness of the theory, its authors have let it run away with them. It cannot of course be denied that astrological conceptions may colour some of the stories in the Old Testament. The three hundred foxes, with firebrands tied to their brushes, with which Samson destroyed the standing corn of the Philistines, find a striking parallel in the ceremonial which took place annually in the circus at Rome during the Cerealia,[4] and may well be regarded as folk-mythology of astrological origin.[5] Elijah's chariot of fire may have been suggested by some astronomical phenomenon, perhaps a comet ; it was probably the product of the same association of ideas as Medea's dragon-chariot, the gift of Helios. But this scarcely prepares us to accept such an allegorizing of details as is proposed in other passages.

[1] Jeremias (op. cit., II., p. 182) connects the name Goliath with Assyr. *galittu*, which he renders "sea," hence the dragon Tiamat ; but *galittu*, though applied to the sea, is merely the feminine of the adj. galtu, "terrible."

[2] I. Samuel, xvii., 4 ; Josephus and some MSS. of the Septuagint read four cubits and a span.

[3] As in so much of their speculation, the members of the astral school have here mixed valuable suggestions with pure theorizing. Certain numbers were specially sacred among the Babylonians and were employed as divine names. Sin, the Moon-god, for example, was the god "Thirty," from the conventional length of the lunar month ; and the gods "Four" and "Seven" may have represented different aspects of the Moon-god, the former the four phases of the moon, the latter the seven-day week as a lunar quarter. If the idea travelled westward, we obtain a satisfactory explanation of such Palestinian names as Kiriath-arba and Be'er-sheba'. On this subject, see especially Prof. Burney's forthcoming work on "Judges" (see above, p. 290, n. 3), p. 43 f. Discussions are there given of other points illustrated by the Babylonian texts, of which special mention may be made of the exhaustive notes on Yahwe (pp. 243 ff.) and the Ashera (pp. 196 ff.), and the valuable sections on early Hebrew poetry.

[4] Ovid, *Fasti*, IV., 679 ff. ; and cf. Frazer, "Spirits of the Corn," I., p. 297 f.

[5] See Burney, op. cit., additional note on "The mythical element in the story of Samson."

Precisely the same principles of interpretation have
been applied to the heroes of Greek legend.   Professor
Jensen of Marburg, in his work on the Babylonian
epic of Gilgamesh, has attempted to trace almost every
figure, not only in the Old Testament, but also in
classical mythology, to a Babylonian source.[1]   But his
rather monotonous method of perceiving on all sides
reflexions of his own hero Gilgamesh has already been
criticized sufficiently, and we will take some examples
from a more recent work by Dr. Carl Fries,[2] who has
made other contributions of a less speculative character
upon Greek and Oriental connexions.   Elaborating a
published suggestion of Professor Jensen, Dr. Fries has
enthusiastically applied the astral method of interpretation to the Odyssey.   Such an episode as the voyage of
Odysseus to Hades, in order to consult the Theban
prophet Teiresias, undoubtedly presents a close parallel
to the journey of Gilgamesh to Xisuthros in Babylonian
legend ; and, though similar traditions are not un-
common in the epics of other races, the Greek form of
the story may perhaps retain an echo from Babylon.
But a far closer relationship than that is suggested.

The section of the Odyssey which is said to have
been principally exposed to Babylonian influence is the
sojourn of Odysseus in Scheria, the whole episode of his
entertainment by the Phæacians being said to reflect the
Babylonian Feast of the New Year.   From the moment
of his awakening on the island we begin to perceive
astral *motifs*.   In Nausicaa's choral game of ball with
her maidens, the ball symbolizes the sun or moon which
revolves from one side of heaven to the other ; when it
falls into the river it is the setting sun or moon.
Odysseus, awakened by the maiden's shrill cry, comes
forth from the darkness of the wood : he is the rising
sun.   The way into the city which Nausicaa describes
to Odysseus corresponds to the sacred Procession Street
in Babylon, along which Marduk was carried from his
temple through the city at the Feast of the New Year.
The cult-image on its journey must be protected from

[1] See "Das Gilgamesch-Epos in der Weltliteratur" (Strassburg, 1906).
[2] "Studien zur Odyssee" in the "Mitteilungen der Vorderasiatischen
Gesellschaft," 1910, Hefte 2–4 ; 1911, Heft 4.

the gaze of unconsecrated eyes ; so Athene sheds a mist about Odysseus lest any of the Phæacians should accost him by the way. Other astral elements are suggested without a specially Babylonian colouring.[1]

We are not here concerned with Dr. Fries' theory on the origin of Greek tragedy, but we may note in passing that Odysseus, in relating his adventures, is the priest-singer at the festival of the Light-god. In other parts of the Odyssey Dr. Fries does not attempt to trace many astral *motifs*, though he certainly remarks that the adventures of Odysseus are merely survivals of astral myths, and, in spite of a hundred transformations, ultimately relate only to the journey of the Light-god over the heavenly ocean.[2] The closing scenes of the Odyssey also receive a thoroughly astrological interpretation, and moon- and sun-*motifs* appear promiscuously. From the speech of Antinous at the trial of the bow we know that the slaying of the wooers took place at the Feast of the New Moon, for after Eurymachus and the other wooers had failed to bend it, he makes the feast an excuse for his proposal to postpone the trial till the morrow. This fact leads to the suggestion that in Odysseus returning at the Feast of the New Moon we are to recognize the Moon-god himself, who triumphs over the darkness with his bow or crescent. On the other hand, the twelve axes, through which the arrow flies, suggest, presumably by their number, the sun. Penelope wooed by the suitors is the moon whom the stars surround, and her weaving and unravelling of the

---

[1] The fifty-two noble youths, for example, whom Alcinous entrusts with the task of preparing the ship and escorting Odysseus homewards may correspond to the fifty-two weeks of the year, sun-heroes who accompany the sun on his voyage through the year. In the challenge of Euryalus to Odysseus and the latter's triumph in the discus-throwing, we are to see a glimmer of the old light-myth. The dance of Halius and Laodamas, with the purple ball which Polybus made for them, again symbolizes the battle of light, the colour of the ball being specially significant. Indeed, there are few limits to be placed to this system of astrological interpretation, since, according to Dr. Fries, even lawn-tennis goes back to the same idea : he remarks that " alles Ballspiel ja bis herab zum Lawn-Tennis auf denselben Gedanken [der Lichtkampf] zurückgeht " (" Studien zur Odyssee," i., p. 324).

[2] One point, at which the colouring is said to be peculiarly Babylonian, is the prophecy that death shall come to Odysseus from the sea ; for this is traced to the Babylonian legend of Oannes, the benefactor of mankind, who ever returns to the sea from which he rose. But here, too, Odysseus is the god of heaven who sinks at the approach of night.

web is a moon-*motif*.   Then Odysseus as the sun draws
near, and all the stars are eclipsed at his appearance.

In such hands the astral theory carries its own
antidote, for one cannot but be struck with the ease
with which it may be applied.   There is generally no
need to prove a mythological setting to the narrative ;
all that is necessary is to assume an astral meaning
beneath the text.[1]   In fact, one way of demonstrating
its unsoundness has been to apply its methods to the
records of the life of a historical personage.[2]   But this
argument amounts at best to a *reductio ad absurdum*,
and the most damaging criticism has been directed from
the purely astronomical side.

It is well known that the different ecliptic constellations which make up the signs of the zodiac do not each
occupy thirty degrees of the ecliptic, but that some are
longer and some shorter than others.   Also, the constellations of the Babylonian astronomers during the
late period did not completely coincide with ours.   For
instance, the most eastern star of our constellation Virgo
was counted by the Babylonians of the Arsacid era as
belonging to the next ecliptic constellation, Leo, since
it was known as " the hind-foot of the lion." [3]   But,
fortunately for our purpose, not much doubt can exist as
to the eastern limit of the Twins and the western limit
of the Ram, which mark the beginning and end of the
three World Ages of the astral mythologists.   For the
two bright stars, Castor and Pollux, from which the
Twins receive their name were undoubtedly reckoned
in that constellation by the Neo-Babylonians.   And the
easternmost star of our constellation of the Fishes (*a*

---

[1] With regard to its application to the Hebrew narratives, the " Church
Quarterly " reviewer of Dr. Jeremias' work (see above, p. 304, n. 1) points
out the resemblance between this procedure and Philo's method of interpretation.

[2] In 1870 the same plan was adopted to discredit Professor Max Müller's
theory of the Solar Myth.   The demonstration, though humorous (since its
subject was the professor himself), constituted a legitimate form of criticism,
and it has been borrowed by Dr. Kugler, the Dutch astronomer, and applied
to the astral theory.   For the astral theory is in essence the old Solar Myth
revived and grafted on to a Babylonian stem.   In his book " Im Bannkreis
Babels " (1910), Dr. Kugler selects at random the historical figure of Louis IX.
of France, and has no difficulty in demonstrating by astral methods that the
extant records of his life and reign are full of solar and astral *motifs*.

[3] Cf. Kugler, *op. cit.*

A NEO-BABYLONIAN TREATISE ON ASTRONOMY.

Brit. Mus., No. 86378.

piscium) was probably well beyond the Babylonian constellation of the Ram.

Working on this assumption, and assuming thirty degrees to each of the three intervening constellations, Dr. Kugler has calculated the years in which the sun entered these signs of the zodiac at the vernal equinox, the points, that is to say, at which the astral World-Ages would have begun and ended. His figures entirely dispose of Winckler's claim to an astronomical basis for his astral system. The Age of the Twins, instead of ending, according to the theory, at about 2800 B.C., really ended in the year 4383 B.C.   Thus the Age of the Bull began over fifteen hundred years before the birth of Sargon I., who is supposed to have inaugurated its beginning ; and it ended in 2232 B.C.— that is, considerably before the birth of Hammurabi, under whom we are told the Bull Age *motifs* were principally developed. Moreover, from the time of the First Dynasty onwards down to the year 81 B.C.—that is to say, during the whole course of her history— Babylon was really living in the Age of the Ram, not in that of the Bull. Thus all the *motifs* and myths, which have been so ingeniously connected with the Bull sign of the zodiac, ought really to have been connected with the Ram   But even the astral mythologists admit that there is not a trace of a Ram-*motif* in the Babylonian mythology. Granting all the assumptions made by Winckler and his school with regard to the astronomical knowledge of the early Babylonians, the theory evolved from them is found to be baseless. Winckler's astronomy was at fault, and his three astrological World-Ages do not really correspond to his periods of history.[1]

Babylon was, indeed, the mother of astronomy no less than of astrology, and classical antiquity was indebted to her in no small measure ; but, strictly speaking, her scientific observations do not date from a very early period.   It is true we have evidence that, as early as the close of the third millennium, the

---

[1] His interpretation of Euripides' story of the Golden Lamb must share the fate of the main structure of his theory ; but the legend itself may well have been of Babylonian origin (see above, p. 293).

astronomers recorded observations of the planet Venus,[1] and there is also a fragment of an early text which shows that they attempted to measure approximately the positions of the fixed stars. But their art of measuring remained for a long time primitive, and it was only the later Babylonians, of the period from the sixth to the first century B.C., who were enabled to fix with sufficient accuracy the movements of the planets, especially those of the moon, and by this means to found a reliable system of time-measurement. The mere fact that the astrological texts, even in the late Assyrian period, treat eclipses as possible on any day of the month, and use the term for any kind of obscuration of the sun and moon, is sufficient evidence that they had not at that time noted their regular occurrence and still had comparatively crude notions of astronomy.[2]

The earliest scientific document in the strict sense of the word dates from the second half of the sixth century, when we find for the first time that the relative positions of the sun and moon were calculated in advance, as well as the conjunction of the moon with the planets and of the planets with each other, their position being noted in the signs of the zodiac. But the tablets afford no evidence that the Babylonian astronomers possessed any knowledge of the precession of the equinoxes before the close of the second century B.C., and the traditional ascription of the discovery to Hipparchus of Nicæa, working between the years 161 and 126 B.C. on the observations of his Babylonian predecessors, may be accepted as accurate.[3]

---

[1] See above, pp. 106 ff.

[2] For an exhaustive discussion of the astrological material contained in the omen-literature, see Jastrow, " Religion Babyloniens und Assyriens," II., pp. 138 ff. (1909–12). A Neo-Babylonian astronomical treatise, recently acquired by the British Museum (see Plate XXXII., opposite p. 310), containing classified and descriptive lists of the principal stars and constellations, with their heliacal risings and settings, culminations in the south, etc., does not suggest a profound knowledge of astronomy on the part of its compiler (cf. King, "Cun. Texts," XXXIII., 1912, pp. 3 ff., and " Proc. Soc. Bibl. Arch.," XXXV., 1913, pp. 41 ff.).

[3] See " Sternkunde und Sterndienst," II., pp. 30 ff. ; cf. also Cumont, " Babylon und der griechische Astrologie," in the " Neue Jahrbücher für das klassische Altertum," Bd. 27 (1911), pp. 6 ff., and the earlier of his " American Lectures on the History of Religions," published under the title " Astrology and Religion among the Greeks and Romans " (1912).

There are, in short, no grounds for the theory that the Babylonians divided the history of the world into astral ages, nor that their myths and legends had any peculiar connexion with successive signs of the zodiac. That astrology formed an important section of the Babylonian religious system from an early period there can be no doubt; but at that time the stars and planets did not exercise any preponderating influence on religious belief, and many features of the system, for which an astral origin has been confidently assumed, must be traced to a simpler and more primitive association of ideas.[1] But the necessary modification of the astral theory still leaves open the possibility that Hebrew literature may have acquired a strong astrological tinge in the Exilic and post-Exilic periods. Were Jewish traditions affected in Babylon, for example, in some such way as the Mithraic legends from Persia? Since the astral theory has no claim to dictate the answer for us, the question must be decided by the ordinary rules of historical and literary evidence.

If we are to assume that Babylonian astrology exerted so marked an influence on the Jews of the Exile, we should at least expect to find some traces of it in practical matters and in terminology. And in this connexion there are certain facts which have never been fairly met by the astral mythologists.[2] It is true that the returning exiles under Zerubbabel had adopted the Babylonian names of the months for civil use; but the idea of hours—that is to say, the division of the day into equal parts—does not seem to have occurred to the Jews till long after the Exile, and even then there is no trace of the Babylonian double hour.[3] The other fact is still more significant. With the exception of a single reference to the planet Saturn by the prophet Amos,[4] none of the Hebrew names for the stars and constellations, which occur in the Old

---

[1] See above, p. 298 f.

[2] They are emphasized by Schiarparelli, in his " Astronomy in the Old Testament " (Engl. transl.), pp. 39 ff., 99 ff., 104 f.

[3] During their pastoral and agricultural life in Palestine the Hebrews found it quite sufficient to refer to time by describing the period of the day see further, Schiarparelli, op. cit., p. 96.

[4] Amos, v., 26.

Testament, correspond to those we know were in use in Babylon. Such a fact is surely decisive against any wholesale adoption of astral mythology from Babylon on the part of the writers or redactors of the Old Testament, whether in pre-Exilic or in post-Exilic times. But it is quite compatible with the view that some of the imagery, and even certain lines of thought, occurring in the poetical and prophetic books of the Hebrews, betray a Babylonian colouring and may find their explanation in the cuneiform literature. There can be no doubt that the Babylonian texts have afforded invaluable assistance in the effort to trace the working of the oriental mind in antiquity.

With regard to the suggested influence of Babylon on Greek religious thought, it is essential to realize that the temperaments of the Babylonian and the Hellene were totally distinct, the fanatic and self-abasing spirit of the East contrasting vividly with the coolness, civic sobriety, and self-confidence of the West. This has been pointed out by Dr. Farnell,[1] who lays special emphasis on the total absence of any trace in Mesopotamian cults of those religious mysteries, which, as he has shown elsewhere, formed so essential a feature in Hellenic and Ægean society.[2] Another fact in which he would see significance is that the use of incense, universal from immemorial times in Babylonia, was not introduced into Greece before the eighth century B.C. This little product, it will be readily admitted, was much easier to import than Babylonian theology. Few will disagree with him in regarding the suggestion, that for long centuries the Hittite empire was a barrier between Mesopotamia and the coast-lands of Asia Minor,[3] as a sufficient reason for this check in the direct spread of Babylonian influence westward. But no political barrier is effective against the tales that are remembered by travelling merchants and are retold around the camp-fires of the caravan. That Babylon should have contributed in some degree to the rich store of legends

[1] Cf. " Greece and Babylon " (published as the Wilde Lectures, 1911).
[2] See his " Cults of the Greek States," Oxford, 1896–1909.
[3] Cf. Hogarth, " Ionia and the East," pp. 27 ff., 64 ff.

current in various forms throughout the region of the eastern Mediterranean is what one would expect.

The cultural influence of Babylonia had from the earliest period penetrated eastward, and the civilization of Elam, her nearest neighbour, had been to a great extent moulded by that of Sumer. But even at that time the trade-routes had been open to the west, and before the rise of Babylon both soldier and merchant had passed from the lower Euphrates into Syria. With the expansion of the Western Semites the two regions were drawn into more intimate relationship, and the political control of the middle Euphrates, first established in the age of Hammurabi, was followed by an increased commercial traffic, which continued with few interruptions into the Neo-Babylonian and later periods. Babylon's foreign policy was always dominated by the necessity of keeping her connexion open with the west; and it was mainly due to her commercial enterprise, and not to any territorial ambitions, that her culture reached the farther limits of Palestine and has left some traces in Greek mythology.

APPENDICES

I.—A COMPARATIVE LIST OF THE DYNASTIES OF
NÎSIN, LARSA AND BABYLON.

II.—A DYNASTIC LIST OF THE KINGS OF BABYLON.

I. A COMPARATIVE LIST OF THE DYNASTIES OF NÎSIN, LARSA, AND BABYLON.

Dynasty of Nîsin (16 kings; 225¼ years).			Dynasty of Larsa (16 kings; 267, or 289, years).			First Dynasty of Babylon (11 kings; c. 300 years).		
	Years.	B.C.		Years.	B.C.		Years.	B.C.
1. Ishbi-Ura,	(32)	2339–2308	1. Naplanum	(21)	2335–2315			
			2. Emiṣu	(28)	2314–2287			
2. Gimil-ilishu,	(10)	2307–2298						
3. Idin-Dagan,	(21)	2297–2277						
			3. Samum	(35)	2286–2252			
4. Ishme-Dagan(,)	(20)	2276–2257						
5. Libit-Ishtar	(11)	2256–2246	4. Zabâia	(9)	2251–2243			
6. Ur-Ninib,	(28)	2245–2218	5. Gungunum	(27)	2242–2216			
						1. Sumu-abum	(14)	2225–2212
7. Bûr-Sin II.,	(21)	2217–2197	6. Abi-sarê	(11)	2215–2205			
						2. Sumu-la-ilum,	(36)	2211–2176
			7. Sumu-ilum	(29)	2204–2176			
8. Itêr-pîsha	(5)	2196–2192						
9. Ura-imitti	(7)	2191–2185						
10. [............]	(½)	2185						

EXPLANATORY NOTE.—A comma after a king's name implies that he was succeeded by his son. The figures within parentheses, which follow a king's name, indicate the number of years he ruled. Contemporaneous reigns are set opposite each other in the parallel columns, but their respective lengths are indicated only approximately by the spacing of the names.

I. A COMPARATIVE LIST OF THE DYNASTIES OF NÎSIN, LARSA, AND BABYLON (continued).

DYNASTY OF NÎSIN (continued).

		YEARS.	B.C.
11.	Enlil-bani	(24)	2184–2161
12.	Zambia	(3)	2160–2158
13.	[..........]	(5)	2157–2153
14.	[..........]	(4)	2152–2149
15.	Sin-magir,	(11)	2148–2138
16.	Damik-ilishu	(23)	2137–2115
	Capture of Nîsin		2115

DYNASTY OF LARSA (continued).

		YEARS.	B.C.
8.	Nûr-Adad	(16)	2175–2160
9.	Sin-idinnam	(7?)	2159–2153
10.	Sin-iribam	(2)	2152–2151
11.	Sin-ikisham	(6?)	2150–2145
12.	Sili-Adad	(1)	2144
13.	Warad-Sin	(12)	2143–2132
14.	Rîm-Sin	(61)	2131–2071
15.	Hammurabi	(12?)	2092–2081
16.	Samsu-iluna	(12 +?)	2080–2069

FIRST DYNASTY OF BABYLON (continued).

		YEARS.	B.C.
3.	Zabum,	(14)	2175–2162
4.	Apil-Sin,	(18)	2161–2144
5.	Sin-muballit,	(20)	2143–2124
6.	Hammurabi,	(43)	2123–2081
7.	Samsu-iluna,	(38)	2080–2043
8.	Abi-eshu',	(28)	2042–2015
9.	Ammi-ditana,	(37)	2014–1978
10.	Ammi-zaduga,	(21)	1977–1957
11.	Samsu-ditana	(31)	1956–1926

EXPLANATORY NOTE.—A comma after a king's name implies that he was succeeded by his son. The figures within parentheses, which follow a king's name, indicate the number of years he ruled. Contemporaneous reigns are set opposite each other in the parallel columns, but their respective lengths are indicated only approximately by the spacing of the names.

CONTEMPORANEOUS RULERS.	DYNASTIES I. AND III.	
	I. FIRST DYNASTY (11 kgs. ; c. 300 yrs.).	B.C.
	1. Sumu-abum (14)	2225–2212
	2. Sumu-la-ilum, (36)	2211–2176
	3. Zabum, (14)	2175–2162
	4. Apil-Sin, (18)	2161–2144
II. SECOND DYNASTY	5. Sin-muballit, (20)	2143–2124
(11 kings).	6. Hammurabi, (43)	2123–2081
1. Iluma-ilum (60)	7. Samsu-iluna, (38)	2080–2043
2. Itti-ili-nibi (55)	8. Abi-eshu', (28)	2042–2015
3. Damki-ilishu (36)	9. Ammi-ditana, (37)	2014–1978
4. Ishkibal (15)	10. Ammi-zaduga, (21)	1977–1957
5. Sushshi (27)	11. Samsu-ditana (31)	1956–1926
6. Gulkishar, (55)		
7. Peshgal-daramash, (50)	**III. THIRD DYNASTY**	
8. A-dara-kalama (28)	(36 kgs. ; 576¾ yrs.).	
9. Akur-ul-ana (26)		
10. Melam-kurkura (7)	1. Gandash, (16)	1760–1745
11. Ea-gamil (9)	2. Agum (22)	1744–1723
	3. Kashtiliash I., (22)	1722–1701
	4. Ushshi (8)	1700–1693
	5. Abi-rattash,	1692
	6. Tashshi-gurumash,	
	7. Agum-kakrime	
	....	
	Kadashman-Kharbe I.,	
	Kurigalzu I.,	
Contemporaneous kings of	Meli-Shipak I.	
Assyria.	....	
Ashur-rîm-nishêshu......	16. Kara-indash I.	c. 1425
	17. Kadashman-Enlil I.,	
	18. [.........]-[Bu]riash	
	19. Kurigalzu II.,	
Puzur-Ashur...............	20. Burna-Buriash (25)	c. 1385
Ashur-uballit	21. Kara-indash II.	
	Nazi-bugash (usurper)	
Enlil-nirari	22. Kurigalzu III., (23)	1357–1335
Adad-nirari I.	23. Nazi-maruttash, (26)	1334–1309
	24. Kadashman-turgu, (17)	1308–1292
	25. Kadashman-Enlil II. (6)	1291–1286
	26. Kudur-Enlil, (9)	1285–1277
	27. Shagarakti-Shuriash, (13)	1276–1264
Tukulti-Ninib I.	28. Kashtiliash II. (8)	1263–1256
	29. Enlil-nadin-shum (1½)	1255–1254
	30. Kadashman-Kharbe II. (1½)	1254–1253
	31. Adad-shum-iddin (6)	1252–1247
Enlil-kudur-usur	32. Adad-shum-usur, (30)	1246–1217
	33. Meli-Shipak II., (15)	1216–1202
	34. Merodach-baladan I. (13)	1201–1189
Ashur-dân I...............	35. Zamama-shum-iddin (1)	1188
	36. Bêl-nadin-[akhi] (3)	1187–1185

N.B. A comma after a king's name implies that he was succeeded by his son.

DYNASTIES IV.–IX.	LATER PERIODS.

IV. FOURTH DYNASTY
(11 kgs. ; 132½ yrs.).

		B.C.
1.	Marduk-[shapik-zêrim] (17)	1184–1168
2.	.... (6)	1167–1162
3.	....	
4.	Nebuchadnezzar I.	c. 1140
5.	Enlil-nadin-apli	
6.	Marduk-nadin-akhê	c. 1110
7.	Marduk-shapik-zêr-mâti	c. 1100
8.	Adad-aplu-iddina (22)	1095–1074
9.	Marduk-akhi-erba (1½)	1073
10.	Marduk-zêr-[......] (12)	1072–1061
11.	Nabû-shum-libur (8)	1060–1053

V. FIFTH DYNASTY
(3 kgs. ; 21$\frac{5}{12}$ yrs.).

1.	Simmash-Shipak (18)	1052–1035
2.	Ea-mukîn-zêr ($\frac{5}{12}$)	1035
3.	Kashshû-nadin-akhi (3)	1034–1032

VI. SIXTH DYNASTY
(3 kgs. ; 20¼ yrs.).

1.	E-ulmash-shakin-shum (17)	1031–1015
2.	Ninib-kudur-uṣur (3)	1014–1012
3.	Shilanum-Shukamuna ($\frac{1}{4}$)	1012

VII. SEVENTH DYNASTY
(1 kg. ; 6 yrs.).

1.	[Ae-aplu-uṣur] (6)	1011–1006

VIII. EIGHTH DYNASTY
(about 13 kgs.).

1.	Nabû-mukîn-apli (36)	1005–970
	....	
	Sibir	
	....	
	Shamash-mudammik	c. 910
	Nabû-shum-ishkun I.,	
	Nabû-aplu-iddina,	c. 885
	Marduk-zakir-shum,	c. 855
	Marduk-balâtsu-iḳbi	c. 830
	Erba-Marduk	
	Bau-akhi-iddina	c. 815
	....	

IX. NINTH DYNASTY
(about 5 kgs.).

	....	
	Nabû-shum-ishkun II.	
	Nabonassar, (14)	747–734
	Nabû-nadin-zêr(,) (2)	733–732
	Nabû-shum-ukîn ($\frac{1}{12}$)	732

X. PERIOD OF ASSYRIAN DOMINATION
(107 years).

		B.C.
1.	Nabû-mukîn-zêr (3)	732–730
2.	Pulu (Tiglath-pileser IV.), (2)	729–727
3.	Ululai (Shalmaneser V.) (5)	727–722
4.	Merodach-baladan II. (12)	721–710
5.	Sargon, (5)	709–705
6.	Sennacherib (2)	704–703
7.	Marduk-zakir-shum ($\frac{1}{12}$)	703–702
8.	Merodach-baladan II. ($\frac{3}{4}$)	703–702
9.	Bêl-ibni (3)	702–700
10.	Ashur-nadin-shum (6) (son of Sennacherib)	699–694
11.	Nergal-ushezib (1½)	693–692
12.	Mushezib-Marduk (4)	692–689
13.	Sennacherib, (8)	688–681
14.	Esarhaddon, (12)	681–669
15.	Shamash-shum-ukîn (20)	668–648
16.	Kandalanu	647–626
17.	Ashur-etil-ilâni	625–c. 618
18.	Sin-shum-lishir	c. 618
19.	Sin-shar-ishkun	c. 616

(Capture of Nineveh by the Medes, 606.)

XI. NEO-BABYLONIAN EMPIRE
(6 kgs. ; 86 yrs.).

1.	Nabopolassar,	625–604
2.	Nebuchadnezzar II.,	604–561
3.	Amêl-Marduk	561–559
4.	Neriglissar,	559–556
5.	Labashi-Marduk	556
6.	Nabonidus	555–539

XII. ACHAEMENIAN KINGS
(11 kgs. ; 208 yrs.).

1.	Cyrus,	539–529
2.	Cambyses	529–522
3.	Darius I. Hystaspis,	522–486
4.	Xerxes I.,	486–465
5.	Artaxerxes I. Longimanus	465–424
6.	Xerxes II. (45 days)	424
7.	Darius II.,	424–404
8.	Artaxerxes II. Mnemon,	404–359
9.	Artaxerxes III. Ochus,	359–338
10.	Arses	338–336
11.	Darius III. Codomanus	336–331

(Capture of Babylon by Alexander, 331)

INDEX